THE WORKS OF
WILLIAM
SHAKESPEARE

VOLUME SIX

AN ELIZABETHAN THEATRE

THE WORKS OF WILLIAM SHAKESPEARE

VOLUME SIX

The Merchant of Venice
The Merry Wives of Windsor
A Mid-Summer Night's Dream
Much Ado about Nothing
Othello, The Moor of Venice

THE PEEBLES CLASSIC LIBRARY
SANDY LESBERG, *Editor*

ISBN 0-85690-044-3

Published by Peebles Press International
U.S.A.: 10 Columbus Circle, New York, NY 10019
U.K.: 12 Thayer Street, London W1M 5LD

Distributed by WHS Distributors

PRINTED AND BOUND IN THE U.S.A.

CONTENTS

THE MERCHANT OF VENICE

DRAMATIS PERSONÆ

DUKE OF VENICE
PRINCE OF MOROCCO } *suitors to Portia*
PRINCE OF ARRAGON }
ANTONIO, *a merchant of Venice*
BASSANIO, *his friend, suitor to Portia*
GRATIANO
SALANIO } *friends to Antonio and Bassanio*
SALARINO
SALERIO
LORENZO, *in love with Jessica*
SHYLOCK, *a Jew*
TUBAL, *a Jew, his friend*
LAUNCELOT GOBBO, *a clown, servant to Shylock, afterwards servant to Bassanio*
OLD GOBBO, *father to Launcelot*
LEONARDO, *servant to Bassanio*
BALTHAZAR } *servants to Portia*
STEPHANO }
PORTIA, *a rich heiress*
NERISSA, *her waiting-maid*
JESSICA, *daughter to Shylock*

Magnificoes of Venice, Officers of the Court of Justice, Gaoler, Servants to Portia, and other Attendants

SCENE.—*Partly at Venice, and partly at Belmont*

THE MERCHANT OF VENICE

ACT ONE

SCENE I.—Venice. A Street

Enter ANTONIO, SALARINO, *and* SALANIO

Ant. In sooth, I know not why I am so sad.
It wearies me; you say, it wearies you;
But how I caught it, found it, or came by it,
What stuff 't is made of, whereof it is born,
I am to learn:
And such a want-wit sadness makes of me,
That I have much ado to know myself.

Salar. Your mind is tossing on the ocean,
There were your argosies with portly sail,
Like signiors and rich burghers on the flood,
Or, as it were, the pageants of the sea,
Do overpeer the petty traffickers
That curt'sy to them, do them reverence
As they fly by them with their woven wings.

Salan. Believe me, sir, had I such venture forth,
The better part of my affections would
Be with my hopes abroad. I should be still
Plucking the grass to know where sits the wind,
Peering in maps for ports, and piers, and roads;
And every object that might make me fear
Misfortune to my ventures, out of doubt
Would make me sad.

Salar.   My wind cooling my broth,
Would blow me to an ague when I thought
What harm a wind too great might do at sea.
I should not see the sandy hour-glass run,
But I should think of shallows and of flats,
And see my wealthy Andrew docked in sand,
Vailing her high-top lower than her ribs
To kiss her burial. Should I go to church,
And see the holy edifice of stone
And not bethink me straight of dangerous rocks,
Which touching but my gentle vessel's side
Would scatter all her spices on the stream,
Enrobe the roaring waters with my silks;
And, in a word, but even now worth this,
And now worth nothing? Shall I have the thought
To think on this, and shall I lack the thought
That such a thing bechanced would make me sad?

But tell not me; I know Antonio
Is sad to think upon his merchandise.
    Ant. Believe me, no. I thank my fortune for it,
My ventures are not in one bottom trusted,
Nor to one place; nor is my whole estate
Upon the fortune of this present year:
Therefore, my merchandise makes me not sad.
    Salar. Why, then you are in love.
    Ant.   Fie, fie!
    Salar. Not in love neither? Then let 's say you are sad
Because you are not merry; and 't were as easy
For you to laugh and leap, and say you are merry
Because you are not sad. Now, by two-headed Janus,
Nature hath framed strange fellows in her time:
Some that will evermore peep through their eyes
And laugh like parrots at a bag-piper;
And other of such vinegar aspéct,
That they 'll not show their teeth in way of smile
Though Nestor swear the jest be laughable.

Enter BASSANIO, LORENZO, *and* GRATIANO

    Salan. Here comes Bassanio, your most noble kinsman,
Gratiano, and Lorenzo. Fare ye well:
We leave you now with better company.
    Salar. I would have stayed till I had made you merry,
If worthier friends had not prevented me.
    Ant.   Your worth is very dear in my regard.
I take it, your own business calls on you,
And you embrace the occasion to depart.
    Salar. Good morrow, my good lords.
    Bass. Good signiors both, when shall we laugh? say,
        when?
You grow exceeding strange: must it be so?
    Salar. We'll make our leisures to attend on yours.
                         [Exeunt Salarina and Salanio
    Lor. My lord Bassanio, since you have found Antonio,
We two will leave you; but at dinner-time,
I pray you, have in mind where we must meet.
    Bass. I will not fail you.
    Gra. You look not well, signior Antonio;
You have too much respect upon the world:
They lose it that do buy it with much care.
Believe me, you are marvellously changed.
    Ant. I hold the world but as the world, Gratiano;
A stage, where every man must play a part,
And mine a sad one.
    Gra.   Let me play the fool:
With mirth and laughter let old wrinkles come,
And let my liver rather heat with wine
Than my heart cool with mortifying groans.

Why should a man whose blood is warm within
Sit like his grandsire cut in alabaster,
Sleep when he wakes, and creep into the jaundice
By being peevish?   I tell thee what, Antonio,—
I love thee, and it is my love that speaks,—
There are a sort of men whose visages
Do cream and mantle like a standing pond,
And do a wilful stillness entertain
With purpose to be dressed in an opinion
Of wisdom, gravity, profound conceit;
As who should say, " I am Sir Oracle,
And when I ope my lips, let no dog bark!"
O, my Antonio, I do know of these,
That therefore only are reputed wise,
For saying nothing; when, I am very sure,
If they should speak, would almost damn those ears,
Which, hearing them, would call their brothers fools.
I'll tell thee more of this another time:
But fish not with this melancholy bait
For this fool-gudgeon, this opinion.—
Come, good Lorenzo.—Fare ye well awhile:
I 'll end my exhortation after dinner.
 Lor.   Well, we will leave you then till dinner-time.
I must be one of these same dumb wise men,
For Gratiano never lets me speak.
 Gra.   Well, keep me company but two years more,
Thou shalt not know the sound of thine own tongue.
 Ant.   Farewell: I'll grow a talker for this gear.
 Gra.   Thanks, i' faith; for silence is only commendable
In a neat tongue dried, and a maid not vendible.
        [*Exeunt Gratiano and Lorenzo*
 Ant.   Is that anything now?
 Bass.   Gratiano speaks an infinite deal of nothing, more
than any man in all Venice. His reasons are as two grains
of wheat hid in two bushels of chaff: you shall seek all day
ere you find them; and when you have them, they are not
worth the search.
 Ant.   Well: tell me now, what lady is the same
To whom you swore a secret pilgrimage,
That you to-day promised to tell me of?
 Bass.   'T is not unknown to you, Antonio,
How much I have disabled mine estate
By something showing a more swelling port
Than my faint means would grant continuance:
Nor do I now make moan to be abridged
From such a noble rate; but my chief care
Is to come fairly off from the great debts
Wherein my time, something too prodigal,
Hath left me gaged.   To you, Antonio,
I owe the most, in money and in love;

And from your love I have a warranty
To unburthen all my plots and purposes
How to get clear of all the debts I owe.
    Ant.   I pray you, good Bassanio, let me know it;
And if it stand as you yourself still do,
Within the eye of honour, be assured,
My purse, my person, my extremest means,
Lie all unlocked to your occasions.
    Bass.   In my school-days, when I had lost one shaft
I shot his fellow of the self-same flight
The self-same way, with more adviséd watch
To find the other forth, and by adventuring both
I oft found both.   I urge this childhood proof
Because what follows is pure innocence.
I owe you much and, like a wilful youth,
That which I owe is lost; but if you please
To shoot another arrow that self way
Which you did shoot the first, I do not doubt,
As I will watch the aim, or to find both
Or bring your latter hazard back again,
And thankfully rest debtor for the first.
    Ant.   You know me well, and herein spend but time
To wind about my love with circumstance;
And, out of doubt, you do me now more wrong
In making question of my uttermost
Than if you had made waste of all I have:
Then do but say to me what I should do,
That in your knowledge may by me be done,
And I am prest unto it: therefore, speak.
    Bass.   In Belmont is a lady richly left,
And she is fair, and fairer than that word,
Of wondrous virtues.   Sometimes from her eyes
I did receive fair speechless messages.
Her name is Portia; nothing undervalued
To Cato's daughter, Brutus' Portia;
Nor is the wide world ignorant of her worth,
For the four winds blow in from every coast
Renownéd suitors; and her sunny locks
Hang on her temples like a golden fleece,
Which makes her seat of Belmont Colchos' strand,
And many Jasons come in quest of her.
O, my Antonio, had I but the means
To hold a rival place with one of them,
I have a mind presages me such thrift
That I should questionless be fortunate.
    Ant.   Thou know'st that all my fortunes are at sea;
Neither have I money, nor commodity
To raise a present sum: therefore, go forth;
Try what my credit can in Venice do:
That shall be racked even to the uttermost,

To furnish thee to Belmont, to fair Portia.
Go presently inquire, and so will I,
Where money is, and I no question make
To have it of my trust, or for my sake.   [*Exeunt*

Scene II.—Belmont. A Room in Portia's House

Enter Portia *and* Nerissa

Por.   By my troth, Nerissa, my little body is aweary of this great world.

Ner.   You would be, sweet madam, if your miseries were in the same abundance as your good fortunes are. And yet, for aught I see, they are as sick that surfeit with too much as they that starve with nothing. It is no mean happiness, therefore, to be seated in the mean: superfluity comes sooner by white hairs, but competency lives longer.

Por.   Good sentences, and well pronounced.

Ner.   They would be better, if well followed.

Por.   If to do were as easy as to know what were good to do, chapels had been churches, and poor men's cottages princes' palaces. It is a good divine that follows his own instructions: I can easier teach twenty what were good to be done, than be one of the twenty to follow mine own teaching. The brain may devise laws for the blood; but a hot temper leaps o'er a cold decree: such a hare is madness, the youth, to skip o'er the meshes of good counsel, the cripple. But this reasoning is not in the fashion to choose me a husband.—O me, the word choose! I may neither choose whom I would, nor refuse whom I dislike; so is the will of a living daughter curbed by the will of a dead father.—Is it not hard, Nerissa, that I cannot choose one, nor refuse none?

Ner.   Your father was ever virtuous, and holy men at their death have good inspirations; therefore, the lottery that he hath devised in these three chests, of gold, silver, and lead, (whereof who chooses his meaning, chooses you,) will, no doubt, never be chosen by any rightly, but one whom you shall rightly love. But what warmth is there in your affection towards any of these princely suitors that are already come?

Por.   I pray thee, over-name them, and as thou namest them I will describe them; and according to my description level at my affection.

Ner.   First, there is the Neapolitan prince.

Por.   Ay, that's a colt, indeed, for he doth nothing but talk of his horse; and he makes it a great appropriation to his own good parts that he can shoe him himself. I am much afraid my lady his mother played false with a smith.

Ner.   Then is there the county Palatine.

Por. He doth nothing but frown, as who should say, "An you will not have me, choose." He hears merry tales and smiles not; I fear he will prove the weeping philosopher when he grows old, being so full of unmannerly sadness in his youth. I had rather be married to a death's-head with a bone in his mouth than to either of these. God defend me from these two!

Ner. How say you by the French lord, Monsieur Le Bon?

Por. God made him, and therefore let him pass for a man. In truth, I know it is a sin to be a mocker, but he! why, he hath a horse better than the Neapolitan's, a better bad habit of frowning than the count Palatine: he is every man in no man; if a throstle sing, he falls straight a capering: he will fence with his own shadow. If I should marry him, I should marry twenty husbands. If he would despise me, I would forgive him; for if he love me to madness, I shall never requite him.

Ner. What say you then to Faulconbridge, the young baron of England?

Por. You know I say nothing to him, for he understands not me nor I him: he hath neither Latin, French, nor Italian; and you will come into the court and swear that I have a poor pennyworth in the English. He is a proper man's picture; but, alas, who can converse with a dumb-show? How oddly he is suited! I think he bought his doublet in Italy, his round hose in France, his bonnet in Germany, and his behaviour everywhere.

Ner. What think you of the Scottish lord, his neighbour?

Por. That he hath a neighbourly charity in him; for he borrowed a box of the ear of the Englishman, and swore he would pay him again, when he was able: I think the Frenchman became his surety, and sealed under for another.

Ner. How like you the young German, the duke of Saxony's nephew?

Por. Very vilely in the morning, when he is sober, and most vilely in the afternoon, when he is drunk: when he is best, he is a little worse than a man; and when he is worst, he is a little better than a beast. An the worst fall that ever fell, I hope I shall make shift to go without him.

Ner. If he should offer to choose, and choose the right casket, you should refuse to perform your father's will, if you should refuse to accept him.

Por. Therefore, for fear of the worst, I pray thee, set a deep glass of Rhenish wine on the contrary casket, for, if the devil be within, and that temptation without, I know he will choose it. I will do anything, Nerissa, ere I will be married to a spunge.

Ner. You need not fear, lady, the having any of these lords: they have acquainted me with their determinations; which is, indeed, to return to their home, and to trouble you with no more suit, unless you may be won by some other sort than your father's imposition, depending on the caskets.

Por. If I live to be as old as Sibylla, I will die as chaste as Diana unless I be obtained by the manner of my father's will. I am glad this parcel of wooers are so reasonable; for there is not one among them but I dote on his very absence, and I pray God grant them a fair departure.

Ner. Do you not remember, lady, in your father's time, a Venetian, a scholar, and a soldier, that came hither in company of the marquess of Montferrat?

Por. Yes, yes, it was Bassanio: as I think, so was he called.

Ner. True, madam: he, of all the men that ever my foolish eyes looked upon, was the best deserving a fair lady.

Por. I remember him well: and I remember him worthy of thy praise.

Enter a Servant

How now? what news?

Serv. The four strangers seek for you, madam, to take their leave; and there is a forerunner come from a fifth, the prince of Morocco, who brings word the prince his master will be here to-night.

Por. If I could bid the fifth welcome with so good heart as I can bid the other four farewell, I should be glad of his approach: if he have the condition of a saint, and the complexion of a devil, I had rather he should shrive me than wive me.

Come, Nerissa.—Sirrah, go before.—

Whiles we shut the gate upon one wooer, another knocks at the door.   [*Exeunt*

SCENE III.—Venice. A public place

Enter BASSANIO *and* SHYLOCK

Shy. Three thousand ducats—well.
Bass. Ay, sir, for three months.
Shy. For three months—well.
Bass. For the which, as I told you, Antonio shall be bound.
Shy. Antonio shall become bound,—well.
Bass. May you stead me? Will you pleasure me? Shall I know your answer?
Shy. Three thousand ducats for three months, and Antonio bound.
Bass. Your answer to that.
Shy. Antonio is a good man.
Bass. Have you heard any imputation to the contrary?
Shy. Ho! no, no, no, no:—my meaning, in saying he

is a good man, is to have you understand me that he is
sufficient: yet his means are in supposition. He hath an
argosy bound to Tripolis, another to the Indies; I understand moreover upon the Rialto, he hath a third at Mexico,
a fourth for England, and other ventures he hath squandered
abroad. But ships are but boards; sailors but men; there
be land-rats and water-rats, water-thieves and land-thieves;
I mean pirates; and then there is the peril of waters, winds,
and rocks; the man is, notwithstanding, sufficient. Three
thousand ducats;—I think, I may take his bond.

    Bass. Be assured you may.

    Shy. I will be assured I may; and, that I may be as-
sured, I will bethink me. May I speak with Antonio?

    Bass. If it please you to dine with us.

    Shy. Yes, to smell pork; to eat of the habitation which
your prophet, the Nazarite, conjured the devil into. I
will buy with you, sell with you, talk with you, walk with
you, and so following: but I will not eat with you, drink
with you, nor pray with you. What news on the Rialto?—
Who is he comes here?

Enter ANTONIO

    Bass. This is Signior Antonio.

    Shy. [*Aside*] How like a fawning publican he looks!
I hate him, for he is a Christian;
But more, for that in low simplicity
He lends out money gratis, and brings down
The rate of usance here with us in Venice.
If I catch him one upon the hip,
I will feed fat the ancient grudge I bear him.
He hates our sacred nation; and he rails,
Even there where merchants most do congregate,
On me, my bargains, and my well-won thrift,
Which he calls interest. Curséd be my tribe
If I forgive him!

    Bass.   Shylock, do you hear?

    Shy. I am debating of my present store,
And, by the near guess of my memory,
I cannot instantly raise up the gross
Of full three thousand ducats. What of that?
Tubal, a wealthy Hebrew of my tribe,
Will furnish me. But soft! how many months
Do you desire?—[*To Antonio*] Rest you fair, good signior;
Your worship was the last man in our mouths.

    Ant. Shylock, albeit I neither lend nor borrow
By taking nor by giving of excess,
Yet to supply the ripe wants of my friend,
I 'll break a custom.—Is he yet possessed
How much ye would?

    Shy.   Ay, ay, three thousand ducats.

Ant. And for three months.
Shy. I had forgot:—three months; you told me so.
Well then, your bond; and let me see,—But hear you:
Methought, you said, you neither lend nor borrow
Upon advantage.
Ant.   I do never use it.
Shy. When Jacob grazed his uncle Laban's sheep,—
This Jacob from our holy Abram was
(As his wise mother wrought in his behalf)
The third possessor; ay, he was the third.—
Ant. And what of him? did he take interest?
Shy. No, not take interest; not as you would say
Directly interest: mark what Jacob did.
When Laban and himself were compromised,
That all the eanlings which were streaked and pied
Should fall as Jacob's hire, the ewes, being rank,
In end of autumn turnéd to the rams,
And when the work of generation was
Between these woolly breeders in the act,
The skilful shepherd peeled me certain wands,
And, in the doing of the deed of kind,
He stuck them up before the fulsome ewes,
Who, then conceiving, did in eaning time
Fall party-coloured lambs, and those were Jacob's.
This was a way to thrive, and he was blest:
And thrift is blessing, if men steal it not.
Ant. This was a venture, sir, that Jacob served for;
A thing not in his power to bring to pass,
But swayed and fashioned by the hand of Heaven.
Was this inserted to make interest good?
Or is your gold and silver ewes and rams?
Shy. I cannot tell: I make it breed as fast.—
But not me, signior.
Ant.   Mark you this, Bassanio;
The devil can cite Scripture for his purpose.
An evil soul producing holy witness
Is like a villain with a smiling cheek,
A goodly apple rotten at the heart.
O, what a goodly outside falsehood hath!
Shy. Three thousand ducats;—'t is a good round sum.
Three months from twelve, then let me see the rate.
Ant. Well, Shylock, shall we be beholding to you?
Shy. Signior Antonio, many a time and oft
In the Rialto you have rated me
About my moneys and my usances:
Still have I borne it with a patient shrug;
For sufferance is the badge of all our tribe.
You call me misbeliever, cut-throat dog,
And spit upon my Jewish gaberdine,
And all for use of that which is mine own.

Well then, it now appears, you need my help:
Go to then; you come to me, and you say,
"Shylock, we would have moneys," you say so;
You, that did void your rheum upon my beard
And foot me as you spurn a stranger cur
Over your threshold: moneys is your suit.
What should I say to you? Should I not say.
"Hath a dog money? Is it possible,
A cur can lend three thousand ducats?" or
Shall I bend low, and in a bondman's key,
With bated breath, and whispering humbleness,
Say this:—
"Fair sir, you spit on me on Wednesday last;
You spurned me such a day; another time
You called me dog; and for these courtesies
I 'll lend you thus much moneys?"
    Ant. I am as like to call thee so again,
To spit on thee again, to spurn thee too.
If thou wilt lend this money, lend it not
As to thy friends; for when did friendship take
A breed of barren metal of his friend?
But lend it rather to thine enemy;
Who, if he break, thou may'st with better face
Exact the penalty.
    Shy.   Why, look you, how you storm!
I would be friends with you, and have your love,
Forget the shames that you have stained me with.
Supply your present wants, and take no doit
Of usance for my moneys, and you 'll not hear me.
This is kind I offer.
    Bass. This were kindness.
    Shy.   This kindness will I show.
Go with me to a notary, seal me there
Your single bond; and, in a merry sport,
If you repay me not on such a day,
In such a place, such sum or sums as are
Expressed in the condition, let the forfeit
Be nominated for an equal pound
Of your fair flesh, to be cut off and taken
In what part of your body pleaseth me.
    Ant. Content, in faith: I 'll seal to such a bond,
And say there is much kindness in the Jew.
    Bass. You shall not seal to such a bond for me:
I 'll rather dwell in my necessity.
    Ant. Why, fear not, man; I will not forfeit it:
Within these two months, that 's a month before
This bond expires, I do expect return
Of thrice three times the value of this bond.
    Shy. O father Abram, what these Christians are,
Whose own hard dealings teaches them suspect

The thoughts of others!—Pray you tell me this:
If he should break his day, what should I gain
By the exaction of the forfeiture?
A pound of man's flesh, taken from a man,
Is not so estimable, profitable neither,
As flesh of muttons, beefs, or goats.   I say,
To buy his favour, I extend this friendship:
And for my love, I pray you, wrong me not.
    Ant.   Yes, Shylock, I will seal unto this bond.
    Shy.   Then meet me forthwith at the notary's,
Give him direction for this merry bond,
And I will go and purse the ducats straight;
See to my house, left in the fearful guard
Of an unthrifty knave; and presently
I will be with you.
    Ant.   Hie thee, gentle Jew.   [*Exit Shylock*
This Hebrew will turn Christian: he grows kind.
    Bass.   I like not fair terms and a villain's mind.
    Ant.   Come on, in this there can be no dismay;
My ships come home a month before the day.   [*Exeunt*

ACT TWO

SCENE I.—Belmont. A Room in PORTIA's House

Enter the PRINCE OF MOROCCO, *and his Followers:* PORTIA,
   NERISSA, *and others of her Train.   Flourish cornets*

    Mor.   Mislike me not for my complexion,
The shadowed livery of the burnished sun
To whom I am a neighbour and near bred.
Bring me the fairest creature northward born,
Where Phœbus' fire scarce thaws the icicles,
And let us make incision for your love
To prove whose blood is reddest, his or mine.
I tell thee, lady, this aspéct of mine
Hath feared the valiant; by my love, I swear,
The best regarded virgins of our clime
Have loved it too.   I would not change this hue,
Except to steal your thoughts, my gentle queen.
    Por.   In terms of choice I am not solely led
By nice direction of a maiden's eyes:
Besides, the lottery of my destiny
Bars me the right of voluntary choosing;
But, if my father had not scanted me
And hedged me by his wit to yield myself
His wife who wins me by that means I told you,
Yourself, renownéd prince, then stood as fair

As any comer I have looked on yet,
For my affection.
  Mor.   Even for that I thank you:
Therefore, I pray you, lead me to the caskets
To try my fortune. By this scimitar,—
That slew the Sophy and a Persian prince
That won three fields of Sultan Solyman,—
I would outstare the sternest eyes that look,
Outbrave the heart most daring on the earth,
Pluck the young suckling cubs from the she-bear,
Yea, mock the lion when he roars for prey,
To win thee, lady. But, alas the while!
If Hercules and Lichas play at dice
Which is the better man, the greater throw
May turn by fortune from the weaker hand,
So is Alcides beaten by his page;
And so may I, blind fortune leading me,
Miss that which one unworthier may attain,
And die with grieving.
  Pro.   You must take your chance,
And either not attempt to choose at all,
Or swear before you choose,—if you choose wrong,
Never speak to lady afterward
In way of marriage: therefore be advised.
  Mor. Nor will not. Come, bring me unto my chance.
  Por. First, forward to the temple: after dinner
Your hazard shall be made.
  Mor.   Good fortune then,
To make me blest or cursed'st among men!
          [Cornets, and exeunt

SCENE II.—Venice. A Street

Enter LAUNCELOT GOBBO

 Laun. Certainly, my conscience will serve me to run
from this Jew my master. The fiend is at mine elbow, and
tempts me, saying to me—"Gobbo, Launcelot Gobbo,
good Launcelot," or "good Gobbo," or "good Launcelot
Gobbo, use your legs, take the start, run away." My conscience says,—"No; take heed, honest Launcelot; take
heed, honest Gobbo"; or, as aforesaid, "honest Launcelot Gobbo; do not run; scorn running with thy heels."
Well, the most courageous fiend bids me pack: "Via!"
says the fiend; "away!" says the fiend; "for the heavens,
rouse up a brave mind," says the fiend, "and run." Well,
my conscience, hanging about the neck of my heart, says
very wisely to me—"My honest friend Launcelot, being
an honest man's son,"—or rather an honest woman's son;
—for, indeed, my father did something smack—something

grow to—he had a kind of taste:—well, my conscience
says, "Launcelot, budge not." "Budge," says the fiend:
"Budge not," says my conscience. "Conscience," say I,
"you counsel well"; "fiend," say I, "you counsel well":
to be ruled by my conscience, I should stay with the Jew my
master, who (God bless the mark) is a kind of devil; and,
to run away from the Jew, I should be ruled by the fiend,
who, saving your reverence, is the devil himself. Certainly,
the Jew is the very devil incarnation, and, in my conscience,
my conscience is but a kind of hard conscience to offer to
counsel me to stay with the Jew. The fiend gives the
more friendly counsel: I will run, fiend; my heels are
at your commandment; I will run.

Enter OLD GOBBO, *with a basket*

Gob. Master, young man, you, I pray you which is the
way to Master Jew's?
Laun. [*Aside*] O heavens, this is my true-begotten
father, who, being more than sand-blind, high gravel-
blind, knows me not:—I will try confusions with him.
Gob. Master, young gentleman, I pray you, which is the
way to Master Jew's?
Laun. Turn up on your right hand at the next turning,
but at the next turning of all, on your left; marry, at the
very next turning, turn of no hand, but turn down in-
directly to the Jew's house.
Gob. By God's sonties, 't will be a hard way to hit.
Can you tell me, whether one Launcelot, that dwells with
him, dwell with him, or no?
Laun. Talk you of young Master Launcelot?—[*Aside*]
Mark me now; now will I raise the waters.—[*To him*]
Talk you of young Master Launcelot?
Gob. No master, sir, but a poor man's son: his father,
though I say it, is an honest exceeding poor man; and,
God be thanked, well to live.
Laun. Well, let his father be what a will, we talk of
young Master Launcelot.
Gob. Your worship's friend, and Launcelot, sir.
Laun. But I pray you, *ergo*, old man, *ergo*, I beseech you,
talk you of young Master Launcelot?
Gob. Of Launcelot, an 't please your mastership.
Laun. Ergo, Master Launcelot. Talk not of Master
Launcelot, father; for the young gentleman (according to
Fates and Destinies, and such odd sayings, the Sisters Three,
and such branches of learning) is, indeed, deceased; or,
as you would say, in plain terms, gone to heaven.
Gob. Marry, God forbid! the boy was the very staff
of my age, my very prop.
Laun. Do I look like a cudgel, or a hovel-post, a staff,
or a prop?—Do you know me, father?

Gob. Alack the day! I know you not, young gentleman; but, I pray you, tell me, is my boy (God rest his soul) alive, or dead?

Laun. Do you not know me, father?

Gob. Alack, sir, I am sand-blind; I know you not.

Laun. Nay, indeed, if you had your eyes, you might fail of the knowing me: it is a wise father that knows his own child. Well, old man, I will tell you news of your son. [*Kneels*] Give me your blessing. Truth will come to light; murder cannot be hid long, a man's son may, but in the end truth will out.

Gob. Pray you, sir, stand up. I am sure you are not Launcelot, my boy.

Laun. Pray you, let's have no more fooling about it, but give me your blessing: I am Launcelot, your boy that was, your son that is, your child that shall be.

Gob. I cannot think you are my son.

Laun. I know not what I shall think of that; but I am Launcelot, the Jew's man, and, I am sure, Margery, your wife, is my mother.

Gob Her name is Margery, indeed: I'll be sworn, if thou be Launcelot, thou art mine own flesh and blood. Lord worshipped might he be! what a beard hast thou got: thou hast got more hair on thy chin than Dobbin, my fill-horse, has on his tail.

Laun. It should seem then that Dobbin's tail grows backward. I am sure he had more hair of his tail than I have of my face, when I last saw him.

Gob. Lord! how art thou changed! How doest thou and thy master agree? I have brought him a present. How gree you now?

Laun. Well, well; but, for mine own part, as I have set up my rest to run away, so I will not rest till I have run some ground. My master's a very Jew: give him a present! give him a halter: I am famished in his service. You may tell every finger I have with my ribs. Father, I am glad you are come: give me your present to one Master Bassanio, who indeed gives rare new liveries; if I serve not him, I will run as far as God has any ground.— O rare fortune, here comes the man:—to him, father; for I am a Jew, if I serve the Jew any longer.

Enter BASSANIO, *with* LEONARDO, *and other Followers*

Bass. You may do so, but let it be so hasted, that supper be ready at the farthest by five of the clock. See these letters delivered, put the liveries to making, and desire Gratiano to come anon to my lodging.

[*Exit a Servant*

Laun. To him, father.

Gob. God bless your worship!

Bass. Gramercy. Wouldst thou aught with me?

Gob. Here's my son, sir, a poor boy,—

Laun. Not a poor boy, sir, but the rich Jew's man,
that would, sir,—as my father shall specify,—

Gob. He hath a great infection, sir, as one would say,
to serve—

Laun. Indeed, the short and the long is, I serve the
Jew, and have a desire,—as my father shall specify,—

Gob. His master and he (saving your worship's reverence) are scarce cater-cousins,—

Laun. To be brief, the very truth is, that the Jew
having done me wrong, doth cause me,—as my father,
being, I hope, an old man, shall frutify unto you,—

Gob. I have here a dish of doves, that I would bestow
upon your worship; and my suit is,—

Laun. In very brief, the suit is impertinent to myself,
as your worship shall know by this honest old man; and,
though I say it, though old man, yet poor man, my father.

Bass. One speak for both.—What would you?

Laun. Serve you, sir.

Gob. That is the very defect of the matter, sir.

Bass. I know thee well; thou hast obtained thy suit:
Shylock, thy master, spoke with me this day,
And have preferred thee, if it be preferment
To leave a rich Jew's service, to become
The follower of so poor a gentleman.

Laun. The old proverb is very well parted between
my master Shylock and you, sir: you have the grace of
God, sir, and he hath enough.

Bass. Thou speak'st it well. Go, father, with thy son.
Take leave of thy old master, and inquire
My lodging out. [*To his Followers*] Give him a livery
More guarded then his fellows': see it done.

Laun. Father, in.—I cannot get a service, no; I have
ne'er a tongue in my head. Well: [*looking on his palm*]
if any man in Italy have a fairer table, which doth offer
to swear upon a book, I shall have good fortune. Go to,
here's a simple line of life, here's a small trifle of wives,
alas, fifteen wives is nothing; eleven widows, and nine
maids, is a simple coming-in for one man: and then, to
'scape drowning thrice, and to be in peril of my life with
the edge of a feather-bed, here are simple 'scapes: well,
if Fortune be a woman, she's a good wench for this gear.—
Father, come; I'll take my leave of the Jew in the twinkling
of an eye. [*Exeunt Launcelot and Old Gobbo*

Bass. I pray thee, good Leonardo, think on this.
These things being bought and orderly bestowed,
Return in haste, for I do feast to-night
My best-esteemed acquaintance: hie thee, go.

Leon. My best endeavours shall be done herein.

27

Enter GRATIANO

Gra.   Where is your master?
Leon.   Yonder, sir, he walks.   [*Exit*
Gra.   Signior Bassanio,—
Bass.   Gratiano.
Gra.   I have a suit to you.
Bass.   You have obtained it.
Gra.   You must not deny me: I must go with you to
Belmont.
Bass.   Why, then you must.   But hear thee, Gratiano:
Thou art too wild, too rude, and bold of voice;
Parts, that become thee happily enough,
And in such eyes as ours appear not faults,
But where thou art not known, why, there they show
Something too liberal.   Pray thee, take pain
To allay with some cold drops of modesty
Thy skipping spirit, lest, through thy wild behaviour,
I be misconstrued in the place I go to,
And lose my hopes.
Gra.   Signior Bassanio, hear me:
If I do not put on a sober habit,
Talk with respect, and swear but now and then,
Wear prayer-books in my pocket, look demurely,
Nay more, while grace is saying, hood mine eyes
Thus with my hat, and sigh, and say amen,
Use all the observance of civility
Like one well studied in a sad ostent
To please his grandam, never trust me more.
Bass.   Well, we shall see your bearing.
Gra.   Nay, but I bar to-night; you shall not gage me
By what we do to-night.
Bass.   No, that were pity.
I would entreat you rather to put on
Your boldest suit of mirth, for we have friends
That purpose merriment.   But fare you well:
I have some business.
Gra.   And I must to Lorenzo and the rest:
But we will visit you at supper-time.   [*Exeunt*

SCENE III.—The Same.   A Room in SHYLOCK'S House

Enter JESSICA *and* LAUNCELOT

Jes.   I am sorry that thou wilt leave my father so:
Our house is hell, and thou, a merry devil,
Didst rob it of some taste of tediousness.
But fare thee well; there is a ducat for thee:
And, Launcelot, soon at supper shalt thou see
Lorenzo, who is thy new master's guest:

Give him this letter, do it secretly:
And so farewell; I would not have my father
See me in talk with thee.

    Laun. Adieu!—tears exhibit my tongue.—Most beautiful pagan, most sweet Jew! If a Christian do not play the knave and get thee, I am much deceived. But, adieu! these foolish drops do somewhat drown my manly spirit: adieu!

    Jes. Farewell, good Launcelot.—   [*Exit Launcelot*
Alack, what heinous sin is it in me,
To be ashamed to be my father's child!
But though I am a daughter to his blood,
I am not to his manners. O Lorenzo,
If thou keep promise, I shall end this strife,
Become a Christian and thy loving wife.   [*Exit*

Scene IV.—The Same. A Street

Enter Gratiano, Lorenzo, Salarino, *and* Salanio

    Lor. Nay, we will slink away in supper-time,
Disguise us at my lodging, and return
All in an hour.

    Gra. We have not made good preparation.

    Salar. We have not spoke us yet of torch-bearers.

    Salan. 'T is vile unless it may be quaintly ordered,
And better, in my mind, not undertook.

    Lor. 'T is now but four o'clock, we have two hours
To furnish us.

Enter Launcelot *with a letter*

                Friend Launcelot, what's the news?

    Laun. An it shall please you to break up this, it shall seem to signify.   [*Giving a letter*

    Lor. I know the hand: in faith, 't is a fair hand,
And whiter than the paper it writ on
Is the fair hand that writ.

    Gra.   Love-news, in faith.

    Laun. By your leave, sir.

    Lor. Whither goest thou?

    Laun. Marry, sir, to bid my old master, the Jew, to sup to-night with my new master, the Christian.

    Lor. Hold here, take this: tell gentle Jessica I will not fail her, speak it privately: [*Exit Launcelot*
Go, Gentlemen,
Will you prepare you for this masque to-night?
I am provided of a torch-bearer.

    Salar. Ay, marry, I'll be gone about it straight.

    Salan. And so will I.

Lor.   Meet me and Gratiano
At Gratiano's lodging some hour hence.
   Salar. 'T is good we do so.
                       [Exeunt Salarino and Salanio
   Gra. Was not that letter from fair Jessica?
   Lor. I must needs tell thee all. She hath directed
How I shall take her from her father's house,
What gold and jewels she is furnished with,
What page's suit she hath in readiness.
If e'er the Jew her father come to Heaven,
It will be for his gentle daughter's sake;
And never dare misfortune cross her foot,
Unless she do it under this excuse,
That she is issue to a faithless Jew.
Come, go with me, pursue this as thou goest:
Fair Jessica shall be my torch-bearer.   *[Exeunt*

Scene V.—The Same. Before Shylock's House

Enter Shylock *and* Launcelot

   Shy. Well, thou shalt see, thy eyes shall be thy judge,
The difference of old Shylock and Bassanio;
What, Jessica!—thou shalt not gormandise
As thou hast done with me;—what, Jessica!
And sleep and snore, and rend apparel out.—
Why, Jessica, I say!
   Laun.   Why. Jessica!
   Shy. Who bids thee call? I do not bid thee call.
I could do nothing without bidding.

Enter Jessica

   Jes. Call you? What is your will?
   Shy. I am bid forth to supper, Jessica:
There are my keys.—But wherefore should I go?
I am not bid for love; they flatter me;
But yet I'll go in hate, to feed upon
The prodigal Christian.—Jessica, my girl,
Look to my house.—I am right loath to go:
There is some ill a-brewing towards my rest,
For I did dream of money-bags to-night.
   Laun. I beseech you, sir, go: my young master doth
expect your reproach.
   Shy. So do I his.
   Laun. And they have conspired together,—I will not
say, you shall see a masque; but if you do, then it was not
for nothing that my nose fell a-bleeding on Black-Monday
last, at six o'clock i' the morning, falling out that year
on Ash-Wednesday was four year in th' afternoon.

Shy. What, are there masques?—Hear you me, Jessica,
Lock up my doors, and when you hear the drum,
And the vile squeaking of the wry-necked fife,
Clamber not you up to the casements then,
Nor thrust your head into the public street
To gaze on Christian fools with varnished faces:
But stop my house's ears, I mean my casements,
Let not the sound of shallow foppery enter
My sober house.—By Jacob's staff I swear,
I have no mind of feasting forth to-night:
But I will go:—Go you before me, sirrah,
Say, I will come.

   Laun. I will go before, sir.—Mistress, look out at window, for all this;

       There will come a Christian by,
       Will be worth a Jewess' eye.   [*Exit*

   Shy. What says that fool of Hagar's offspring? ha!
   Jes. His words were "Farewell, mistress"; nothing else.

   Shy. The patch is kind enough, but a huge feeder,
Snail-slow in profit, and he sleeps by day
More than the wild cat: drones hive not with me,
Therefore I part with him, and part with him
To one that I would have him help to waste
His borrowed purse.—Well, Jessica, go in,
Perhaps I will return immediately.
Do as I bid you; shut the door after you:
Fast bind, fast find;
A proverb never stale in thrifty mind.   [*Exit*

   Jes. Farewell; and if my fortune be not crost,
I have a father, you a daughter, lost.   [*Exit*

Scene VI.—The same

Enter Gratiano *and* Salarino, *masqued*

   Gra. This is the penthouse, under which Lorenzo
Desired us to make stand.
   Salar.   His hour is almost past.
   Gra. And it is marvel he outdwells his hour,
For lovers ever run before the clock.
   Salar. O! ten times faster Venus' pigeons fly
To seal love's bonds new made, than they are wont
To keep obligéd faith unforfeited!
   Gra. That ever holds: who riseth from a feast
With that keen appetite that he sits down?
Where is the horse that doth untread again
His tedious measures with the unbated fire
That he did pace them first? All things that are,
Are with more spirit chaséd than enjoyed.

How like a younker or a prodigal
The scarféd bark puts from her native bay,
Hugged and embracéd by the strumpet wind!
How like the prodigal doth she return,
With over-weathered ribs and ragged sails,
Lean, rent, and beggared by the strumpet wind!

Enter LORENZO

Salar.   Here comes Lorenzo: more of this hereafter.
   Lor.   Sweet friends, your patience for my long abode;
Not I, but my affairs, have made you wait:
When you shall please to play the thieves for wives
I'll watch as long for you then,—Approach;
Here dwells my father Jew.—Ho, who's within?

Enter JESSICA *above, in boy's clothes*

   Jes.   Who are you?   Tell me for more certainty,
Albeit I'll swear that I do know your tongue.
   Lor.   Lorenzo, and thy love.
   Jes.   Lorenzo, certain; and my love, indeed,
For who love I so much?   And now who knows
But you, Lorenzo, whether I am yours?
   Lor.   Heaven and thy thoughts are witness that thou art.
   Jes.   Here, catch this casket; it is worth the pains.
I am glad 't is night, you do not look on me,
For I am much ashamed of my exchange:
But love is blind, and lovers cannot see
The pretty follies that themselves commit;
For if they could, Cupid himself would blush
To see me thus transforméd to a boy.
   Lor.   Descend, for you must be my torch-bearer.
   Jes.   What, must I hold a candle to my shames?
They in themselves, good sooth, are too light.
Why, 't is an office of discovery, love,
And I should be obscured.
   Lor.   So are you, sweet,
Even in the lovely garnish of a boy.
But come at once;
For the close night doth play the runaway,
And we are stayed for at Bassanio's feast.
   Jes.   I will make fast the doors, and gild myself
With some more ducats, and be with you straight.
                                        [*Exit from above*
   Gra.   Now, by my hood, a Gentile, and no Jew.
   Lor.   Beshrew me, but I love her heartily;
For she is wise, if I can judge of her,
And fair she is, if that mine eyes be true,
And true she is, as she hath proved herself;
And therefore, like herself, wise, fair, and true,
Shall she be placéd in my constant soul.

32

Enter JESSICA

What, art thou come?—On gentlemen; away!
Our masquing mates by this time for us stay.
                                    [*Exit with Jessica and Salarino*

Enter ANTONIO

  Ant. Who's there?
  Gra. Signior Antonio!
  Ant. Fie, fie, Gratiano, where are all the rest?
'T is nine o'clock, our friends all stay for you:
No masque to-night: the wind is come about,
Bassanio presently will go aboard;
I have sent twenty out to seek for you.
  Gra. I am glad on 't, I desire no more delight
Than to be under sail and gone to-night.   [*Exeunt*

SCENE VII.—Belmont. An Apartment in PORTIA's House

Enter PORTIA, *with the* PRINCE OF MOROCCO, *and their
Trains*

  Por. Go, draw aside the curtains, and discover
The several caskets to this noble prince:—
Now make your choice.
  Mor.   The first, of gold, who this inscription bears,
"Who chooseth me shall gain what many men desire."
The second, silver, which this promise carries,
"Who chooseth me shall get as much as he deserves."
This third, dull lead, with warning all as blunt,
"Who chooseth me must give and hazard all he hath."
How shall I know if I do choose the right?
  Por.   The one of them contains my picture, prince:
If you choose that, then I am yours withal.
  Mor.   Some god direct my judgment! Let me see:—
I will survey the inscriptions back again.
What says this leaden casket?
"Who chooseth me must give and hazard all he hath."
Must give—for what? for lead? hazard for lead?
This casket threatens.   Men that hazard all
Do it in hope of fair advantages:
A golden mind stoops not to shows of dross,
I'll then nor give, nor hazard, aught for lead.
What says the silver with her virgin hue?
"Who chooseth me shall get as much as he deserves."
As much as he deserves?—Pause there, Morocco,
And weigh thy value with an even hand.
If thou beest rated by thy estimation,
Thou dost deserve enough; and yet enough
May not extend so far as to the lady;

And yet to be afeared of my deserving
Were but a weak disabling of myself.
As much as I deserve!—Why, that's the lady:
I do in birth deserve her, and in fortunes,
In graces, and in qualities of breeding;
But more than these, in love I do deserve.
What if I strayed no further, but chose here?—
Let's see once more this saying graved in gold:
"Who chooseth me shall gain what many men desire."
Why, that's the lady: all the world desires her.
From the four corners of the earth they come
To kiss this shrine, this mortal-breathing saint.
The Hyrcanian deserts, and the vasty wilds
Of wild Arabia, are as thoroughfares now
For princes to come view fair Portia.
The watery kingdom, whose ambitious head
Spits in the face of heaven, is no bar
To stop the foreign spirits, but they come,
As o'er a brook, to see fair Portia.
One of these three contains her heavenly picture.
Is't like, that lead contains her? 'T were damnation
To think so base a thought: it were too gross
To rib her cerecloth in the obscure grave.
Or shall I think in silver she's immured,
Being ten times undervalued to tried gold?
O sinful thought! Never so rich a gem
Was set in worse than gold. They have in England
A coin, that bears the figure of an angel
Stampéd in gold, but that's insculped upon;
But here an angel in a golden bed
Lies all within. Deliver me the key:
Here do I choose, and thrive I as I may!
　　Por.   There, take it, prince; and if my form lie there,
Then I am yours.   [*He unlocks the golden casket*
　　Mor.   O hell! what have we here?
A carrion death, within whose empty eye
There is a written scroll. I'll read the writing,
[*Reads*]   *All that glisters is not gold;*
　　　　　Often have you heard that told:
　　　　　Many a man his life hath sold
　　　　　But my outside to behold:
　　　　　Gilded tombs do worms infold.
　　　　　Had you been as wise as bold,
　　　　　Young in limbs, in judgment old,
　　　　　Your answer had not been inscroll'd,
　　　　　" Fare you well, your suit is cold."
Cold, indeed. and labour lost:
Then, farewell, heat, and, welcome, frost!
Portia, adieu.   I have too grieved a heart,
To take a tedious leave: thus losers part.   [*Exit*

Por.   A gentle riddance.   Draw the curtains; go.
Let all of his complexion choose me so.   [*Exeunt*

Scene VIII.—Venice.   A Street

Enter Salarino *and* Salanio

Salar.   Why, man, I saw Bassanio under sail:
With him is Gratiano gone along;
And in their ship, I'm sure, Lorenzo is not.
Salan.   The villain Jew with outcries raised the Duke,
Who went with him to search Bassanio's ship.
Salar.   He came too late, the ship was under sail:
But there the Duke was given to understand
That in a gondola were seen together
Lorenzo and his amorous Jessica.
Besides, Antonio certified the Duke
They were not with Bassanio in his ship.
Salan.   I never heard a passion so confused,
So strange, outrageous, and so variable,
As the dog Jew did utter in the streets:
"My daughter!—O my ducats!—O my daughter!
Fled with a Christian!—O my Christian ducats!
Justice! the law! my ducats, and my daughter!
A sealéd bag, two sealéd bags of ducats,
Of double ducats, stolen from me by my daughter!
And jewels, two stones, two rich and precious stones,
Stolen by my daughter!—Justice! find the girl!
She hath the stones upon her, and the ducats!"
Salar.   Why, all the boys in Venice follow him,
Crying, his stones, his daughter, and his ducats.
Salan.   Let good Antonio look he keep his day,
Or he shall pay for this.
Salar.   Marry, well remembered.
I reasoned with a Frenchman yesterday,
Who told me, in the narrow seas that part
The French and English, there miscarriéd
A vessel of our country richly fraught.
I thought upon Antonio when he told me,
And wished in silence that it were not his.
Salan.   You were best to tell Antonio what you hear;
Yet do not suddenly, for it may grieve him.
Salar.   A kinder gentleman treads not the earth.
I saw Bassanio and Antonio part:
Bassanio told him he would make some speed
Of his return: he answered—"Do not so;
Slubber not business for my sake, Bassanio,
But stay the very riping of the time;
And for the Jew's bond which he hath of me,
Let it not enter in your mind of love;

35

Be merry, and employ your chiefest thoughts
To courtship and such fair ostents of love
As shall conveniently become you there."
And even there, his eye being big with tears,
Turning his face, he put his hands behind him,
And with affection wondrous sensible
He wrung Bassanio's hand; and so they parted.
    Salan. I think he only loves the world for him.
I pray thee, let us go and find him out,
And quicken his embracéd heaviness
With some delight or other.
    Salar.   **Do** we so.   *[Exeunt*

SCENE IX.—Belmont.—A Room in PORTIA'S House

Enter NERISSA, *with a Servitor*

    Ner. Quick, quick, I pray thee, draw the curtain straight,
The prince of Arragon hath ta'en his oath,
And comes to his election presently.

Enter the PRINCE OF ARRAGON, PORTIA, *and their Trains.*
Flourish Cornets

    Por. Behold, there stand the caskets, noble prince:
If you choose that wherein I am contained,
Straight shall our nuptial rites be solemnised;
But if you fail, without more speech, my lord,
You must be gone from hence immediately.
    Ar. I am enjoined by oath to observe three things:
First, never to unfold to any one
Which casket 't was I chose; next, if I fail
Of the right casket, never in my life
To woo a maid in way of marriage;
Lastly,
If I do fail in fortune of my choice,
Immediately to leave you and be gone.
    Por. To these injunctions every one doth swear
That come to hazard for my worthless self.
    Ar. And so have I addressed me. Fortune now
To my heart's hope!—Gold, silver, and base lead,
  "Who chooseth me must give and hazard all he hath":
You shall look fairer, ere I give, or hazard.
What says the golden chest? ha! let me see:—
"Who chooseth me shall gain what many men desire."
What many men desire:—that many may be meant
By the fool multitude, that choose by show,
Not learning more than the fond eye doth teach,
Which pries not to the interior, but, like the martlet,
Builds in the weather on the outward wall,
Even in the force and road of casualty.

I will not choose what many men desire,
Because I will not jump with common spirits
And rank me with the barbarous multitudes.
Why, then to thee, thou silver treasure-house;
Tell me once more what title thou dost bear:
"Who chooseth me shall get as much as he deserves."
And well said too; for who shall go about
To cozen fortune and be honourable
Without the stamp of merit?   Let none presume
To wear an undeservéd dignity:
O! that estates, degrees, and offices,
Were not derived corruptly, and that clear honour
Were purchased by the merit of the wearer!
How many then should cover that stand bare;
How many be commanded that command;
How much low peasantry would then be gleaned
From the true seed of honour; and how much honour
Picked from the chaff and ruin of the times,
To be new-varnished!   Well, but to my choice:
"Who chooseth me shall get as much as he deserves."
I will assume desert.—Give me a key for this,
And instantly unlock my fortunes here.

> [*He opens the silver casket*

   Por.   Too long a pause for that which you find there.
   Ar.   What's here? the portrait of a blinking idiot,
Presenting me a schedule!   I will read it.
How much unlike art thou to Portia!
How much unlike my hopes and my deservings!
"Who chooseth me shall have as much as he deserves:"
Did I deserve no more than a fool's head?
Is that my prize? are my deserts no better?
   Por.   To offend and judge are distinct offices,
And of opposéd natures.
   Ar.   What is here?
[*Reads*]   *The fire seven times tried this:*
        Seven times tried that judgment is
        That did never choose amiss.
        Some there be that shadows kiss;
        Such have but a shadow's bliss:
        There be fools alive, I wis,
        Silvered o'er, and so was this:
        Take what wife you will to bed,
        I will ever be your head:
        So be gone; you are sped.
Still more fool I shall appear
By the time I linger here:
With one fool's head I came to woo,
But I go away with two,—
Sweet, adieu.   I'll keep my oath,
Patiently to bear my wroth.   [*Exeunt Arragon and Train*

Por. Thus hath the candle singed the moth.
O, these deliberate fools, when they do choose
They have the wisdom by their wit to lose.
Ner. The ancient saying is no heresy,
Hanging and wiving goes by destiny.
Por. Come, draw the curtain, Nerissa.

Enter a Messenger

Mess. Where is my lady?
Por.   Here, what would my lord?
Mess. Madam, there is alighted at your gate
A young Venetian, one that comes before
To signify the approaching of his lord,
From whom he bringeth sensible regrets,
To wit (beside commends and courteous breath)
Gifts of rich value.   Yet I have not seen
So likely an ambassador of love:
A day in April never came so sweet,
To show how costly summer was at hand,
As this fore-spurrer comes before his lord.
Por. No more, I pray thee, I am half afeard
Thou wilt say anon he is some kin to thee.
Thou spend'st such high-day wit in praising him.
Come, come, Nerissa, for I long to see
Quick Cupid's post that comes so mannerly.
Ner. Bassanio lord,—Love, if thy will it be!   [*Exeunt*

ACT THREE

SCENE I.—Venice. A Street

Enter SALANIO *and* SALARINO

Salan. Now, what news on the Rialto?
Salar. Why, yet it lives there unchecked, that Antonio
hath a ship of rich lading wrecked on the narrow seas;
the Goodwins, I think they call the place, a very dangerous
flat, and fatal, where the carcases of many a tall ship lie
buried, as they say, if my gossip Report be an honest
woman of her word.
Salan. I would she were as lying a gossip in that as
ever knapped ginger or made her neighbours believe she
wept for the death of a third husband. But it is true,
without any slips of prolixity, or crossing the plain highway
of talk, that the good Antonio, the honest Antonio—O,
that I had a title good enough to keep his name company—
Salar. Come, the full stop.
Salan. Ha, what sayest thou? Why, the end is, he
hath lost a ship.

Salar. I would it might prove the end of his losses.

Salan. Let me say "amen" betimes, lest the devil cross my prayer, for here he comes in the likeness of a Jew.

Enter SHYLOCK

How now, Shylock, what news among the merchants?

Shy. You knew, none so well, none so well as you, of my daughter's flight.

Salar. That's certain: I, for my part, knew the tailor that made the wings she flew withal.

Salan. And Shylock, for his own part, knew the bird was fledged; and then it is the complexion of them all to leave the dam.

Shy. She is damned for it.

Salar. That's certain, if the devil may be her judge.

Shy. My own flesh and blood to rebel!

Salan. Out upon it, old carrion, rebels it at these years?

Shy. I say my daughter is my flesh and blood.

Salar. There is more difference between thy flesh and hers than between jet and ivory; more between your bloods than there is between red wine and rhenish. But tell us, do you hear whether Antonio have had any loss at sea or no?

Shy. There I have another bad match; a bankrupt, a prodigal, who dare scarce show his head on the Rialto; a beggar, that used to come so smug upon the mart: Let him look to his bond: he was wont to call me usurer; let him look to his bond: he was wont to lend money for a Christian courtesy; let him look to his bond.

Salar. Why, I am sure, if he forfeit, thou wilt not take his flesh; what's that good for?

Shy. To bait fish withal; if it will feed nothing else, it will feed my revenge. He hath disgraced me, and hindered me half a million, laughed at my losses, mocked at my gains, scorned my nation, thwarted my bargains, cooled my friends, heated mine enemies; and what's his reason? I am a Jew. Hath not a Jew eyes? hath not a Jew hands, organs, dimensions, senses, affections, passions? fed with the same food, hurt with the same weapons, subject to the same diseases, healed by the same means, warmed and cooled by the same winter and summer, as a Christian is? If you prick us, do we not bleed? if you tickle us, do we not laugh? if you poison us, do we not die? and if you wrong us, shall we not revenge? If we are like you in the rest, we will resemble you in that. If a Jew wrong a Christian, what is his humility? revenge. If a Christian wrong a Jew, what should his sufferance be by Christian example? why, revenge. The villainy you teach me, I will execute; and it shall go hard but I will better the instruction.

Enter a Servant

Serv. Gentlemen, my master Antonio is at his house, and desires to speak with you both.

Salar. We have been up and down to seek him.

Salan. Here comes another of the tribe; a third cannot be matched, unless the devil himself turn Jew.

     [*Exeunt Salanio, Salarino, and Servant*

Enter TUBAL

Shy. How now, Tubal? what news from Genoa? Hast thou found my daughter?

Tub. I often came where I did hear of her, but cannot find her.

Shy. Why there, there, there, there! a diamond gone, cost me two thousand ducats in Frankfort. The curse never fell upon our nation till now; I never felt it till now; two thousand ducats in that, and other precious, precious jewels. I would my daughter were dead at my foot, and the jewels in her ear! would she were hearsed at my foot, and the ducats in her coffin! No news of them?—Why so; and I know not what's spent in the search: why, thou loss upon loss! the thief gone with so much, and so much to find the thief, and no satisfaction, no revenge; nor no ill luck stirring, but what lights o' my shoulders; no sighs, but o' my breathing; no tears, but o' my shedding.

Tub. Yes, other men have ill luck too. Antonio, as I heard in Genoa—

Shy. What, what, what? ill luck, ill luck?

Tub. —hath an argosy cast away, coming from Tripolis.

Shy. I thank God! I thank God! Is it true? is it true?

Tub. I spoke with some of the sailors that escaped the wreck.

Shy. I thank thee, good Tubal. Good news, good news: —Ha, ha! . . . hear . . . in Genoa?

Tub. Your daughter spent in Genoa, as I heard, one night, fourscore ducats.

Shy. Thou stick'st a dagger in me. I shall never see my gold again. Fourscore ducats at a sitting! fourscore ducats!

Tub. There came divers of Antonio's creditors in my company to Venice, that swear he cannot choose but break.

Shy. I am very glad of it: I'll plague him; I'll torture him; I am glad of it.

Tub. One of them showed me a ring that he had of your daughter for a monkey.

Shy. Out upon her! Thou torturest me, Tubal: it was my turquoise; I had it of Leah, when I was a bachelor. I would not have given it for a wilderness of monkeys.

Tub. But Antonio is certainly undone.

Shy. Nay, that's true, that's very true. Go, Tubal, fee me an officer, bespeak him a fortnight before. I will have the heart of him, if he forfeit; for were he out of Venice, I can make what merchandise I will. Go, go, Tubal, and meet me at our synagogue: go, good Tubal; at our synagogue, Tubal.   [*Exeunt*

SCENE II.—Belmont. A Room in PORTIA'S House

Enter BASSANIO, PORTIA, GRATIANO, NERISSA, *and Attendants*

Por.   I pray you, tarry; pause a day or two
Before you hazard, for in choosing wrong
I lose your company; therefore, forbear awhile.
There's something tells me, but it is not love,
I would not lose you,—and you know yourself,
Hate counsels not in such a quality;
But lest you should not understand me well
(And yet a maiden hath no tongue but thought)
I would detain you here some month or two
Before you venture for me.   I could teach you
How to choose right,—but then I am forsworn;
So will I never be: so may you miss me;
But if you do, you'll make me wish a sin,
That I had been forsworn.   Beshrew your eyes,
They have o'erlooked me, and divided me:
One half of me is yours, the other half yours,
Mine own, I would say; but if mine, then yours,
And so all yours.   O, these naughty times
Put bars between the owners and their rights;
And so, though yours, not yours;—prove it so,
Let fortune go to hell for it, not I.
I speak too long; but 't is to peise the time,
To eke it, and to draw it out in length,
To stay you from election.
Bass.   Let me choose.
For as I am, I live upon the rack.
Por.   Upon the rack, Bassanio: then confess
What treason there is mingled with your love.
Bass.   None, but that ugly treason of mistrust
Which makes me fear the enjoying of my love.
There may as well be amity and life
'Tween snow and fire as treason and my love.
Por.   Ay, but I fear you speak upon the rack,
Where men enforcéd do speak anything.
Bass.   Promise me life, and I'll confess the truth.
Por.   Well then, confess and live.
Bass.   Confess and love,

41

Had been the very sum of my confession:
O happy torment, when my torturer
Doth teach me answers for deliverance:
But let me to my fortune and the caskets.
                    [*Curtain drawn from before the caskets*
  Por. Away then, I am locked in one of them,
If you do love me, you will find me out.
Nerissa and the rest, stand all aloof.
Let music sound, while he doth make his choice,
Then, if he lose, he makes a swan-like end,
Fading in music. That the comparison
May stand more proper, my eye shall be the stream
And watery death-bed for him. He may win;
And what is music then? then music is
Even as the flourish when true subjects bow
To a new-crownéd monarch; such it is,
As are those dulcet sounds in break of day
That creep into the dreaming bridegroom's ear,
And summon him to marriage.—Now he goes,
With no less presence but with much more love
Than young Alcides when he did redeem
The virgin tribute paid by howling Troy
To the sea-monster: I stand for sacrifice,
The rest aloof are the Dardanian wives,
With blearéd visages, come forth to view
The issue of the exploit: go, Hercules,
Live thou, I live:—with much, much more dismay,
I view the fight than thou that mak'st the fray.

A song, the whilst Bassanio comments on the caskets to
himself

> *Tell me where is fancy bred,*
> *Or in the heart, or in the head?*
> *How begot, how nourishéd?*
>   *Reply, reply.*
> *It is engendered in the eyes,*
> *With gazing fed, and fancy dies*
> *In the cradle where it lies,*
>   *Let us all ring fancy's knell:*
>   *I'll begin it,—Ding, dong, bell.*

  All. Ding, dong, bell.
  Bass. So may the outward shows be least themselves:
The world is still deceived with ornament.
In law, what plea so tainted and corrupt
But, being seasoned with a gracious voice,
Obscures the show of evil? In religion,
What damnéd error but some sober brow
Will bless it and approve it with a text,
Hiding the grossness with fair ornament?

There is no vice so simple but assumes
Some mark of virtue on his outward parts.
How many cowards, whose hearts are all as false
As stairs of sand, wear yet upon their chins
The beards of Hercules and frowning Mars,
Who, inward searched, have livers white as milk,
And these assume but valour's excrement,
To render them redoubted.   Look on beauty,
And you shall see 't is purchased by the weight,
Which therein works a miracle in nature,
Making them lightest that wear most of it:
So are those crispéd snaky golden locks,
Which make such wanton gambols with the wind
Upon supposéd fairness, often known
To be the dowry of a second head,
The skull that bred them in the sepulchre.
Thus ornament is but the guiléd shore
To a most dangerous sea; the beauteous scarf
Veiling an Indian beauty; in a word,
The seeming truth which cunning times put on
To entrap the wisest.   Therefore, thou gaudy gold,
Hard food for Midas, I will none of thee;
Nor none of thee, thou pale and common drudge
'Tween man and man: but thou, thou meagre lead,
Which rather threat'nest than dost promise aught,
Thy plainness moves me more than eloquence,
And here choose I.   Joy be the consequence!
   Por.   How all the other passions fleet to air,
As doubtful thoughts, and rash-embraced despair,
And shuddering fear, and green-eyed jealousy!
O love, be moderate, allay thy ecstacy,
In measure rain thy joy, scant this excess:
I feel too much thy blessing! make it less,
For fear I surfeit!
   Bass.   What find I here?

                    [*Opening the leaden casket*
Fair Portia's counterfeit.   What demi-god
Hath come so near creation?   Move these eyes?
Or whether, riding on the balls of mine,
Seem they in motion?   Here are severed lips
Parted with sugar breath, so sweet a bar
Should sunder such sweet friends.   Here in her hairs,
The painter plays the spider and hath woven
A golden mesh to entrap the hearts of men
Faster than gnats in cobwebs.   But her eyes,
How could he see to do them? having made one
Methinks it should have power to steal both his,
And leave itself unfurnished: yet look, how far
The substance of my praise doth wrong this shadow
In underprizing it, so far this shadow

Doth limp behind the substance.   Here's the scroll,
The continent and summary of my fortune:
[*Reads*]   *You that choose not by the view,*
                   Chance as fair, and choose as true,
                   Since this fortune falls to you,
                   Be content, and seek no new.
                   If you be well pleased with this,
                   And hold your fortune for your bliss,
                   Turn you where your Lady is,
                   And claim her with a loving kiss.
A gentle scroll.—Fair lady, by your leave,
I come by note, to give and to receive.   [*Kissing her*
Like one of two contending in a prize,
That thinks he hath done well in people's eyes,
Hearing applause, and universal shout,
Giddy in spirit, still gazing in a doubt,
Whether those pearls of praise be his or no:
So, thrice fair lady, stand I, even so,
As doubtful whether what I see be true,
Until confirmed, signed, ratified by you.
     Por.   You see me, Lord Bassanio, where I stand,
Such as I am: though for myself alone
I would not be ambitious in my wish,
To wish myself much better, yet for you
I would be trebled twenty times myself;
A thousand times more fair, ten thousand times more rich;
That, only to stand high in your account,
I might in virtues, beauties, livings, friends,
Exceed account: but the full sum of me
Is sum of nothing; which, to term in gross,
Is an unlessoned girl, unschooled, unpractised,
Happy in this, she is not yet so old
But she may learn; happier than this,
She is not bred so dull but she can learn;
Happiest of all is, that her gentle spirit
Commits itself to yours to be directed,
As from her lord, her governor, her king.
Myself, and what is mine, to you and yours
Is now converted: but now I was the lord
Of this fair mansion, master of my servants,
Queen o'er myself; and even now, but now,
This house, these servants, and this same myself,
Are yours, my lord.   I give them with this ring,
Which when you part from, lose, or give away,
Let it pressage the ruin of your love
And be my vantage to exclaim on you.
     Bass.   Madam, you have bereft me of all words,
Only my mouth speaks to you in my veins,
And there is such confusion in my powers
As after some oration, fairly spoke

By a beloved prince, there doth appear
Among the buzzing pleaséd multitude;
Where every something, being blent together,
Turns to a wild of nothing, save of joy,
Expressed, and not expressed.   But when this ring
Parts from this finger, then parts life from hence:
O, then be bold to say, Bassanio's dead.
   Ner.   My lord and lady, it is now our time,
That have stood by and seen our wishes prosper,
To cry, good joy.   Good joy, my lord and lady!
   Gra.   My Lord Bassanio, and my gentle lady,
I wish you all the joy that you can wish;
For, I am sure, you can wish none from me,
And, when your honours mean to solemnise
The bargain of your faith, I do beseech you
Even at that time I may be married too.
   Bass.   With all my heart, so thou canst get a wife.
   Gra.   I thank your lordship, you have got me one,
My eyes, my lord, can look as swift as yours,—
You saw the mistress, I beheld the maid;
You loved, I loved for intermission.
No more pertains to me, my lord, than you.
Your fortune stood upon the caskets there,
And so did mine too, as the matter falls;
For wooing here until I sweat again,
And swearing till my very roof was dry
With oaths of love, at last, if promise last,
I got a promise of this fair one here,
To have her love, provided that your fortune
Achieved her mistress.
   Por.   Is this true, Nerissa?
   Ner.   Madam, it is, so you stand pleased withal.
   Bass.   And do you, Gratiano, mean good faith?
   Gra.   Yes, faith, my lord.
   Bass.   Our feast shall be much honoured in your marriage.
   Gra.   We'll play with them the first boy for a thousand
      ducats.
   Ner.   What, and stake down?
   Gra.   No, we shall ne'er win at that sport, and stake down.
But who comes here?   Lorenzo, and his infidel?
What! and my old Venetian friend Salerio?

        Enter LORENZO, JESSICA, *and* SALERIO

   Bass.   Lorenzo and Salerio, welcome hither.
If that the youth of my new interest here
Have power to bid you welcome.   By your leave
I bid my very friends and countrymen,
Sweet Portia, welcome.
   Por.   So do I, my lord;
They are entirely welcome.

Lor.   I thank your honour.—For my part, my lord,
My purpose was not to have seen you here;
But meeting with Salerio by the way,
He did entreat me, past all saying nay,
To come with him along.
          Saler.   I did, my lord,
And I have reason for it.—Signior Antonio
Commends him to you.   [*Gives Bassanio a letter*
          Bass.   Ere I ope his letter,
I pray you, tell me how my good friend doth.
          Saler.   Not sick, my lord, unless it be in mind;
Nor well, unless in mind; his letter there
Will show you his estate.   [*Bassanio reads the letter*
          Gra.   Nerissa, cheer yon stranger; bid her welcome.
Your hand, Salerio.   What's the news from Venice?
How doth that royal merchant, good Antonio?
I know he will be glad of our success;
We are the Jasons, we have won the fleece.
          Saler.   I would you had won the fleece that he hath lost!
          Por.   There are some shrewd contents in yon same paper,
That steals the colour from Bassanio's cheek:
Some dear friend dead, else nothing in the world
Could turn so much the constitution
Of any constant man.   What, worse and worse?—
With leave, Bassanio; I am half yourself,
And I must freely have the half of anything
That this same paper brings you.
          Bass.   O sweet Portia,
Here are a few of the unpleasant'st words
That ever blotted paper.   Gentle lady,
When I did first impart my love to you,
I freely told you, all the wealth I had
Ran in my veins,—I was a gentleman:
And then I told you true, and yet, dear lady,
Rating myself at nothing, you shall see
How much I was a braggart.   When I told you,
My state was nothing, I should then have told you,
That I was worse than nothing; for indeed,
I have engaged myself to a dear friend,
Engaged my friend to his mere enemy,
To feed my means.   Here is a letter, lady;
The paper as the body of my friend.
And every word in it a gaping wound,
Issuing life-blood.   But is it true, Salerio?
Hath all his ventures failed?   What, not one hit
From Tripolis, from Mexico, and England,
From Lisbon, Barbary, and India,
And not one vessel scape the dreadful touch
Of merchant-marring rocks?
          Saler.   Not one, my lord,

Besides, it should appear, that if he had
The present money to discharge the Jew,
He would not take it.   Never did I know
A creature, that did bear the shape of man,
So keen and greedy to confound a man:
He plies the Duke at morning and at night,
And doth impeach the freedom of the state
If they deny him justice.   Twenty merchants,
The Duke himself, and the magnificoes
Of greatest port, have all persuaded with him,
But none can drive him from the envious plea
Of forfeiture, of justice, and his bond.
   Jes.   When I was with him I have heard him swear
To Tubal, and to Chus, his countrymen,
That he would rather have Antonio's flesh
Than twenty times the value of the sum
That he did owe him; and I know, my lord,
If law, authority, and power deny not,
It will go hard with poor Antonio.
   Por.   Is it your dear friend that is thus in trouble?
   Bass.   The dearest friend to me, the kindest man,
The best-conditioned and unwearied spirit
In doing courtesies; and one in whom
The ancient Roman honour more appears,
Than any that draws breath in Italy.
   Por.   What sum owes he the Jew?
   Bass.   For me, three thousand ducats.
   Por.   What, no more?
Pay him six thousand and deface the bond:
Double six thousand, and then treble that,
Before a friend of this description
Shall lose a hair through Bassanio's fault.
First go with me to church, and call me wife,
And then away to Venice to your friend;
For never shall you lie by Portia's side
With an unquiet soul.   You shall have gold
To pay the petty debt twenty times over.
When it is paid, bring your true friend along;
My maid Nerissa, and myself, meantime,
Will live as maids and widows.   Come away,
For you shall hence upon your wedding-day.
Bid your friends welcome, show a merry cheer;
Since you are dear bought, I will love you dear.—
But let me hear the letter of your friend.
   Bass.   [Reads]   *Sweet Bassanio, My ships have all mis-
carried, my creditors grow cruel, my estate is very low; my
bond to the Jew is forfeit, and since in paying it, it is impossible
I should live, all debts are cleared between you and I if I might
but see you at my death. Notwithstanding, use your pleasure:
if your love do not persuade you to come, let not my letter.*

Por.   O, love, despatch all business, and be gone.
Bass.   Since I have your good leave to go away,
I will make haste; but till I come again,
No bed shall e'er be guilty of my stay,
Nor rest be interposer 'twixt us twain.   [*Exeunt*

SCENE III.—Venice.   A Street

Enter SHYLOCK, SALARINO, ANTONIO, *and* *Gaoler*

Shy.   Gaoler, look to him: tell not me of mercy.
This is the fool that lent out money gratis.
Gaoler, look to him.
Ant.   Hear me yet, good Shylock.
Shy.   I'll have my bond; speak not against my bond.
I have sworn an oath that I will have my bond.
Thou call'dst me dog before thou hadst a cause,
But since I am a dog, beware my fangs.
The Duke shall grant me justice.   I do wonder,
Thou naughty gaoler, that thou art so fond
To come abroad with him at his request.
Ant.   I pray thee, hear me speak.
Shy.   I'll have my bond: I will not hear thee speak:
I'll have my bond: and therefore speak no more.
I'll not be made a soft and dull-eyed fool,
To shake the head, relent, and sigh, and yield
To Christian intercessors.   Follow not;
I'll have no speaking: I will have my bond.   [*Exit*
Salar.   It is the most impenetrable cur
That ever kept with men.
Ant.   Let him alone:
I'll follow him no more with bootless prayers.
He seeks my life; his reason well I know;
I oft delivered from his forfeitures
Many that have at times made moan to me;
Therefore he hates me.
Salar.   I am sure, the Duke
Will never grant this forfeiture to hold.
Ant.   The Duke cannot deny the course of law:
For the commodity that strangers have
With us in Venice, if it be denied,
Will much impeach the justice of the state,
Since that the trade and profit of the city
Consisteth of all nations.   Therefore, go:
These griefs and losses have so bated me
That I shall hardly spare a pound of flesh
To-morrow to my bloody creditor.—
Well, gaoler, on.—Pray God, Bassanio come
To see me pay his debt, and then I care not!   [*Exeunt*

SCENE IV.—Belmont. A Room in PORTIA's House

Enter PORTIA, NERISSA, LORENZO, JESSICA, *and*
BALTHAZAR

  Lor. Madam, although I speak it in your presence,
You have a noble and a true conceit
Of god-like amity; which appears most strongly
In bearing thus the absence of your lord.
But, if you knew to whom you show this honour,
How true a gentleman you send relief,
How dear a lover of my lord, your husband,
I know, you would be prouder of the work
Than customary bounty can enforce you.
  Por. I never did repent for doing good,
Nor shall not now: for in companions
That do converse and waste the time together,
Whose souls do bear an equal yoke of love,
There must be needs a like proportion
Of lineaments, of manners, and of spirit;
Which makes me think that this Antonio,
Being the bosom lover of my lord,
Must needs be like my lord.   If it be so,
How little is the cost I have bestowed
In purchasing the semblance of my soul
From out of the state of hellish cruelty!
This comes too near the praising of myself;
Therefore, no more of it: hear other things.
Lorenzo, I commit into your hands
The husbandry and manage of my house
Until my lord's return: for mine own part,
I have toward heaven breathed a secret vow
To live in prayer and contemplation
Only attended by Nerissa here,
Until her husband and my lord's return.
There is a monastery two miles off,
And there we will abide.   I do desire you
Not to deny this imposition
The which my love and some necessity
Now lays upon you.
  Lor.   Madam, with all my heart
I shall obey you in all fair commands.
  Por. My people do already know my mind,
And will acknowledge you and Jessica
In place of Lord Bassanio and myself.
So fare you well till we shall meet again.
  Lor. Fair thoughts and happy hours attend on you!
  Jes. I wish your ladyship all heart's content.
  Por. I thank you for your wish, and am well pleased
To wish it back on you: fare you well, Jessica.
                            [Exeunt Jessica and Lorenzo

Now, Balthazar,
As I have ever found thee honest-true,
So let me find thee still.   Take this same letter,
And use thou all the endeavour of a man
In speed to Padua: see thou render this
Into my cousin's hand, doctor Bellario;
And look, what notes and garments he doth give thee,
Bring them, I pray thee, with imagined speed
Unto the tranect, to the common ferry
Which trades to Venice.   Waste no time in words,
But get thee gone: I shall be there before thee.
    Bal.   Madam, I go with all convenient speed.   [*Exit*
    Por.   Come on, Nerissa: I have work in hand
That you yet know not of.   We'll see our husbands
Before they think of us.
    Ner.   Shall they see us?
    Por.   They shall, Nerissa; but in such a habit,
That they shall think we are accomplishéd
With that we lack.   I'll hold thee any wager,
When we are both accoutred like young men,
I'll prove the prettier fellow of the two;
And wear my dagger with the braver grace;
And speak between the change of man and boy
With a reed voice; and turn two mincing steps
Into a manly stride; and speak of frays,
Like a fine bragging youth; and tell quaint lies,
How honourable ladies sought my love,
Which I denying, they fell sick and died,
I could not do withal: then I'll repent,
And wish, for all that, that I had not killed them.
And twenty of these puny lies I'll tell,
That men shall swear I have discontinued school
Above a twelvemonth.   I have within my mind
A thousand raw tricks of these bragging Jacks,
Which I will practise.
    Ner.   Why, shall we turn to men?
    Por.   Fie, what a question's that,
If thou wert near a lewd interpreter!
But come, I'll tell thee all my whole device
When I am in my coach, which stays for us
At the park gate; and therefore haste away,
For we must measure twenty miles to-day.   [*Exeunt*

SCENE V.—The Same.   A Garden

Enter LAUNCELOT *and* JESSICA

    Laun.   Yes, truly; for, look you, the sins of the father
are to be laid upon the children; therefore, I promise you,
I fear you.   I was always plain with you, and so now I

speak my agitation of the matter: therefore, be of good
cheer; for, truly, I think you are damned. There is but
one hope in it that can do you any good, and that is but
a kind of bastard hope neither.

Jes. And what hope is that, I pray thee?

Laun. Marry, you may partly hope that your father
got you not, that you are not the Jew's daughter.

Jes. That were a kind of bastard hope, indeed: so the
sins of my mother should be visited upon me.

Laun. Truly then I fear you are damned both by father
and mother: thus when I shun Scylla, your father, I fall
into Charybdis, your mother. Well, you are gone, both
ways.

Jes. I shall be saved by my husband; he hath made me
a Christian.

Laun. Truly, the more to blame he: we were Christians enow before; e'en as many as could well live one by
another. The making of Christians will raise the price of
hogs: if we grow all to be pork-eaters, we shall not shortly
have a rasher on the coals for money.

Jes. I'll tell my husband, Launcelot, what you say:
here he comes.

Enter LORENZO

Lor. I shall grow jealous of you shortly, Launcelot, if
you thus get my wife into corners.

Jes. Nay, you need not fear us, Lorenzo, Launcelot and
I are out. He tells me flatly, there is no mercy for me in
heaven, because I am a Jew's daughter: and he says, you
are no good member of the commonwealth, for, in con-
verting Jews to Christians you raise the price of pork.

Lor. I shall answer that better to the commonwealth
than you can the getting up of the negro's belly: the Moor
is with child by you, Launcelot.

Laun. It is much, that the Moor should be more than
reason; but if she be less than an honest woman, she is,
indeed, more than I took her for.

Lor. How every fool can play upon the word! I think,
the best grace of wit will shortly turn into silence, and discourse grow commendable in none only but parrots. Go
in, sirrah; bid them prepare for dinner.

Laun. That is done, sir; they have all stomachs.

Lor. Goodly Lord, what a wit-snapper are you! then bid
them prepare dinner.

Laun. That is done too, sir; only, cover is the word.

Lor. Will you cover then, sir?

Laun. Not so, sir, neither; I know my duty.

Lor. Yet more quarrelling with occasion? Wilt thou
show the whole wealth of thy wit in an instant? I pray
thee, understand a plain man in his plain meaning: go to

thy fellows, bid them cover the table, serve in the meat,
and we will come in to dinner.

Laun.   For the table, sir, it shall be served in; for the
meat, sir, it shall be covered; for your coming in to dinner,
sir, why, let it be as humours and conceits shall govern.

[Exit

Lor.   O dear discretion, how his words are suited!
The fool hath planted in his memory
An army of good words; and I do know
A many fools, that stand in better place,
Garnished like him, that for tricksy word
Defy the matter. How cheer'st thou, Jessica?
And now, good sweet, say thy opinion,
How dost thou like the Lord Bassanio's wife?

Jes.   Past all expressing. It is very meet
The Lord Bassanio live an upright life,
For, having such a blessing in his lady,
He finds the joys of heaven here on earth;
And, if on earth he do not mean it, then
In reason he should never come to heaven.
Why, if two gods should play some heavenly match,
And on the wager lay two earthly women,
And Portia one, there must be something else
Pawned with the other, for the poor rude world
Hath not her fellow.

Lor.   Even such a husband
Hast thou of me, as she is for a wife.

Jes.   Nay, but ask my opinion too of that.

Lor.   I will anon; first, let us go to dinner.

Jes.   Nay, let me praise you while I have a stomach.

Lor.   No, pray thee, let it serve for table-talk;
Then, howsoe'er thou speak'st, 'mong other things
I shall digest it.

Jes.   Well, I'll set you forth.   [*Exeunt*

ACT FOUR

Scene I.—Venice. A Court of Justice

Enter the Duke; *the Magnificoes;* Antonio, Bassanio,
Gratiano, Salarino, Salerio, *and others*

Duke.   What, is Antonio here?

Ant.   Ready, so please your grace.

Duke.   I am sorry for thee: thou art come to answer
A stony adversary, an inhuman wretch
Uncapable of pity, void and empty
From any dram of mercy.

Ant.   I have heard

52

Your grace hath ta'en great pains to qualify
His rigorous course; but since he stands obdurate,
And that no lawful means can carry me
Out of his envy's reach, I do oppose
My patience to his fury, and am armed
To suffer with a quietness of spirit
The very tyranny and rage of his.
　　Duke.　Go one, and call the Jew into the court.
　　Salar.　He's ready at the door.　He comes, my lord.

Enter SHYLOCK

　　Duke.　Make room, and let him stand before our face.
Shylock, the world thinks, and I think so too,
That thou but lead'st this fashion of thy malice
To the last hour of act; and then, 't is thought,
Thou 'lt show thy mercy and remorse more strange
Than in thy strange apparent cruelty;
And where thou now exact'st the penalty,
Which is a pound of this poor merchant's flesh,
Thou wilt not only loose the forfeiture,
But, touched with human gentleness and love,
Forgive a moiety of the principal;
Glancing an eye of pity on his losses
That have of late so huddled on his back,
Enow to press a royal merchant down
And pluck commiseration of his state
From brassy bosoms and rough hearts of flint,
From stubborn Turks and Tartars, never trained
To offices of tender courtesy.
We all expect a gentle answer, Jew.
　　Shy.　I have possessed your grace of what I purpose;
And by our holy Sabbath have I sworn
To have the due and forfeit of my bond:
If you deny it, let the danger light
Upon your charter and your city's freedom.
You 'll ask me, why I rather choose to have
A weight of carrion flesh, than to receive
Three thousand ducats?　I 'll not answer that,
But, say, it is my humour: is it answered?
What if my house be troubled with a rat,
And I be pleased to give ten thousand ducats
To have it baned?　What, are you answered yet?
Some men there are love not a gaping pig;
Some that are mad if they behold a cat;
And others, when the bagpipe sings i' the nose,
Cannot contain their urine: for affection,
Master of passion, sways it to the mood
Of what it likes or loathes.　Now, for your answer.
As there is no firm reason to be rendered,
Why he cannot abide a gaping pig;

Why he, a harmless necessary cat;
Why he, a woollen bagpipe, but of force
Must yield to such inevitable shame
As to offend himself, being offended;
So can I give no reason, nor I will not,
More than a lodged hate, and a certain loathing
I bear Antonio, that I follow thus
A losing suit against him.   Are you answered?
   Bass.   This is no answer, thou unfeeling man,
To excuse the current of thy cruelty.
   Shy.   I am not bound to please thee with my answer.
   Bass.   Do all men kill the things they do not love?
   Shy.   Hates any man the thing he would not kill?
   Bass.   Every offence is not a hate at first.
   Shy.   What, wouldst thou have a serpent sting thee
    twice?
   Ant.   I pray you, think you question with the Jew.
You may as well go stand upon the beach
And bid the main flood bate his usual height;
You may as well use question with the wolf
Why he hath made the ewe bleat for the lamb;
You may as well forbid the mountain pines
To wag their high tops, and to make no noise
When they are fretted with the gusts of heaven;
You may as well do anything most hard
As seek to soften that (than which what's harder?)
His Jewish heart.   Therefore, I do beseech you,
Make no more offers, use no further means;
But with all brief and plain conveniency,
Let me have judgment, and the Jew his will.
   Bass.   For thy three thousand ducats here is six.
   Shy.   If every ducat in six thousand ducats
Were in six parts, and every part a ducat,
I would not draw them: I would have my bond.
   Duke.   How shalt thou hope for mercy, rendering none?
   Shy.   What judgment shall I dread, doing no wrong?
You have among you many a purchased slave,
Which, like your asses, and your dogs, and mules,
You use in abject, and in slavish parts
Because you bought them:—shall I say to you,
Let them be free; marry them to your heirs?
Why sweat they under burdens? let their beds
Be made as soft as yours, and let their palates
Be seasoned with such viands?   You will answer,
The slaves are ours.   So do I answer you:
The pound of flesh which I demand of him
Is dearly bought; 't is mine, and I will have it.
If you deny me, fie upon your law!
There is no force in the decrees of Venice.
I stand for judgment: answer; shall I have it?

Duke. Upon my power I may dismiss this court,
Unless Bellario, a learned doctor
Whom I have sent for to determine this,
Come here to-day.
    Salar.   My lord, here stays without
A messenger with letters from the doctor,
New come from Padua.
    Duke. Bring us the letters; call the messenger.
    Bass. Good cheer, Antonio! What, man, courage yet!
The Jew shall have my flesh, blood, bones, and all,
Ere thou shalt lose for me one drop of blood.
    Ant. I am a tainted wether of the flock,
Meetest for death: the weakest kind of fruit
Drops earliest to the ground, and so let me.
You cannot better be employed, Bassanio,
Than to live still, and write mine epitaph.

Enter NERISSA, *dressed like a lawyer's clerk*

    Duke. Came you from Padua, from Bellario?
    Ner. From both, my lord. Bellario greets your grace.
        [Presents a letter
    Bass. Why dost thou whet thy knife so earnestly?
    Shy. To cut the forfeiture from that bankrupt there.
    Gra. Not on thy sole, but on thy soul, harsh Jew,
Thou mak'st thy knife keen; but no metal can,
No, not the hangman's axe, bear half the keenness
Of thy sharp envy. Can no prayers pierce thee?
    Shy. No, none that thou hast wit enough to make.
    Gra. O, be thou damned, inexorable dog,
And for thy life let justice be accursed!
Thou almost mak'st me waver in my faith,
To hold opinion with Pythagoras
That souls of animals infuse themselves
Into the trunks of men: thy currish spirit
Governed a wolf, who, hanged for human slaughter,
Even from the gallows did his fell soul fleet,
And whilst thou lay'st in thy unhallowed dam
Infused itself in thee; for thy desires
Are wolfish, bloody, starved, and ravenous.
    Shy. Till thou canst rail the seal from off my bond,
Thou but offend'st thy lungs to speak so loud.
Repair thy wit, good youth, or it will fall
To cureless ruin,—I stand here for law.
    Duke. This letter from Bellario doth commend
A young and learned doctor to our court.
Where is he?
    Ner.   He attendeth here hard by
To know your answer, whether you 'll admit him.
    Duke. With all my heart. Some three or four of you

Go give him courteous conduct to this place.
Meantime, the court shall hear Bellario's letter.
    Clerk. [*Reads*] *Your grace shall understand, that, at
the receipt of your letter, I am very sick ; but in the instant
that your messenger came, in loving visitation was with me
a young doctor of Rome ; his name is Balthazar. I acquainted him with the cause in controversy between the Jew
and Antonio, the merchant ; we turned o'er many books
together; he is furnished with my opinion, which, bettered
with his own learning, the greatness whereof I cannot enough
commend, comes with him, at my importunity, to fill up your
grace's request in my stead. I beseech you, let his lack of
years be no impediment to let him lack a reverend estimation,
for I never knew so young a body with so old a head. I leave
him to your gracious acceptance, whose trial shall better
publish his commendation.*
    Duke. You hear the learn'd Bellario, what he writes:
And here, I take it, is the doctor come.

Enter PORTIA *for* BALTHAZAR

Give me your hand. Came you from old Bellario?
    Por. I did, my lord.
    Duke.   You are welcome; take your place.
Are you acquainted with the difference
That holds this present question in the court?
    Por. I am informéd th'roughly of the cause.
Which is the merchant here, and which the Jew?
    Duke. Antonio and old Shylock, both stand forth.
    Por. Is your name Shylock?
    Shy.   Shylock is my name.
    Por. Of a strange nature is the suit you follow;
Yet in such rule, that the Venetian law
Cannot impugn you, as you do proceed.
[*To Antonio*] You stand within his danger, do you not?
    Ant. Ay, so he says.
    Por.   Do you confess the bond?
    Ant. I do.
    Por.   Then must the Jew be merciful.
    Shy. On what compulsion must I? tell me that.
    Por. The quality of mercy is not strained,
It droppeth as the gentle rain from heaven
Upon the place beneath: it is twice blessed:
It blesseth him that gives, and him that takes.
'Tis mightiest in the mightiest, it becomes
The thronéd monarch better than his crown:
His sceptre shows the force of temporal power,
The attribute to awe and majesty,
Wherein doth sit the dread and fear of kings;
But mercy is above this sceptred sway,

It is enthronéd in the hearts of kings,
It is an attribute to God himself,
And earthly power doth then show likest God's
When mercy seasons justice. Therefore Jew,
Though justice be thy plea, consider this,
That in the course of justice none of us
Should see salvation: we do pray for mercy,
And that some prayer doth teach us all to render
The deeds of mercy. I have spoken thus much
To mitigate the justice of thy plea,
Which if thou wilt follow, this strict court of Venice
Must needs give sentence 'gainst the merchant there.
    Shy. My deeds upon my head! I crave the Law,
The penalty and forfeit of my bond.
    Por. Is he not able to discharge the money?
    Bass. Yes, here I tender it for him in the court;
Yea, twice the sum; if that will not suffice,
I will be bound to pay it ten times o'er,
On forfeit of my hands, my head, my heart.
If this will not suffice, it must appear
That malice bears down truth. And I beseech you,
Wrest once the law to your authority:
To do a great right, do a little wrong,
And curb this cruel devil of his will.
    Por. It must not be: there is no power in Venice
Can alter a decree establishéd;
'T will be recorded for a precedent,
And many an error, by the same example,
Will rush into the state: it cannot be.
    Shy. A Daniel come to judgment! yea, a Daniel!
O wise young judge, how I do honour thee!
    Por. I pray you let me look upon the bond.
    Shy. Here 't is, most reverend doctor, here it is.
    Por. Shylock, there's thrice thy money offered thee.
    Shy. An oath, an oath, I have an oath in heaven,
Shall I lay perjury upon my soul?
No, not for Venice.
    Por.   Why, this bond is forfeit,
And lawfully by this the Jew may claim
A pound of flesh, to be by him cut off
Nearest the merchant's heart. Be merciful:
Take thrice thy money; bid me tear the bond.
    Shy. When it is paid, according to the tenour.
It doth appear you are a worthy judge;
You know the law, your exposition
Hath been most sound: I charge you by the Law,
Whereof you are a well-deserving pillar,
Proceed to judgment. By my soul I swear,
There is no power in the tongue of man
To alter me. I stay here on my bond.

Ant.   Most heartily I do beseech the court
To give the judgment.
   Por.   Why, then, thus it is:
You must prepare your bosom for his knife.
   Shy.   O noble judge!   O excellent young man!
   Por.   For the intent and purpose of the law
Hath full relation to the penalty,
Which here appeareth due upon the bond.
   Shy.   'T is very true.   O wise and upright judge!
How much more elder art thou than thy looks!
   Por.   Therefore, lay bare your bosom.
   Shy.   Ay, his breast;
So says the bond:—doth it not, noble judge?—
"Nearest his heart:" those are the very words.
   Por.   It is so.   Are there balance here to weigh
The flesh?
   Shy.   I have them ready.
   Por.   Have by some surgeon, Shylock, on your charge,
To stop his wounds, lest he do bleed to death.
   Shy.   Is it so nominated in the bond?
   Por.   It is not so expressed; but what of that?
'T were good you do so much for charity.
   Shy.   I cannot find it: 't is not in the bond?
   Por.   You, merchant, have you anything to say?
   Ant.   But little; I am armed and well prepared.
Give me your hand, Bassanio: fare you well.
Grieve not that I am fallen to this for you;
For herein Fortune shows herself more kind
Than is her custom: it is still her use
To let the hollow man outlive his wealth
To view with hollow eye and wrinkled brow
An age of poverty; from which lingering penance
Of such misery doth she cut me off.
Commend me to your honourable wife:
Tell her the process of Antonio's end;
Say how I loved you, speak me fair in death;
And, when the tale is told, bid her be judge
Whether Bassanio had not once a love.
Repent not you that you shall lose your friend,
And he repents not that he pays your debt;
For, if the Jew do cut but deep enough,
I'll pay it instantly with all my heart.
   Bass.   Antonio, I am married to a wife
Which is dear to me as life itself;
But life itself, my wife, and all the world,
Are not with me esteemed above thy life;
I would lose all, ay, sacrifice them all
Here to this devil, to deliver you.
   Por.   Your wife would give you little thanks for that,
If she were by to hear you make the offer.

Gra. I have a wife whom I protest I love:
I would she were in heaven, so she could
Entreat some power to change this currish Jew.
   Ner. 'T is well you offer it behind her back;
The wish would make else an unquiet house.
   Shy. These be the Christian husbands. I have a
                                        daughter;
'Would any of the stock of Barrabas
Had been her husband, rather than a Christian.
We trifle time; I pray thee, pursue sentence.
   Por. A pound of that same merchant's flesh is thine:
The Court awards it, and the Law doth give it.
   Shy. Most rightful judge!
   Por. And you must cut this flesh from off his breast:
The Law allows it, and the Court awards it.
   Shy. Most learned judge!—A sentence! come, prepare!
   Por. Tarry a little; there is something else.
This bond doth give thee here no jot of blood;
The words expressly are, a pound of flesh:
Take then thy bond, take thou thy pound of flesh;
But in the cutting it, if thou dost shed
One drop of Christian blood, thy lands and goods
Are, by the laws of Venice, confiscate
Unto the state of Venice.
   Gra. O upright judge!—Mark, Jew:—O learned judge!
   Shy. Is that the law?
   Por.   Thyself shalt see the Act;
For, as thou urgest justice, be assured,
Thou shalt have justice, more than thou desirest.
   Gra. O learned judge!—Mark, Jew:—a learned judge!
   Shy. I take this offer then; pay the bond thrice,
And let the Christian go.
   Bass.   Here is the money.
   Por. Soft!
The Jew shall have all justice;—soft! —no haste:
He shall have nothing but the penalty.
   Gra. O Jew, an upright judge, a learned judge!
   Por. Therefore prepare thee to cut off the flesh.
Shed thou no blood; nor cut thou less nor more
But just a pound of flesh: if thou takest more
Or less than a just pound,—be it but so much
As makes it light, or heavy in the substance
Or the division of the twentieth part
Of one poor scruple, nay if the scale do turn
But in the estimation of a hair,
Thou diest, and all thy goods are confiscate.
   Gra. A second Daniel, a Daniel, Jew!
Now, infidel, I have thee on the hip.
   Por. Why doth the Jew pause! take thy forfeiture.
   Shy. Give me my principal, and let me go.

Bass.   I have it ready for thee; here it is.
Por.   He hath refused it in the open court:
He shall have merely justice, and his bond.
Gra.   A Daniel, still say I; a second Daniel!
I thank thee Jew, for teaching me that word.
Shy.   Shall I not have barely my principal?
Por.   Thou shalt have nothing but the forfeiture,
To be so taken at thy peril, Jew.
Shy.   Why then the devil give him good of it!
I'll stay no longer question.
Por.   Tarry, Jew:
The Law hath yet another hold on you.
It is enacted in the laws of Venice,
If it be proved against an alien,
That, by direct or indirect attempts.
He seek the life of any citizen,
That party against the which he doth contrive
Shall seize one half his goods; the other half
Comes to the privy coffer of the State,
And the offender's life lies in the mercy
Of the Duke only, against all other voice.
In which predicament, I say, thou stand'st;
For it appears by manifest proceeding,
That indirectly and directly too,
Thou hast contrived against the very life
Of the defendant, and thou hast incurred
The danger formerly by me rehearsed.
Down, therefore, and beg mercy of the Duke.
Gra.   Beg, that thou may'st have leave to hang thy-
          self;
And yet, thy wealth being forfeit to the State,
Thou hast not left the value of a cord;
Therefore thou must be hanged at the State's charge.
Duke.   That thou shalt see the difference of our spirits,
I pardon thee thy life before thou ask it.
For half thy wealth, it is Antonio's:
The other half comes to the general State,
Which humbleness may drive into a fine.
Por.   Ay, for the State; not for Antonio.
Shy.   Nay, take my life and all; pardon not that:
You take my house, when you do take the prop
That doth sustain my house; you take my life,
When you do take the means whereby I live.
Por.   What mercy can you render him, Antonio?—
Gra.   A halter gratis, nothing else, for God's sake.—
Ant.   So please my lord the Duke, and all the Court,
To quit the fine for one half of his goods,
I am content so he will let me have
The other half in use, to render it
Upon his death unto the gentleman

That lately stole his daughter:
Two things provided more,—that, for this favour,
He presently become a Christian;
The other, that he do record a gift,
Here in the court, of all he dies possessed
Unto his son Lorenzo and his daughter.
    Duke.   He shall do this, or else I do recant
The pardon, that I late pronouncéd here.
    Por.   Art thou contented, Jew? what dost thou say?
    Shy.   I am content.
    Por.   Clerk, draw a deed of gift.
    Shy.   I pray you give me leave to go from hence.
I am not well.   Send the deed after me,
And I will sign it.
    Duke.   Get thee gone, but do it.
    Gra.   In christening thou shalt have two godfathers,
Had I been judge, thou shouldst have had ten more,
To bring thee to the gallows, not the font.   *[Exit Shylock*
    Duke.   Sir, I entreat you home with me to dinner.
    Por.   I humbly do desire your grace of pardon,
I must away this night toward Padua,
And it is meet I presently set forth.
    Duke.   I am sorry that your leisure serves you not.
Antonio, gratify this gentleman,
For, in my mind, you are much bound to him.
                [Exeunt Duke and his Train
    Bass.   Most worthy gentleman, I and my friend
Have by your wisdom been this day acquitted
Of grievous penalties; in lieu whereof,
Three thousand ducats, due unto the Jew,
We freely cope your courteous pains withal.
    Ant.   And stand indebted, over and above,
In love and service to you evermore.
    Por.   He is well paid that is well satisfied;
And I, delivering you, am satisfied,
And therein do account myself well paid:
My mind was never yet more mercenary.
I pray you, know me when we meet again:
I wish you well, and so I take my leave.
    Bass.   Dear sir, of force I must attempt you further:
Take some remembrance of us, as a tribute
Not as a fee.   Grant me two things, I pray you;
Not to deny me, and to pardon me.
    Por.   You press me far, and therefore I will yield.
Give me your gloves, I'll wear them for your sake;
And, for your love, I'll take this ring from you.
Do not draw back your hand; I'll take no more;
And you in love shall not deny me this.
    Bass.   This ring, good sir? alas, it is a trifle;
I will not shame myself to give you this.

Por.   I will have nothing else but only this;
And now, methinks, I have a mind to it.
  Bass.   There 's more depends on this than on the value.
The dearest ring in Venice will I give you,
And find it out by proclamation:
Only for this, I pray you, pardon me.
  Por.   I see, sir, you are liberal in offers.
You taught me first to beg, and now, methinks,
You teach me how a beggar should be answered.
  Bass.   Good, sir, this ring was given me by my wife:
And when she put it on, she made me vow
That I should neither sell, nor give, nor lose it.
  Por.   That 'scuse serves many men to save their gifts.
An if your wife be not a mad-woman,
And know how well I have deserved this ring,
She would not hold out enemy for ever,
For giving it to me.   Well, peace be with you.
                              [*Exeunt Portia and Nerissa*
  Ant.   My lord Bassanio, let him have the ring:
Let his deservings, and my love withal,
Be values 'gainst your wife's commandment.
  Bass.   Go, Gratiano; run and overtake him,
Give him the ring; and bring him, if thou canst,
Unto Antonio's house.   Away! make haste.
                              [*Exit Gratiano*

Come, you and I will thither presently,
And in the morning early will we both
Fly toward Belmont.   Come, Antonio.   [*Exeunt*

SCENE II.—The Same.   A Street

Enter PORTIA *and* NERISSA

Por.   Inquire the Jew's house out, give him this deed,
And let him sign it; we'll away to-night,
And be a day before our husbands home.
This deed will be well welcome to Lorenzo.

Enter GRATIANO

Gra.   Fair sir, you are well o'erta'en.
My lord Bassanio, upon more advice,
Hath sent you here this ring, and doth entreat
Your company at dinner.
  Por.   That cannot be.
His ring I do accept most thankfully,
And so I pray you, tell him: furthermore,
I pray you, show my youth old Shylock's house.
  Gra.   That will I do.
  Ner.   Sir, I would speak with you.—
[*To Portia*]   I'll see if I can get my husband's ring,
Which I did make him swear to keep for ever.

Por. [*To Nerissa*] Thou may'st, I warrant.
    We shall have old swearing
That they did give the rings away to men;
But we'll outface them and outswear them too.
[*Aloud*] A way! make haste: thou know'st where I will
    tarry.
  Ner. Come, good sir, will you show me to this house?
                            [*Exeunt*

ACT FIVE

SCENE I.—Belmont. The Avenue to PORTIA'S House

Enter LORENZO *and* JESSICA

  Lor. The moon shines bright.   In such a night as this,
When the sweet wind did gently kiss the trees,
And they did make no noise, in such a night,
Troilus, methinks, mounted the Trojan walls
And sighed his soul towards the Grecian tents,
Where Cressid lay that night.
  Jes.   In such a night
Did Thisbe fearfully o'ertrip the dew,
And saw the lion's shadow ere himself,
And ran dismayed away.
  Lor.   In such a night
Stood Dido with a willow in her hand
Upon the wild sea-banks, and waved her love
To come again to Carthage.
  Jes.   In such a night
Medea gathered the enchanted herbs
That did renew old Æson.
  Lor.   In such a night
Did Jessica steal from the wealthy Jew,
And with an unthrift love did run from Venice,
As far as Belmont.
  Jes.   In such a night
Did young Lorenzo swear he loved her well,
Stealing her soul with many vows of faith
And ne'er a true one.
  Lor.   In such a night
Did pretty Jessica, like a little shrew,
Slander her love, and he forgave her.
  Jes. I would out-night you did no body come;
But hark, I hear the footing of a man.

Enter STEPHANO

  Lor. Who comes so fast in silence of the night?
  Steph. A friend.

Lor.   A friend? what friend? your name, I pray you,
friend?

   Steph.   Stephano is my name; and I bring word
My mistress will before the break of day
Be here at Belmont; she doth stray about
By holy crosses, where she kneels and prays
For happy wedlock hours.

   Lor.   Who comes with her?

   Steph.   None, but a holy hermit, and her maid.
I pray you, is my master yet returned?

   Lor.   He is not, nor we have not heard from him.
But go we in, I pray thee, Jessica,
And ceremoniously let us prepare
Some welcome for the mistress of the house.

Enter LAUNCELOT

   Laun.   Sola, sola! wo ha, ho! sola, sola!

   Lor.   Who calls?

   Laun.   Sola! did you see Master Lorenzo, and Mistress
Lorenzo? sola, sola!

   Lor.   Leave holloing, man;—here.

   Laun.   Sola! where? where?

   Lor.   Here.

   Laun.   Tell him, there's a post come from my master,
with his horn full of good news: now my master will be here
ere morning.   [*Exit*

   Lor.   Sweet soul, let's in, and there expect their coming.
And yet no matter; why should we go in?
My friend Stephano, signify, I pray you,
Within the house, your mistress is at hand;
And bring your music forth into the air.   [*Exit Stephano*
How sweet the moonlight sleeps upon this bank!
Here we sit, and let the sounds of music
Creep in our ears: soft stillness and the night
Become the touches of sweet harmony.
Sit, Jessica: look, how the floor of heaven
Is thick inlaid with patines of bright gold.
There's not the smallest orb which thou behold'st
But in his motion like an angel sings,
Still quiring to the young-eyed cherubins:
Such harmony is in immortal souls:
But, whilst this muddy vesture of decay
Doth grossly close it in, we cannot hear it.

Enter Musicians

Come, ho, and wake Diana with a hymn:
With sweetest touches pierce your mistress' ear,
And draw her home with music.   [*Music*

Jes. I am never merry when I hear sweet music.
  Lor. The reason is, your spirits are attentive:
For do but note a wild and wanton herd,
Or race of youthful and unhandled colts,
Fetching mad bounds, bellowing and neighing loud,
Which is the hot condition of their blood;
If they but hear perchance a trumpet sound,
Or any air of music touch their ears,
You shall perceive them make a mutual stand,
Their savage eyes turned to a modest gaze
By the sweet power of music: therefore the poet
Did feign that Orpheus drew trees, stones, and floods;
Since nought so stockish, hard, and full of rage,
But music for the time doth change his nature.
The man that hath no music in himself,
Nor is not moved with concord, of sweet sounds,
Is fit for treasons, stratagems, and spoils;
The motions of his spirit are dull as night,
And his affections dark as Erebus;
Let no such man be trusted: Mark the music.

Enter PORTIA *and* NERISSA, *at a distance*

  Por. That light we see is burning in my hall.
How far that little candle throws his beams!
So shines a good deed in a naughty world.
  Ner. When the moon shone we did not see the candle.
  Por. So doth the greater glory dim the less:
A substitute shines brightly as a king,
Until a king be by; and then his state
Empties itself, as doth an inland brook
Into the main of waters:—Music; hark!
  Ner. It is your music, madam, of the house.
  Por. Nothing is good, I see, without respect.
Methinks it sounds much sweeter than by day.
  Ner. Silence bestows that virtue on it, madam.
  Por. The crow doth sing as sweetly as the lark
When neither is attended; and, I think,
The nightingale, if she should sing by day,
When every goose is cackling, would be thought
No better musician than the wren.
How many things by season seasoned are
To their right praise, and true perfection!—
Peace, ho!—the moon sleeps with Endymion,
And would not be awaked.
  Lor.   That is the voice,
Or I am much deceived, of Portia.
  Por. He knows me as the blind man knows the cuckoo,
By the bad voice.
  Lor.   Dear lady, welcome home.

Por.   We have been praying for our husband's welfare,
Which speed, we hope, the better for our words.
Are they returned?
   Lor.   Madam, they are not yet;
But there is come a messenger before,
To signify their coming.
   Por.   Go in, Nerissa;
Give orders to my servants, that they take
No note at all of our being absent hence;
Nor you, Lorenzo; Jessica, nor you.   [*A tucket sounded*
   Lor.   Your husband is at hand; I hear his trumpet.
We are no tell-tales, madam; fear you not.
   Por.   This night, methinks, is but the daylight sick;
It looks a little paler: 't is a day,
Such as the day is when the sun is hid.

Enter BASSANIO, ANTONIO, GRATIANO, *and their Followers*

   Bass.   We should hold day with the Antipodes
If you would walk in absence of the sun.
   Por.   Let me give light, but let me not be light;
For a light wife doth make a heavy husband,
And never be Bassanio so for me:
But God sort all!   You are welcome home, my lord.
   Bass.   I thank you, madam.   Give welcome to my
      friend:
This is the man, this is Antonio,
To whom I am so infinitely bound.
   Por.   You should in all sense be much bound to him,
For, as I hear, he was much bound for you.
   Ant.   No more than I am well acquitted of.
   Por.   Sir, you are very welcome to our house:
It must appear in other ways than words,
Therefore I scant this breathing courtesy.
   Gra. [*To Nerissa*] By yonder moon, I swear, you do me
      wrong;
In faith, I gave it to the judge's clerk:
Would he were gelt that had it, for my part,
Since you do take it, love, so much at heart.
   Por.   A quarrel, ho, already! what 's the matter?
   Gra.   About a hoop of gold, a paltry ring
That she did give me, whose posy was
For all the world like cutler's poetry
Upon a knife, *Love me, and leave me not.*
   Ner.   What talk you of the posy or the value?
You swore to me when I did give it you
That you would wear it till your hour of death,
And that it should lie with you in your grave:
Though not for me, yet for your vehement oaths,
You should have been respective and have kept it.

Gave it a judge's clerk! no, God's my judge,
The clerk will ne'er wear hair on 's face that had it.
   Gra. He will, an if he live to be a man.
   Ner. Ay, if a woman live to be a man.
   Gra. Now, by this hand, I gave it to a youth,
A kind of boy, a little scrubbéd boy,
No higher than thyself, the judge's clerk;
A prating boy, that begged it as a fee:
I could not for my heart deny it him.
   Por. You were to blame, I must be plain with you,
To part so slightly with your wife's first gift;
A thing stuck on with oaths upon your finger,
And so riveted with faith unto your flesh.
I gave my love a ring, and made him swear
Never to part with it; and here he stands:
I dare be sworn for him, he would not leave it
Nor pluck it from his finger for the wealth
That the world masters.   Now, in faith, Gratiano,
You give your wife too unkind a cause of grief:
An 't were to me, I should be mad at it.
   Bass. [*Aside*] Why, I were best to cut my left hand off,
And swear I lost the ring defending it.
   Gra. My lord Bassanio gave his ring away
Unto the judge that begged it, and, indeed,
Deserved it too; and then the boy, his clerk,
That took some pains in writing, he begged mine;
And neither man nor master would take aught
But the two rings.
   Por.   What ring gave you, my lord?
Not that, I hope, which you received of me.
   Bass. If I could add a lie unto a fault,
I would deny it; but you see, my finger
Hath not the ring upon it: it is gone.
   Por. Even so void is your false heart of truth.
By heaven, I will ne'er come in your bed
Until I see the ring.
   Ner.   Nor I in yours,
Till I again see mine.
   Bass.   Sweet Portia,
If you did know to whom I gave the ring,
If you did know for whom I gave the ring,
And would conceive for what I gave the ring,
And how unwillingly I left the ring,
When naught would be accepted but the ring,
You would abate the strength of your displeasure.
   Por. If you had known the virtue of the ring,
Or half her worthiness that gave the ring,
Or your own honour to contain the ring,
You would not then have parted with the ring.
What man is there so much unreasonable,

If you had pleased to have defended it
With any terms of zeal, wanted the modesty
To urge the thing held as a ceremony?
Nerissa teaches me what to believe:
I 'll die for 't but some woman had the ring.
    Bass. No, by mine honour, madam, by my soul,
No woman had it; but a civil doctor,
Which did refuse three thousand ducats of me,
And begged the ring, which I did deny him,
And suffered him to go displeased away,
Even he that had held up the very life
Of my dear friend. What should I say, sweet lady?
I was enforced to send it after him;
I was beset with shame and courtesy;
My honour would not let ingratitude
So much besmear it. Pardon me, good lady,
For, by these blesséd candles of the night,
Had you been there, I think, you would have begged
The ring of me to give the worthy doctor.
    Por. Let not that doctor e'er come near my house.
Since he hath got the jewel that I loved,
And that which you did swear to keep for me,
I will become as liberal as you:
I'll not deny him any thing I have;
No, not my body, nor my husband's bed.
Know him I shall, I am sure of it:
Lie not a night from home; watch me like Argus;
If you do not, if I be left alone,
Now, by mine honour, which is yet mine own,
I'll have that doctor for my bedfellow.
    Ner. And I his clerk; therefore, be well advised
How do you leave me to mine own protection.
    Gra. Well, do you so: let not me take him then;
For, if I do, I'll mar the young clerk's pen.
    Ant. I am the unhappy subject of these quarrels.
    Por. Sir, grieve not you; you are welcome notwith-
        standing.
    Bass. Portia, forgive me this enforcéd wrong;
And in the hearing of these many friends
I swear to thee, even by thine own fair eyes,
Wherein I see myself—
    Por.   Mark you but that!
In both my eyes he doubly sees himself;
In each eye, one:—swear by your double self,
And there 's an oath of credit.
    Bass.   Nay, but hear me.
Pardon this fault, and by my soul I swear,
I never more will break an oath with thee.
    Ant. I once did lend my body for his wealth,
Which, but for him that had your husband's ring,

Had quite miscarried: I dare be bound again,
My soul upon the forfeit, that your lord
Will never more break faith advisedly.
   Por.   Then you shall be his surety.   Give him this,
And bid him keep it better than the other.
   Ant.   Here, Lord Bassanio; swear to keep this ring.
   Bass.   By heaven, it is the same I gave the doctor.
   Por.   I had it of him: pardon me, Bassanio,
For, by this ring, the doctor lay with me.
   Ner.   And pardon me, my gentle Gratiano,
For that same scrubbed boy, the doctor's clerk,
In lieu of this, last night did lie with me.
   Gra.   Why, this is like the mending of high ways
In summer where the ways are fair enough.
What, are we cuckolds ere we have deserved it?
   Por.   Speak not so grossly.   You are all amazed;
Here is a letter, read it at your leisure;
It comes from Padua, from Bellario:
There you shall find that Portia was the doctor,
Nerissa there, her clerk.   Lorenzo here
Shall witness, I set forth as soon as you,
And even but now returned; I have not yet
Entered my house.   Antonio, you are welcome;
And I have better news in store for you,
Than you expect: unseal this letter soon;
There you shall find, three of your argosies
Are richly come to harbour suddenly.
You shall not know by what strange accident
I chancéd on this letter.
   Ant.   I am dumb.
   Bass.   Were you the doctor, and I knew you not?
   Gra.   Were you the clerk that is to make me cuckold?
   Ner.   Ay; but the clerk that never means to do it,
Unless he live until he be a man.
   Bass.   Sweet doctor, you shall be my bedfellow:
When I am absent, then lie with my wife.
   Ant.   Sweet lady, you have given me life and living;
For here I read for certain that my ships
Are safely come to road.
   Por.   How now, Lorenzo?
My clerk hath some good comforts too for you.
   Ner.   Ay, and I'll give them him without a fee,
There do I give to you and Jessica,
From the rich Jew, a special deed of gift,
After his death, of all he dies possessed of.
   Lor.   Fair ladies, you drop manna in the way
Of starvéd people.
   Por.   It is almost morning,
And yet I am sure you are not satisfied
Of these events at full.   Let us go in;

And charge us there upon inter'gatories,
And we will answer all things faithfully.
   Gra. Let it be so: the first inter'gatory,
That my Nerissa shall be sworn on, is,
Whether till the next night she had rather stay,
Or go to bed now, being two hours to day:
But were the day come, I should wish it dark,
Till I were couching with the doctor's clerk.
Well, while I live, I 'll fear no other thing
So sore, as keeping safe Nerissa's ring.   *[Exeunt*

THE MERRY WIVES OF WINDSOR

DRAMATIS PERSONÆ

SIR JOHN FALSTAFF
FENTON, *a young gentleman*
SHALLOW, *a country justice*
SLENDER, *cousin to Shallow*
FORD }
PAGE } *two gentlemen dwelling at Windsor*
WILLIAM PAGE, *a boy, son to Page*
SIR HUGH EVANS, *a Welsh parson*
DOCTOR CAIUS, *a French physician*
Host of the Garter Inn
BARDOLPH }
PISTOL } *followers of Falstaff*
PYM }
ROBIN, *page to Falstaff*
SIMPLE, *servant to Slender*
RUGBY, *servant to Doctor Caius*

MISTRESS FORD
MISTRESS PAGE
ANNE PAGE, *her daughter*
MISTRESS QUICKLY, *servant to Doctor Caius*

Servants to Page, Ford, etc.

SCENE.—*Windsor, and the neighbourhood*

THE MERRY WIVES OF WINDSOR

ACT ONE

Scene I.—Windsor. Before Page's House

Enter Justice Shallow, Slender, *and* Sir Hugh Evans

Shal. Sir Hugh, persuade me not; I will make a Star-Chamber matter of it: if he were twenty Sir John Falstaffs, he shall not abuse Robert Shallow, esquire.

Slen. In the county of Gloster, justice of peace, and *coram.*

Shal. Ay, cousin Slender, and *cist-alorum.*

Slen. Ay, and *Ratolorum* too; and a gentleman born, master parson; who writes himself *Armigero,* in any bill, warrant, quittance, or obligation, *Armigero.*

Shal. Ay, that I do; and have done any time these three hundred years.

Slen. All his successors, gone before him, hath done 't; and all his ancestors, that come after him, may: they may give the dozen white luces in their coat.

Shal. It is an old coat.

Eva. The dozen white louses do become an old coat well; it agrees well, passant; it is a familiar beast to man, and signifies love.

Shal. The luce is the fresh fish; the salt fish is an old coat.

Slen. I may quarter, coz?

Shal. You may, by marrying.

Eva. It is marring, indeed, if he quarter it.

Shal. Not a whit.

Eva. Yes, pyr-lady; if he has a quarter of your coat, there is but three skirts for yourself, in my simple conjectures, but that is all one: if Sir John Falstaff have committed disparagements unto you, I am of the church, and will be glad to do my benevolence to make atonements and compromises between you.

Shal. The Council shall hear it: it is a riot.

Eva. It is not meet the Council hear a riot; there is no fear of Got in a riot: the Council, look you, shall desire to hear the fear of Got, and not to hear a riot; take your vizaments in that.

Shal. Ha! o' my life, if I were young again, the sword should end it.

Eva. It is petter that friends is the sword, and end it: and there is also another device in my prain, which, per-

73

adventure, prings goot discretions with it: there is Anne Page, which is daughter to Master George Page, which is pretty virginity.

Slen.   Mistress Anne Page! She has brown hair, and speaks small like a woman.

Eva.   It is that fery person for all the orld: as just as you will desire, and seven hundred pounds of moneys, and gold and silver, is her grandsire, upon his death's-bed (Got deliver to a joyful resurrections!) give, when she is able to overtake seventeen years old. It were a goot motion if we leave our pribbles and prabbles, and desire a marriage between Master Abraham and Mistress Anne Page.

Shal.   Did her grandsire leave her seven hundred pound?

Eva.   Ay, and her father is make her a petter penny.

Shal.   I know the young gentlewoman; she has good gifts.

Eva.   Seven hundred prounds and possibilities is good gifts.

Shal.   Well, let us see honest Master Page. Is Falstaff there?

Eva.   Shall I tell you a lie? I do despise a liar as I do despise one that is false, or, as I despise one that is not true. The knight, Sir John, is there: and, I beseech you, be ruled by your well-willers. I will peat the door for Master Page. [*Knocks*] What, hoa! Got pless your house here!

Page.   [*Within*] Who 's there?

Eva.   Here is Got's plessing and your friend, and Justice Shallow; and here young Master Slender, that, peradventures, shall tell you another tale, if matters grow to your likings.

Enter PAGE

Page.   I am glad to see your worships well. I thank you for my venison, Master Shallow.

Shal.   Master Page, I am glad to see you: much good do it your good heart! I wished your venison better; it was ill killed.—How doth good Mistress Page?—and I thank you always with my heart, la; with my heart.

Page.   Sir, I thank you.

Shal.   Sir, I thank you; by yea, and no, I do.

Page.   I am glad to see you, good Master Slender.

Slen.   How does your fallow greyhound, sir? I heard say, he was outrun on Cotsol'.

Page.   It could not be judged, sir.

Slen.   You 'll not confess, you 'll not confess.

Shal.   That he will not.—'T is your fault, 't is your fault:—'t is a good dog.

Page.   A cur, sir.

Shal. Sir, he's a good dog, and a fair dog; can there be more said? he is good, and fair.—Is Sir John Falstaff here?

Page. Sir, he is within; and I would I could do a good office between you.

Eva. It is spoke as a Christians ought to speak.

Shal. He hath wronged me, Master Page.

Page. Sir, he doth in some sort confess it.

Shal. If it be confessed, it is not redressed: is not that so, Master Page? He hath wronged me; indeed, he hath; —at a word, he hath;—believe me;—Robert Shallow, esquire, saith, he is wronged.

Page. Here comes Sir John.

Enter SIR JOHN FALSTAFF, BARDOLPH, NYM, *and* PISTOL

Fal. Now, Master Shallow, you 'll complain of me to the king?

Shal. Knight, you have beaten my men, killed my deer, and broke open my lodge.

Fal. But not kissed your keeper's daughter?

Shal. Tut, a pin, this shall be answered.

Fal. I will answer it straight:—I have done all this.— That is now answered

Shal. The Council shall know this.

Fal. 'T were better for you, if it were known in counsel; you'll be laughed at.

Eva. *Pauca verba*, Sir John; goot worts.

Fal. Goot worts? good cabbage.—Slender, I broke your head: what matter have you against me?

Slen. Marry, sir, I have matter in my head against you; and against your cony-catching rascals, Bardolph, Nym, and Pistol. They carried me to the tavern, and made me drunk, and afterwards picked my pocket.

Bard. You Banbury cheese!

Slen. Ay, it is no matter.

Pist. How now, Mephostophilus?

Slen. Ay, it is no matter.

Nym. Slice, I say! *pauca, pauca;* slice! that's my humour.

Slen. Where 's Simple, my man?—can you tell, cousin?

Eva. Peace! I pray you. Now let us understand: there is three umpires in this matter, as I understand: that is—Master Page, *fidelicet*, Master Page; and there is myself, *fidelicet*, myself; and the three party is, lastly and finally, mine host of the Garter.

Page. We three, to hear it, and end it between them.

Eva. Fery goot: I will make a prief of it in my note-book; and we will afterwards ork upon the cause, with as great discreetly as we can.

Fal. Pistol,—

Pist. He hears with ears.

Eva. The tevil and his tam! what phrase is this, "He hears with ear?" Why, it is affectations.

Fal. Pistol, did you pick Master Slender's purse?

Slen. Ay, by these gloves, did he—or I would I might never come in mine own great chamber again else—of seven groats in mill six-pences, and two Edward shovel-boards, that cost me two shilling and two pence a-piece of Yead Miller;—by these gloves.

Fal. Is this true, Pistol?

Eva. No; it is false, if it is a pick-purse.

Pist. Ha, thou mountain-foreigner!—Sir John and master challenge of this latten bilbo.—
Word of denial in thy labras here;
Word of denial:—froth and scum, thou liest.

Slen. By these gloves, then, 't was he.

Nym. Be avised, sir, and pass good humours: I will say, "marry trap," with you, if you run the nut-hook's humour on me; that is the very note of it.

Slen. By this hat, then, he in the red face had it; for though I cannot remember what I did when you made me drunk, yet I am not altogether an ass.

Fal. What say you, Scarlet and John?

Bard. Why, sir, for my part, I say, the gentleman had drunk himself out of his five sentences,—

Eva. It is his five senses: fie, what the ignorance is!

Bard. And being fap, sir, was, as they say, cashiered; and so conclusions passed the careers.

Slen. Ay, you spake in Latin then too; but 't is no matter. I'll ne'er be drunk whilst I live again but in honest, civil, godly company, for this trick; if I be drunk, I'll be drunk with those that have the fear of God, and not with drunken knaves.

Eva. So Got udge me, that is a virtuous mind.

Fal. You hear all these matters denied, gentlemen; you hear it.

Enter ANNE PAGE, *with wine;* MISTRESS FORD *and* MISTRESS PAGE *following*

Page. Nay, daughter, carry the wine in; we'll drink within.   [*Exit Anne Page*

Slen. O Heaven! this is Mistress Anne Page.

Page. How now, Mistress Ford?

Fal. Mistress Ford, by my troth, you are very well met: by your leave, good mistress.   [*Kissing her*

Page. Wife, bid these gentlemen welcome.—
Come, we have a hot venison pasty to dinner: come, gentlemen, I hope we shall drink down all unkindness.
                    [*Exeunt all but Shallow, Slender, and Evans*

76

Slen. I had rather than forty shillings, I had my Book of Songs and Sonnets here.

Enter SIMPLE

How now, Simple? Where have you been? I must wait on myself, must I? You have not the Book of Riddles about you, have you?

Sim. Book of Riddles! why, did you not lend it to Alice Shortcake upon All-hallowmas last, a fortnight afore Michaelmas?

Shal. Come, coz; come, coz; we stay for you. A word with you, coz; marry, this coz: there is, as 't were, a tender, a kind of tender, made afar off by Sir Hugh here: do you understand me?

Slen. Ay, sir, you shall find me reasonable: if it be so, I shall do that that is reason.

Shal. Nay, but understand me.

Slen. So I do, sir.

Eva. Give ear to his motions, Master Slender. I will description the matter to you, if you be capacity of it.

Slen. Nay, I will do as my cousin Shallow says. I pray you pardon me; he's a justice of peace in his country, simple though I stand here.

Eva. But that is not the question: the question is concerning your marriage.

Shal. Ay, that 's the point, sir.

Eva. Marry, is it, the very point of it; to Mistress Anne Page.

Slen. Why, if it be so, I will marry her upon any reasonable demands.

Eva. But can you affection the oman? Let us command to know that of your mouth, or of your lips; for divers philosophers hold, that the lips is parcel of the mouth: therefore, precisely, can you carry your good will to the maid?

Shal. Cousin Abraham Slender, can you love her?

Slen. I hope, sir, I will do as it shall become one that would do reason.

Eva. Nay, Got's lords and his ladies, you must speak positable, if you can carry her your desires towards her.

Shal. That you must. Will you, upon good dowry, marry her?

Slen. I will do a greater thing than that, upon your request, cousin, in any reason.

Shal. Nay, conceive me, conceive me, sweet coz; what I do, is to pleasure you, coz. Can you love the maid?

Slen. I will marry her, sir, at your request; but if there be no great love in the beginning, yet Heaven may decrease it upon better acquaintance, when we are married

77

and have more occasion to know one another: I hope, upon
familiarity will grow more contempt: but if you say,
"marry her," I will marry her; that I am freely dissolved,
and dissolutely.

Eva. It is a fery discretion answer; save the faul is
in the ort dissolutely: the ort is, according to our meaning,
resolutely: his meaning is goot.

Shal. Ay, I think my cousin meant well.

Slen. Ay, or else I would I might be hanged, la!

Shal. Here comes fair Mistress Anne.—

Re-enter ANNE PAGE

'Would I were young for your sake, Mistress Anne!

Anne. The dinner is on the table; my father desires
your worship's company.

Shal. I will wait on him, fair Mistress Anne.

Eva. Od's plessed will! I will not be absence at the
grace.   [*Exeunt Shallow and Evans*

Anne. Will 't please your worship to come in, sir?

Slen. No, I thank you, forsooth, heartily; I am very
well.

Anne. The dinner attends you, sir.

Slen. I am not a-hungry, I thank you, forsooth.—Go,
sirrah, for all you are my man, go, wait upon my cousin
Shallow. [*Exit Simple*] A justice of peace sometime may
be beholding to his friend for a man.—I keep but three men
and a boy yet, till my mother be dead; but what though?
yet I live like a poor gentleman born.

Anne. I may not go in without your worship; they will
not sit, till you come.

Slen. I' faith, I 'll eat nothing; I thank you as much
as though I did.

Anne. I pray you, sir, walk in.

Slen. I had rather walk here, I thank you. I bruised
my shin th' other day with playing at sword and dagger
with a master of fence—three veneys for a dish of stewed
prunes; and, by my troth, I cannot abide the smell of hot
meat since.—Why do your dogs bark so? be there bears
i' the town?

Anne. I think there are, sir; I heard them talked of.

Slen. I love the sport well; but I shall as soon quarrel
at it as any man in England. You are afraid, if you see
the bear loose, are you not?

Anne. Ay, indeed, sir.

Slen. That 's meat and drink to me now. I have seen
Sackerson loose twenty times, and have taken him by the
chain; but, I warrant you, the women have so cried and
shrieked at it that it passed—but women, indeed, cannot
abide 'em; they are very ill-favoured rough things.

Re-enter PAGE

Page. Come, gentle Master Slender, come; we stay for you.

Slen. I 'll eat nothing, I thank you, sir.

Page. By cock and pie, you shall not choose, sir: come, come.

Slen. Nay, pray you, lead the way.

Page. Come on, sir.

Slen. Mistress Anne, yourself shall go first.

Anne. Not I, sir; pray you, keep on.

Slen. Truly, I will not go first: truly, la, I will not do you that wrong.

Anne. I pray you, sir.

Slen. I 'll rather be unmannerly, than troublesome. You do yourself wrong, indeed, la!   [*Exeunt*

SCENE II.—An outer Room in PAGE's House.

Enter SIR HUGH EVANS *and* SIMPLE

Eva. Go your ways, and ask of Doctor Caius' house which is the way; and there dwells one Mistress Quickly, which is in the manner of his nurse, or his try nurse, or his cook, or his laundry, his washer and his wringer.

Sim. Well, sir.

Eva. Nay, it is petter yet.—Give her this letter; for it is a oman that altogether's acquaintance with Mistress Anne Page: and the letter is, to desire and require her to solicit your master's desires to Mistress Anne Page. I pray you, be gone: I will make an end of my dinner: there 's pippins and cheese to come.   [*Exeunt*

SCENE III.—A Room in the Garter Inn

Enter FALSTAFF, *Host*, BARDOLPH, NYM, PISTOL, *and* ROBIN

Fal. Mine host of the Garter,—

Host. What says my bully-rook? Speak scholarly and wisely.

Fal. Truly, mine host, I must turn away some of my followers.

Host. Discard, bully Hercules; cashier: let them wag; trot, trot.

Fal. I sit at ten pounds a week.

Host. Thou 'rt an emperor, Cæsar, Keisar, and Pheezar. I will entertain Bardolph; he shall draw, he shall tap: said I well, bully Hector?

Fal. Do so, good mine host.

Host. I have spoke; let him follow.—Let me see thee froth and lime: I am at a word; follow.   [*Exit Host*

79

Fal.   Bardolph, follow him. A tapster is a good trade:
an old cloak makes a new jerkin; a withered serving-man
a fresh tapster. Go; adieu.

Bard.   It is a life that I have desired: I will thrive.

Pist.   O base Gongarian wight! wilt thou the spigot
wield?   [*Exit Bardolph*

Nym.   He was gotten in drink; is not the humour con-
ceited?

Fal.   I am glad I am so acquit of this tinder-box: his
thefts were too open; his filching was like an unskilful
singer,—he kept not time.

Nym.   The good humour is to steal at a minim's rest.

Pist.   Convey, the wise it call. "Steal?" foh! a fico for
the phrase!

Fal.   Well, sirs, I am almost out at heels.

Pist.   Why, then let kibes ensue.

Fal.   There is no remedy; I must cony-catch; I must shift.

Pist.   Young ravens must have food.

Fal.   Which of you know Ford of this town?

Pist.   I ken the wight: he is of substance good.

Fal.   My honest lads, I will tell you what I am about.

Pist.   Two yards, and more.

Fal.   No quips now, Pistol: indeed, I am in the waist
two yards about; but I am now about no waste, I am
about thrift. Briefly, I do mean to make love to Ford's
wife. I spy entertainment in her; she discourses, she
carves, she gives the leer of invitation: I can construe the
action of her familiar style; and the hardest voice of her
behaviour, to be Englished rightly, is, "I am Sir John
Falstaff's."

Pist.   He hath studied her well, and translated her well,
—out of honesty into English.

Nym.   The anchor is deep: will that humour pass?

Fal.   Now, the report goes, she has all the rule of her
husband's purse—he hath a legion of angels.

Pist.   As many devils entertain; and "To her, boy,"
say I.

Nym.   The humour rises; it is good: humour me the
angels.

Fal.   I have writ me here a letter to her: and here
another to Page's wife, who even now gave me good eyes
too, examined my parts with most judicious oullads;
sometimes the beam of her view gilded my foot, sometimes
my portly belly.

Pist.   Then did the sun on dunghill shine.

Nym.   I thank thee for that humour.

Fal.   O, she did so course o'er my exteriors with such
a greedy intention, that the appetite of her eye did seem
to scorch me up like a burning-glass. Here 's another
letter to her: she bears the purse too; she is a region in

Guiana, all gold and bounty. I will be cheaters to them
both, and they shall be exchequers to me: they shall be
my East and West Indies, and I will trade to them both.
Go, bear thou this letter to Mistress Page; and thou this
to Mistress Ford. We will thrive, lads, we will thrive.

    Pist.   Shall I Sir Pandarus of Troy become,
And by my side wear steel? then, Lucifer take all!

    Nym.   I will run no base humour: here take the humour-
letter.   I will keep the haviour of réputation.

    Fal.   [*To Robin*] Hold, sirrah, bear you these letters
        tightly;
Sail like my pinnance to the golden shores.—
Rogues, hence! avaunt! vanish like hailstones, go;
Trudge, plod away o' the hoof; seek shelter, pack!
Falstaff will learn the humour of the age,
French thrift, you rogues; myself, and skirted page.
                     [*Exeunt Falstaff and Robin*

    Pist.   Let vultures gripe thy guts! for gourd and fullam
        holds,
And high and low beguile the rich and poor.
Tester I 'll have in pouch when thou shalt lack,
Base Phrygian Turk.

    Nym.   I have operations in my head which be humours
of revenge.

    Pist.   Wilt thou revenge?

    Nym.   By welkin, and her star.

    Pist.   With wit, or steel?

    Nym.   With both the humours, I:
I will discuss the humour of this love to Page.

    Pist.   And I to Ford shall eke unfold
        How Falstaff, varlet vile,
        His dove will prove, his gold will hold,
        And his soft couch defile.

    Nym.   My humour shall not cool: I will incense Page
to deal with poison; I will possess him with yellowness: for
this revolt of mine is dangerous; that is my true humour.

    Pist.   Thou art the Mars of malcontents: I second thee;
troop on.   [*Exeunt*

SCENE IV.—A Room in DOCTOR CAIUS'S House

Enter MISTRESS QUICKLY *and* SIMPLE

    Quick.   What, John Rugby!—

Enter RUGBY

I pray thee, go to the casement, and see if you can see
my master, Master Doctor Caius, coming: if he do, i' faith,
and find anybody in the house, here will be an old abusing
of God's patience and the king's English.

81

Rug. I 'll go watch.

Quick. Go; and we 'll have a posset for 't soon at night, in faith, at the latter end of a sea-coal fire.   [*Exit Rugby*] An honest, willing, kind fellow, as ever servant shall come in house withal; and, I warrant you, no tell-tale, nor no breed-bate: his worst fault is, that he is given to prayer; he is something peevish that way; but nobody but has his fault;—but let that pass.—Peter Simple you say your name is?

Sim. Ay, for fault of a better.

Quick. And Master Slender 's your master?

Sim. Ay, forsooth.

Quick. Does he not wear a great round beard, like a glover's paring-knife?

Sim. No, forsooth: he hath but a little wee face, with a little yellow beard,—a cane-coloured beard.

Quick. A softly-sprighted man, is he not?

Sin. Ay, forsooth; but he is as tall a man of his hands as any is between this and his head: he hath fought with a warrener.

Quick. How say you?—O, I should remember him: does he not hold up his head, as it were, and strut in his gait?

Sim. Yes, indeed, does he.

Quick. Well, Heaven send Anne Page no worse fortune! Tell Master Parson Evans, I will do what I can for your master: Anne is a good girl, and I wish—

Re-enter RUGBY

Rug. Out, alas! here comes my master.

Quick. We shall all be shent.   [*Exit Rugby*] Run in here, good young man; go into this closet. [*Shuts Simple in the closet.*]   He will not stay long.—What, John Rugby! John, what, John, I say!—Go, John, go inquire for my master; I doubt, he be not well, that he comes not home. [*Sings*] *And down, down, adown-a, etc.*

Enter DOCTOR CAIUS

Caius. Vat is you sing? I do not like dese toys. Pray you, go and vetch me in my closet *un boitier vert ;* a box, a green-a box: do intend vat I speak? a green-a box.

Quick. Ay, forsooth; I'll fetch it you. [*Aside*] I am glad he went not in himself: if he had found the young man, he would have been horn-mad.

Caius. Fe, fe, fe, fe! ma foi, il fait fort chaud. *Je me'en vais à la cour,—la grande affaire.*

Quick. Is it this, sir?

Caius. Ouy, mette le au mon pocket; *dépéche, quickly.* —Vere is dat knave Rugby?

Quick. What, John Rugby! John!

Re-enter RUGBY

Rug. Here, sir.

Caius. You are John Rugby, and you are Jack Rogeby: come, take-a your rapier, and come after my heel to de court.

Rug. 'T is ready, sir, here in the porch.

Caius. By my trot, I tarry too long.—Od's me! *Qu'ay j'oublié?* dere is some simples in my closet, dat I vit not for de varld I shall leave behind.

Quick. Ay me! he 'll find the young man there, and be mad.

Caius. *O diable! diable!* vat is in my closet?—Villainy! *larron!* [*Pulling Simple out*] Rugby; my rapier!

Quick. Good master, be content.

Caius. Verefore shall I be content-a?

Quick. The young man is an honest man.

Caius. Vat shall de honest man do in my closet? dere is no honest man dat shall come in my closet.

Quick. I beseech you, be not so phlegmatic; hear the truth of it: he came of an errand to me from Parson Hugh.

Caius. Vell.

Sim. Ay, forsooth, to desire her to—

Quick. Peace, I pray you.

Caius. Peace-a young tongue! Speak-a your tale.

Sim. To desire this honest gentlewoman, your maid, to speak a good word to Mistress Anne Page for my master in the way of marriage.

Quick. This is all, indeed, la; but I'll ne'er put my finger in the fire, and need not.

Caius. Sir Hugh send-a you?—Rugby, *baillez* me some paper: tarry you a little-a while.   [*Writes*

Quick. I am glad he is so quiet: if he had been thoroughly moved, you should have heard him so loud and so melancholy.—But notwithstanding, man, I 'll do you your master what good I can; and the very yea and the no is, the French doctor, my master,—I may call him my master, look you, for I keep his house; and I wash, wring, brew, bake, scour, dress meat and drink, make the beds, and do all myself;—

Sim. 'T is a great charge, to come under one body's hand.

Quick. Are you avised o' that? you shall find it a great charge: and to be up early and down late;—but notwithstanding, to tell you in your ear—I would have no words of it—my master himself is in love with Mistress Anne Page, but nothingstanding that, I know Anne's mind, that 's neither here nor there.

Caius. You jack'nape,—give-a dis letter to Sir Hugh; by gar, it is a shallenge: I will cut his troat in de park and I vill teach a scurvy jackanape priest to meddle or make.—You may be gone; it is not good you tarry here:—by gar, I vill cut all his two stones; by gar, he shall not have a stone to throw at his dog.   [*Exit Simple*

Quick. Alas! he speaks but for his friend.

Caius. It is no matter-a for dat:—do not you tell-a me, dat I shall have Anne Page for myself?—By gar, I vill kill de Jack priest; and I have appointed mine host of de Jarteer to measure our weapon.—By gar, I vill myself have Anne Page.

Quick. Sir, the maid loves you, and all shall be well. We must give folks leave to prate: what the good-jer!

Caius. Rugby, come to the court vit me.—By gar, if I have not Anne Page, I shall turn your head out of my door.—Follow my heels, Rugby.   [*Exeunt Caius and Rugby*

Quick. You shall have An fool's-head of your own. No, I know Anne's mind for that: never a woman in Windsor knows more of Anne's mind than I do, nor can do more than I do with her, I thank Heaven.

Fent. [*Within*] Who 's within there? ho!

Quick. Who 's there, I trow? Come near the house, I pray you.

Enter FENTON

Fent. How now, good woman? how dost thou?

Quick. The better, that it pleases your good worship to ask.

Fent. What news? how does pretty Mistress Anne?

Quick. In truth, sir, and she is pretty, and honest, and gentle; and one that is your friend, I can tell you that by the way; I praise Heaven for it.

Fent. Shall I do any good, thinkest thou? Shall I not lose my suit?

Quick. Troth, sir, all is in His hands above; but notwithstanding, Master Fenton, I 'll be sworn on a book, she loves you.—Have not your worship a wart above your eye?

Fent. Yes, marry, have I; what of that?

Quick. Well, thereby hangs a tale:—good faith, it is such another Nan;—but, I detest, an honest maid as ever broke bread:—we had an hour's talk of that wart:—I shall never laugh but in that maid's company!—but, indeed, she is given too much to allicholly and musing: but for you—well, go to.

Fent. Well, I shall see her to-day. Hold, there 's money for thee; let me have thy voice in my behalf: if thou see'st her before me, commend me.

Quick. Will I? i' faith, that we will; and I will tell your worship more of the wart the next time we have confidence, and of other wooers.

Fent. Well, farewell; I am in great haste now.   [*Exit*

Quick. Farewell to your worship.—Truly an honest gentleman: but Anne loves him not; for I know Anne's mind as well as another does.—Out upon 't! what have I forgot?   [*Exit*

ACT TWO

SCENE I.—Before PAGE's House

Enter MISTRESS PAGE *with a letter*

Mrs. Page. What, have I scaped love-letters in the holiday-time of my beauty, and am I now a subject for them? Let me see.   [*Reads*
"Ask me no reason why I love you; for though Love use Reason for his physician, he admits him not for his counsellor. You are not young, no more am I; go to then, there 's sympathy: you are merry, so am I; ha, ha! then, there 's more sympathy: you love sack, and so do I; would you desire better sympathy? Let it suffice thee, Mistress Page,—at the least, if the love of a soldier can suffice,—that I love thee. I will not say, pity me,—'t is not a soldier-like phrase; but I say, love me. By me,

> Thine own true knight,
> By day or night,
> Or any kind of light,
> With all his might
> For thee to fight,   JOHN FALSTAFF."

What a Herod of Jewry is this!—O wicked, wicked world! —one that is well nigh worn to pieces with age, to show himself a young gallant! What unweighed behaviour hath this Flemish drunkard picked, with the devil's name, out of my conversation, that he dares in this manner assay me? Why, he hath not been thrice in my company.— What should I say to him?—I was then frugal of my mirth: —Heaven forgive me!—Why, I 'll exhibit a bill in the parliament for the putting down of men. How shall I be revenged on him? for revenged I will be, as sure as his guts are made of puddings.

Enter MISTRESS FORD

Mrs. Ford. Mistress Page! trust me, I was going to your house.
Mrs. Page. And, trust me, I was coming to you. You look very ill.
Mrs. Ford. Nay, I 'll ne'er believe that; I have to show to the contrary.
Mrs. Page. Faith, but you do, in my mind.
Mrs. Ford. Well, I do then; yet, I say, I could show you to the contrary. O Mistress Page, give me some counsel.

Mrs. Page. What 's the matter, woman?

Mrs. Ford. O woman, if it were not for one trifling respect, I could come to such honour!

Mrs. Page. Hang the trifle, woman; take the honour. What is it?—dispense with trifles;—what is it?

Mrs. Ford. If I would but go to hell for an eternal moment or so, I could be knighted.

Mrs. Page. What?—thou liest.—Sir Alice Ford!—These knights will hack; and so, thou shouldst not alter the article of the gentry.

Mrs. Ford. We burn daylight:—here, read, read:—perceive how I might be knighted.—I shall think the worse of fat men, as long as I have an eye to make difference of men's liking: and yet he would not swear; praised women's modesty; and gave such orderly and well-behaved reproof to all uncomeliness, that I would have sworn his disposition would have gone to the truth of his words; but they do no more adhere, and keep place together, than the Hundredth Psalm to the tune of "Green Sleeves." What tempest, I trow, threw this whale, with so many tuns of oil in his belly, ashore at Windsor? How shall I be revenged on him? I think, the best way were to entertain him with hope, till the wicked fire of lust have melted him in his own grease.—Did you ever hear the like?

Mrs. Page. Letter for letter, but that the name of Page and Ford differs!—To thy great comfort in this mystery of ill opinions, here 's the twin-brother of thy letter: but let thine inherit first; for, I protest, mine never shall. I warrant, he hath a thousand of these letters, writ with blank space for different names—sure more—and these are of the second edition. He will print them, out of doubt; for he cares not what he puts into the press, when he would put us two: I had rather be a giantess, and lie under Mount Pelion. Well, I will find you twenty lascivious turtles, ere one chaste man.

Mrs. Ford. Why, this is the very same; the very hand, the very words. What doth he think of us?

Mrs. Page. Nay, I know not: it makes me almost ready to wrangle with mine own honesty. I 'll entertain myself like one that I am not acquainted withal; for sure, unless he know some strain in me that I know not myself, he would never have boarded me in this fury.

Mrs. Ford. Boarding, call you it? I 'll be sure to keep him above deck.

Mrs. Page. So will I: if he come under my hatches, I 'll never to sea again. Let 's be revenged on him: let 's appoint him a meeting; give him a show of comfort in his suit; and lead him on with a fine-baited delay, till he hath pawned his horses to mine host of the Garter.

Mrs. Ford. Nay, I will consent to act any villainy against him that may not sully the chariness of our honesty. O, that my husband saw this letter! it would give eternal food to his jealousy.

Mrs. Page. Why, look, where he comes; and my good man, too: he's as far from jealousy, as I am from giving him cause; and that, I hope, is an unmeasurable distance.

Mrs. Ford. You are the happier woman.

Mrs. Page. Let's consult together against this greasy knight. Come hither.   [*They retire*

Enter FORD, PISTOL, PAGE, *and* NYM

Ford. Well, I hope, it be not so.

Pist. Hope is a curtal dog in some affairs: Sir John affects thy wife.

Ford. Why, sir, my wife is not young.

Pist. He wooes both high and low, both rich and poor,
Both young and old, one with another, Ford.
He loves the gallimaufry: Ford, perpend.

Ford. Love my wife?

Pist. With liver burning hot: prevent, or go thou,
Like Sir Actæon he, with Ringwood at thy heels:—
O, odious is the name.

Ford. What name, sir?

Pist. The horn, I say. Farewell:
Take heed; have open eye; for thieves do foot by night:
Take heed, ere summer comes, or cuckoo-birds do sing.—
Away, Sir Corporal Nym:—
Believe it, Page; he speaks sense.   [*Exit*

Ford. [*Aside*] I will be patient; I will find out this.

Nym [*To Page*] And this is true; I like not the humour of lying. He hath wronged me in some humours: I should have borne the humoured letter to her; but I have a sword, and it shall bite upon my necessity. He loves your wife; there's the short and the long. My name is Corporal Nym: I speak, and I avouch 't is true:—my name is Nym, and Falstaff loves your wife.—Adieu. I love not the humour of bread and cheese; and there's the humour of it. Adieu.
                                                                [*Exit*

Page. [*Aside*] "The humour of it," quoth 'a! here's a fellow frights humour out of his wits.

Ford. [*Aside*] I will seek out Falstaff.

Page. [*Aside*] I never heard such a drawling, affecting rogue.

Ford. [*Aside*] If I do find it:—well.

Page. [*Aside*] I will not believe such a Cataian, though the priest o' the town commanded him for a true man.

Ford. [*Aside*] 'T was a good sensible fellow: well.

Page. How now, Meg?

Mrs. Page. Whither go you, George?—Hark you.

Mrs. Ford How now, sweet Frank? why art thou melancholy?

Ford. I melancholy! I am not melancholy.—Get you home, go.

Mrs. Ford. 'Faith, thou hast some crotchets in thy head now.—Will you go, Mistress Page?

Mrs. Page. Have with you.—You'll come to dinner, George?—[*Aside to Mrs. Ford*] Look, who comes yonder: she shall be our messenger to this paltry knight.

Mrs. Ford. Trust me, I thought on her: she 'll fit it.

Enter MISTRESS QUICKLY

Mrs. Page. You are come to see my daughter Anne?

Quick. Ay, forsooth; and, I pray, how does good Mistress Anne?

Mrs. Page. Go in with us, and see; we have an hour's talk with you.

[*Exeunt Mrs. Page, Mrs. Ford, and Mrs. Quickly*

Page. How now, Master Ford?

Ford. You heard what this knave told me, did you not?

Page. Yes; and you heard what the other told me.

Ford. Do you think there is truth in them?

Page. Hang 'em slaves; I do not think the knight would offer it: but these that accuse him, in his intent towards our wives, are a yoke of his discarded men; very rogues, now they be out of service.

Ford. Were they his men?

Page. Marry, were they.

Ford. I like it never the better for that.—Does he lie at the Garter?

Page. Ay, marry, does he. If he should intend this voyage towards my wife, I would turn her loose to him; and what he gets more of her than sharp words, let it lie on my head.

Ford. I do not misdoubt my wife, but I would be loath to turn them together. A man may be too confident: I would have nothing lie on my head: I cannot be thus satisfied.

Page. Look, where my ranting host of the Garter comes. There is either liquor in his pate, or money in his purse, when he looks so merrily.—

Enter Host

How now, mine host?

Host. How now, bully-rook! thou 'rt a gentleman.—Cavalero-justice, I say,—

Enter SHALLOW

Shal. I follow, mine host, I follow.—Good-even and twenty, Good Master Page. Master Page, will you go with us? we have sport in hand.

Host. Tell him, cavalero-justice; tell him, bully-rook.

Shal. Sir, there is a fray to be fought between Sir Hugh
the Welsh priest and Caius the French doctor.

Ford. Good mine host o' the Garter, a word with you.

Host. What say'st thou, my bully-rook?

[*They go aside*

Shal. [*To Page*] Will you go with us to behold it?
My merry host hath had the measuring of their weapons,
and, I think, hath appointed them contrary places; for,
believe me, I hear the parson is no jester. Hark, I will tell
you what our sport shall be.

Host. Hast thou no suit against my knight, my guest-
cavalier?

Ford. None, I protest: but I'll give you a pottle of
burnt sack to give me recourse to him and tell him my
name is Brook, only for a jest.

Host. My hand, bully: thou shalt have egress and
regress; said I well? and thy name shall be Brook. It
is a merry knight.—Will you go, mynheers?

Shal. Have with you, mine host.

Page. I have heard the Frenchman hath good skill in
his rapier.

Shal. Tut, sir! I could have told you more: in these
times you stand on distance, your passes, stoccadoes, and
I know not what: 't is the heart, Master Page; 't is here,
't is here. I have seen the time, with my long sword, I
would have made you four tall fellows skip like rats.

Host. Here, boys, here, here! shall we wag?

Page. Have with you.—I had rather hear them scold
than fight.   [*Exeunt Host, Shallow, and Page*

Ford. Though Page be a secure fool, and stands so
firmly on his wife's frailty, yet I cannot put off my opinion
so easily. She was in his company at Page's house, and what
they made there, I know not. Well, I will look further
into 't; and I have a disguise to sound Falstaff. If I find
her honest, I lose not my labour; if she be otherwise, 't is
labour well bestowed.   [*Exit*

Scene II.—A Room in the Garter Inn

Enter Falstaff *and* Pistol

Fal. I will not lend thee a penny.

Pist. Why, then the world 's mine oyster, which I with
sword will open.

Fal. Not a penny. I have been content, sir, you should
lay my countenance to pawn: I have grated upon my good
friends for three reprieves for you and your coach-fellow
Nym; or else you had looked through the grate, like a
geminy of baboons. I am damned in hell for swearing to

gentlemen, my friends, you were good soldiers, and tall
fellows; and when Mistress Bridget lost the handle of her
fan, I took 't upon mine honour thou hadst it not.

Pist. Didst thou not share? hadst thou not fifteen
pence?

Fal. Reason, you rogue, reason: think'st thou I'll
endanger my soul gratis? At a word, hang no more about
me, I am no gibbet for you:—go:—a short knife and a
throng:—to your manor of Pickt-hatch, go.—You'll not
bear a letter for me, you rogue!—you stand upon your
honour!—Why, thou unconfinable baseness, it is as much
as I can do, to keep the terms of my honour precise: I, I,
I myself sometimes, leaving the fear of Heaven on the left
hand, and hiding mine honour in my necessity, am fain
to shuffle, to hedge, and to lurch; and yet you, rogue, will
ensconce your rags, your cat-a-mountain looks, your red-
lattice phrases, and your bull-baiting oaths, under the
shelter of your honour! You will not do it, you?

Pist. I do relent: what would thou more of man?

Enter ROBIN

Rob. Sir, here's a woman would speak with you.
Fal. Let her approach.

Enter MISTRESS QUICKLY

Quick. Give your worship good morrow.
Fal. Good morrow, good wife.
Quick. Not so, an 't please your worship.
Fal. Good maid, then.
Quick. I'll be sworn; as my mother was, the first hour
I was born.
Fal. I do believe the swearer. What with me?
Quick. Shall I vouchsafe your worship a word or two?
Fal. Two thousand, fair woman: and I'll vouchsafe
thee the hearing.
Quick. There is one Mistress Ford, sir:—I pray, come
a little nearer this ways:—I myself dwell with Master
Doctor Caius.
Fal. Well, on: Mistress Ford you say,—
Quick. Your worship says very true:—I pray your
worship, come a little nearer this ways.
Fal. I warrant thee, nobody hears: mine own people,
mine own people.
Quick. Are they so? Heaven bless them, and make
them His servants!
Fal. Well: Mistress Ford;—what of her?
Quick. Why, sir, she's a good creature. Lord, Lord!
your worship's a wanton! well Heaven forgive you and
all of us, I pray!
Fal. Mistress Ford;—come, Mistress Ford,—

Quick. Marry, this is the short and the long of it. You have brought her into such a canaries, as 't is wonderful. The best courtier of them all, when the court lay at Windsor, could never have brought her to such a canary. Yet there has been knights, and lords, and gentlemen, with their coaches; I warrant you, coach after coach, letter after letter, gift after gift; smelling so sweetly,—all musk,—and so rushling, I warrant you, in silk and gold; and in such alligant terms; and such wine and sugar of the best, and the fairest, that would have won any woman's heart, and, I warrant you, they could never get an eye-wink of her.—I had myself twenty angels given me this morning; but I defy all angels,—in any such sort, as they say—but in the way of honesty:—and, I warrant you, they could never get her so much as sip on a cup with the proudest of them all; and yet there had been earls, nay, which is more, pensioners; but, I warrant you, all is one with her.

Fal. But what says she to me? be brief, my good she-Mercury.

Quick. Marry, she hath received your letter; for the which she thanks you a thousand times; and she gives you to notify, that her husband will be absence from his house between ten and eleven.

Fal. Ten and eleven.

Quick. Ay, forsooth; and then you may come and see the picture, she says, that you wot of; Master Ford, her husband, will be from home. Alas! the sweet woman leads an ill life with him! he's a very jealousy man; she leads a very frampold life with him, good heart.

Fal. Ten and eleven:—woman, commend me to her; I will not fail her.

Quick. Why, you say well. But I have another messenger to your worship. Mistress Page hath her hearty commendations to you, too;—and let me tell you in your ear, she's as fartuous a civil modest wife, and one, I tell you, that will not miss you morning nor evening prayer, as any is in Windsor, whoe'er be the other:—and she bade me tell your worship, that her husband is seldom from home; but she hopes there will come a time. I never knew a woman so dote upon a man: surely, I think you have charms, la; yes, in truth.

Fal. Not I, I assure thee; setting the attractions of my good parts aside, I have no other charms.

Quick. Blessing on your heart for 't!

Fal. But, I pray thee, tell me this,—has Ford's wife, and Page's wife, acquainted each other how they love me?

Quick. That were a jest, indeed!—they have not so little grace, I hope:—that were a trick, indeed!—But Mistress Page would desire you to send her your little page, of all loves: her husband has a marvellous infection to the

91

little page; and, truly, Master Page is an honest man.
Never a wife in Windsor leads a better life than she does:
do what she will, say what she will, take all, pay all, go to
bed when she list, rise when she list, all is as she will: and,
truly, she deserves it; for if there be a kind woman in
Windsor, she is one. You must send her your page; no
remedy.

Fal. Why, I will.

Quick. Nay, but do so, then: and, look you, he may
come and go between you both; and, in any case, have a
nayword, that you may know one another's mind, and the
boy never need to understand anything; for 't is not good
that children should know any wickedness: old folks, you
know, have discretion, as they say, and know the world.

Fal. Fare thee well: commend me to them both.
There's my purse; I am yet thy debtor.—Boy, go along
with this woman. [*Exeunt Mistress Quickly and Robin*]
—This news distracts me.

Pist. This punk is one of Cupid's carriers.—
Clap on more sails; pursue; up with your fights;
Give fire! She is my prize, or ocean whelm them all!
                                        [*Exit*

Fal. Sayest thou so, old Jack? Go thy ways; I'll
make more of thy body than I have done. Will they yet
look after thee? Wilt thou, after the expense of so much
money, be now a gainer? Good body, I thank thee: let
them say, 't is grossly done; so it be fairly done, no matter.

Enter BARDOLPH, *with a cup of sack*

Bard. Sir John, there's one Master Brook below would
fain speak with you, and be acquainted with you; and
hath sent your worship a morning's draught of sack.

Fal. Brook is his name?

Bard. Ay, sir.

Fal. Call him in. [*Exit Bardolph*] Such Brooks are
welcome to me, that o'erflow such liquor. Ah, ha!
Mistress Ford and Mistress Page, have I encompassed you?
go to; *via!*

Re-enter BARDOLPH, *with* FORD *disguised*

Ford. Bless you, sir.

Fal. And you, sir: would you speak with me?

Ford. I make bold to press with so little preparation
upon you.

Fal. You're welcome. What's your will?
—Give us leave, drawer.   [*Exit Bardolph*

Ford. Sir, I am a gentleman that have spent much:
my name is Brook.

Fal. Good Master Brook, I desire more acquaintance
of you.

Ford. Good Sir John, I sue for yours; not to charge you; for I must let you understand I think myself in better plight for a lender than you are; the which hath something emboldened me to this unseasoned intrusion; for they say, if money go before, all ways do lie open.

Fal. Money is a good soldier, sir, and will on.

Ford. Troth, and I have a bag of money here troubles me: if you will help to bear it, Sir John, take all, or half, for easing me of the carriage.

Fal. Sir, I know not how I may deserve to be your porter.

Ford. I will tell you, sir, if you will give me the hearing.

Fal. Speak, good Master Brook: I shall be glad to be your servant.

Ford. Sir, I hear you are a scholar,—I will be brief with you;—and you have been a man long known to me, though I had never so good means, as desire, to make myself acquainted with you. I shall discover a thing to you, wherein I must very much lay open mine own imperfection: but, good Sir John, as you have one eye upon my follies, as you hear them unfolded, turn another into the register of your own; that I may pass with a reproof the easier, sith with yourself know how easy it is to be such an offender.

Fal. Very well, sir; proceed.

Ford. There is a gentlewoman in this town, her husband's name is Ford.

Fal. Well, sir.

Ford. I have long loved her, and, I protest to you, bestowed much on her; followed her with a doting observance; engrossed opportunities to meet her; fee'd every slight occasion, that could but niggardly give me sight of her; not only bought many presents to give her, but have given largely to many, to know what she would have given; briefly, I have pursued her, as love hath pursued me; which hath been, on the wing of all occasions. But whatsoever I have merited, either in my mind, or in my means, meed, I am sure, I have received none, unless experience be a jewel; that I have purchased at an infinite rate, and that hath taught me to say this:

Love like a shadow flies when substance love pursues;
Pursuing that that flies, and flying what pursues.

Fal. Have you received no promise of satisfaction at her hands?

Ford. Never.

Fal. Have you importuned her to such a purpose?

Ford. Never.

Fal. Of what quality was your love then?

Ford. Like a fair house built upon another man's

93

ground; so that I have lost my edifice by mistaking the place where I erected it.

Fal. To what purpose have you unfolded this to me?

Ford. When I have told you that, I have told you all. Some say, that though she appear honest to me, yet in other places she enlargeth her mirth so far that there is shrewd construction made of her. Now, Sir John, here is the heart of my purpose: you are a gentleman of excellent breeding, admirable discourse, of great admittance, authentic in your place and person, generally. allowed for your many war-like, court-like, and learned preparations,—

Fal. O, sir!

Ford. Believe it, for you know it.—There is money; spend it, spend it; spend more; spend all I have, only give me so much of your time in exchange of it, as to lay an amiable siege to the honesty of this Ford's wife: use your art of wooing; win her to consent to you: if any man may, you may as soon as any.

Fal. Would it apply well to the vehemency of your affection, that I should win what you would enjoy? Methinks you prescribe to yourself very preposterously.

Ford. O, understand my drift. She dwells so securely on the excellency of her honour, that the folly of my soul dares not present itself: she is too bright to be looked against. Now, could I come to her with any detection in my hand, my desires had instance and argument to commend themselves; I could drive her then from the ward of her purity, her reputation, her marriage-vow, and a thousand other her defences, which now are too strongly embattled against me. What say you to 't, Sir John?

Fal. Master Brook, I will first make bold with your money; next, give me your hand; and last, as I am a gentleman, you shall, if you will, enjoy Ford's wife.

Ford. O good sir!

Fal. I say you shall.

Ford. Want no money, Sir John; you shall want none.

Fal. Want no Mistress Ford, Master Brook; you shall want none. I shall be with her—I may tell you—by her own appointment; even as you came in to me, her assistant, or go-between, parted from me: I say, I shall be with her between ten and eleven; for at that time the jealous rascally knave, her husband, will be forth. Come you to me at night; you shall know how I speed.

Ford. I am blest in your acquaintance. Do you know Ford, sir?

Fal. Hang him, poor cuckoldly knave! I know him not.— Yet I wrong him, to call him poor; they say, the jealous wittolly knave hath masses of money, for the which his wife seems to be well-favoured. I will use her as the key of the cuckoldly rogue's coffer; and there's my harvest home.

Ford. I would you knew Ford, sir, that you might avoid him, if you saw him.

Fal. Hang him, mechanical salt-butter rogue! I will stare him out of his wits; I will awe him with my cudgel,— it shall hang like a meteor o'er the cuckold's horns. Master Brook, thou shalt know I will predominate over the peasant, and thou shalt lie with his wife.—Come to me soon at night.—Ford's a knave, and I will aggravate his style; thou, Master Brook, shalt know him for a knave and cuckold:—come to me soon at night. [*Exit*

Ford. What a damned Epicurean rascal is this!—My heart is ready to crack with impatience.—Who says, this is improvident jealousy? my wife hath sent to him, the hour is fixed, the match is made. Would any man have thought this?—See the hell of having a false woman! my bed shall be abused, my coffers ransacked, my reputation gnawn at; and I shall not only receive this villainous wrong, but stand under the adoption of abominable terms, and by him that does me this wrong. Terms! names!— Amaimon sounds well; Lucifer, well; Barbason, well; yet they are devils' additions, the names of fiends: but cuckold! wittol-cuckold! the devil himself hath not such a name. Page is an ass, a secure ass; he will trust his wife, he will not be jealous, I will rather trust a Fleming with my butter, Parson Hugh the Welshman with my cheese, an Irishman with my aqua-vitæ bottle, or a thief to walk my ambling gelding than my wife with herself: then she plots, then she ruminates, then she devises; and what they think in their hearts they may effect, they will break their hearts but they will effect, Heaven be praised for my jealousy!—Eleven o'clock the hour: I will prevent this, detect my wife, be revenged on Falstaff, and laugh at Page. I will about it; better three hours too soon, than a minute too late. Fie, fie, fie! cuckold! cuckold! cuckold!
[*Exit*

SCENE III.—Windsor Park

Enter CAIUS *and* RUGBY

Caius. Jack Rugby!

Rug. Sir.

Caius. Vat is de clock, Jack?

Rug. 'T is past the hour, sir, that Sir Hugh promised to meet.

Caius. By gar, he has save his soul, dat he is no come: he has pray his Pible vell, dat he is no come. By gar, Jack Rugby, he is dead already, if he be come.

Rug. He is wise, sir; he knew your worship would kill him, if he came.

Caius. By gar, de herring is no dead so as I vill kill

him. Take your rapier, Jack; I vill tell you how I vill
kill him.

Rug.   Alas, sir, I cannot fence.

Caius.   Villainy, take your rapier.

Rug.   Forbear; here's company.

Enter HOST, SHALLOW, SLENDER, *and* PAGE

Host.   Bless thee, bully doctor.

Shal.   Save you, Master Doctor Caius.

Page.   Now, good master doctor!

Slen.   Give you good morrow, sir.

Caius.   Vat be all you, one, two, tree, four, come for?

Host.   To see thee fight, to see thee foin, to see the
traverse, to see thee here, to see thee there; to see thee
pass thy punto, thy stock, thy reverse, thy distance, thy
montânt. Is he dead, my Ethiopian? is he dead, my
Francisco? ha, bully! What says my Æsculapius? my
Galen? my heart of elder? ha! is he dead, bully Stale?
is he dead?

Caius.   By gar, he is de coward Jack priest of de vorld;
he is not show his face.

Host.   Thou art a Castilian, King Urinal! Hector of
Greece, my boy!

Caius.   I pray you, bear vitness that me have stay six
or seven, two, tree hours for him, and he is no come.

Shal.   He is the wiser man, master doctor: he is the
curer of souls, and you a curer of bodies; if you should
fight, you go against the hair of your professions.—Is it
not true, Master Page?

Page.   Master Shallow, you have yourself been a great
fighter, though now a man of peace.

Shal.   Bodikins, Master Page, though I now be old, and
of the peace, if I see a sword out, my finger itches to make
one. Though we are justices, and doctors, and churchmen,
Master Page, we have some salt of our youth in us; we
are the sons of women, Master Page.

Page.   'T is true, Master Shallow.

Shal.   It will be found so, Master Page.—Master Doctor
Caius, I am come to fetch you home. I am sworn of the
peace: you have showed yourself a wise physician, and
Sir Hugh hath shown himself a wise and patient churchman.
You must go with me, master doctor.

Host.   Pardon, guest-justice:—a word, Monsieur Mock-
water.

Caius.   Mock-vater! vat is dat?

Host.   Mock-water, in our English tongue, is valour, bully.

Caius.   By gar, then I have as much mock-vater as de
Englishman.—Scurvy jack-dog priest! by gar, me vill cut
his ears.

Host.   He will clapper-claw thee tightly, bully.

Caius.   Clapper-de-claw! vat is dat?
Host.   That is, he will make thee amends.
Caius.   By gar, me do look, he shall clapper-de-claw
me; for, by gar, me vill have it.
Host.   And I will provoke him to 't, or let him wag.
Caius.   Me tank you for dat.
Host.   And moreover, bully,—but first, master guest,
and Master Page, and eke Cavalero Slender, go you through
the town to Frogmore.   [*Aside to them*
Page.   Sir Hugh is there, is he?
Host.   He is there: see what humour he is in, and I will
bring the doctor about by the fields. Will it do well?
Shal.   We will do it.
Page, Shal., and Slen.   Adieu, good master doctor.
                    [*Exeunt Page, Shallow, and Slender*
Caius.   By gar, me vill kill de priest, for he speak for a
jack-an-ape to Anne Page.
Host.   Let him die. Sheathe thy impatience; throw
cold water on thy choler. Go about the fields with me
through Frogmore; I will bring thee where Mistress Anne
Page is, at a farmhouse a-feasting, and thou shalt woo her.
Cried I aim? said I well?
Caius.   By gar, me tank you vor dat: by gar, I love
you; and I shall procure-a you de good guest, de earl, de
knight, de lords, de gentlemen, my patients.
Host.   For the which I will be thy adversary toward
Anne Page: said I well?
Caius.   By gar, 't is good; vell said.
Host.   Let us wag, then.
Caius.   Come at my heels. Jack Rugby.   [*Exeunt*

ACT THREE

Scene I.—A Field near Frogmore

Enter Sir Hugh Evans *and* Simple

Eva.   I pray you now, good Master Slender's serving
man, and friend Simple by your name, which way have
you looked for Master Caius, that calls himself doctor of
physic?
Sim.   Marry, sir, the Pitty-ward, the Park-ward, every
way; old Windsor way, and every way but the town way.
Eva.   I most fehemently desire you, you will also look
that way.
Sim.   I will, sir.   [*Retiring*
Eva.   Pless my soul! how full of cholers I am, and
trempling of mind!—I shall be glad if he have deceived
me.—How melancholies I am!—I will knog his urinals

about his knave's costard, when I have good opportunities
for the 'ork:—pless my soul!   [*Sings*

> *To shallow rivers, to whose falls*
> *Melodious pirds sing madrigals ;*
> *There will we make our peds of roses,*
> *And a thousand fragrant posies.*
> *To shallow—*

Mercy on me! I have a great dispositions to cry.

> *Melodious pirds sing madrigals ;—*
> *Whenas I sat in Pabylon,—*
> *And a thousand vagram posies.*
> *To shallow—*

Sim. [*Coming forward*] Yonder he is coming, this way,
Sir Hugh!
Eva. He's welcome.—

> *To shallow rivers, to whose falls—*

Heaven prosper the right!—What weapons is he?
Sim. No weapons, sir. There comes my master, Master
Shallow, and another gentleman, from Frogmore, over the
stile, this way.
Eva. Pray you, give me my gown; or else keep it in
your arms.
                                              [*Reads in a book*

Enter PAGE, SHALLOW, *and* SLENDER

Shal. How now, master parson? Good morrow, good
Sir Hugh. Keep a gamester from the dice, and a good
student from his book, and it is wonderful.
Slen. [*Aside*] Ah, sweet Anne Page!
Page. Save you, good Sir Hugh.
Eva. Pless you from his mercy sake, all of you!
Shal. What, the sword and the word? do you study
them both, master parson?
Page. And youthful still, in your doublet and hose this
raw rheumatic day!
Eva. There is reasons and causes for it.
Page. We are come to you to do a good office, master
parson.
Eva. Fery well: what is it?
Page. Yonder is a most reverend gentleman who, belike,
having received wrong by some person, is at most odds
with his own gravity and patience that ever you saw.
Shal. I have lived forescore years and upward; I never
heard a man of his place, gravity, and learning, so wide of
his own respect.
Eva. What is he?
Page. I think you know him; Master Doctor Caius,
the renowned French physician.

Eva. Got's will, and his passion of my heart! I had as
lief you would tell me of a mess of porridge.

Page. Why?

Eva. He has no more knowledge in Hibbocrates and
Galen,—and he is a knave besides; a cowardly knave, as
you would desires to be acquainted withal.

Page. I warrant you, he's the man should fight with
him.

Slen. [*Aside*] O, sweet Anne Page!

Shal. It appears so, by his weapons.—Keep them
asunder:—here comes Doctor Caius.

Enter Host, CAIUS, *and* RUGBY

Page. Nay, good master parson, keep in your weapon.

Shal. So do you, good master doctor.

Host. Disarm them, and let them question: let them
keep their limbs whole, and hack our English.

Caius. I pray you, let-a me speak a word vit your ear:
verefore vill you not meet-a me?

Eva. [*Aside to Caius*] Pray you, use your patience: in
good time.

Caius. By gar, you are de coward, de Jack dog, John ape.

Eva. [*Aside to Caius*] Pray you, let us not be laughing-
stogs to other men's humours; I desire you in friendship,
and I will one way or other make you amends.—[*Aloud*] I
will knog your urinals about your knave's cogscomb for
missing your meetings and appointments.

Caius. *Diable!* Jack Rugby,—mine host *de Jartiere,*
have I not stay for him to kill him? have I not, at de place
I did appoint?

Eva. As I am a Christian soul, now, look you, this
is the place appointed. I'll be judgment by mine host of
the Garter.

Host. Peace, I say! Gallia and Guallia, French and
Welsh, soul-curer and body curer.

Caius. Ay, dat is very good; excellent.

Host. Peace, I say! hear mine host of the Garter. Am
I politic? am I subtle? am I Machiavel? Shall I lose
my doctor? no; he gives me the potions and the motions.
Shall I lose my parson? my priest? my Sir Hugh? no;
he gives me the proverbs and the noverbs.—Give me thy
hand, terrestrial; so.—Give me thy hand, celestial; so.—
Boys of art, I have deceived you both; I have directed you
to wrong places: your hearts are mighty, your skins are
whole, and let burnt sack be the issue.—Come, lay their
swords to pawn.—Follow me, lads of peace; follow, follow,
follow.

Shal. Trust me, a mad host.—Follow, gentlemen, follow.

Slen. [*Aside*] O, sweet Anne Page!

[*Exeunt Shallow, Slender, Page and Host*

Caius. Ha! do I perceive dat? have you make-a de sot of us? ha, ha!

Eva. This is well; he has made us his vlouting-stog. —I desire you, that we may be friends, and let us knog our prains together to be revenge on this same scall, scurvy, cogging companion, the host of the Garter.

Caius. By gar, vit all my heart. He promised to bring me vere is Anne Page: by gar, he deceive me too.

Eva. Well, I will smite his noddles.—Pray you, follow.

[*Exeunt*

SCENE II.—A Street in Windsor

Enter MISTRESS PAGE *and* ROBIN

Mrs. Page. Nay, keep your way, little gallant: you were wont to be a follower, but now you are a leader. Whether had you rather lead mine eyes, or eye your master's heels?

Rob. I had rather, forsooth, go before you like a man, than follow him like a dwarf.

Mrs. Page. O! you are a flattering boy: now I see you'll be a courtier.

Enter FORD

Ford. Well met, Mistress Page. Whither go you?

Mrs. Page. Truly, sir, to see your wife: is she at home?

Ford. Ay; and as idle as she may hang together, for want of company. I think, if your husbands were dead, you two would marry.

Mrs. Page. Be sure of that,—two other husbands.

Ford. Where had you this pretty weathercock?

Mrs. Page. I cannot tell what the dickens his name is,—my husband had him of—What do you call your knight's name, sirrah?

Rob. Sir John Falstaff.

Ford. Sir John Falstaff!

Mrs. Page. He, he; I can never hit on 's name.—There is such a league between my good man and he! Is your wife at home indeed!

Ford. Indeed, she is.

Mrs. Page. By your leave, sir: I am sick till I see her.

[*Exeunt Mrs. Page and Robin*

Ford. Has Page any brains? hath he any eyes? hath he any thinking? Sure, they sleep; he hath no use of them. Why, this boy will carry a letter twenty miles, as easy as a cannon will shoot point-blank twelve score. He pieces out his wife's inclination; he gives her folly motion and advantage: and now she's going to my wife, and Falstaff's boy with her. A man may hear this shower sing in

the wind:—and Falstaff's boy with her?—Good plots!—
they are laid; and our revolted wives share damnation
together.   Well; I will take him, then torture my wife,
pluck the borrowed veil of modesty from the so seeming
Mistress Page, divulge Page himself for a secure and wilful
Actæon; and to these violent proceedings all my neighbours shall cry aim.   [*Clock strikes*]   The clock gives me
my cue, and my assurance bids me search: there I shall
find Falstaff: I shall be rather praised for this than mocked;
for it is as positive as the earth is firm, that Falstaff is there:
I will go.

Enter PAGE, SHALLOW, SLENDER, *Host,* SIR HUGH EVANS,
CAIUS, *and* RUGBY

Page, Shal., etc.   Well met, Master Ford.
Ford.   Trust me, a good knot.   I have good cheer at
home, and I pray you all go with me.
Shal.   I must excuse myself, Master Ford.
Slen.   And so must I, sir: we have appointed to dine
with Mistress Anne, and I would not break with her for
more money than I'll speak of.
Shal.   We have lingered about a match between Anne
Page and my cousin Slender, and this day we shall have our
answer.
Slen.   I hope, I have your good will, father Page.
Page.   You have, Master Slender; I stand wholly for
you:—but my wife, master doctor, is for you altogether.
Caius.   Ay, by gar; and de maid is love-a me: my
nursh-a Quickly tell me so mush.
Host.   What say you to young Master Fenton? he capers,
he dances, he has eyes of youth, he writes verses, he speaks
holiday, he smells April and May: he will carry 't, he will
carry 't; 't is in his buttons; he will carry 't.
Page.   Not by my consent, I promise you.   The gentleman is of no having: he kept company with the wild
prince and Poins; he is of too high a region; he knows too
much.   No, he shall not knit a knot in his fortunes with the
finger of my substance: if he take her, let him take her
simply; the wealth I have waits on my consent, and my
consent goes not that way.
Ford.   I beseech you, heartily, some of you go home
with me to dinner: besides your cheer, you shall have sport;
I will show you a monster.—Master doctor, you shall go:
—so shall you, Master Page,—and you, Sir Hugh.
Shal.   Well, fare you well.—We shall have the freer
wooing at Master Page's.   [*Exeunt Shallow and Slender*
Caius.   Go home, John Rugby; I come anon.
[*Exit Rugby*
Host.   Farewell, my hearts.   I will to my honest knight
Falstaff, and drink canary with him.   [*Exit*

Ford. [*Aside*] I think, I shall drink in pipe-wine first with him; I'll make him dance. Will you go, gentles?
All.   Have with you, to see this monster.   [*Exeunt*

SCENE III.—A Room in FORD's House

Enter MISTRESS FORD *and* MISTRESS PAGE

Mrs. Ford.   What, John! what, Robert!
Mrs. Page.   Quickly, quickly:— is the buck-basket—
Mrs. Ford.   I warrant.—What, Robin, I say!

Enter Servants with a basket

Mrs. Page.   Come, come, come.
Mrs. Ford.   Here, set it down.
Mrs. Page.   Give your men the charge; we must be brief.
Mrs. Ford.   Marry, as I told you before, John, and Robert, be ready here hard by in the brew-house; and when I suddenly call you, come forth, and without any pause or staggering take this basket on your shoulders: that done, trudge with it in all haste, and carry it among the whitsters in Datchet-mead, and there empty it in the muddy ditch close by the Thames side.
Mrs. Page.   You will do it?
Mrs. Ford.   I ha' told them over and over; they lack no direction. Be gone, and come when you are called.
                                    [*Exeunt Servants*
Mrs. Page.   Here comes little Robin.

Enter ROBIN

Mrs. Ford.   How now, my eyas-musket? what news with you?
Rob.   My master, Sir John, is come in at your back-door, Mistress Ford, and requests your company.
Mrs. Page.   You little Jack-a-Lent, have you been true to us?
Rob.   Ay, I'll be sworn. My master knows not of your being here, and hath threatened to put me into everlasting liberty, if I tell you of it; for he swears he 'll turn me away.
Mrs. Page.   Thou 'rt a good boy; this secrecy of thine shall be a tailor to thee, and shall make thee a new doublet and hose.—I'll go hide me.
Mrs. Ford.   Do so.—Go, tell thy master I am alone.
[*Exit Robin*]—Mistress Page, remember you your cue.
Mrs. Page.   I warrant thee; if I do not act it, hiss me.
                                    [*Exit*
Mrs. Ford.   Go to, then: we'll use this unwholesome humidity, this gross watery pumpion;—we'll teach him to know turtles from jays.

Enter FALSTAFF

Fal. Have I caught my heavenly jewel? Why, now let me die, for I have lived long enough: this is the period of my ambition: O this blessed hour!

Mrs. Ford. O sweet Sir John!

Fal. Mistress Ford, I cannot cog, I cannot prate, mistress Ford. Now shall I sin in my wish,—I would thy husband were dead: I'll speak it before the best lord, I would make thee my lady.

Mrs. Ford. I your lady, Sir John! alas, I should be a pitiful lady.

Fal. Let the court of France show me such another. I see how thine eye would emulate the diamond: thou hast the right arched beauty of the brow that becomes the ship-tire, the tire-valiant, or any tire of Venetian admittance.

Mrs. Ford. A plain kerchief, Sir John: my brows become nothing else; nor that well neither.

Fal. By the Lord, thou art a tyrant to say so: thou wouldst make an absolute courtier; and the firm fixture of thy foot would give an excellent motion to thy gait, in a semi-circled farthingale. I see what thou wert, if Fortune thy foe were not, Nature thy friend: come, thou canst not hide it.

Mrs. Ford. Believe me, there's no such thing in me.

Fal. What made me love thee? let that persuade thee, there's something extraordinary in thee. Come; I cannot cog, and say thou art this and that, like a many of these lisping hawthorn-buds, that come like women in man's apparel, and smell like Bucklersbury in simple time: I cannot; but I love thee, none but thee, and thou deservest it.

Mrs. Ford. Do not betray me, sir. I fear, you love Mistress Page.

Fal. Thou mightst as well say, I love to walk by the Counter-gate, which is as hateful to me as the reek of a lime-kiln.

Mrs. Ford. Well, Heaven knows how I love you; and you shall one day find it.

Fal. Keep in that mind; I'll deserve it.

Mrs. Ford. Nay, I must tell you, so you do; or else I could not be in that mind.

Rob. [*Within*] Mistress Ford! Mistress Ford! here's Mistress Page at the door, sweating, and blowing, and looking wildly, and would needs speak with you presently.

Fal. She shall not see me: I will ensconce me behind the arras.

Mrs. Ford. Pray you, do so: she's a very tattling woman.—   [*Falstaff hides himself behind the arras*

Re-enter MISTRESS PAGE *and* ROBIN

What's the matter? how now!

Mrs. Page. O Mistress Ford! what have you done? You're shamed, you are overthrown, you're undone for ever.

Mrs. Ford. What's the matter, good Mistress Page?

Mrs. Page. O well-a-day, Mistress Ford! having an honest man to your husband, to give him such cause of suspicion!

Mrs. Ford. What cause of suspicion?

Mrs. Page. What cause of suspicion!—Out upon you! how am I mistook in you!

Mrs. Ford. Why, alas, what's the matter?

Mrs. Page. Your husband's coming hither, woman, with all the officers in Windsor, to search for a gentleman, that, he says, is here now in the house, by your consent, to take an ill advantage of his absence: you are undone.

Mrs. Ford. 'T is not so, I hope.

Mrs. Page. Pray Heaven it be not so, that you have such a man here! but 't is most certain your husband's coming, with half Windsor at his heels, to search for such a one: I come before to tell you. If you know yourself clear, why, I am glad of it: but if you have a friend here, convey him out. Be not amazed; call all your senses to you; defend your reputation, or bid farewell to your good life for ever.

Mrs. Ford. What shall I do?—There is a gentleman, my dear friend; and I fear not mine own shame so much as his peril: I had rather than a thousand pound he were out of the house.

Mrs. Page. For shame! never stand "you had rather," and "you had rather:" your husband's here at hand; bethink you of some conveyance: in the house you cannot hide him.—O, how have you deceived me!—Look, here is a basket: if he be of any reasonable stature, he may creep in here; and throw foul linen upon him, as if it were going to bucking: or,—it is whiting-time,—send him by your two men to Datchet-mead.

Mrs. Ford. He's too big to go in there. What shall I do?

Re-enter FALSTAFF

Fal. Let me see 't, let me see 't, O, let me see 't! I'll in, I'll in.—Follow your friend's counsel:—I'll in.

Mrs. Page. What! Sir John Falstaff? Are these your letters, knight?

Fal. I love thee and none but thee: help me away; let me creep in here; I'll never—

[*He gets into the basket ; they cover him with foul linen*
Mrs. Page. Help to cover your master, boy. Call your men, Mistress Ford.—You dissembling knight!

Mrs. Ford. What, John! Robert! John!

[*Exit Robin*

Re-enter Servants

Go take up these clothes here, quickly:—where's the cowl-staff?—look, how you drumble: carry them to the laundress in Datchet-mead; quickly, come.

Enter FORD, PAGE, CAIUS, *and* SIR HUGH EVANS

Ford.   Pray you, come near; if I suspect without cause, why, then make sport at me, then let me be your jest; I deserve it.—How now? whither bear you this?

Serv.   To the laundress, forsooth.

Mrs. Ford.   Why, what have you to do whither they bear it?   You were best meddle with buck-washing.

Ford.   Buck!—I would I could wash myself of the buck! —Buck, buck, buck?   Ay, buck; I warrant you, buck, and of the season too, it shall appear. [*Exeunt Servants with the basket.*] Gentlemen, I have dreamed to-night: I'll tell you my dream.   Here, here, here be my keys: ascend my chambers, search, seek, find out: I'll warrant, we'll un-kennel the fox.—Let me stop this way first. [*Locks the door.*] So, now uncape.

Page.   Good Master Ford, be contented: you wrong yourself too much.

Ford.   True, Master Page.—Up, gentlemen; you shall see sport anon: follow me, gentlemen.   [*Exit*

Eva.   This is fery fantastical humours and jealousies.

Caius.   By gar, 't is no de fashion of France; it is not jealous in France.

Page.   Nay, follow him, gentlemen; see the issue of his search.   [*Exeunt Page, Caius, and Evans*

Mrs. Page.   Is there not a double excellency in this?

Mrs. Ford.   I know not which pleases me better, that my husband is deceived, or Sir John.

Mrs. Page.   What a taking was he in, when your husband asked what was in the basket!

Mrs. Ford.   I am half afraid he will have need of washing; so, throwing him into the water will do him a benefit.

Mrs. Page.   Hang him, dishonest rascal!   I would all of the same strain were in the same distress.

Mrs. Ford.   I think, my husband hath some special sus-picion of Falstaff's being here; for I never saw him so gross in his jealousy till now.

Mrs. Page.   I will lay a plot to try that; and we will yet have more tricks with Falstaff: his dissolute disease will scarce obey this medicine.

Mrs. Ford.   Shall we send that foolish carrion, Mistress Quickly, to him, and excuse his throwing into the water; and give him another hope, to betray him to another punish-ment?

Mrs. Page.   We'll do it: let him be sent for to-morrow eight o'clock, to have amends.

Re-enter FORD, PAGE, CAIUS, *and* SIR HUGH EVANS

Ford.   I cannot find him: may be, the knave bragged of
that he could not compass.
   Mrs. Page.   [*Aside to Mrs. Ford*] Heard you that?
   Mrs. Ford.   [*Aside to Mrs. Page*] Ay, ay, peace.—You
use me well, Master Ford, do you?
   Ford.   Ay, I do so.
   Mrs. Ford.   Heaven make you better than your thoughts!
   Ford.   Amen.
   Mrs. Page.   You do yourself mighty wrong, Master Ford.
   Ford.   Ay, ay, I must bear it.
   Eva.   If there be anypody in the house, and in the
chambers, and in the coffers, and in the presses, Heaven
forgive my sins at the day of judgment!
   Caius.   By gar, nor I too: dere is no bodies.
   Page.   Fie, fie, Master Ford! are you not ashamed?
What spirit, what devil suggest this imagination? I
would not have your distemper in this kind for the wealth
of Windsor Castle.
   Ford.   'T is my fault, Master Page: I suffer for it.
   Eva.   You suffer for a pad conscience: your wife is as
honest a omans as I will desires among five thousand, and
five hundred too.
   Caius.   By gar, I see 't is an honest woman.
   Ford.   Well; I promised you a dinner:—come, come,
walk in the park: I pray you, pardon me; I will hereafter
make known to you, why I have done this.—Come wife;—
come, Mistress Page.—I pray you, pardon me; pray
heartily, pardon me.
   Page.   Let's go in, gentlemen; but, trust me, we'll mock
him. I do invite you to-morrow morning to my house to
breakfast: after, we'll a-birding together; I have a fine
hawk for the bush.   Shall it be so?
   Ford.   Anything.
   Eva.   If there is one, I shall make two in the company.
   Caius.   If dere be one or two, I shall make-a de turd.
   Ford.   Pray you go, Master Page.
   Eva.   I pray you now, remembrance to-morrow on the
lousy knave, mine host.
   Caius.   Dat is good; by gar, vit all my heart.
   Eva.   A lousy knave! to have his gibes and his mock-
eries!   [*Exeunt*

SCENE IV.—A Room in PAGE'S House

Enter FENTON *and* ANNE PAGE

Fent.   I see, I cannot get thy father's love;
Therefore, no more turn me to him, sweet Nan.
   Anne.   Alas! how then?

106

Fent.   Why, thou must be thyself.
He doth object, I am too great of birth;
And that, my state being galled with my expense,
I seek to heal it only by his wealth;
Besides, these other bars he lays before me,—
My riots past, my wild societies,
And tells me, 't is a thing impossible
I should love thee, but as a property.
    Anne.   May be, he tells you true.
    Fent.   No, Heaven so speed me in my time to come!
Albeit I will confess thy father's wealth
Was the first motive that I wooed thee, Anne:
Yet, wooing thee, I found thee of more value
Than stamps in gold or sums in sealéd bags;
And 't is the very riches of thyself
That now I aim at.
    Anne.   Gentle Master Fenton,
Yet seek my father's love; still seek it, sir:
If opportunity and humblest suit
Cannot attain it, why, then—hark you hither.
                          [*They converse apart*

Enter SHALLOW, SLENDER, *and* MISTRESS QUICKLY

    Shal.   Break their talk, Mistress Quickly: my kinsman
shall speak for himself.
    Slen.   I'll make a shaft or a bolt on 't: slid, 't is but
venturing.
    Shal.   Be not dismayed.
    Slen.   No, she shall not dismay me: I care not for
that,—but that I am afeared.
    Quick.   Hark ye; Master Slender would speak a word
with you.
    Anne.   I come to him.—[*Aside*] This is my father's choice.
O, what a world of vile ill-favoured faults
Looks handsome in three hundred pounds a year!
    Quick.   And how does good Master Fenton? Pray you,
a word with you.
    Shal.   She's coming; to her, coz. O boy, thou hadst a
father!
    Slen.   I had a father, Mistress Anne; my uncle can
tell you good jests of him.—Pray you, uncle, tell Mistress
Anne the jest, how my father stole two geese out of a
pen, good uncle.
    Shal.   Mistress Anne, my cousin loves you.
    Slen.   Ay, that I do; as well as I love any woman in
Glostershire.
    Shal.   He will maintain you like a gentlewoman.
    Slen.   Ay, that I will, come cut and longtail, under
the degree of a squire.

Shal. He will make you a hundred and fifty pounds jointure.

Anne. Good Master Shallow, let him woo for himself.

Shal. Marry, I thank you for it; I thank you for that good comfort.—She calls you, coz: I'll leave you.

Anne. Now, Master Slender,—

Slen. Now, good Mistress Anne,—

Anne. What is your will?

Slen. My will? od's heartlings, that's a pretty jest, indeed. I ne'er made my will yet, I thank Heaven; I am not such a sickly creature, I give Heaven praise.

Anne. I mean, Master Slender, what would you with me?

Slen. Truly, for mine own part, I would little or nothing with you. Your father, and my uncle, have made motions: if it be my luck, so; if not, happy man be his dole! They can tell you how things go better than I can: you may ask your father; here he comes.

Enter PAGE *and* MISTRESS PAGE

Page. Now, Master Slender:—Love him, daughter Anne.—
Why, how now? what does Master Fenton here?
You wrong me, sir, thus still to haunt my house:
I told you, sir, my daughter is disposed of.

Fent. Nay, Master Page, be not impatient.

Mrs. Page. Good Master Fenton, come not to my child.

Page. She is no match for you.

Fent. Sir, will you hear me?

Page.   No, good Master Fenton.—
Come, Master Shallow; come, son Slender, in.—
Knowing my mind, you wrong me, Master Fenton.
                    [*Exeunt Page, Shallow, and Slender*

Quick. Speak to Mistress Page.

Fent. Good Mistress Page, for that I love your daughter
In such a righteous fashion as I do,
Perforce, against all checks, rebukes, and manners,
I must advance the colours of my love,
And not retire: let me have your good will.

Anne. Good mother, do not marry me to yond fool.

Mrs. Page. I mean it not; I seek you a better husband.

Quick. That's my master, master doctor.

Anne. Alas! I had rather be set quick i' the earth,
And bowled to death with turnips.

Mrs. Page.   Come, trouble not
            yourself.—Good Master Fenton,
I will not be your friend nor enemy:
My daughter will I question how she loves you,
And as I find her, so am I affected.
Till then, farewell, sir: she must needs go in;
Her father will be angry   [*Exeunt Mrs. Page and Anne*

Fent. Farewell, gentle mistress.—Farewell, Nan.
Quick. This is my doing, now.—"Nay," said I, "will
you cast away your child on a fool, and a physician? look
on Master Fenton."—This is my doing.
Fent. I thank thee; and I pray thee, once to-night
Give my sweet Nan this ring.   There's for thy pains.
                                                        [*Exit*
Quick. Now, Heaven send thee good fortune!   A kind
heart he hath: a woman would run through fire and water
for such a kind heart.   But yet I would my master had
Mistress Anne; or I would Master Slender had her; or,
in sooth, I would Master Fenton had her.   I will do what
I can for them all three; for so I have promised, and I'll
be as good as my word; but speciously for Master Fenton.
Well, I must of another errand to Sir John Falstaff from
my two mistresses: what a beast I am to slack it!   [*Exit*

SCENE V.—A Room in the Garter Inn

Enter FALSTAFF *and* BARDOLPH

Fal. Bardolph, I say,—
Bard. Here, sir.
Fal. Go fetch me a quart of sack; put a toast in 't.
[*Exit Bardolph*] Have I lived to be carried in a basket,
like a barrow of butcher's offal, and to be thrown in the
Thames?   Well, if I be served such another trick, I'll
have my brains ta'en out, and buttered, and give them
to a dog for a new year's gift.   The rogues slighted me
into the river with as little remorse as they would have
drowned a bitch's blind puppies, fifteen i' the litter; and
you may know by my size, that I have a kind of alacrity
in sinking; if the bottom were as deep as hell, I should
down.   I had been drowned, but that the shore was shelvy
and shallow;—a death that I abhor; for the water swells
a man, and what a thing should I have been, when I had
been swelled!   I should have been a mountain of mummy.

Re-enter BARDOLPH *with the wine*

Bard. Here's Mistress Quickly, sir, to speak with you.
Fal. Come, let me pour in some sack to the Thames
water; for my belly's as cold as if I had swallowed snow-
balls for pills to cool the reins.   Call her in.
Bard. Come in, woman.

Enter MISTRESS QUICKLY

Quick. By your leave.—I cry you mercy: give your
worship good morrow.
Fal. Take away these chalices.   Go, brew me a pottle
of sack finely.
Bard. With eggs, sir?

109

Fal. Simple of itself; I'll no pullet-sperm in my brewage. [*Exit Bardolph*]—How now?

Quick. Marry, sir, I come to your worship from Mistress Ford.

Fal. Mistress Ford! I have had ford enough; I was thrown into the ford; I have my belly full of ford.

Quick. Alas the day! good heart, that was not her fault: she does so take on with her men; they mistook their erection.

Fal. So did I mine, to build upon a foolish woman's promise.

Quick. Well, she laments, sir, for it, that it would yearn your heart to see it. Her husband goes this morning a-birding: she desires you once more to come to her; between eight and nine. I must carry her word quickly: she'll make you amends, I warrant you.

Fal. Well, I will visit her: tell her so; and bid her think, what a man is: let her consider his frailty, and then judge of my merit.

Quick. I will tell her.

Fal. Do so. Between nine and ten, say'st thou?

Quick. Eight and nine, sir.

Fal. Well, be gone: I will not miss her.

Quick. Peace be with you, sir.   [*Exit*

Fal. I marvel, I hear not of Master Brook: he sent me word to stay within: I like his money well.—O, here he comes.

Enter FORD

Ford. Bless you, sir.

Fal. Now, Master Brook,—you come to know what hath passed between me and Ford's wife?

Ford. That indeed, Sir John, is my business.

Fal. Master Brook, I will not lie to you. I was at her house the hour she appointed me.

Ford. And sped you, sir?

Fal. Very ill-favouredly, Master Brook.

Ford. How so, sir? Did she change her determination?

Fal. No, Master Brook; but the peaking Cornuto her husband, Master Brook, dwelling in a continual 'larum of jealousy, comes me in the instant of our encounter, after we had embraced, kissed, protested, and, as it were, spoke the prologue of our comedy; and at his heels a rabble of his companions, thither provoked and instigated by his distemper, and, forsooth, to search his house for his wife's love.

Ford. What, while you were there?

Fal. While I was there.

Ford. And did he search for you, and could not find you?

Fal. You shall hear. As good luck would have it, comes in one Mistress Page; gives intelligence of Ford's approach; and in her invention and Ford's wife's distraction, they conveyed me into a buck-basket.

Ford. A buck-basket!

Fal. By the Lord, a buck-basket!—rammed me in with foul shirts and smocks, socks, foul stockings, and greasy napkins; that, Master Brook, there was the rankest compound of villainous smell, that ever offended nostril.

Ford. And how long lay you there?

Fal. Nay, you shall hear, Master Brook, what I have suffered to bring this woman to evil for your good. Being thus crammed in the basket, a couple of Ford's knaves, his hinds, were called forth by their mistress to carry me in the name of foul clothes to Datchet Lane: they took me on their shoulders; met the jealous knave their master in the door, who asked them once or twice what they had in their basket. I quaked for fear, lest the lunatic knave would have searched it; but fate, ordaining he should be a cuckold, held his hand. Well; on went he for a search, and away went I for foul clothes. But mark the sequel, Master Brook: I suffered the pangs of three several deaths: first, an intolerable fright, to be detected with a jealous rotten bell-wether; next, to be compassed, like a good bilbo, in the circumference of a peck, hilt to point, heel to head; and then, to be stopped in, like a strong distillation, with stinking clothes that fretted in their own grease: think of that,—a man of my kidney,—think of that; that am as subject to heat as butter; a man of continual dissolution and thaw;—it was a miracle, to escape suffocation. And in the height of this bath, when I was more than half stewed in grease, like a Dutch dish, to be thrown into the Thames, and cooled, glowing hot, in that surge, like a horseshoe; think of that,—hissing hot,—think of that, Master Brook.

Ford. In good sadness, sir, I am sorry that for my sake you have suffered all this. My suit then is desperate; you'll undertake her no more?

Fal. Master Brook, I will be thrown into Etna, as I have been into Thames, ere I will leave her thus. Her husband is this morning gone a-birding: I have received from her another embassy of meeting; 'twixt eight and nine is the hour, Master Brook.

Ford. 'T is past eight already, sir.

Fal. Is it? I will then address me to my appointment. Come to me at your convenient leisure, and you shall know how I speed; and the conclusion shall be crowned with your enjoying her. Adieu. You shall have her, Master Brook; Master Brook, you shall cuckold Ford.   [*Exit*

Ford. Hum,—ha! is this a vision? is this a dream? do I sleep? Master Ford, awake! awake, Master Ford! there's a hole made in your best coat, Master Ford. This 't is to be married: this 't is to have linen, and buck-baskets.—Well, I will proclaim myself what I am: I will now take the lecher; he is at my house; he cannot 'scape

me; 't is impossible he should; he cannot creep into a
halfpenny purse, nor into a pepper-box; but, lest the
devil that guides him should aid him, I will search impossible places.   Though what I am I cannot avoid, yet
to be what I would not, shall not make me tame: if I have
horns to make one mad, let the proverb go with me,—I'll
be horn-mad.   [*Exit*

ACT FOUR

SCENE I.—The Street

Enter MISTRESS PAGE, MISTRESS QUICKLY, *and* WILLIAM

Mrs. Page.   Is he at Master Ford's already, think'st thou?
Quick.   Sure, he is by this, or will be presently: but
truly, he is very courageous mad about his throwing into
the water.   Mistress Ford desires you to come suddenly.
Mrs. Page.   I'll be with her by-and-by: I'll but bring
my young man here to school.   Look where his master
comes; 't is a playing-day I see.

Enter SIR HUGH EVANS

How now, Sir Hugh? no school to-day?
Eva.   No; Master Slender is let the boys leave to play.
Quick.   Blessing of his heart!
Mrs. Page.   Sir Hugh, my husband says, my son profits
nothing in the world at his book: I pray you, ask him
some questions in his accidence.
Eva.   Come hither, William; hold up your head; come.
Mrs. Page.   Come on, sirrah; hold up your head; answer
your master, be not afraid.
Eva.   William, how many numbers is in nouns?
Will.   Two.
Quick.   Truly, I thought there had been one number
more, because they say, Od's nouns.
Eva.   Peace your tattlings!—What is *fair*, William?
Will.   *Pulcher.*
Quick.   Polecats! there are fairer things than polecats,
sure.
Eva.   You are a very simplicity oman: I pray you,
peace.—What is *lapis*, William?
Will.   A stone.
Eva.   And what is a stone, William?
Will.   A pebble.
Eva.   No, it is *lapis :* I pray you remember in your prain.
Will.   *Lapis.*
Eva.   That is good, William.   What is he, William,
that does lend articles?
Will.   Articles are borrowed of the pronoun; and be
thus declined, *Singulariter, nominativo, hic, haec, hoc.*

Eva. Nominativo, *hig, hag, hog;*—pray you, mark:
genitivo, hujus. Well, what is your accusative case?
Will. Accusativo, hunc.
Eva. I pray you, have your remembrance, child:
accusativo, hung, hang, hog.
Quick. Hang-hog is Latin for bacon, I warrant you.
Eva. Leave your prabbles, oman.—What is the focative
case, William?
Will. O—vocativo, O.
Eva. Remember, William; focative is, *caret.*
Quick. And that's a good root.
Eva. Oman, forbear.
Mrs. Page. Peace!
Eva. What is your genitive case plural, William?
Will. Genitive case?
Eva. Ay.
Will. Genitive,—*horum, harum, horum.*
Quick. Vengeance of Jenny's case! fie on her!—Never
name her, child, if she be a whore.
Eva. For shame, oman!
Quick. You do ill to teach the child such words.—He
teaches him to hick and to hack, which they'll do fast
enough of themselves; and to call whorum,—fie upon you!
Eva. Oman, art thou lunatics? hast thou no under-
standings for thy cases, and the numbers of the genders?
Thou art as foolish Christian creatures as I would desires.
Mrs. Page. Pr'ythee, hold thy peace.
Eva. Show me now, William, some declensions of your
pronouns.
Will. Forsooth, I have forgot.
Eva. It is *qui, quæ, quod;* if you forget your *quies,*
your *quæs,* and your *quods,* you must be preeches. Go
your ways, and play; go.
Mrs. Page. He is a better scholar than I thought he was.
Eva. He is a good sprag memory. Farewell, Mistress Page.
Mrs. Page. Adieu, good Sir Hugh. [*Exit Sir Hugh*]
Get you home, boy.—Come, we stay too long. [*Exeunt*

Scene II.—A Room in Ford's House

Enter Falstaff *and* Mistress Ford

Fal. Mistress Ford, your sorrow hath eaten up my
sufferance. I see, you are obsequious in your love, and
I profess requital to a hair's-breadth; not only, Mistress
Ford, in the simple office of love, but in all the accoutre-
ment, complement, and ceremony of it. But are you
sure of your husband now?
Mrs. Ford. He's a-birding, sweet Sir John.
Mrs. Page. [*Within*] What ho! gossip Ford! what ho!

Mrs. Ford.   Step into the chamber, Sir John.

[Exit Falstaff

Enter MISTRESS PAGE

Mrs. Page.   How now, sweetheart? who's at home besides yourself?

Mrs. Ford.   Why, none but mine own people.

Mrs. Page.   Indeed?

Mrs. Ford.   No, certainly.—[*Aside to her*] Speak louder.

Mrs. Page.   Truly, I am so glad you have nobody here.

Mrs. Ford.   Why?

Mrs. Page.   Why, woman, your husband is in his old lunes again: he so takes on yonder with my husband; so rails against all married mankind; so curses all Eve's daughters, of what complexion soever; and so buffets himself on the forehead, crying, "Peer out, peer out!" that any madness I ever yet beheld seemed but tameness, civility, and patience, to this his distemper he is in now.   I am glad the fat knight is not here.

Mrs. Ford.   Why, does he talk of him?

Mrs. Page.   Of none but him; and swears, he was carried out, the last time he searched for him, in a basket: protests to my husband he is now here, and hath drawn him and the rest of their company from their sport, to make another experiment of his suspicion.   But I am glad the knight is not here; now he shall see his own foolery.

Mrs. Ford.   How near is he, Mistress Page?

Mrs. Page.   Hard by; at street end; he will be here anon.

Mrs. Ford.   I am undone! the knight is here.

Mrs. Page.   Why, then you are utterly shamed, and he's but a dead man.   What a woman are you!—Away with him, away with him: better shame than murder.

Mrs. Ford.   Which way should he go? how should I bestow him?   Shall I put him into the basket again?

Re-enter FALSTAFF

Fal.   No, I'll come no more i' the basket.   May I not go out, ere he come?

Mrs. Page.   Alas, three of Master Ford's brothers watch the door with pistols, that none shall issue out; otherwise you might slip away ere he came.   But what make you here?

Fal.   What shall I do?—I'll creep up into the chimney.

Mrs. Ford.   There they always use to discharge their birding-pieces.

Mrs. Page.   Creep into the kiln-hole.

Fal.   Where is it?

Mrs. Ford.   He will seek there, on my word.   Neither press, coffer, chest, trunk, well, vault, but he hath an abstract for the remembrance of such places; and goes to them by his note: there is no hiding you in the house.

Fal.   I'll go out then.

114

Mrs. Page.   If you go out in your own semblance, you die, Sir John.   Unless you go out disguised,—

Mrs. Ford.   How might we disguise him?

Mrs. Page.   Alas the day!   I know not.   There is no woman's gown big enough for him; otherwise he might put on a hat, a muffler, and a kerchief, and so escape.

Fal.   Good hearts, devise something: any extremity rather than a mischief.

Mrs. Ford.   My maid's aunt, the fat woman of Brentford, has a gown above.

Mrs. Page.   On my word, it will serve him; she's as big as he is, and there's her thrummed hat, and her muffler too.—Run up, Sir John.

Mrs. Ford.   Go, go, sweet Sir John: Mistress Page and I will look some linen for your head.

Mrs. Page.   Quick, quick! we'll come dress you straight; put on the gown the while.   [*Exit Falstaff*

Mrs. Ford.   I would, my husband would meet him in this shape: he cannot abide the old woman of Brentford; he swears she's a witch; forbade her my house, and hath threatened to beat her.

Mrs. Page.   Heaven guide him to thy husband's cudgel, and the devil guide his cudgel afterwards!

Mrs. Ford.   But is my husband coming?

Mrs. Page.   Ay, in good sadness, is he; and talks of the basket too, howsoever he hath had intelligence.

Mrs. Ford.   We'll try that; for I'll appoint my men to carry the basket again, to meet him at the door with it, as they did last time.

Mrs. Page.   Nay, but he'll be nere presently: let's go dress him like the witch of Brentford.

Mrs. Ford.   I'll first direct my men, what they shall do with the basket.   Go up, I'll bring linen for him straight.
[*Exit*

Mrs. Page.   Hang him, dishonest varlet! we cannot misuse him enough.

We'll leave a proof, by that which we will do,
Wives may be merry, and yet honest too:
We do not act, that often jest and laugh;
'T is old but true, Still swine eat all the draff.   [*Exit*

Re-enter MISTRESS FORD *with two Servants*

Mrs. Ford.   Go, sirs, take the basket again on your shoulders: your master is hard at door; if he bid you set it down, obey him.   Quickly; despatch.   [*Exit*

First Serv.   Come, come, take it up.

Sec. Serv.   Pray Heaven, it be not full of knight again.

First Serv.   I hope not; I had as lief bear so much lead.

Enter FORD, PAGE, SHALLOW, CAIUS, *and* SIR HUGH EVANS

Ford.   Ay, but if it prove true, Master Page, have you

any way then to unfool me again?—Set down the basket,
villains!—Somebody call my wife.—Youth in a basket!
O you panderly rascals! there's a knot, a ging, a pack, a
conspiracy against me: now shall the devil be shamed.—
What, wife, I say!—Come, come forth!—Behold what
honest clothes you send forth to bleaching.

Page.   Why, this passes! Master Ford, you are not to
go loose any longer; you must be pinioned.

Eva.   Why, this is lunatics; this is mad as a mad dog.

Shal.   Indeed, Master Ford, this is not well; indeed.

Ford.   So say I too, sir.

Re-enter MISTRESS FORD

Come hither, Mistress Ford; Mistress Ford, the honest
woman, the modest wife, the virtuous creature, that hath
the jealous fool to her husband!—I suspect without cause,
mistress, do I?

Mrs. Ford.   Heaven be my witness, you do, if you
suspect me in any dishonesty.

Ford.   Well said, brazen-face; hold it out.—Come forth,
sirrah.   [*Pulls the clothes out of the basket*

Page.   This passes!

Mrs. Ford.   Are you not ashamed? let the clothes alone.

Ford.   I shall find you anon.

Eva.   'T is unreasonable. Will you take up your wife's
clothes? Come away.

Ford.   Empty the basket, I say.

Mrs. Ford.   Why, man, why,—

Ford.   Master Page, as I am a man, there was one conveyed out of my house yesterday in this basket: why may
not he be there again. In my house I am sure he is: my
intelligence is true; my jealousy is reasonable.—Pluck me
out all the linen.

Mrs. Ford.   If you find a man there, he shall die a flea's death.

Page.   Here's no man.

Shal.   By my fidelity, this is not well, Master Ford;
this wrongs you.

Eva.   Master Ford, you must pray, and not follow the
imaginations of your own heart: this is jealousies.

Ford.   Well, he's not here I seek for.

Page.   No, nor nowhere else, but in your brain.

Ford.   Help to search my house this one time: if I find
not what I seek, show no colour for my extremity; let me
for ever be your table-sport; let them say of me, "As
jealous as Ford, that searched a hollow walnut for his wife's
leman." Satisfy me once more; once more search with me.

Mrs. Ford.   What ho! Mistress Page! come you and the
old woman down; my husband will come into the chamber.

Ford.   Old woman! What old woman's that?

Mrs. Ford.   Why, it is my maid's aunt of Brentford.

116

Ford. A witch, a quean, an old cozening quean! Have I not forbid her my house? She comes of errands, does she? We are simple men; we do not know what's brought to pass under the profession of fortune-telling. She works by charms, by spells, by the figure, and such daubery as this is beyond our element: we know nothing.—Come down, you witch, you hag you; come down, I say.

Mrs. Ford. Nay, good, sweet husband.—Good gentlemen, let him not strike the old woman.

Re-enter FALSTAFF *in woman's clothes, led by* MISTRESS PAGE

Mrs. Page. Come, Mother Prat; come, give me your hand.

Ford. I'll prat her.—Out of my door, you witch [*beats him*] you hag, you baggage, you polecat, you ronyon: out! out! I'll conjure you, I'll fortune-tell you.   [*Exit Falstaff*

Mrs. Page. Are you not ashamed? I think, you have killed the poor woman.

Mrs. Ford. Nay, he will do it.—'Tis a goodly credit for you.

Ford. Hang her, witch!

Eva. By yea and no, I think, the oman is a witch indeed: I like not when a oman has a great peard; I spy a great peard under her muffler.

Ford. Will you follow, gentlemen? I beseech you, follow: see but the issue of my jealousy. If I cry out thus upon no trail, never trust me when I open again.

Page. Let's obey his humour a little further. Come, gentlemen.   [*Exeunt Ford, Page, Shallow, and Evans*

Mrs. Page. Trust me, he beat him most pitifully.

Mrs. Ford. Nay, by the mass, that he did not; he beat him most unpitifully, methought.

Mrs. Page. I'll have the cudgel hallowed, and hung o'er the altar: it hath done meritorious service.

Mrs. Ford. What think you? May we, with the warrant of womanhood, and the witness of a good conscience, pursue him with any further revenge?

Mrs. Page. The spirit of wantonness is, sure, scared out of him: if the devil have him not in fee-simple, with fine and recovery, he will never, I think, in the way of waste, attempt us again.

Mrs. Ford. Shall we tell our husbands how we have served him?

Mrs. Page. Yes, by all means; if it be but to scrape the figures out of your husband's brains. If they can find in their hearts the poor unvirtuous fat knight shall be any further afflicted we two will still be the ministers.

Mrs. Ford. I'll warrant, they'll have him publicly shamed; and, methinks, there would be no period to the jest, should he not be publicly shamed.

Mrs. Page. Come, to the forge with it, then; shape it: I would not have things cool.   [*Exeunt*

SCENE III.—A Room in the Garter Inn

Enter Host and BARDOLPH

Bard.   Sir, the Germans desire to have three of your horses: the duke himself will be to-morrow at court, and they are going to meet him.

Host.   What duke should that be, comes so secretly?   I hear not of him in the court.   Let me speak with the gentlemen:—they speak English?

Bard.   Ay, sir; I'll call them to you.

Host.   They shall have my horses, but I'll make them pay; I'll sauce them: they have had my house a week at command; I have turned away my other guests: they must come off; I'll sauce them.   Come.   [*Exeunt*

SCENE IV.—A Room in FORD's House

Enter PAGE, FORD, MISTRESS PAGE, MISTRESS FORD, *and* SIR HUGH EVANS

Eva.   'T is one of the pest discretions of a oman as ever I did look upon.

Page.   And did he send you both these letters at an instant?

Mrs. Page.   Within a quarter of an hour.

Ford.   Pardon me, wife.   Henceforth do what thou wilt; I rather will suspect the sun with cold
Than thee with wantonness: now doth thy honour stand,
In him that was of late an heretic,
As firm as faith.

Page.   'T is well, 't is well; no more.
Be not as extreme in submission
As in offence;
But let our plot go forward: let our wives
Yet once again, to make us public sport,
Appoint a meeting with this old fat fellow,
Where we may take him, and disgrace him for it.

Ford.   There is no better way than that they spoke of.

Page.   How? to send him word they'll meet him in the park at midnight?   Fie, fie! he'll never come.

Eva.   You say, he has been thrown in the rivers, and has been grievously peaten, as an old oman: methinks, there should be terrors in him, that he should not come; methinks, his flesh is punished, he shall have no desires.

Page.   So think I too.

Mrs. Ford.   Devise but how you'll use him when he comes,
And let us two devise to bring him thither.

Mrs. Page.   There is an old tale goes, that Herne the hunter,
Sometime a keeper here in Windsor Forest,
Doth all the winter-time, at still midnight,
Walk round about an oak, with great ragg'd horns;

And there he blasts the tree, and takes the cattle;
And makes milch-kine yield blood, and shakes a chain
In a most hideous and dreadful manner:
You've heard of such a spirit; and well you know,
The superstitious idle-headed eld
Received and did deliver to our age
This tale of Herne the hunter for a truth.
    Page. Why, yet there want not many that do fear
In deep of night to walk by this Herne's oak.
But what of this!
    Mrs. Ford.   Marry, this is our device;
That Falstaff at that oak shall meet with us,
Disguised like Herne, with huge horns on his head.
    Page. Well, let it not be doubted but he'll come:
And in this shape when you have brought him thither,
What shall be done with him? what is your plot?
    Mrs. Page. That likewise have we thought upon, and
        thus:
Nan Page my daughter, and my little son,
And three or four more of their growth, we'll dress
Like urchins, ouphs, and fairies, green and white,
With rounds of waxen tapers on their heads,
And rattles in their hands. Upon a sudden,
As Falstaff, she, and I, are newly met,
Let them from forth a sawpit rush at once
With some diffuséd song: upon their sight,
We two in great amazedness will fly:
Then let them all encircle him about,
And, fairy-like, to pinch the unclean knight;
And ask him, why, that hour of fairy revel,
In their so sacred paths he dares to tread
In shape profane.
    Mrs. Ford.   And till he tell the truth,
Let the supposéd fairies pinch him sound,
And burn him with their tapers.
    Mrs. Page.   The truth being known,
We'll all present ourselves, dis-horn the spirit,
And mock him home to Windsor.
    Ford.   The children must
Be practised well to this, or they'll ne'er do't.
    Eva. I will teach the children their behaviours; I will
be like a jack-an-apes also, to burn the knight with my taber.
    Ford. That will be excellent. I'll go buy them vizards.
    Mrs. Page. My Nan shall be the queen of all the fairies,
Finely attiréd in a robe of white.
    Page. That silk will I go buy;—[*aside*] and in that tire
Shall Master Slender steal my Nan away,
And marry her at Eton.—Go send to Falstaff straight.
    Ford. Nay, I'll to him again in name of Brook;
He'll tell me all his purpose. Sure, he'll come.

Mrs. Page. Fear not you that. Go, get us properties,
And tricking for our fairies.

Eva. Let us about it: it is admirable pleasures, and
fery honest knaveries.   [*Exeunt Page, Ford, and Evans*

Mrs. Page. Go, Mistress Ford,
Send quickly to Sir John, to know his mind.

[*Exit Mrs. Ford*

I'll to the doctor: he hath my good will,
And none but he, to marry with Nan Page.
That Slender, though well landed, is an idiot,
And he my husband best of all affects:
The doctor is well moneyed, and his friends
Potent at court: he, none but he, shall have her,
Though twenty thousand worthier come to crave her. [*Exit*

SCENE V.—A Room in the Garter Inn

Enter Host and SIMPLE

Host. What wouldst thou have, boor? what, thick-
skin? speak, breathe, discuss; brief, short, quick, snap.

Sim. Marry, sir, I come to speak with Sir John Falstaff
from Master Slender.

Host. There's his chamber, his house, his castle, his
standing-bed, and truckle-bed: 't is painted about with
the story of the Prodigal, fresh and new. Go, knock and
call: he'll speak like an Anthropophaginian unto thee:
knock, I say.

Sim. There's an old woman, a fat woman, gone up into
his chamber: I'll be so bold as stay, sir, till she come
down; I come to speak with her, indeed.

Host. Ha! a fat woman? the knight may be robbed:
I'll call.—Bully knight! Bully Sir John! speak from
thy lungs military: art thou there? it is thine host, thine
Ephesian, calls.

Fal. [*Above*] How now, mine host!

Host. Here's a Bohemian-Tartar tarries the coming
down of thy fat woman. Let her descend, bully, let her
descend; my chambers are honourable: fie! privacy? fie!

Enter FALSTAFF

Fal. There was, mine host, an old fat woman even now
with me, but she's gone.

Sim. Pray you, sir, was't not the wise woman of
Brentford?

Fal. Ay, marry, was it, mussel-shell: what would you
with her?

Sim. My master, sir,   Master Slender, sent to her,
seeing her go through the streets, to know, sir, whether one
Nym, sir, that beguiled him of a chain, had the chain, or no.

Fal. I spake with the old woman about it.

Sim. And what says she, I pray, sir?

Fal. Marry, she says, that the very same man that beguiled Master Slender of his chain cozened him of it.

Sim. I would I could have spoken with the woman herself: I had other things to have spoken with her too from him.

Fal. What are they? let us know.

Host. Ay, come; quick.

Sim. I may not conceal them, sir.

Host. Conceal them, and thou diest.

Sim. Why, sir, they were nothing but about Mistress Anne Page; to know, if it were my master's fortune to have her or no.

Fal. 'T is, 't is his fortune.

Sim. What, sir?

Fal. To have her,—or no. Go; say, the woman told me so.

Sim. May I be bold to say so, sir?

Fal. Ay, sir; like who more bold.

Sim. I thank your worship. I shall make my master glad with these tidings. [*Exit*

Host. Thou art clerkly, thou art clerkly, Sir John. Was there a wise woman with thee?

Fal. Ay, that there was, mine host; one, that hath taught me more wit than ever I learned before in my life: and I paid nothing for it neither, but was paid for my learning.

Enter Bardolph

Bard. Out, alas, sir! cozenage; mere cozenage!

Host. Where be my horses? speak well of them, varletto.

Bard. Run away with the cozeners; for so soon as I came beyond Eton, they threw me off from behind one of them, in a slough of mire; and set spurs, and away, like three German devils, three Doctor Faustuses.

Host. They are gone but to meet the duke, villain. Do not say, they be fled; Germans are honest men.

Enter Sir Hugh Evans

Eva. Where is mine host?

Host. What is the matter, sir?

Eva. Have a care of your entertainments: there is a friend of mine come to town, tells me, there is three cozen-germans, that has cozened all the hosts of Readings, of Maidenhead, of Colebrook, of horses and money. I tell you for good will, look you: you are wise, and full of gibes and vlouting-stogs, and 't is not convenient you should be cozened. Fare you well. [*Exit*

Enter Doctor Caius

Caius. Vere is mine host de Jarteere?

Host. Here, master doctor, in perplexity, and doubtful dilemma.

121

Caius. I cannot tell vat is dat; but it is tell-a me, dat
you make grand preparation for a duke de Jarmany: by
my trot, dere is no duke dat de court is know to come. I
tell you for good vill: adieu.   [*Exit*
Host. Hue and cry, villain! go.—Assist me, knight.
I am undone.—Fly, run, hue and cry, villain!—I am
undone!   [*Exeunt Host and Bardolph*
Fal. I would all the world might be cozened, for I have
been cozened, and beaten too. If it should come to the
ear of the court how I have been transformed, and how
my transformation hath been washed and cudgelled, they
would melt me out of my fat drop by drop, and liquor
fishermen's boots with me: I warrant, they would whip
me with their fine wits till I were as crest-fallen as a dried
pear. I never prospered since I forswore myself at primero.
Well, if my wind were but long enough to say my prayers,
I would repent.

Enter MISTRESS QUICKLY

Now, whence come you?
Quick. From the two parties, forsooth.
Fal. The devil take one party, and his dam the other!
and so they shall be both bestowed. I have suffered more
for their sakes, more than the villainous inconstancy of
man's disposition is able to bear.
Quick. And have not they suffered? Yes, I warrant;
speciously one of them: Mistress Ford, good heart, is
beaten black and blue, that you cannot see a white spot
about her.
Fal. What tell'st thou me of black and blue? I was
beaten myself into all the colours of the rainbow; and I
was like to be apprehended for the witch of Brentford: but
that my admirable dexterity of wit, my counterfeiting the
action of an old woman, delivered me, the knave constable
had set me i' the stocks, i' the common stocks, for a witch.
Quick. Sir, let me speak with you in your chamber;
you shall hear how things go, and, I warrant, to your content. Here is a letter will say somewhat. Good hearts!
what ado here is to bring you together! Sure, one of you
does not serve Heaven well, that you are so crossed.
Fal. Come up into my chamber.   [*Exeunt*

SCENE VI.—Another Room in the Garter Inn

Enter FENTON *and Host*

Host. Master Fenton, talk not to me; my mind is
heavy: I will give over all.
Fent. Yet hear me speak. Assist me in my purpose,
And, as I am a gentleman, I'll give thee
A hundred pound in gold more than your loss.

Host. I will hear you, Master Fenton; and I will, at the least, keep your counsel.

Fent. From time to time I have acquainted you
With the dear love I bear to fair Anne Page;
Who, mutually, hath answered my affection,
So far forth as herself might be her chooser,
Even to my wish. I have a letter from her
Of such contents as you will wonder at;
The mirth whereof so larded with my matter,
That neither singly can be manifested
Without the show of both; wherein fat Falstaff
Hath a great scene: the image of the jest
I'll show you here at large. Hark, good mine host:
To-night at Herne's oak, just 'twixt twelve and one,
Must my sweet Nan present the fairy queen;
The purpose why, is here: in which disguise,
While other jests are something rank on foot,
Her father hath commanded her to slip
Away with Slender, and with him at Eton
Immediately to marry: she hath consented.
Now, sir,
Her mother, ever strong against that match,
And firm for Doctor Caius, hath appointed
That he shall likewise shuffle her away,
While other sports are tasking of their minds,
And at the deanery, where a priest attends,
Straight marry her: to this her mother's plot
She, seemingly obedient, likewise hath
Made promise to the doctor.—Now, thus it rests:
Her father means she shall be all in white;
And in that habit, when Slender sees his time
To take her by the hand, and bid her go,
She shall go with him:—her mother hath intended,
The better to denote her to the doctor,—
For they must all be masked and vizarded,—
That quaint in green she shall be loose enrobed
With ribands pendent, flaring 'bout her head;
And when the doctor spies his vantage ripe,
To pinch her by the hand, and on that token
The maid hath given consent to go with him.

Host. Which means she to deceive? father or mother?

Fent. Both, my good host, to go along with me:
And here it rests,—that you'll procure the vicar
To stay for me at church 'twixt twelve and one,
And, in the lawful name of marrying,
To give our hearts united ceremony.

Host. Well, husband your device: I'll to the vicar.
Bring you the maid, you shall not lack a priest.

Fent. So shall I evermore be bound to thee;
Besides, I'll make a present recompense.   [*Exeunt*

ACT FIVE

Scene I.—A Room in the Garter Inn

Enter Falstaff *and* Mistress Quickly

Fal. Pr'ythee, no more prattling;—go:—I'll hold.
This is the third time; I hope, good luck lies in odd numbers. Away, go. They say, there is divinity in odd
numbers, either in nativity, chance, or death.—Away.

Quick. I'll provide you a chain; and I'll do what I
can to get you a pair of horns.

Fal. Away, I say; time wears: hold up your head, and
mince.   [*Exit Mrs. Quickly*

Enter Ford

How now, Master Brook! Master Brook, the matter
will be known to-night, or never. Be you in the park
about midnight, at Herne's oak, and you shall see wonders.

Ford. Went you not to her yesterday, sir, as you told
me you had appointed?

Fal. I went to her, Master Brook, as you see, like a
poor old man; but I came from her, Master Brook, like
a poor old woman. That same knave Ford, her husband,
hath the finest mad devil of jealousy in him, Master Brook,
that ever governed frenzy:—I will tell you:—he beat me
grievously, in the shape of a woman; for in the shape of
man, Master Brook, I fear not Goliath with a weaver's
beam; because I know also, life is a shuttle. I am in haste;
go along with me; I'll tell you all, Master Brook. Since I
plucked geese, played truant, and whipped top, I knew
not what 't was to be beaten, till lately. Follow me: I'll
tell you strange things of this knave Ford, on whom to-night
I will be revenged, and I will deliver his wife into your
hand.—Follow:—strange things in hand, Master Brook:
follow.   [*Exeunt*

Scene II.—Windsor Park

Enter Page, Shallow, *and* Slender

Page. Come, come: we'll couch i' the castle ditch,
till we see the light of our fairies.—Remember, son Slender,
my daughter.

Slen. Ay, forsooth; I have spoke with her, and we have
a nay-word, how to know one another. I come to her in
white, and cry, "mum;" she cries, "budget;" and by
that we know one another.

Shal. That's good too: but what needs either your
"mum" or her "budget?" the white will decipher her
well enough.—It hath struck ten o'clock.

Page. The night is dark; light and spirits will become
it well. Heaven prosper our sport! No man means evil

but the devil, and we shall know by his horns. Let's away; follow me.   [*Exeunt*

SCENE III.—A Street leading to the Park

Enter MISTRESS PAGE, MISTRESS FORD, *and* DOCTOR CAIUS

Mrs. Page. Master doctor, my daughter is in green: when you see your time, take her by the hand, away with her to the deanery, and despatch it quickly. Go before into the Park: we two must go together.

Caius. I know vat I have to do. Adieu.

Mrs. Page. Fare you well, sir. [*Exit Caius.*] My husband will not rejoice so much at the abuse of Falstaff, as he will chafe at the doctor's marrying my daughter: but 't is no matter; better a little chiding than a great deal of heart-break.

Mrs. Ford. Where is Nan now, and her troop of fairies? and the Welsh devil, Hugh?

Mrs. Page. They are all couched in a pit hard by Herne's oak, with obscured lights; which, at the very instant of Falstaff's and our meeting, they will at once display to the night.

Mrs. Ford. That cannot choose but amaze him.

Mrs. Page. If he be not amazed, he will be mocked; if he be amazed, he will every way be mocked.

Mrs. Ford. We 'll betray him finely.

Mrs. Page. Against such lewdsters and their lechery, Those that betray them do no treachery.

Mrs. Ford. The hour draws on. To the oak, to the oak!
                                                 [*Exeunt*

SCENE IV.—Windsor Park

Enter SIR HUGH EVANS, *and Fairies*

Eva. Trib, trib, fairies: come; and remember your parts. Be pold, I pray you; follow me into the pit, and when I give the watch-'ords, do as I pid you. Come, come; trib, trib.   [*Exeunt*

SCENE V.—Another Part of the Park

Enter FALSTAFF *disguised as Herne, with a buck's head on*

Fal. The Windsor bell hath struck twelve; the minute draws on. Now, the hot-blooded gods assist me!— Remember, Jove, thou wast a bull for thy Europa; love set on thy horns.—O powerful love! that, in some respects, makes a beast a man; in some other, a man a beast.—You were also, Jupiter, a swan, for the love of Leda:—O, omnipotent love! how near the god drew to the complexion of a goose!—A fault done first in the form of a beast;—O Jove, a beastly fault! and then another fault in the semblance of a fowl: think on 't, Jove; a foul fault.—When gods have hot backs, what shall poor men do? For me, I am here a Windsor stag; and the fattest, I think, i' the forest.—Send me a cool rut time, Jove, or who can blame me to piss my tallow? Who comes here? my doe?

Enter MISTRESS FORD *and* MISTRESS PAGE

Mrs. Ford. Sir John? art thou there, my deer? my male deer?

Fal. My doe with the black scut!—Let the sky rain potatoes; let it thunder to the tune of "Green Sleeves;" hail kissing-comfits, and snow eringoes; let there come a tempest of provocation, I will shelter me here.
           [*Embracing her*

Mrs. Ford. Mistress Page is come with me, sweet-heart.

Fal. Divide me like a bribed buck, each a haunch: I will keep my sides to myself, my shoulders for the fellow of this walk, and my horns I bequeath your husbands. Am I a woodman? ha! Speak I like Herne the hunter?—Why, now is Cupid a child of conscience; he makes restitution. As I am a true spirit, welcome.   [*Noise within*

Mrs. Page. Alas, what noise?

Mrs. Ford. Heaven forgive our sins!

Fal. What should this be?

Mrs. Ford. }
Mrs. Page. }   Away, away!   [*They run off*

Fal. I think, the devil will not have me damned, lest the oil that's in me should set hell on fire; he would never else cross me thus.

Enter SIR HUGH EVANS, *as a Satyr; another Person as Hobgoblin;* ANNE PAGE, *as the Fairy Queen, attended by her Brother and others, dressed like Fairies, with waxen tapers on their heads*

Anne. Fairies, black, grey, green, and white.
You moonshine revellers, and shades of night,
You orphan heirs of fixéd destiny,
Attend your office, and your quality.—
Crier Hobgoblin, make the fairy oyes.

Hobgoblin. Elves, list your names: silence, you airy toys!
Cricket, to Windsor chimneys shalt thou leap:
Where fires thou find'st unraked, and hearths unswept,
There pinch the maids as blue as bilberry:
Our radiant queen hates sluts and sluttery.

Fal. They're fairies; he that speaks to them shall die:
I'll wink and couch; no man their works must eye.
        [*Lies down upon his face*

Eva. Where's Pead?—Go you, and where you find a maid
That, ere she sleep, has thrice her prayers said,
Rein up the organs of her fantasy,
Sleep she as sound as careless infancy;

But those as sleep and think not on their sins,
Pinch them, arms, legs, backs, shoulders, sides, and shins.
   Anne. About, about;
Search Windsor castle, elves, within and out:
Strew good luck, ouphs, on every sacred room,
That it may stand till the prepetual doom,
In state as wholesome, as in state 't is fit,
Worthy the owner, and the owner it.
The several chairs of order look you scour
With juice of balm, and every precious flower:
Each fair instalment, coat, and several crest,
With loyal blazon, ever more be blest!
And nightly, meadow-fairies, look, you sing,
Like to the Garter's compass, in a ring:
The expressure that it bears, green let it be,
More fertile fresh than all the field to see;
And *Honi soit qui mal y pense*, write
In emerald tufts, flowers purple, blue, and white;
Like sapphire, pearl, and rich embroidery,
Buckle below fair knighthood's bending knee:—
Fairies use flowers for their charactery.
Away! disperse!   But, till 't is one o'clock,
Our dance of custom round about the oak
Of Herne the hunter let us not forget.
   Eva. Pray you, lock hand in hand: yourselves in order set;
And twenty glow-worms shall our lanterns be,
To guide our measure round about the tree.
But, stay! I smell a man of middle-earth.
   Fal. Heavens defend me from that Welsh fairy, lest he
transform me to a piece of cheese!
   Hobgoblin. Vile worm, thou wast o'erlooked even in thy
      birth.
   Anne. With trial-fire touch me his finger-end.
If he be chaste, the flame will back descend
And turn him to no pain; but if he start,
It is the flesh of a corrupted heart.
   Hobgoblin. A trial! come.
   Eva. Come, will this wood take fire?
                         [They burn him with their tapers
   Fal. Oh, oh, oh!
   Anne. Corrupt, corrupt, and tainted in desire!
About him, fairies, sing a scornful rhyme;
And, as you trip, still pinch him to your time.

SONG

> *Fie on sinful fantasy!*
> *Fie on lust and luxury!*
> *Lust is but a bloody fire,*
> *Kindled with unchaste desire,*
> *Fed in heart; whose flames aspire,*

As thoughts do blow them higher and higher.
Pinch him, fairies, mutually;
Pinch him for his villainy;
Pinch him, and burn him, and turn him about,
Till candles, and star-light, and moonshine be out.

[*During this song the Fairies pinch* FALSTAFF. DOCTOR CAIUS
comes one way, and steals away a Fairy in green;
SLENDER *another way, and takes off a Fairy in white;*
and FENTON *comes, and steals away* ANNE PAGE. *A*
noise of hunting is heard within.   All the Fairies run
away. FALSTAFF *pulls off his buck's head, and rises*]

Enter PAGE, FORD, MISTRESS PAGE, *and* MISTRESS FORD.
They lay hold on FALSTAFF

Page. Nay do not fly; I think, we've watched you now.
Will none but Herne the hunter serve your turn?
Mrs. Page. I pray you, come; hold up the jest no higher.—
Now, good Sir John, how like you Windsor wives?
See you these, husband? do not these fair yokes
Become the forest better than the town?
Ford. Now, sir, who's a cuckold now?—Master Brook,
Falstaff's a knave, a cuckoldy knave; here are his horns,
Master Brook: and, Master Brook, he hath enjoyed nothing
of Ford's but his buck-basket, his cudgel, and twenty
pounds of money, which must be paid to Master Brook;
his horses are arrested for it, Master Brook.
Mrs. Ford. Sir John, we have had ill luck; we could
never meet. I will never take you for my love again;—
but I will always count you my deer.
Fal. I do begin to perceive, that I am made an ass.
Ford. Ay, and an ox too; both the proofs are extant.
Fal. And these are not fairies? I was three or four
times in the thought, they were not fairies; and yet the
guiltiness of my mind, the sudden surprise of my powers,
drove the grossness of the foppery into a received belief,
in despite of the teeth of all rhyme and reason, that they
were fairies.   See now, how wit may be made a Jack-a-Lent,
when 't is upon ill employment!
Eva. Sir John Falstaff, serve Got, and leave your desires,
and fairies will not pinse you.
Ford. Well said, fairy Hugh.
Eva. And leave you your jealousies too, I pray you.
Ford. I will never mistrust my wife again, till thou art
able to woo her in good English.
Fal. Have I laid my brain in the sun, and dried it, that
it wants matter to prevent so gross o'er-reaching as this?
Am I ridden with a Welsh goat too? shall I have a coxcomb
of frieze? 'T is time I were choked with a piece of toasted
cheese.

Eva.   Seese is not good to give putter: your pelly is all putter.

Fal.   Seese and putter! have I lived to stand at the taunt of one that makes fritters of English? This is enough to be the decay of lust and late-walking through the realm.

Mrs. Page.   Why, Sir John, do you think, though we would have thrust virtue out of our hearts by the head and shoulders, and have given ourselves without scruple to hell, that ever the devil could have made you our delight?

Ford.   What, a hodge-pudding? a bag of flax?

Mrs. Page.   A puffed man?

Page.   Old, cold, withered, and of intolerable entrails?

Ford.   And one that is as slanderous as Satan?

Page.   And as poor as Job?

Ford.   And as wicked as his wife?

Eva.   And given to fornications, and to taverns, and sack, and wine, and metheglins, and to drinkings, and swearings, and starings, pribbles and prabbles?

Fal.   Well, I am your theme: you have the start of me; I am dejected; I am not able to answer the Welsh flannel; ignorance itself is a plummet o'er me: use me as you will.

Ford.   Marry, sir, we'll bring you to Windsor, to one Master Brook, that you have cozened of money, to whom you should have been a pander: over and above that you have suffered, I think to repay that money will be a biting affliction.

Page.   Yet be cheerful, knight: thou shalt eat a posset to-night at my house; where I will desire thee to laugh at my wife, that now laughs at thee. Tell her, Master Slender hath married her daughter.

Mrs. Page.   [*Aside*] Doctors doubt that: if Anne Page be my daughter, she is, by this, Doctor Caius' wife.

Enter SLENDER

Slen.   Whoo, ho! ho! father Page!

Page.   Son, how now? how now, son? have you despatched?

Slen.   Despatched!—I'll make the best in Glostershire know on 't; would I were hanged, la, else.

Page.   Of what, son?

Slen.   I came yonder at Eton to marry Mistress Anne Page, and she's a great lubberly boy. If it had not been i' the church, I would have swinged him, or he should have swinged me. If I did not think it had been Anne Page, would I might never stir!—and 't is a postmaster's boy.

Page.   Upon my life, then, you took the wrong.

Slen.   What need you tell me that? I think so, when I took a boy for a girl. If I had been married to him, for all he was in woman's apparel, I would not have had him.

Page.   Why, this is your own folly. Did not I tell you, how you should know my daughter by her garments?

Slen. I went to her in white, and cried, "mum," and she cried, "budget," as Anne and I had appointed; and yet it was not Anne, but a postmaster's boy.

Mrs. Page. Good George, be not angry: I knew of your purpose; turned my daughter into green; and indeed, she is now with the doctor at the deanery, and there married.

Enter DOCTOR CAIUS

Caius. Vere is Mistress Page? By gar, I am cozened; I ha' married *un garçon,* a boy; *un paysan,* by gar, a boy; it is not Anne Page; by gar, I am cozened.

Mrs. Page. Why, did you take her in green?

Caius. Ay, by gar, and 't is a boy: by gar, I 'll raise all Windsor.   [*Exit*

Ford. This is strange. Who hath got the right Anne?

Page. My heart misgives me. Here comes Master Fenton.

Enter FENTON *and* ANNE PAGE

How now, Master Fenton?

Anne. Pardon, good father! good my mother, pardon!

Page. Now, mistress; how chance you went not with Master Slender?

Mrs. Page. Why went you not with master doctor, maid?

Fent. You do amaze her: hear the truth of it.
You would have married her most shamefully,
Where there was no proportion held in love.
The truth is, she and I, long since contracted,
Are now so sure, that nothing can dissolve us.
The offence is holy that she hath committed,
And this deceit loses the name of craft,
Of disobedience, or unduteous title,
Since therein she doth evitate and shun
A thousand irreligious cursèd hours,
Which forcèd marriage would have brought upon her.

Ford. Stand not amazèd: here is no remedy.—
In love, the heavens themselves do guide the state:
Money buys lands, and wives are sold by fate.

Fal. I am glad, though you have ta'en a special stand to strike at me, that your arrow hath glanced.

Page. Well, what remedy? Fenton, Heaven give thee joy!
What cannot be eschewed, must be embraced.

Fal. When night-dogs run, all sorts of deer are chased.

Mrs. Page. Well, I will muse no further. Master Fenton,
Heaven give you many, many merry days.—
Good husband, let us every one go home,
And laugh this sport o'er by a country fire;
Sir John and all.

Ford.   Let it be so.—Sir John,
To Master Brook you yet shall hold your word:
For he, to-night, shall lie with Mistress Ford.   [*Exeunt*

A MIDSUMMER-NIGHT'S DREAM

DRAMATIS PERSONÆ

THESEUS, *duke of Athens*
EGEUS, *father to Hermia*
LYSANDER
DEMETRIUS } *in love with Hermia*
PHILOSTRATE, *master of the revels to Theseus*
QUINCE, *a carpenter*
SNUG, *a joiner*
BOTTOM, *a weaver*
FLUTE, *a bellows-mender*
SNOUT, *a tinker*
STARVELING, *a tailor*

HIPPOLYTA, *queen of the Amazons, betrothed to Theseus*
HERMIA, *daughter to Egeus, in love with Lysander*
HELENA, *in love with Demetrius*

OBERON, *king of the Fairies*
TITANIA, *queen of the Fairies*
PUCK, *or Robin Good-fellow*
PEASE-BLOSSOM
COBWEB
MOTH } *Fairies*
MUSTARD-SEED

Other fairies attending their king and queen. Attendants on Theseus and Hippolyta

SCENE.—*Athens and a Wood near it*

A MIDSUMMER-NIGHT'S DREAM

ACT ONE

SCENE I.—Athens. A Room in the Palace of THESEUS

Enter THESEUS, HIPPOLYTA, PHILOSTRATE, *and Attendants*

   The. Now, fair Hippolyta, our nuptial hour
Draws on apace; four happy days bring in
Another moon: but, O, methinks, how slow
This old moon wanes! she lingers my desires,
Like to a step-dame, or a dowager,
Long withering out a young man's revenue.
   Hip. Four days will quickly steep themselves in nights;
Four nights will quickly dream away the time;
And then the moon, like to a silver bow
New-bent in heaven, shall behold the night
Of our solemnities.
   The.   Go, Philostrate,
Stir up the Athenian youth to merriments;
Awake the pert and nimble spirit of mirth:
Turn melancholy forth to funerals,
The pale companion is not for our pomp. [*Exit Philostrate*
Hippolyta, I wooed thee with my sword,
And won thy love doing thee injuries;
But I will wed thee in another key,
With pomp, with triumph, and with revelling.

   Enter EGEUS, HERMIA, LYSANDER, *and* DEMETRIUS

   Ege. Happy be Theseus, our renownéd duke!
   The. Thanks, good Egeus: what's the news with thee?
   Ege. Full of vexation come I, with complaint
Against my child, my daughter Hermia.—
Stand forth, Demetrius:—My noble lord,
This man hath my consent to marry her.—
Stand forth, Lysander:—and, my gracious duke,
This man hath witched the bosom of my child.
Thou, thou, Lysander, thou hast given her rhymes,
And interchanged love-tokens with my child;
Thou hast by moonlight at her window sung,
With feigning voice, verses of feigning love;
And stolen the impression of her fantasy
With bracelets of thy hair, rings, gawds, conceits,
Knacks, trifles, nosegays, sweetmeats,—messengers
Of strong prevailment in unhardened youth;
With cunning hast thou filched my daughter's heart,
Turned her obedience, which is due to me,

To stubborn harshness:—and, my gracious duke,
Be it so she will not here before your grace
Consent to marry with Demetrius,
I beg the ancient privilege of Athens,—
As she is mine, I may dispose of her:
Which shall be either to this gentleman
Or to her death, according to our law
Immediately provided in that case.
    The. What say you, Hermia? be advised, fair maid.
To you your father should be as a god;
One that composed your beauties; yea, and one
To whom you are but as a form in wax,
By him imprinted, and within his power
To leave the figure or disfigure it.—
Demetrius is a worthy gentleman.
    Her. So is Lysander.
    The.   In himself he is;
But in this kind, wanting your father's voice,
The other must be held the worthier.
    Her. I would, my father looked but with my eyes!
    The. Rather your eyes must with his judgment look.
    Her. I do entreat your grace to pardon me.
I know not by what power I am made bold,
Nor how it may concern my modesty,
In such a presence here, to plead my thoughts;
But I beseech your grace that I may know
The worst that may befall me in this case,
If I refuse to wed Demetrius.
    The. Either to die the death, or to abjure
For ever the society of men.
Therefore, fair Hermia, question your desires;
Know of your youth, examine well your blood,
Whether, if you yield not to your father's choice,
You can endure the livery of a nun;
For aye to be in shady cloister mewed,
To live a barren sister all your life,
Chanting faint hymns to the cold fruitless moon.
Thrice blessèd they that master so their blood,
To undergo such maiden pilgrimage;
But earthlier happy is the rose distilled
Than that which, withering on the virgin thorn,
Grows, lives, and dies in single blessedness.
    Her. So will I grow, so live, so die, my lord,
Ere I will yield my virgin patent up
Unto his lordship to whose unwished yoke
My soul consents not to give sovereignty.
    The. Take time to pause; and by the next new moon,—
The sealing-day betwixt my love and me
For everlasting bond of fellowship,—
Upon that day, either prepare to die

For disobedience to your father's will;
Or else to wed Demetrius, as he would;
Or on Diana's altar to protest
For aye austerity and single life.
    Dem. Relent, sweet Hermia;—and, Lysander, yield
Thy crazéd title to my certain right.
    Lys. You have her father's love, Demetrius;
Let me have Hermia's: do you marry him.
    Ege. Scornful Lysander! true, he hath my love,
And what is mine my love shall render him;
And she is mine, and all my right of her
I do estate unto Demetrius.
    Lys. I am, my lord, as well derived as he;
As well possessed; my love is more than his;
My fortunes every way as fairly ranked—
If not with vantage—as Demetrius';
And, which is more than all these boasts can be,
I am beloved of beauteous Hermia.
Why should not I then prosecute my right?
Demetrius, I'll avouch it to his head,
Made love to Nedar's daughter, Helena,
And won her soul; and she, sweet lady, dotes,
Devoutly dotes, dotes in idolatry,
Upon this spotted and inconstant man.
    The. I must confess, that I have heard so much,
And with Demetrius thought to have spoken thereof;
But, being over-full of self-affairs,
My mind did lose it.—But, Demetrius, come;
And come, Egeus: you shall go with me,
I have some private schooling for you both.—
For you, fair Hermia, look you arm yourself
To fit your fancies to your father's will,
Or else the law of Athens yields you up—
Which by no means we may extenuate—
To death, or to a vow of single life.—
Come, my Hippolyta: what cheer, my love?—
Demetrius and Egeus, go along:
I must employ you in some business
Against our nuptial, and confer with you
Of something nearly that concerns yourselves.
    Ege. With duty and desire we follow you.
                 [Exeunt all but Lysander and Hermia
    Lys. How now, my love? Why is your cheek so pale?
How chance the roses there do fade so fast?
    Her. Belike for want of rain, which I could well
Beteem them from the tempest of mine eyes.
    Lys. Ay me! for aught that ever I could read,
Could ever hear by tale or history,
The course of true love never did run smooth;
But, either it was different in blood,

Her. O cross! too high to be enthrall'd to low!—
Lys. Or else misgraffèd in respect of years,
Her. O spite! too old to be engaged to young!—
Lys. Or else it stood upon the choice of friends,—
Her. O hell! to choose love by another's eyes!—
Lys. Or, if there were a sympathy in choice,
War, death, or sickness did lay siege to it,
Making it momentary as a sound,
Swift as a shadow, short as any dream,
Brief as the lightning in the collied night,
That, in a spleen, unfolds both heaven and earth,
And ere a man hath power to say,—"Behold!"
The jaws of darkness do devour it up:
So quick bright things come to confusion.
    Her. If then true lovers have been ever crossed,
It stands as an edict in destiny:
Then let us teach our trial patience,
Because it is a customary cross
As due to love as thoughts, and dreams, and sighs,
Wishes, and tears, poor fancy's followers.
    Lys. A good persuasion: therefore, hear me, Hermia.
I have a widow aunt, a dowager
Of great revenue, and she hath no child:
From Athens is her house remote seven leagues;
And she respects me as her only son.
There, gentle Hermia, may I marry thee;
And to that place the sharp Athenian law
Cannot pursue us. If thou lov'st me, then,
Steal forth thy father's house to-morrow night,
And in the wood, a league without the town,
Where I did meet thee once with Helena,
To do observance to a morn of May,
There will I stay for thee.
    Her.   My good Lysander!
I swear to thee, by Cupid's strongest bow;
By his best arrow with the golden head;
By the simplicity of Venus' doves;
By that which knitteth souls and prospers loves;
And by that fire which burned the Carthage queen,
When the false Trojan under sail was seen;
By all the vows that ever men have broke,
In number more than ever women spoke;
In that same place thou hast appointed me,
To-morrow truly will I meet with thee.
    Lys. Keep promise, love,—Look, here comes Helena.

Enter HELENA

Her. God speed fair Helena! Whither away?
Hel. Call you me fair? that fair again unsay.
Demetrius loves your fair: O happy fair!

Your eyes are lode-stars, and your tongue's sweet air
More tuneable than lark to shepherd's ear
When wheat is green, when hawthorn buds appear.
Sickness is catching: O, were favour so,
Yours would I catch, fair Hermia, ere I go;
My ear should catch your voice, my eye your eye,
My tongue should catch your tongue's sweet melody.
Were the world mine, Demetrius being bated,
The rest I'd give to be to you translated.
O, teach me how you look, and with what art
You sway the motion of Demetrius' heart.

 Her. I frown upon him, yet he loves me still.
 Hel. O, that your frowns would teach my smiles such
  skill!
 Her. I give him curses, yet he gives me love.
 Hel. O, that my prayers could such affection move!
 Her. The more I hate, the more he follows me.
 Hel. The more I love, the more he hateth me.
 Her. His folly, Helena, 's no fault of mine.
 Hel. None, but your beauty: would that fault were
  mine!
 Her. Take comfort: he no more shall see my face;
Lysander and myself will fly this place.
Before the time I did Lysander see,
Seemed Athens as a paradise to me:
O, then, what graces in my love do dwell,
That he hath turned a heaven unto a hell!

 Lys. Helen, to you our minds we will unfold:
To-morrow night, when Phœbe doth behold
Her silver visage in the watery glass,
Decking with liquid pearl the bladed grass,—
A time that lovers' flights doth still conceal—
Through Athens' gates have we devised to steal.

 Her. And in the wood, where often you and I
Upon faint primrose-beds were wont to lie,
Emptying our bosoms of their counsel sweet,
There my Lysander and myself shall meet;
And thence, from Athens turn away our eyes,
To seek new friends and stranger companies.
Farewell, sweet playfellow: pray thou for us,
And good luck grant thee thy Demetrius!—
Keep word, Lysander: we must starve our sight
From lovers' food, till morrow deep midnight.

 Lys. I will, my Hermia. [*Exit Herm.*]—Helena, adieu:
As you on him, Demetrius dote on you!   [*Exit*

 Hel. How happy some o'er other some can be!
Through Athens I am thought as fair as she;
But what of that? Demetrius thinks not so;
He will not know what all but he do know;
And as he errs, doting on Hermia's eyes,

So I, admiring of his qualities.
Things base and vile, holding no quantity,
Love can transpose to form and dignity:
Love looks not with the eyes, but with the mind,
And therefore is winged Cupid painted blind:
Nor hath Love's mind of any judgment taste;
Wings and no eyes, figure unheedy haste:
And therefore is Love said to be a child,
Because in choice he is so oft beguiled.
As waggish boys in game themselves forswear,
So the boy Love is perjured every where;
For ere Demetrius looked on Hermia's eyne,
He hailed down oaths that he was only mine;
And when this hail some heat from Hermia felt,
So he dissolved, and showers of oaths did melt.—
I will go tell him of fair Hermia's flight:
Then to the wood will he to-morrow night
Pursue her; and for this intelligence
If I have thanks, it is a dear expense:
But herein mean I to enrich my pain,
To have his sight thither and back again.   [*Exit*

SCENE II.—Athens. A Room in QUINCE'S House

Enter QUINCE, SNUG, BOTTOM, FLUTE, SNOUT, *and*
STARVELING

Quin. Is all our company here?
Bot. You were best to call them generally, man by man,
according to the scrip.
Quin. Here is the scroll of every man's name which is
thought fit, through all Athens, to play in our interlude
before the duke and the duchess on his wedding-day at night.
Bot. First, good Peter Quince, say what the play treats
on; then read the names of the actors; and so grow to a
point.
Quin. Marry, our play is—The most lamentable comedy
and most cruel death of Pyramus and Thisbe.
Bot. A very good piece of work, I assure you, and a
merry.—Now, good Peter Quince, call forth your actors by
the scroll.—Masters, spread yourselves.
Quin. Answer, as I call you.—Nick Bottom the weaver.
Bot. Ready. Name what part I am for, and proceed.
Quin. You, Nick Bottom, are set down for Pyramus.
Bot. What is Pyramus? a lover, or a tyrant?
Quin. A lover, that kills himself most gallantly for love.
Bot. That will ask some tears in the true performing of
it: if I do it, let the audience look to their eyes; I will
move storms, I will condole in some measure. To the rest:

—yet my chief humour is for a tyrant: I could play Ercles rarely, or a part to tear a cat in, to make all split.

> "The raging rocks
> And shivering shocks
> Shall break the locks
>   Of prison gates;
> And Phibbus' car
> Shall shine from far,
> And make and mar
>   The foolish Fates."

This was lofty.—Now name the rest of the players.—This is Ercles' vein, a tyrant's vein; a lover is more condoling.

Quin.   Francis Flute the bellows-mender.

Flu.   Here, Peter Quince.

Quin.   You must take Thisbe on you.

Flu.   What is Thisbe? a wandering knight?

Quin.   It is the lady that Pyramus must love.

Flu.   Nay, faith, let me not play a woman; I have a beard coming.

Quin.   That's all one. You shall play it in a mask, and you may speak as small as you will.

Bot.   An I may hide my face, let me play Thisbe too. I'll speak in a monstrous little voice:—"Thisne, Thisne,"—"Ah, Pyramus, my lover dear! thy Thisbe dear, and lady dear!"

Quin.   No, no; you must play Pyramus;—and, Flute, you Thisbe.

Bot.   Well, proceed.

Quin.   Robin Starveling the tailor.

Star.   Here, Peter Quince.

Quin.   Robin Starveling, you must play Thisbe's mother.—Tom Snout the tinker.

Snout.   Here, Peter Quince.

Quin.   You, Pyramus's father; myself, Thisbe's father.—Snug, the joiner, you, the lion's part:—and, I hope, here is a play fitted.

Snug.   Have you the lion's part written? pray you, if it be, give it me, for I am slow of study.

Quin.   You may do it extempore, for it is nothing but roaring.

Bot.   Let me play the lion too: I will roar, that I will do any man's heart good to hear me; I will roar, that I will make the duke say, "Let him roar again, let him roar again."

Quin.   An you should do it too terribly, you would fright the duchess and the ladies, that they would shriek; and that were enough to hang us all.

All.   That would hang us, every mother's son.

Bot.   I grant you, friends, if that you should fright the ladies out of their wits, they would have no more discretion but to hang us; but I will aggravate my voice so, that I will roar you as gently as any sucking dove; I will roar you an 't were any nightingale.

Quin. You can play no part but Pyramus:—for Pyramus is a sweet-faced man,—a proper man, as one shall see in a summer's day,—a most lovely, gentleman-like man:—therefore, you must needs play Pyramus.

Bot. Well, I will undertake it. What beard were I best to play it in?

Quin. Why, what you will.

Bot. I will discharge it in either your straw-colour beard, your orange-tawny beard, your purple-in-grain beard, or your French-crown-colour beard, your perfect yellow.

Quin. Some of your French crowns have no hair at all, and then you will play bare-faced.—But, masters, here are your parts: and I am to entreat you, request you, and desire you, to con them by to-morrow night, and meet me in the palace wood, a mile without the town, by moon-light: there will we rehearse, for if we meet in the city, we shall be dogged with company, and our devices known. In the meantime I will draw a bill of properties, such as our play wants. I pray you, fail me not.

Bot. We will meet; and there we may rehearse more obscenely and courageously. Take pains; be perfect; adieu.

Quin. At the duke's oak we meet.

Bot. Enough; hold, or cut bowstrings.   [*Exeunt*

ACT TWO

Scene I.—A Wood near Athens

Enter, from opposite sides, a Fairy, and Puck

Puck. How now, spirit, whither wander you?
Fai. Over hill, over dale.
Thorough bush, thorough brier,
Over park, over pale,
Thorough flood, thorough fire,
I do wander everywhere,
Swifter than the moony sphere;
And I serve the fairy queen,
To dew her orbs upon the green:
The cowslips tall her pensioners be;
In their gold coats spots you see,—
Those be rubies, fairy favours,
In those freckles live their savours;
I must go seek some dew-drops here,
And hang a pearl in every cowslip's ear.
Farewell, thou lob of spirits; I'll be gone;
Our queen and all her elves come here anon.
     Puck. The king doth keep his revels here to-night:

Take heed the queen come not within his sight;
For Oberon is passing fell and wrath,
Because that she as her attendant hath
A lovely boy, stol'n from an Indian king,
She never had so sweet a changeling,
And jealous Oberon would have the child
Knight of his train, to trace the forests wild;
But she perforce withholds the lovéd boy,
Crowns him with flowers, and makes him all her joy:
And now they never meet in grove or green,
By fountain clear or spangled starlight sheen,
But they do square, that all their elves, for fear,
Creep into acorn cups and hide them there.
   Fai.   Either I mistake your shape and making quite,
Or else you are that shrewd and knavish sprite
Called Robin Good-fellow.   Are you not he
That frights the maidens of the villagery;
Skim milk, and sometimes labour in the quern,
And bootless make the breathless housewife churn;
And sometime make the drink to bear no barm;
Mislead night-wanderers, laughing at their harm?
Those that Hobgoblin call you, and sweet Puck,
You do their work, and they shall have good luck:
Are not you he?
   Puck.   Fairy, thou speak'st aright;
I am that merry wanderer of the night.
I jest to Oberon, and make him smile,
When I a fat and bean-fed horse beguile,
Neighing in likeness of a filly foal;
And sometime lurk I in a gossip's bowl,
In very likeness of a roasted crab,
And when she drinks, against her lips I bob,
And on her withered dewlap pour the ale.
The wisest aunt, telling the saddest tale,
Sometime for three-foot stool mistaketh me,
Then slip I from her bum, down topples she,
And "tailor" cries, and falls into a cough,
And then the whole quire hold their hips and laugh;
And waxen in their mirth and neeze and swear
A merrier hour was never wasted there.—
But room now, Fairy: here comes Oberon.
   Fai.   And here my mistress.—Would that he were gone!

Scene II

Enter, from one side, Oberon *with his Train, and
from the other,* Titania *with hers*

   Obe.   Ill met by moonlight, proud Titania.
   Tita.   What, jealous Oberon!   Fairies, skip hence:
I have forsworn his bed and company.

Obe. Tarry, rash wanton. Am not I thy lord?
  Tita. Then I must be thy lady: but I know
When thou hast stol'n away from fairy land
And in the shape of Corin sat all day,
Playing on pipes of corn and versing love
To amorous Phillida. Why art thou here,
Come from the farthest steep of India,
But that, forsooth, the bouncing Amazon,
Your buskined mistress and your warrior love,
To Theseus must be wedded? and you come
To give their bed joy and prosperity.
  Obe. How canst thou thus, for shame, Titania,
Glance at my credit with Hippolyta,
Knowing I know thy love to Theseus?
Didst thou not lead him through the glimmering night
From Perigenia, whom he ravishéd?
And make him with fair Ægle break his faith,
With Ariadne, and Antiopa?
  Tita. These are the forgeries of jealousy:
And never, since the middle summer's spring,
Met we on hill, in dale, forest, or mead,
By pavéd fountain, or by rushy brook,
Or in the beachéd margin of the sea,
To dance our ringlets to the whistling wind,
But with thy brawls thou hast disturbed our sport.
Therefore the winds, piping to us in vain,
As in revenge, have sucked up from the sea
Contagious fogs, which, falling in the land,
Have every pelting river made so proud,
That they have overborne their continents;
The ox hath therefore stretched his yoke in vain,
The ploughman lost his sweat, and the green corn
Hath rotted ere his youth attained a beard:
The fold stands empty in the drownéd field,
And crows are fatted with the murrain flock:
The nine men's morris is filled up with mud;
And the quaint mazes in the wanton green
For lack of tread are undistinguishable:
The human mortals want their winter here,
No night is now with hymn or carol blest,
Therefore the moon, the governess of floods,
Pale in her anger, washes all the air,
That rheumatic diseases do abound:
And thorough this distemperature we see
The seasons alter: hoary-headed frosts
Fall in the fresh lap of the crimson rose;
And on old Hiems' thin and icy crown
An odorous chaplet of sweet summer buds
Is, as in mockery, set. The spring, the summer,
The chiding autumn, angry winter, change

Their wonted liveries; and the mazéd world,
By their increase, now knows not which is which.
And this same progeny of evils comes
From our debate, from our dissension;
We are their parents and original.
   Obe. Do you amend it, then; it lies in you.
Why should Titania cross her Oberon?
I do but beg a little changeling boy
To be my henchman.
   Tita.   Set your heart at rest,
The fairy land buys not the child of me.
His mother was a votaress of my order:
And, in the spicéd Indian air, by night,
Full often hath she gossiped by my side,
And sat with me on Neptune's yellow sands,
Marking the embarkéd traders on the flood
When we have laughed to see the sails conceive
And grow big-bellied with the wanton wind;
Which she, with pretty and with swimming gait
Following,—her womb then rich with my young squire—
Would imitate, and sail upon the land
To fetch me trifles, and return again,
As from a voyage, rich with merchandise.
But she, being mortal, of that boy did die;
And for her sake I do rear up her boy,
And for her sake I will not part with him.
   Obe. How long within this wood intend you stay?
   Tita. Perchance, till after Theseus' wedding-day.
If you will patiently dance in our round,
And see our moonlight revels, go with us;
If not, shun me, and I will spare your haunts.
   Obe. Give me that boy, and I will go with thee.
   Tita. Not for thy fairy kingdom.—Fairies, away!
We shall chide downright, if I longer stay.
                [*Exit Titania, with her Train*
   Obe. Well, go thy way: thou shalt not from this grove
Till I torment thee for this injury.—
My gentle Puck, come hither: thou remember'st
Since once I sat upon a promontory,
And heard a mermaid on a dolphin's back
Uttering such dulcet and harmonious breath,
That the rude sea grew civil at her song,
And certain stars shot madly from their spheres,
To hear the sea-maid's music.
   Puck.   I remember.
   Obe. That very time I saw—but thou couldst not—
Flying between the cold moon and the earth,
Cupid all armed; a certain aim he took
At a fair vestal thronéd by the west,
And loosed his love-shaft smartly from his bow

As it should pierce a hundred thousand hearts:
But I might see young Cupid's fiery shaft
Quenched in the chaste beams of the watery moon,
And the imperial votaress passed on,
In maiden meditation, fancy-free.
Yet marked I where the bolt of Cupid fell:
It fell upon a little western flower,
Before milk-white, now purple with love's wound,
And maidens call it Love-in-idleness.
Fetch me that flower; the herb I showed thee once:
The juice of it, on sleeping eyelids laid,
Will make or man or woman madly dote
Upon the next live creature that it sees.
Fetch me this herb; and be thou here again
Ere the leviathan can swim a league.
    Puck.   I'll put a girdle round about the earth
In forty minutes.   [*Exit*
    Obe.   Having once this juice,
I'll watch Titania when she is asleep,
And drop the liquor of it in her eyes.
The next thing then she waking looks upon—
Be it on lion, bear, or wolf, or bull,
On meddling monkey, or on busy ape—
She shall pursue it with the soul of love.
And ere I take this charm off from her sight—
As I can take it with another herb—
I'll make her render up her page to me.
But who comes here? I am invisible;
And I will overhear their conference.

Enter DEMETRIUS, HELENA *following him*

    Dem.   I love thee not, therefore pursue me not.
Where is Lysander and fair Hermia?
The one I'll slay, the other slayeth me.
Thou toldst me, they were stol'n into this wood;
And here am I, and wood within this wood
Because I cannot meet my Hermia.
Hence, get thee gone, and follow me no more.
    Hel.   You draw me, you hard-hearted adamant;
But yet you draw not iron, for my heart
Is true as steel: leave you your power to draw,
And I shall have no power to follow you.
    Dem.   Do I entice you? do I speak you fair?
Or, rather, do I not in plainest truth
Tell you I do not nor I cannot love you?
    Hel.   And even for that do I love you the more.
I am your spaniel; and, Demetrius,
The more you beat me, I will fawn on you:
Use me but as your spaniel, spurn me, strike me,
Neglect me, lose me; only give me leave,

144

Unworthy as I am, to follow you.
What worser place can I beg in your love,—
And yet a place of high respect with me,—
Than to be uséd as you use your dog?
    Dem.   Tempt not too much the hatred of my spirit,
For I am sick when I do look on thee.
    Hel.   And I am sick when I look not on you.
    Dem.   You do impeach your modesty too much,
To leave the city, and commit yourself
Into the hands of one that loves you not;
To trust the opportunity of night
And the ill counsel of a desert place
With the rich worth of your virginity.
    Hel.   Your virtue is my privilege for that.
It is not night when I do see your face,
Therefore I think I am not in the night;
Nor doth this wood lack worlds of company,
For you, in my respect, are all the world,
Then how can it be said I am alone,
When all the world is here to look on me?
    Dem.   I'll run from thee and hide me in the brakes,
And leave thee to the mercy of wild beasts.
    Hel.   The wildest hath not such a heart as you.
Run when you will, the story shall be changed,—
Apollo flies, and Daphne holds the chase;
The dove pursues the griffin; the mild hind
Makes speed to catch the tiger. Bootless speed,
When cowardice pursues, the valour flies!
    Dem.   I will not stay thy questions: let me go;
Or, if thou follow me, do not believe
But I shall do thee mischief in the wood.
    Hel.   Ay, in the temple, in the town, the field,
You do me mischief. Fie, Demetrius!
Your wrongs do set a scandal on my sex.
We cannot fight for love, as men may do;
We should be wooed, and were not made to woo.
I'll follow thee, and make a heaven of hell,
To die upon the hand I love so well.
                [Exeunt Demetrius and Helena
    Obe.   Fare thee well, nymph: ere he do leave this grove,
Thou shalt fly him, and he shall seek thy love.

Re-enter PUCK

Hast thou the flower there?   Welcome, wanderer.
    Puck.   Ay, there it is.
    Obe.   I pray thee, give it me.
I know a bank whereon the wild thyme blows,
Where oxlips and the nodding violet grows;
Quite over-canopied with lush woodbine,
With sweet musk-roses, and with eglantine:

There sleeps Titania, some time of the night,
Lulled in these flowers with dances and delight;
And there the snake throws her enamelled skin,
Weed wide enough to wrap a fairy in:
And with the juice of this I'll streak her eyes,
And make her full of hateful fantasies.
Take thou some of it, and seek through this grove.
A sweet Athenian lady is in love
With a disdainful youth: anoint his eyes;
But do it, when the next thing he espies
May be the lady.   Thou shalt know the **man**
By the Athenian garments he hath on.
Effect it with some care, that he may prove
More fond on her than she upon her love.
And look thou, meet me ere the first cock crow.
    Puck.   Fear not, my lord, your servant shall do so.
                            [Exeunt

Scene III.—Another part of the Wood

Enter Titania, *with her Train*

    Tita.   Come, now a roundel and a fairy song;
Then, for the third part of a minute, hence;
Some, to kill cankers in the musk-rose buds;
Some, war with rere-mice for their leathern wings
To make my small elves coats; and some, keep back
The clamorous owl that nightly hoots and wonders
At our quaint spirits.   Sing me now asleep;
Then to your offices, and let me rest.

The Fairies Sing

I

First Fai.   *You spotted snakes with double tongue,*
      Thorny hedge-hogs, be not seen;
  Newts and blind-worms, do no wrong,
      Come not near our fairy queen.

Chorus

    Philomel, with melody
    Sing in our sweet lullaby;
Lulla, lulla, lullaby; lulla, lulla, lullaby;
    Never harm,
    Nor spell nor charm,
Come our lovely lady nigh;
So, good night, with lullaby.

II

Sec. Fai. *Weaving spiders, come not here*
  Hence, you long-legged spinners, hence!
  Beetles black, approach not near;
  Worm nor snail do no offence.

Chorus

  Philomel, with melody, etc.
Fir. Fai. Hence, away! now all is well.
  One, aloof, stand sentinel.
  [*Exeunt Fairies.   Titania sleeps*

Enter OBERON, *and squeezes the flower on* TITANIA's *eyelids*

Obe. What thou seest, when thou dost wake,
  Do it for thy true-love take;
  Love, and languish for his sake:
  Be it ounce, or cat, or bear,
  Pard, or boar with bristled hair,
  In thy eye that shall appear
  When thou wak'st, it is thy dear:
  Wake when some vile thing is near.   [*Exit*

Enter LYSANDER *and* HERMIA

Lys. Fair love, you faint with wandering in the wood;
And, to speak troth, I have forgot our way:
We'll rest us, Hermia, if you think it good,
And tarry for the comfort of the day.
  Her. Be it so, Lysander: find you out a bed;
For I upon this bank will rest my head.
  Lys. One turf shall serve as pillow for us both;
One heart, one bed, two bosoms, and one troth.
  Her. Nay, good Lysander; for my sake, my dear,
Lie further off yet, do not lie so near.
  Lys. O, take the sense, sweet, of my innocence!
Love takes the meaning in love's conference.
I mean, that my heart unto yours is knit,
So that but one heart we can make of it;
Two bosoms interchainéd with an oath;
So then, two bosoms and a single troth.
Then by your side no bed-room me deny,
For, lying so, Hermia, I do not lie.
  Her. Lysander riddles very prettily:—
Now much beshrew my manners and my pride,
If Hermia meant to say Lysander lied.
But, gentle friend, for love and courtesy
Lie further off; in human modesty,
Such separation as may well be said
Becomes a virtuous bachelor and a maid:

So far be distant; and good night, sweet friend:
Thy love ne'er alter till thy sweet life end!
    Lys.   Amen, Amen, to that fair prayer, say I;
And then end life when I end loyalty!
Here is my bed: sleep give thee all his rest!
    Her.   With half that wish the wisher's eyes be pressed!

Enter PUCK

                                                          [They sleep

  Puck.   Through the forest have I gone,
            But Athenian found I none,
            On whose eyes I might approve
            This flower's force in stirring love.—
            Night and silence! Who is here?
            Weeds of Athens he doth wear:
            This is he, my master said
            Despiséd the Athenian maid;
            And here the maiden, sleeping sound
            On the dank and dirty ground.
            Pretty soul! she durst not lie
            Nearer this lack-love, this kill-courtesy.
            Churl, upon thy eyes I throw
            All the power this charm doth owe.
                    [Squeezes the flower on Lysander's eyelids
            When thou wak'st, let love forbid
            Sleep his seat on thy eyelid:
            So awake when I am gone;
            For I must now to Oberon.   *[Exit*

Enter DEMETRIUS and HELENA, running

  Hel.   Stay, though thou kill me, sweet Demetrius.
  Dem.   I charge thee, hence, and do not haunt me thus.
  Hel.   O, wilt thou darkling leave me? do not so.
  Dem.   Stay, on thy peril: I alone will go.   *[Exit*
  Hel.   O, I am out of breath in this fond chase!
The more my prayer, the lesser is my grace.
Happy is Hermia, wheresoe'er she lies;
For she hath blesséd and attractive eyes.
How came her eyes so bright? Not with salt tears:
If so, my eyes are oftener washed than hers.
No, no, I am as ugly as a bear;
For beasts, that meet me, run away for fear:
Therefore no marvel though Demetrius
Do, as a monster, fly my presence thus.
What wicked and dissembling glass of mine
Made me compare with Hermia's sphery eyne?—
But who is here?—Lysander! on the ground!
Dead? or asleep?—I see no blood, no wound.—
Lysander! If you live, good sir, awake.
    Lys. *[Awaking]* And run through fire I will, for thy
      sweet sake.

148

Transparent Helena! Nature here shows art,
That through thy bosom makes me see thy heart.
Where is Demetrius? O, how fit a word
Is that vile name to perish on my sword!

   Hel. Do not say so, Lysander; say not so.
What though he love your Hermia? Lord, what though?
Yet Hermia still loves you: then be content.

   Lys. Content with Hermia! No; I do repent
The tedious minutes I with her have spent.
Not Hermia, but Helena now I love.
Who will not change a raven for a dove?
The will of man is by his reason swayed,
And reason says you are the worthier maid.
Things growing are not ripe until their season,
So I, being young, till now ripe not to reason;
And touching now the point of human skill,
Reason becomes the marshal to my will,
And leads me to your eyes; where I o'erlook
Love's stories written in love's richest book.

   Hel. Wherefore was I to this keen mockery born?
When at your hands did I deserve this scorn?
Is 't not enough, is 't not enough, young man,
That I did never, no, nor never can,
Deserve a sweet look from Demetrius' eye,
But you must flout my insufficiency?
Good troth, you do me wrong,—good sooth, you do,—
In such disdainful manner me to woo.
But fare you well: perforce I must confess
I thought you lord of more true gentleness.
O, that a lady of one man refused
Should of another therefore be abused!   [*Exit*

   Lys. She sees not Hermia.—Hermia, sleep thou there:
And never may'st thou come Lysander near!
For, as a surfeit of the sweetest things
The deepest loathing to the stomach brings;
Or, as the heresies that men do leave
Are hated most of those they did deceive;
So thou, my surfeit and my heresy,
Of all be hated, but the most of me.
And, all my powers, address your love and might
To honour Helen, and to be her knight.   [*Exit*

   Her. [*Awaking*] Help me, Lysander, help me! do thy
     best
To pluck this crawling serpent from my breast!
Ay me, for pity!—what a dream was here!
Lysander, look how I do quake with fear.
Methought a serpent ate my heart away,
And you sat smiling at his cruel prey.—
Lysander! what, removed? Lysander! lord!—
What, out of hearing? gone? no sound, no word?

Alack! where are you? speak, an if you hear;
Speak, of all loves! I swoon almost with fear.
No?—then I well perceive you are not nigh:
Either death, or you, I'll find immediately.   [*Exit*

ACT THREE

SCENE I.—The Wood. TITANIA lying asleep

Enter QUINCE, SNUG, BOTTOM, FLUTE, SNOUT, *and*
STARVELING

Bot. Are we all met?
Quin. Pat, pat; and here's a marvellous convenient place for our rehearsal. This green plot shall be our stage, this hawthorn-brake our tiring-house; and we will do it in action, as we will do it before the duke.
Bot. Peter Quince,—
Quin. What say'st thou, bully Bottom?
Bot. There are things in this comedy of "Pyramus and Thisbe," that will never please. First, Pyramus must draw a sword to kill himself, which the ladies cannot abide. How answer you that?
Snout. By'r lakin, a parlous fear.
Star. I believe, we must leave the killing out, when all is done.
Bot. Not a whit: I have a device to make all well. Write me a prologue; and let the prologue seem to say, we will do no harm with our swords, and that Pyramus is not killed indeed; and, for the more better assurance, tell them that I, Pyramus, am not Pyramus, but Bottom the weaver. This will put them out of fear.
Quin. Well, we will have such a prologue, and it shall be written in eight and six.
Bot. No, make it two more: let it be written in eight and eight.
Snout. Will not the ladies be afeard of the lion?
Star. I fear it, I promise you.
Bot. Masters, you ought to consider with yourselves: to bring in,—God shield us!—a lion among ladies, is a most dreadful thing; for there is not a more fearful wild-fowl than your lion living; and we ought to look to it.
Snout. Therefore another prologue must tell he is not a lion.
Bot. Nay, you must name his name, and half his face must be seen through the lion's neck; and he himself must speak through, saying thus, or to the same defect,—"Ladies," or, "Fair ladies;—I would wish you,"—or, "I would request you,"—or, "I would entreat you,—not to fear, not to tremble: my life for yours. If you think

I come hither as a lion, it were pity of my life: no, I am
no such thing; I am a man as other men are:"—and
there, indeed, let him name his name, and tell them plainly
he is Snug, the joiner.

Quin. Well, it shall be so. But there is two hard
things:—that is, to bring the moonlight into a chamber;
for, you know, Pyramus and Thisbe meet by moonlight.

Snug. Doth the moon shine that night we play our play?

Bot. A calendar, a calendar! look in the almanac;
find out moonshine, find out moonshine.

Quin. Yes, it doth shine that night.

Bot. Why, then you may leave a casement of the great
chamber-window, where we play, open; and the moon
may shine in at the casement.

Quin. Ay; or else one must come in with a bush of
thorns and a lantern, and say, he comes to disfigure, or
to present, the person of Moonshine.—Then, there is
another thing: we must have a wall in the great chamber;
for Pyramus and Thisbe, says the story, did talk through
the chink of a wall.

Snug. You can never bring in a wall.—What say you,
Bottom?

Bot. Some man or other must present Wall; and let
him have some plaster, or some loam, or some rough-cast
about him, to signify wall; and let him hold his fingers
thus, and through that cranny shall Pyramus and Thisbe
whisper.

Quin. If that may be, then all is well. Come, sit down,
every mother's son, and rehearse your parts. Pyramus,
you begin. When you have spoken your speech, enter
into that brake;—and so every one according to his cue.

Enter PUCK *behind*

Puck. What hempen home-spuns have we swaggering
　　　　here,
So near the cradle of the fairy queen?
What, a play toward? I'll be an auditor;
An actor too, perhaps, if I see cause.

Quin. Speak, Pyramus.—Thisbe, stand forth.

Pyr. "Thisbe, the flowers of odious savours sweet."—

Quin. "Odours," "odours."

Pyr. "Odours savours sweet:
So hath thy breath, my dearest Thisbe, dear.
But, hark, a voice! stay thou but here awhile,
And by and by I will to thee appear."　　　　　　*[Exit*

Puck. A stranger Pyramus than e'er played here! *[Exit*

This. Must I speak now?

Quin. Ay, marry, must you; for you must understand, he goes but to see a noise that he heard, and is to
come again.

This. "Most radiant Pyramus, most lily-white of hue,
Of colour like the red rose on triumphant brier
Most brisky juvenal, and eke most lovely Jew,
As true as truest horse, that yet would never tire,
I 'll meet thee, Pyramus, at Ninny's tomb."
    Quin. "Ninus' tomb," man. Why, you must not
speak that yet; that you answer to Pyramus. You speak
all your part at once, cues and all.—Pyramus, enter: your
cue is past; it is "never tire."

Re-enter PUCK, *and* BOTTOM, *with an ass's head*

This. O!—"As true as truest horse, that yet would
        never tire."
    Pyr. "If I were fair, Thisbe, I were only thine."—
    Quin. O monstrous! O strange! we are haunted—
Pray, masters!—fly, masters!—help!   [*Exeunt Clowns*
    Puck. I 'll follow you, I 'll lead you 'bout a round,
Through bog, through bush, through brake, through brier:
Sometime a horse I 'll be, sometime a hound,
    A hog, a headless bear, sometime a fire;
And neigh, and bark, and grunt, and roar, and burn,
Like horse, hound, hog, bear, fire, at every turn.   [*Exit*
    Bot. Why do they run away? this is a knavery of
them to make me afeard.

Re-enter SNOUT

    Snout. O Bottom! thou art changed! what do I see
on thee?   [*Exit*
    Bot. What do you see? you see an asshead of your
own, do you?

Re-enter QUINCE

    Quin. Bless thee, Bottom! bless thee! thou art
translated.   [*Exit*
    Bot. I see their knavery. This is to make an ass of
me; to fright me, if they could. But I will not stir from
this place, do what they can. I will walk up and down
here, and I will sing, that they shall hear I am not afraid.
        [*Sings*

> *The ousel-cock, so black of hue,*
>   *With orange-tawny bill;*
>*The throstle with his note so true,*
>   *The wren with little quill;*—

    Tita. [*Awaking*] What angel wakes me from my
flowery bed?

>*Bot.*   *The finch, the sparrow, and the lark;*
>   *The plain-song cuckoo gray,*
>*Whose note full many a man doth mark,*
>   *And dares not answer, nay;*—

152

for, indeed, who would set his wit to so foolish a bird? who
would give a bird the lie, though he cry "cuckoo" never so?

Tita. I pray thee, gentle mortal, sing again:
Mine ear is much enamoured of thy note;
So is mine eye enthrallèd to thy shape;
And thy fair virtue's force, perforce, doth move me,
On the first view, to say, to swear, I love thee.

Bot. Methinks, mistress, you should have little reason
for that: and yet, to say the truth, reason and love keep
little company together now-a-days:—the more the pity,
that some honest neighbours will not make them friends.
Nay, I can gleek upon occasion.

Tita. Thou art as wise as thou art beautiful.

Bot. Not so, neither; but if I had wit enough to get
out of this wood, I have enough to serve mine own turn.

Tita. Out of this wood do not desire to go:
Thou shalt remain here, whether thou wilt or no.
I am a spirit of no common rate,—
The summer still doth tend upon my state,—
And I do love thee: therefore, go with me;
I'll give thee fairies to attend on thee;
And they shall fetch thee jewels from the deep,
And sing while thou on pressèd flowers dost sleep:
And I will purge thy mortal grossness so,
That thou shalt like an airy spirit go.—
Pease-blossom! Cobweb! Moth! and Mustard-seed!

Enter Four Fairies

First Fai. Ready.
Sec. Fai.   And I.
Third Fai.   And I.
Fourth Fai.   Where shall we go?

Tita. Be kind and courteous to this gentleman:
Hop in his walks, and gambol in his eyes;
Feed him with apricocks, and dewberries,
With purple grapes, green figs, and mulberries,
The honey-bags steal from the humble-bees,
And for night-tapers crop their waxen thighs,
And light them at the fiery glow-worm's eyes,
To have my love to bed, and to arise;
And pluck the wings from painted butterflies,
To fan the moonbeams from his sleeping eyes.
Nod to him, elves, and do him courtesies.

First Fai. Hail, mortal!
Sec. Fai. Hail!
Third Fai. Hail!
Four Fai. Hail!

Bot. I cry your worships mercy, heartily.—I beseech
your worship's name.

Cob. Cobweb.

Bot. I shall desire you of more acquaintance, good
Master Cobweb. If I cut my finger, I shall make bold with
you. Your name, honest gentleman?

Peas. Pease-blossom.

Bot. I pray you, commend me to Mistress Squash, your
mother, and to Master Peascod, your father. Good Master
Pease-blossom, I shall desire you of more acquaintance too.
—Your name, I beseech you, sir?

Mus. Mustard-seed.

Bot. Good Master Mustard-seed, I know your patience
well: that same cowardly, giant-like ox-beef hath de-
voured many a gentleman of your house. I promise you,
your kindred hath made my eyes water ere now. I desire
you more acquaintance, good Master Mustard-seed.

Tita. Come, wait upon him; lead him to my bower.
The moon, methinks, looks with a watery eye;
And when she weeps, weeps every little flower,
Lamenting some enforcéd chastity.
Tie up my love's tongue, bring him silently.   [*Exeunt*

Scene II.—Another Part of the Wood

Enter Oberon

Obe. I wonder, if Titania be awaked;
Then, what it was that next came in her eye,
Which she must dote on in extremity.
Here comes my messenger.

Enter Puck

How now, mad spirit?
What night-rule now about this haunted grove?

Puck. My mistress with a monster is in love.
Near to her close and consecrated bower,
While she was in her dull and sleeping hour,
A crew of patches, rude mechanicals,
That work for bread upon Athenian stalls,
Were met together to rehearse a play,
Intended for great Theseus' nuptial day.
The shallowest thick-skin of that barren sort,
Who Pyramus presented in their sport,
Forsook his scene, and entered in a brake,
When I did him at this advantage take;
And ass's nowl I fixéd on his head:
Anon, his Thisbe must be answeréd.
And forth my mimic comes. When they him spy
As wild geese that the creeping fowler eye,
Or russet-pated choughs, many in sort,
Rising and cawing at the gun's report,
Sever themselves, and madly sweep the sky,
So, at his sight, away his fellows fly,

And, at our stamp, here o'er and o'er one falls;
He murder cries, and help from Athens calls.
Their sense thus weak, lost with their fears thus strong,
Made senseless things begin to do them wrong;
For briers and thorns at their apparel snatch;
Some, sleeves,—some, hats,—from yielders all things catch.
I led them on in this distracted fear,
And left sweet Pyramus translated there:
When in that moment—so it came to pass—
Titania waked, and straightway loved an ass.
   Obe.   This falls out better than I could devise.
But hast thou yet latched the Athenian's eyes
With the love-juice, as I did bid thee do?
   Puck.   I took him sleeping—that is finished too—
And the Athenian woman by his side,
That, when he waked, of force she must be eyed.

Enter DEMETRIUS *and* HERMIA

   Obe.   Stand close; this is the same Athenian.
   Puck.   This is the woman; but not this the man.
   Dem.   O, why rebuke you him that loves you so?
Lay breath so bitter on your bitter foe.
   Her.   Now I but chide; but I should use thee worse,
For thou, I fear, hast given me cause to curse,
If thou hast slain Lysander in his sleep,
Being o'er shoes in blood, plunge in knee deep,
And kill me too.
The sun was not so true unto the day
As he to me.   Would he have stolen away
From sleeping Hermia? I 'll believe as soon
This whole earth may be bored, and that the moon
May through the centre creep, and so displease
Her brother's noontide with the Antipodes.
It cannot be but thou has murdered him;
So should a murderer look, so dead, so grim.
   Dem.   So should the murdered look, and so should I,
Pierced through the heart with your stern cruelty;
Yet you, the murderer, look as bright, as clear,
As yonder Venus in her glimmering sphere.
   Her.   What 's this to my Lysander? where is he?
Ah, good Demetrius, wilt thou give him me?
   Dem.   I had rather give his carcass to my hounds.
   Her.   Out, dog! out, cur! thou driv'st me past the bounds
Of maiden's patience.   Hast thou slain him then?
Henceforth be never numbered among men!
O, once tell true, tell true, e'en for my sake!
Durst thou have looked upon him, being awake,
And hast thou killed him sleeping? O brave touch!
Could not a worm, an adder, do so much?

155

An adder did it; for with double tongue
Than thine, thou serpent, never adder stung.
   Dem.   You spend your passion on a misprised mood:
I am not guilty of Lysander's blood;
Nor is he dead, for aught that I can tell.
   Her.   I pray thee, tell me then, that he is well.
   Dem.   An if I could, what should I get therefore?
   Her.   A privilege never to see me more.—
And from thy hated presence part I so;
See me no more, whether he be dead or no.   *[Exit*
   Dem.   There is no following her in this fierce vein:
Here, therefore, for a while I will remain.
So sorrow's heaviness doth heavier grow
For debt that bankrupt sleep doth sorrow owe;
Which now in some slight measure it will pay,
If for his tender here I make some stay.   *[Lies down*
   Obe.   What hast thou done? thou hast mistaken quite,
And laid the love-juice on some true-love's sight:
Of thy misprision must perforce ensue
Some true-love turned, and not a false turned true.
   Puck.   Then fate o'errules, that, one man holding troth,
A million fail, confounding oath on oath.
   Obe.   About the wood go swifter than the wind,
And Helena of Athens look thou find:
All fancy-sick she is, and pale of cheer
With sighs of love, that cost the fresh blood dear.
By some illusion see thou bring her here:
I 'll charm his eyes against she do appear.
   Puck.   I go, I go; look how I go,—
Swifter than arrow from the Tartar's bow.   *[Exit*
   Obe.   Flower of this purple die,
         Hit with Cupid's archery,
            [Squeezes the flower on Demetrius's eyelids
         Sink in apple of his eye!
         When his love he doth espy,
         Let her shine as gloriously
         As the Venus of the sky.—
         When thou wak'st, if she be by,
         Beg of her for remedy.

Re-enter PUCK

   Puck.   Captain of our fairy band,
         Helena is here at hand;
         And the youth, mistook by me,
         Pleading for a lover's fee.
         Shall we their fond pageant see?—
         Lord, what fools these mortals be!
   Obe.   Stand aside: the noise they make
         Will cause Demetrius to awake.

Puck. Then will two at once woo one,—
That must needs be sport alone;
And those things do best please me
That befall preposterously.

Enter LYSANDER *and* HELENA

Lys. Why should you think that I should woo in scorn?
Scorn and derision never come in tears:
Look, when I vow, I weep; and vows so born,
In their nativity all truth appears.
How can these things in me seem scorn to you,
Bearing the badge of faith to prove them true?
Hel. You do advance your cunning more and more.
When truth kills truth, O devilish-holy fray!
These vows are Hermia's: will you give her o'er?
Weigh oath with oath, and you will nothing weigh:
Your vows, to her and me, put in two scales,
Will even weigh, and both as light as tales.
Lys. I had no judgment, when to her I swore.
Hel. Nor none, in my mind, now you give her o'er.
Lys. Demetrius loves her, and he loves not you.
Dem. [*Awaking*] O Helen, goddess, nymph, perfect, divine!
To what, my love, shall I compare thine eyne?
Crystal is muddy. O, how ripe in show
Thy lips, those kissing cherries, tempting grow!
That pure congealéd white, high Taurus' snow,
Fanned with the eastern wind, turns to a crow,
When thou hold'st up thy hand. O, let me kiss
This pureness of pure white, this seal of bliss!
Hel. O spite! O hell! I see, you all are bent
To set against me, for your merriment:
If you were civil and knew courtesy
You would not do me thus much injury.
Can you not hate me, as I know you do,
But you must join in souls to mock me too?
If you were men, as men you are in show,
You would not use a gentle lady so;
To vow, and swear, and superpraise my parts,
When I am sure you hate me with your hearts.
You both are rivals, and love Hermia;
And now both rivals, to mock Helena:
A trim exploit, a manly enterprise,
To conjure tears up in a poor maid's eyes
With your derision! none of noble sort
Would so offend a virgin, and extort
A poor soul's patience, all to make you sport.
Lys. You are unkind, Demetrius; be not so;
For you love Hermia; this you know I know:
And here, with all good will, with all my heart,

In Hermia's love I yield you up my part;
And yours of Helena to me bequeath,
Whom I do love, and will do till my death.
    Hel.   Never did mockers waste more idle breath.
    Dem.   Lysander, keep thy Hermia; I will none:
If e'er I loved her, all that love is gone.
My heart to her but as guest-wise sojourned,
And now to Helen is it home returned,
There to remain.
    Lys.   Helen, it is not so.
    Dem.   Disparage not the faith thou dost not know,
Lest to thy peril thou aby it dear.—
Look, where thy love comes; yonder is thy dear.

Re-enter HERMIA

    Her.   Dark night, that from the eye his function takes,
The ear more quick of apprehension makes;
Wherein it doth impair the seeing sense,
It pays the hearing double recompense.—
Thou art not by mine eye, Lysander, found;
Mine ear, I thank it, brought me to thy sound.
But why unkindly didst thou leave me so?
    Lys.   Why should he stay, whom love doth press to go?
    Her.   What love could press Lysander from my side?
    Lys.   Lysander's love, that would not let him bide,
Fair Helena, who more engilds the night
Than all yon fiery O's and eyes of light.
Why seek'st thou me? could not this make thee know,
The hate I bear thee made me leave thee so?
    Her.   You speak not as you think: it cannot be.
    Hel.   Lo, she is one of this confederacy!
Now I perceive they have conjoined all three,
To fashion this false sport in spite of me.
Injurious Hermia! most ungrateful maid!
Have you conspired, have you with these contrived
To bait me with this foul derision?
Is all the counsel that we two have shared,
The sisters' vows, the hours that we have spent,
When we have chid the hasty-footed time
For parting us,—O, and is all forgot?
All school-days' friendship, childhood innocence?
We, Hermia, like two artificial gods,
Have with our neelds created both one flower,
Both on one sampler, sitting on one cushion,
Both warbling of one song, both in one key,
As if our hands, our sides, voices, and minds,
Had been incorporate. So we grew together,
Like to a double cherry, seeming parted,
But yet an union in partition;

Two lovely berries moulded on one stem;
So, with two seeming bodies, but one heart;
Two of the first, like coats in heraldry,
Due but to one, and crownéd with one crest.
And will you rend our ancient love asunder,
To join with men in scorning your poor friend?
It is not friendly, 't is not maidenly:
Our sex, as well as I, may chide you for 't,
Though I alone do feel the injury.
    Her.   I am amazéd at your passionate words.
I scorn you not: it seems that you scorn me.
    Hel.   Have you not set Lysander, as in scorn,
To follow me, and praise my eyes and face?
And made your other love, Demetrius,—
Who even but now did spurn me with his foot,—
To call me goddess, nymph, divine, and rare,
Precious, celestial?   Wherefore speaks he this
To her he hates? and wherefore doth Lysander
Deny your love, so rich within his soul,
And tender me, forsooth, affection,
But by your setting on, by your consent?
What though I be not so in grace as you,
So hung upon with love, so fortunate;
But miserable most to love unloved?
This you should pity rather than despise.
    Her.   I understand not what you mean by this.
    Hel.   Ay, do, perséver, counterfeit sad looks,
Make mouths upon me when I turn my back;
Wink at each other; hold the sweet jest up:
This sport, well carried, shall be chronicled.
If you have any pity, grace, or manners,
You would not make me such an argument.
But, fare ye well: 't is partly mine own fault,
Which death or absence soon shall remedy.
    Lys.   Stay, gentle Helena; hear my excuse:
My love, my life, my soul, fair Helena!
    Hel.   O excellent!
    Her.   Sweet, do not scorn her so.
    Dem.   If she cannot entreat, I can compel.
    Lys.   Thou canst compel no more than she entreat:
Thy threats have no more strength than her weak prayers.—
Helen, I love thee; by my life, I do:
I swear by that which I will lose for thee,
To prove him false that says I love thee not.
    Dem.   I say, I love thee more than he can do.
    Lys.   If thou say so, withdraw, and prove it too.
    Dem.   Quick, come,—
    Her.   Lysander, whereto tends all this?
    Lys.   Away, you Ethiop!
    Dem.   No, no; he will

Seem to break loose, take on, as he would follow,
But yet come not.—You are a tame man, go!
    Lys.   Hang off, thou cat, thou burr! vile thing, let loose,
Or I will shake thee from me like a serpent.
    Her. Why are you grown so rude? what change is this,
Sweet love?
    Lys.   Thy love? Out, tawny Tartar, out!
Out, loathéd medicine! O hated potion, hence!
    Her. Do you not jest?
    Hel.   Yes, sooth! and so do you!
    Lys. Demetrius, I will keep my word with thee.
    Dem. I would I had your bond; for I perceive
A weak bond holds you; I 'll not trust your word.
    Lys. What? should I hurt her, strike her, kill her
       dead!
Although I hate her, I 'll not harm her so.
    Her. What can you do me greater harm than hate?
Hate me? wherefore? O me, what news, my love?
Am not I Hermia? Are not you Lysander?
I am as fair now as I was erewhile.
Since night you loved me; yet, since night you left me.
Why, then you left me,—O, the gods forbid!—
In earnest, shall I say?
    Lys.   Ay, by my life;
And never did desire to see thee more.
Therefore, be out of hope, of question, doubt;
Be certain nothing truer: 't is no jest
That I do hate thee, and love Helena.
    Her. O me!—you juggler! you canker-blossom!
You thief of love! what have you come by night,
And stol'n my love's heart from him.
    Hel.   Fine, i' faith!
Have you no modesty, no maiden shame,
No touch of bashfulness? What, will you tear
Impatient answers from my gentle tongue?
Fie, fie! you counterfeit, you puppet, you!
    Her. "Puppet!" why, so; ay, that way goes the
       game:
Now I perceive that she hath made compare
Between our statures; she hath urged her height,
And with her personage, her tall personage,
Her height, forsooth, she hath prevailed with him.—
And are you grown so high in his esteem,
Because I am so dwarfish, and so low?
How low am I, thou painted maypole? speak:
How low am I? I am not yet so low
But that my nails can reach unto thine eyes.
    Hel. I pray you, though you mock me, gentlemen,
Let her not hurt me: I was never curst;
I have no gift at all in shrewishness;

I am a right maid for my cowardice:
Let her not strike me. You, perhaps, may think,
Because she is something lower than myself,
That I can match her.
    Her.   "Lower!" hark, again.
    Hel.   Good Hermia, do not be so bitter with me.
I evermore did love you, Hermia,
Did ever keep your counsels, never wronged you;
Save that, in love unto Demetrius,
I told him of your stealth unto this wood.
He followed you; for love, I followed him;
But he hath chid me hence, and threatened me
To strike me, spurn me, nay, to kill me too:
And now, so you will let me quiet go,
To Athens will I bear my folly back,
And follow you no further. Let me go:
You see how simple and how fond I am
    Her.   Why, get you gone. Who is 't tha hinders you?
    Hel.   A foolish heart, that I leave here behind.
    Her.   What, with Lysander?
    Hel.   With Demetrius.
    Lys.   Be not afraid: she shall not harm thee, Helena.
    Dem.   No, sir; she shall not, though you take her part.
    Hel.   O, when she 's angry, she is keen and shrewd.
She was a vixen, when she went to school;
And, though she be but little, she is fierce.
    Her.   "Little" again? nothing but "low" and
    "little!"—
Why will you suffer her to flout me thus?
Let me come to her.
    Lys.   Get you gone, you dwarf;
You minimus, of hindering knot-grass made;
You bead, you acorn.
    Dem.   You are too officious
In her behalf that scorns your services.
Let her alone; speak not of Helena;
Take not her part; for if thou dost intend
Never so little show of love to her,
Thou shalt aby it.
    Lys.   Now she holds me not;
Now follow, if thou dar'st, to try whose right,
Of thine or mine, is most in Helena.
    Dem.   Follow? nay, I'll go with thee, cheek by jole.
                      [*Exeunt Lysander and Demetrius*
    Her.   You, mistress, all this coil is 'long of you.
Nay, go not back.
    Hel.   I will not trust you, I,
Nor longer stay in your curst company.
Your hands than mine are quicker for a fray;
My legs are longer though, to run away.   [*Exit*

Her. I am amazed, and know not what to say.   [*Exit*
Obe. This is thy negligence: still thou mistak'st,
Or else committ'st thy knaveries wilfully.
    Puck. Believe me, king of shadows, I mistook.
Did not you tell me, I should know the man
By the Athenian garments he had on?
And so far blameless proves my enterprise,
That I have 'nointed an Athenian's eyes:
And so far am I glad it so did sort,
As this their jangling I esteem a sport.
    Obe. Thou seest, these lovers seek a place to fight:
Hie therefore, Robin, overcast the night;
The starry welkin cover thou anon
With drooping fog, as black as Acheron;
And lead these testy rivals so astray,
As one come not within another's way.
Like to Lysander sometime frame thy tongue,
Then stir Demetrius up with bitter wrong;
And sometime rail thou like Demetrius;
And from each other look thou lead them thus,
Till 'oer their brows death-counterfeiting sleep
With leaden legs and batty wings doth creep:
Then crush this herb into Lysander's eye;
Whose liquor hath this virtuous property,
To take from thence all error with his might,
And make his eyeballs roll with wonted sight.
When they next wake, all this derision
Shall seem a dream and fruitless vision;
And back to Athens shall the lovers wend,
With league whose date till death shall never end.
Whiles I in this affair do thee employ,
I 'll to my queen, and beg her Indian boy;
And then I will her charméd eye release
From monster's view, and all things shall be peace.
    Puck. My fairy lord, this must be done with haste,
For night's swift dragons cut the clouds full fast,
And yonder shines Aurora's harbinger,
At whose approach, ghosts, wandering here and there,
Troop home to churchyards; damnéd spirits all,
That in crossways and floods have burial,
Already to their wormy beds are gone;
For fear lest day should look their shames upon,
They wilfully themselves exile from light
And must for aye consort with black-browed night.
    Obe. But we are spirits of another sort.
I with the morning's love have oft made sport;
And, like a forester, the groves may tread,
Even till the eastern gate, all fiery-red,
Opening on Neptune with fair blesséd beams,
Turns into yellow gold his salt green streams.

But, notwithstanding, haste; make no delay:
We may effect this business yet ere day.   [*Exit*

   Puck.   Up and down, up and down,
          I will lead them up and down:
          I am feared in field and town;
          Goblin, lead them up and down.
Here comes one.

Re-enter LYSANDER

   Lys. Where art thou, proud Demetrius? speak thou now.
   Puck. Here, villain! drawn and ready.
          Where art thou?
   Lys. I will be with thee straight.
   Puck.   Follow me then
To plainer ground.   [*Exit Lysander, as following the voice*

Re-enter DEMETRIUS

   Dem.   Lysander, speak again.
Thou runaway, thou coward, art thou fled?
Speak! In some bush? Where dost thou hide thy head?
   Puck. Thou coward, art thou bragging to the stars,
Telling the bushes that thou look'st for wars,
And wilt not come? Come, recreant; come, thou child;
I'll whip thee with a rod.   He is defiled,
That draws a sword on thee.
   Dem.   Yea; art thou there?
   Puck. Follow my voice: we'll try no manhood here.
                            [*Exeunt*

Re-enter LYSANDER

   Lys. He goes before me, and still dares me on;
When I come where he calls, then he is gone.
The villain is much lighter-heeled than I:
I followed fast, but faster he did fly,
That fallen am I in dark uneven way,
And here will rest me. [*Lies down*]   Come, thou gentle day!
For if but once thou show me thy grey light,
I'll find Demetrius, and revenge this spite.   [*Sleeps*

Re-enter PUCK and DEMETRIUS

   Puck. Ho, ho, ho, ho! Coward, why com'st thou not?
   Dem. Abide me, if thou dar'st; for well I wot,
Thou runn'st before me, shifting every place,
And dar'st not stand, nor look me in the face.
Where art thou now?
   Puck.   Come hither: I am here.
   Dem. Nay, then, thou mock'st me. Thou shalt buy
          this dear,
If ever I thy face by day-light see:
Now, go thy way. Faintness constraineth me
To measure out my length on this cold bed.
By day's approach look to be visited. [*Lies down and sleeps*

Re-enter HELENA

Hel.   O weary night, O long and tedious night,
  Abate thy hours: shine, comforts, from the east,
That I may back to Athens, by day-light,
  From these that my poor company detest.
And sleep that sometimes shuts up sorrow's eye,
Steal me awhile from mine own company.   [*Sleeps*
Puck.   Yet but three? Come one more;
      Two of both kinds make up four.
      Here she comes, curst and sad.
      Cupid is a knavish lad,
      Thus to make poor females mad.

Re-enter HERMIA

Her.   Never so weary, never so in woe,
  Bedabbled with the dew, and torn with briers:
I can no further crawl, no further go:
  My legs can keep no pace with my desires.
Here will I rest me till the break of day.
Heaven shield Lysander if they mean a fray.   [*Lies down*
Puck.   On the ground
          Sleep sound:
          I'll apply
          To your eye,
      Gentle lover, remedy.
              [*Squeezing the juice on Lysander's eyes*
          When thou wak'st,
          Thou tak'st
          True delight
          In the sight
      Of thy former lady's eye:
      And the country proverb known,
      That every man should take his own,
      In your waking shall be shown:
          Jack shall have Jill;
          Nought shall go ill;
      The man shall have his mare again,
          And all shall be well.   [*Exit Puck*

ACT FOUR

SCENE I.—The Wood. DEMETRIUS, HELENA, LYSANDER,
          HERMIA, *lying asleep*

Enter TITANIA *and* BOTTOM, *Fairies attending;* OBERON
          behind unseen

Tita.   Come, sit thee down upon this flowery bed,
While I thy amiable cheeks do coy,
And stick musk-roses in thy sleek smooth head,
And kiss thy fair large ears, my gentle joy.

Bot. Where 's Pease-blossom?

Peas. Ready.

Bot. Scratch my head, Pease-blossom.—Where's Monsieur Cobweb?

Cob. Ready.

Bot. Monsieur Cobweb, good monsieur, get your weapons in your hand, and kill me a red-hipped humble-bee, on the top of a thistle; and, good monsieur, bring me the honey-bag. Do not fret yourself too much in the action, monsieur; and, good monsieur, have a care the honey-bag break not; I would be loath to have you over-flown with a honey-bag, signior.—Where's Monsieur Mustard-seed?

Must. Ready.

Bot. Give me your neif, Monsieur Mustard-seed. Pray you, leave your courtesy, good monsieur.

Must. What's your will?

Bot. Nothing, good monsieur, but to help Cavalery Pease-blossom to scratch. I must to the barber's, monsieur; for, methinks, I am marvellous hairy about the face, and I am such a tender ass, if my hair do but tickle me, I must scratch.

Tita. What, wilt thou hear some music, my sweet love?

Bot. I have a reasonable good ear in music: let's have the tongs and the bones.

[Music, Tongs, Rural Music

Tita. Or, say, sweet love, what thou desir'st to eat.

Bot. Truly a peck of provender; I could munch your good dry oats. Methinks, I have a great desire to a bottle of hay; good hay, sweet hay, hath no fellow.

Tita. I have a venturous fairy that shall seek
The squirrel's hoard, and fetch thee thence new nuts.

Bot. I had rather have a handful or two of dried peas. But, I pray you, let none of your people stir me: I have an exposition of sleep come upon me.

Tita. Sleep thou, and I will wind thee in my arms.
Fairies, be gone, and be all ways away.   *[Exeunt Fairies*
So doth the woodbine the sweet honey-suckle
Gently entwist; the female ivy so
Enrings the barky fingers of the elm.
O, how I love thee! how I dote on thee!   *[They sleep*

Enter PUCK

Obe. [*Advancing*] Welcome, good Robin.   Seest thou this sweet sight?
Her dotage now I do begin to pity:
For, meeting her of late behind the wood,
Seeking sweet favours for this hateful fool,
I did upbraid her, and fall out with her;
For she his hairy temples then had rounded
With coronet of fresh and fragrant flowers;

And that same dew, which sometime on the buds
Was wont to swell like round and orient pearls,
Stood now within the pretty flowerets' eyes,
Like tears that did their own disgrace bewail.
When I had at my pleasure taunted her,
And she in mild terms begged my patience,
I then did ask of her her changeling child;
Which straight she gave me, and her fairy sent
To bear him to my bower in fairy land.
And now I have the boy, I will undo
This hateful imperfection of her eyes:
And, gentle Puck, take this transforméd scalp
From off the head of this Athenian swain,
That, he awaking when the other do,
May all to Athens back again repair,
And think no more of this night's accidents,
But as the fierce vexation of a dream:—
But first I will release the fairy queen.

                [*Touching her eyes with an herb*

       Be, as thou wast wont to be;
       See, as thou wast wont to see:
       Dian's bud o'er Cupid's flower
       Hath such force and blessed power.
Now, my Titania, wake you, my sweet queen!
  Tita. My Oberon! what visions have I seen!
Methought, I was enamoured of an ass.
  Obe. There lies your love.
  Tita.   How came these things to pass?
O, how mine eyes do loathe his visage now!
  Obe. Silence awhile.—Robin, take off this head.—
Titania, music call, and strike more dead
Than common sleep of all these five the sense.
  Tita. Music, ho, music, such as charmeth sleep!

                     [*Still music*
  Puck. Now, when thou wak'st, with thine own fool's
      eyes peep.   [*Takes off the ass's head*
  Obe. Sound, music! Come, my queen, take hands with
      me,
And rock the ground whereon these sleepers be.

                    [*Fairy Dance*
Now thou and I are new in amity,
And will to-morrow midnight solemnly
Dance in Duke Theseus' house triumphantly,
And bless it to all fair posterity.
There shall the pairs of faithful lovers be
Wedded, with Theseus, all in jollity.
  Puck. Fairy king, attend, and mark,
         I do hear the morning lark.
  Obe. Then, my queen, in silence sad,
         Trip we after the night's shade;

We the globe can compass soon,
Swifter than the wandering moon.
Tita.   Come, my lord, and in our flight
Tell me how it came this night,
That I sleeping here was found
With these mortals on the ground.
[*Exeunt Fairies.   Sleepers lie still.   Horns sound within*

Enter THESEUS, HIPPOLYTA, EGEUS, *and Train*

The.   Go, one of you, find out the forester,
For now our observation is performed;
And since we have the vaward of the day,
My love shall hear the music of my hounds.—
Uncouple in the western valley; let them go!—
Despatch, I say, and find the forester.—
We will, fair queen, up to the mountain's top,
And mark the musical confusion
Of hounds and echo in conjunction.
Hip.   I was with Hercules and Cadmus once,
When, in a wood of Crete, they bayed the bear
With hounds of Sparta: never did I hear
Such gallant chiding; for, besides the groves,
The skies, the fountains, every region near
Seemed all one mutual cry.   I never heard
So musical a discord, such sweet thunder.
The.   My hounds are bred out of the Spartan kind,
So flewed, so sanded; and their heads are hung
With ears that sweep away the morning dew;
Crook-kneed, and dew-lapped like Thessalian bulls;
Slow in pursuit, but matched in mouth like bells,
Each under each.   A cry more tuneable
Was never halloo'd to, nor cheered with horn,
In Crete, in Sparta, nor in Thessaly:
Judge, when you hear.—But, soft! what nymphs are these?
Ege.   My lord, this is my daughter here asleep;
And this, Lysander; this Demetrius is;
This Helena, old Nedar's Helena:
I wonder of their being here together.
The.   No doubt, they rose up early, to observe
The rite of May, and, hearing our intent,
Came here in grace of our solemnity.—
But speak, Egeus, is not this the day
That Hermia should give answer of her choice?
Ege.   It is, my lord.
The.   Go, bid the huntsmen wake them with their horns.
[*Horns, and shout within.   Lysander, Hermia, Demetrius,*
and Helena wake and start up.
The.   Good morrow, friends.   St. Valentine is past;
Begin these wood-birds but to couple now?

Lys.   Pardon, my lord.   *[He and the rest kneel to Theseus*
The.   I pray you all, stand up.
I know, you two are rival enemies:
How comes this gentle concord in the world,
That hatred is so far from jealousy,
To sleep by hate, and fear no enmity?
    Lys.   My lord, I shall reply amazedly,
Half 'sleep, half waking: but as yet, I swear,
I cannot truly say how I came here;
But, as I think—for truly would I speak,—
And now I do bethink me, so it is,—
I came with Hermia hither: our intent
Was to be gone from Athens, where we might be
Without the peril of the Athenian law.
    Ege.   Enough, enough! my lord, you have enough:
I beg the law, the law, upon his head.
They would have stol'n away, they would, Demetrius,
Thereby to have defeated you and me;
You, of your wife, and me, of my consent,
Of my consent, that she should be your wife.
    Dem.   My lord, fair Helen told me of their stealth,
Of this their purpose hither to this wood;
And I in fury hither followed them,
Fair Helena in fancy following me.
But, my good lord, I wot not by what power—
But by some power it is—my love to Hermia,
Melted as doth the snow, seems to me now
As the remembrance of an idle gaud
Which in my childhood I did dote upon;
And all the faith, the virtue of my heart,
The object and the pleasure of mine eye,
Is only Helena.   To her, my lord,
Was I betrothed ere I saw Hermia:
But, like a sickness, did I loathe this food;
But, as in health come to my natural taste,
Now do I wish it, love it, long for it,
And will for evermore be true to it.
    The.   Fair lovers, you are fortunately met:
Of this discourse we more will hear anon.—
Egeus, I will overbear your will,
For in the temple, by and by, with us,
These couples shall eternally be knit.
And, for the morning now is something worn,
Our purposed hunting shall be set aside.
Away, with us, to Athens!   Three and three,
We'll hold a feast in great solemnity.—
Come, Hippolyta.
               [Exeunt Theseus, Hippolyta, Egeus, and Train
    Dem.   These things seem small and undistinguishable,
Like far-off mountains turnéd into clouds.

Her.   Methinks, I see these things with parted eye,
When every thing seems double.
    Hel.   So methinks:
And I have found Demetrius, like a jewel,
Mine own, and not mine own.
    Dem.   It seems to me
That yet we sleep, we dream.—Do not you think
The duke was here, and bid us follow him?
    Her.   Yea, and my father.
    Hel.   And Hippolyta.
    Lys.   And he did bid us follow to the temple.
    Dem.   Why then, we are awake.   Let 's follow him;
And by the way let us recount our dreams.   [*Exeunt*
    Bot.   [*Waking*]   When my cue comes, call me, and I
will answer:—my next is, "Most fair Pyramus."—Hey, ho!
—Peter Quince!   Flute, the bellows-mender!   Snout, the
tinker!   Starveling!   God's my life, stolen hence, and left
me asleep.—I have had a most rare vision.   I have had a
dream—past the wit of man to say what dream it was:
man is but an ass, if he go about to expound this dream.
Methought I was—there is no man can tell what.   Methought I was, and methought I had—but man is but a
patched fool, if he will offer to say what methought I had.
The eye of man hath not heard, the ear of man hath not
seen, man's hand is not able to taste, his tongue to conceive,
nor his heart to report, what my dream was.   I will get
Peter Quince to write a ballad of this dream: it shall be
called Bottom's Dream, because it hath no bottom; and
I will sing it in the latter end of a play, before the duke:
peradventure, to make it the more gracious, I shall sing it
at her death.   [*Exit*

SCENE II.—Athens.   A Room in QUINCE'S House

Enter QUINCE, FLUTE, SNOUT, *and* STARVELING

    Quin.   Have you sent to Bottom's house? is he come
home yet?
    Star.   He cannot be heard of.   Out of doubt, he is
transported.
    Flu.   If he come not, then the play is marred.   It goes
not forward, doth it?
    Quin.   It is not possible: you have not a man in all
Athens able to discharge Pyramus, but he.
    Flu.   No; he hath simply the best wit of any handicraft
man in Athens.
    Quin.   Yea, and the best person too; and he is a very
paramour for a sweet voice.
    Flu.   You must say, paragon: a paramour is, God bless
us! a thing of naught.

Enter Snug

Snug. Masters, the duke is coming from the temple, and there is two or three lords and ladies more married. If our sport had gone forward, we had all been made men.
Flu. O sweet bully Bottom! Thus hath he lost six-pence a day during his life; he could not have 'scaped sixpence a day: an the duke had not given him sixpence a day for playing Pyramus, I 'll be hanged; he would have deserved it: sixpence a day in Pyramus, or nothing.

Enter Bottom

Bot. Where are these lads? where are these hearts?
Quin. Bottom!—O most courageous day! O most happy hour!
Bot. Masters, I am to discourse wonders; but ask me not what; for, if I tell you, I am no true Athenian, I will tell you everything, right as it fell out.
Quin. Let us hear, sweet Bottom.
Bot. Not a word of me. All that I will tell you is, that the duke hath dined. Get your apparel together, good strings to your beards, new ribbons to your pumps: meet presently at the palace; every man look o'er his part; for the short and the long is, our play is preferred. In any case, let Thisbe have clean linen, and let not him that plays the lion pare his nails, for, they shall hang out for the lion's claws. And, most dear actors, eat no onions, nor garlic, for we are to utter sweet breath, and I do not doubt, but to hear them say, it is a sweet comedy. No more words: away! go! away!   [*Exeunt*

ACT FIVE

Scene I.—The Same. An Apartment in the Palace of Theseus

Enter Theseus, Hippolyta, Philostrate, *Lords, and Attendants*

Hip. 'T is strange, my Theseus, that these lovers speak of.
The. More strange than true: I never may believe
These antick fables nor these fairy toys:
Lovers and madmen have such seething brains,
Such shaping fantasies, that apprehend
More than cool reason ever comprehends.
The lunatic, the lover, and the poet
Are of imagination all compact:
One sees more devils than vast hell can hold;
That is the madman: the lover, all as frantic,
Sees Helen's beauty in a brow of Egypt:

The poet's eye, in a fine frenzy rolling
Doth glance from heaven to earth, from earth to heaven;
And, as imagination bodies forth
The forms of things unknown, the poet's pen
Turns them to shapes, and gives to airy nothing
A local habitation and a name.
Such tricks hath strong imagination,
That, if it would but apprehend some joy,
It comprehends some bringer of that joy:
Or in the night, imagining some fear,
How easy is a bush supposed a bear?
    Hip.   But all the story of the night told over,
And all their minds transfigured so together,
More witnesseth than fancy's images,
And grows to something of great constancy;
But, howsoever, stranger, and admirable.
    The.   Here comes the lovers, full of joy and mirth.

Enter LYSANDER, HERMIA, DEMETRIUS, *and* HELENA

Joy, gentle friends! joy, and fresh days of love,
Accompany your hearts!
    Lys.   More than to us
Wait in your royal walks, your board, your bed!
    The.   Come now; what masques, what dances shall we
        have,
To wear away this long age of three hours
Between our after-supper and bed-time?
Where is our usual manager of mirth?
What revels are in hand?   Is there no play,
To ease the anguish of a torturing hour?
Call Philostrate.
    Phil.   Here, mighty Theseus.
    The.   Say, what abridgment have you for this evening?
What masque? what music?   How shall we beguile
The lazy time, if not with some delight?
    Phil.   There is a brief how many sports are ripe;
Make choice of which your highness will see first.
                             [Giving a paper
    The. [*Reads*] "The battle with the Centaurs, to be sung
By an Athenian eunuch to the harp."
We 'll none of that: that have I told my love,
In glory of my kinsman Hercules.
"The riot of the tipsy Bacchanals,
Tearing the Thracian singer in their rage."
That is an old device; and it was played
When I from Thebes came last a conqueror.
"The thrice three Muses mourning for the death
Of Learning, late deceased in beggary."
That is some satire, keen and critical,
Not sorting with a nuptial ceremony.

"A tedious brief scene of young Pyramus,
And his love Thisbe; very tragical mirth."
Merry and tragical! Tedious and brief!
That is, hot ice, and wonderous strange snow.
How shall we find the concord of this discord?
   Phil.   A play there is, my lord, some ten words long,
Which is as brief as I have known a play;
But by ten words, my lord, it is too long,
Which makes it tedious; for in all the play
There is not one word apt, one player fitted.
And tragical, my noble lord, it is,
For Pyramus therein doth kill himself.
Which when I saw rehearsed, I must confess,
Made mine eyes water; but more merry tears
The passion of loud laughter never shed.
   The.   What are they that do play it?
   Phil.   Hard-handed men, that work in Athens here,
Which never laboured in their minds till now,
And now have toiled their unbreathed memories
With this same play against your nuptial.
   The.   And we will hear it.
   Phil.   No, my noble lord;
It is not for you: I have heard it over,
And it is nothing, nothing in the world,
Unless you can find sport in their intents,
Extremely stretched and conned with cruel pain,
To do you service.
   The.   I will hear that play:
For never anything can be amiss
When simpleness and duty tender it.
Go, bring them in;—and take your places, ladies.
                              [Exit Philostrate
   Hip.   I love not to see wretchedness o'ercharged,
And duty in his service perishing.
   The.   Why, gentle sweet, you shall see no such thing.
   Hip.   He says, they can do nothing in this kind.
   The.   The kinder we, to give them thanks for nothing.
Our sport shall be to take what they mistake:
And what poor duty cannot reach to do,
Noble respect takes it in might, not merit.
Where I have come, great clerks have purposéd
To greet me with premeditated welcomes;
Where I have seen them shiver and look pale,
Make periods in the midst of sentences,
Throttle their practised accent in their fears,
And, in conclusion, dumbly have broke off,
Not paying me a welcome. Trust me, sweet,
Out of this silence yet I picked a welcome;
And in the modesty of fearful duty
I read as much as from the rattling tongue

Of saucy and audacious eloquence.
Love, therefore, and tongue-tied simplicity,
In least speak most, to my capacity.

Re-enter PHILOSTRATE

Phil.   So please your grace, the Prologue is addrest.
The.   Let him approach.   [*Flourish of Trumpets*

Enter the Prologue

Prol.   "If we offend, it is with our good will.
That you should think, we come not to offend,
But with good will.   To show our simple skill,
That is the true beginning of our end.
Consider then, we come but in despite.
We do not come as minding to content you,
Our true intent is.   All for your delight,
We are not here.   That you should here repent you,
The actors are at hand; and, by their show,
You shall know all that you are like to know."
    The.   This fellow doth not stand upon points.
    Lys.   He hath rid his prologue like a rough colt; he
knows not the stop.   A good moral, my lord: it is not
enough to speak, but to speak true.
    Hip.   Indeed, he hath played on this prologue like a
child on a recorder; a sound, but not in government.
    The.   His speech was like a tangled chain;
Nothing impaired, but all disordered.—
Who is next?

Enter PYRAMUS *and* THISBE.   *Wall, Moonshine, and Lion,
as in dumb-show*

Prol.   "Gentles, perchance, you wonder at this show;
    But wonder on, till truth make all things plain.
This man is Pyramus, if you would know;
    This beauteous lady Thisbe is, certain.

This man, with lime and rough-cast, doth present
    Wall, that vile Wall which did these lovers sunder;
And through Wall's chink, poor souls, they are content
    To whisper, at the which let no man wonder.

This man, with lantern, dog, and bush of thorn,
    Presenteth Moonshine; for, if you will know,
By moonshine did these lovers think no scorn
    To meet at Ninus' tomb, there, there to woo.

This grisly beast, which by name Lion hight,
The trusty Thisbe, coming first by night,
Did scare away, or rather did affright;

And, as she fled, her mantle she did fall,
  Which Lion vile with bloody mouth did stain.
Anon comes Pyramus, sweet youth and tall,
  And finds his trusty Thisbe's mantle slain:

Whereat with blade, with bloody blameful blade,
  He bravely broached his boiling bloody breast;
And Thisbe, tarrying in mulberry shade,
  His dagger drew, and died.   For all the rest,

Let Lion, Moonshine, Wall, and lovers twain,
At large discourse, while here they do remain."
  [*Exeunt Prologue, Pyramus, Thisbe, Lion, and Moonshine*
  The.   I wonder, if the lion be to speak.
  Dem.   No wonder, my lord: one lion may, when many
asses do.
  Wall.   "In this same interlude it doth befall,
That I, one Snout by name, present a wall;
And such a wall, as I would have you think,
That had in it a crannied hole, or chink,
Through which the lovers, Pyramus and Thisbe,
Did whisper often very secretly.
This lime, this rough-cast, and this stone, doth show
That I am that same wall; the truth is so;
And this the cranny is, right and sinister,
Through which the fearful lovers are to whisper."
  The.   Would you desire lime and hair to speak better?
  Dem.   It is the wittiest partition that ever I heard dis-
course, my lord.
  The.   Pyramus draws near the wall: silence!

Re-enter PYRAMUS

  Pyr.   "O grim-looked night! O night with hue so
          black!
O night, which ever art, when day is not!
O night! O night! alack, alack, alack!
I fear my Thisbe's promise is forgot.—
And thou, O wall! O sweet, O lovely wall,
That stand'st between her father's ground and mine;
Thou wall, O wall! O sweet and lovely wall!
Show me thy chink to blink through with mine eyne.
                    [*Wall holds up his fingers*
Thanks, courteous wall: Jove shield thee well for this!
But what see I?   No Thisbe do I see.
O wicked wall, through whom I see no bliss;
Cursed be thy stones for thus deceiving me!"
  The.   The wall, methinks, being sensible, should curse
again.
  Pyr.   No, in truth, sir, he should not.—"Deceiving me,"
is Thisbe's cue: she is to enter now, and I am to spy her

through the wall. You shall see, it will fall pat as I told
you.—Yonder she comes.

Re-enter THISBE

This. "O wall, full often hast thou heard my moans,
For parting my fair Pyramus and me:
My cherry lips have often kissed thy stones,
Thy stones with lime and hair knit up in thee."
Pyr. "I see a voice: now will I to the chink,
To spy an I can hear my Thisbe's face.
Thisbe!"
This. "My love! thou art my love, I think."
Pyr. "Think what thou wilt, I am thy lover's grace;
And like Limander am I trusty still."
This. "And I like Helen, till the Fates me kill."
Pyr. "Not Shafalus to Procrus was so true."
This. "As Shafalus to Procrus, I to you."
Pyr. "O! kiss me through the hole of this vile wall."
This. "I kiss the wall's hole, not your lips at all."
Pyr. "Wilt thou at Ninny's tomb meet me straight-
        way?"
This. "'Tide life, 'tide death, I come without delay."
Wall. "Thus have I, Wall, my part discharged so;
And, being done, thus Wall away doth go."
                              [*Exeunt Wall, Pyramus and Thisbe*
The. Now is the mural down between the two neigh-
bours.
Dem. No remedy, my lord, when walls are so wilful to
hear without warning.
Hip. This is the silliest stuff that e'er I heard.
The. The best in this kind are but shadows; and the
worst are no worse, if imagination amend them.
Hip. It must be your imagination then, and not theirs.
The. If we imagine no worse of them than they of them-
selves, they may pass for excellent men. Here come two
noble beasts in: a moon and a lion.

Enter Lion and Moonshine

Lion. "You, ladies, you, whose gentle hearts do fear
The smallest monstrous mouse that creeps on floor,
May now perchance both quake and tremble here,
When lion rough in wildest rage doth roar.
Then know, that I, one Snug the joiner am,
A lion fell, nor else no lion's dam:
For, if I should as lion come in strife
Into this place, 't were pity on my life."
The. A very gentle beast, and of a good conscience.
Dem. The very best at a beast, my lord, that e'er I saw.
Lys. This lion is a very fox for his valour.
The. True; and a goose for his discretion.

Dem. Not so, my lord; for his valour cannot carry his discretion, and the fox carries the goose.

The. His discretion, I am sure, cannot carry his valour, for the goose carries not the fox. It is well: leave it to his discretion, and let us listen to the moon.

Moon. "This lantern doth the hornéd moon present."

Dem. He should have worn the horns on his head.

The. He is no crescent, and his horns are invisible within the circumference.

Moon. "This lantern doth the hornéd moon present; Myself the man i' the moon do seem to be."

The. This is the greatest error of all the rest. The man should be put into the lantern: how is it else the man i' the moon?

Dem. He dares not come there for the candle; for, you see, it is already in snuff.

Hip. I am aweary of this moon: 'would, he would change!

The. It appears by his small light of discretion, that he is in the wane; but yet, in courtesy, in all reason, we must stay the time.

Lys. Proceed, Moon.

Moon. "All that I have to say is, to tell you, that the lantern is the moon; I, the man in the moon; this thorn-bush, my thorn-bush; and this dog, my dog."

Dem. Why, all these should be in the lantern; for all these are in the moon. But, silence! here comes Thisbe.

Re-enter THISBE

This. "This is old Ninny's tomb. Where is my love?"

Lion. "Oh———!" [*The Lion roars.—Thisbe runs off*

Dem. Well roared, Lion.

The. Well run, Thisbe.

Hip. Well shone, Moon.—Truly, the moon shines with a good grace. [*The Lion tears Thisbe's mantle, and exit*

The. Well moused, Lion.

Dem. And then came Pyramus.

Lys. And so the lion vanished.

Re-enter PYRAMUS

Pyr. "Sweet moon, I thank thee for thy sunny beams:
I thank thee, moon, for shining now so bright.
For, by thy gracious, golden, glittering streams,
    I trust to taste of truest Thisbe's sight.
        But stay;—O spite!—
        But mark, poor knight,
     What dreadful dole is here?
        Eyes, do you see?
        How can it be?
   O dainty duck! O dear!

Thy mantle good,
What, stained with blood!
Approach, ye Furies fell!
O Fates, come, come:
Cut thread and thrum;
Quail, crush, conclude, and quell!"

The. This passion, and the death of a dear friend, would
go near to make a man look sad.

Hip. Beshrew my heart, but I pity the man.

Pyr. "O, wherefore, Nature, didst thou lions frame,
Since lion vile hath here defloured my dear?
Which is—no, no—which was the fairest dame,
That lived, that loved, that liked, that looked with cheer.
Come, tears, confound;
Out, sword and wound
The pap of Pyramus:
Ay, that left pap,
Where heart doth hop:—   *[Stabs himself*
Thus die I, thus, thus, thus!
Now am I dead;
Now am I fled;
My soul is in the sky:
Tongue, lose thy light!
Moon, take thy flight!   *[Exit Moonshine*
Now die, die, die, die, die."   *[Dies*

Dem. No die, but an ace, for him; for he is but one.

Lys. Less than an ace, man, for he is dead; he is
nothing.

The. With the help of a surgeon, he might yet recover,
and yet prove an ass.

Hip. How chance Moonshine is gone, before Thisbe
comes back and finds her lover?

The. She will find him by starlight.—Here she comes,
and her passion ends the play.

Re-enter THISBE

Hip. Methinks, she should not use a long one for such a
Pyramus; I hope she will be brief.

Dem. A mote will turn the balance, which Pyramus,
which Thisbe, is the better; he for a man, God warrant us;
she for a woman, God bless us.

Lys. She hath spied him already with those sweet eyes.

Dem. And thus she moans, *videlicet ;—*

This. "Asleep, my love?
What, dead, my dove?
O Pyramus, arise!
Speak, speak!   Quite dumb?
Dead, dead?   A tomb
Must cover thy sweet eyes,

> These lily lips,
> This cherry nose,
> These yellow cowslip cheeks,
> Are gone, are gone!
> Lovers, make moan!
> His eyes were green as leeks.
> O Sisters Three,
> Come, come to me,
> With hands as pale as milk;
> Lay them in gore,
> Since you have shore
> With shears his thread of silk.
> Tongue, not a word:
> Come, trusty sword;
> Come, blade, my breast imbrue: [*Stabs herself*
> And farewell, friends.—
> Thus Thisbe ends:—
> Adieu, adieu, adieu."   [*Dies*

The. Moonshine and Lion are left to bury the dead.

Dem. Ay, and Wall too.

Bot. No, I assure you: the wall is down, that parted their fathers. Will it please you to see the epilogue, or to hear a Bergomask dance between two of our company.

The. No epilogue, I pray you; for your play needs no excuse. Never excuse; for when the players are all dead, there need none to be blamed. Marry, if he that write it had played Pyramus, and hanged himself in Thisbe's garter, it would have been a fine tragedy:—and so it is, truly; and very notably discharged. But come, your Bergomask: let your epilogue alone.   [*A dance*
The iron tongue of midnight hath told twelve.—
Lovers, to bed: 't is almost fairy time.
I fear we shall outsleep the coming morn,
As much as we this night have overwatched.
This palpable gross play hath well beguiled
The heavy gait of night.—Sweet friends, to bed.—
A fortnight hold we this solemnity
In nightly revels and new jollity.   [*Exeunt*

Enter PUCK *with a broom*

> *Puck.* Now the hungry lion roars,
> And the wolf behowls the moon,
> Whilst the heavy ploughman snores,
> All with weary task fordone.
> Now the wasted brands do glow,
> Whilst the screech-owl, screeching loud,
> Puts the wretch, that lies in woe,
> In remembrance of a shroud.
> Now it is the time of night,
> That the graves, all gaping wide,

Every one lets forth his sprite,
    In the church-way paths to glide:
And we fairies, that do run
    By the triple Hecate's team,
From the presence of the sun,
    Following darkness like a dream,
Now are frolic; not a mouse
Shall disturb this hallowed house:
I am sent with broom before,
To sweep the dust behind the door.

Enter OBERON *and* TITANIA, *with their Train*

Obe.   Through the house give glimmering light,
    By the dead and drowsy fire;
Every elf and fairy sprite
    Hop as light as bird from brier:
And this ditty, after me,
Sing and dance it trippingly.

Tita.   First, rehearse your song by rote,
To each word a warbling note:
Hand in hand, with fairy grace,
Will we sing, and bless this place.
                                    [*Song and dance*

Obe.   Now, until the break of day,
Through this house each fairy stray.
To the best bride-bed will we,
Which by us shall blessèd be;
And the issue there create
Ever shall be fortunate.
So shall all the couples three
Ever true in loving be;
And the blots of Nature's hand
Shall not in their issue stand;
Never mole, hare-lip, nor scar,
Nor mark prodigious, such as are
Despisèd in nativity,
Shall upon their children be.
With this field-dew consecrate,
Every fairy take his gait,
And each several chamber bless,
Through this palace, with sweet peace;
Ever shall 't in safety rest,
And the owner of it blest.
            Trip away;
            Make no stay;
Meet me all by break of day.
                        [*Exeunt Oberon, Titania, and Train*

Puck   If we shadows have offended,
Think but this, and all is mended,—
That you have but slumbered here,

179

While these visions did appear.
And this weak and idle theme,
No more yielding but a dream,
Gentles, do not reprehend:
If you pardon, we will mend.
And, as I 'm an honest Puck,
If we have unearnéd luck
Now to 'scape the serpent's tongue,
We will make amends ere long;
Else the Puck a liar call:
So, good night unto you all.
Give me your hands, if we be friends,
And Robin shall restore amends.   *[Exit*

MUCH ADO ABOUT NOTHING

DRAMATIS PERSONÆ

DON PEDRO, *prince of Aragon*
DON JOHN, *his bastard brother*
CLAUDIO, *a young lord of Florence*
BENEDICK, *a young lord of Padua*
LEONATO, *governor of Messina*
ANTONIO, *his brother*
BALTHAZAR, *attendant on Don Pedro*
BORACHIO }
CONRADE } *followers of Don John*
DOGBERRY }
VERGES } *two officers*
FRIAR FRANCIS
A Sexton
A Boy

HERO, *daughter to Leonato*
BEATRICE, *niece to Leonato*
MARGARET }
URSULA } *gentlewomen attending on Hero*

Messengers, Watchmen, and Attendants

SCENE.—*Messina*

MUCH ADO ABOUT NOTHING

ACT ONE

Scene I.—Before Leonato's House

Enter Leonato, Hero *and* Beatrice *with a Messenger*

Leon. I learn in this letter, that Don Pedro of Aragon comes this night to Messina.

Mess. He is very near by this: he was not three leagues off when I left him.

Leon. How many gentlemen have you lost in this action?

Mess. But few of any sort, and none of name.

Leon. A victory is twice itself, when the achiever brings home full numbers. I find here that Don Pedro hath bestowed much honour on a young Florentine called Claudio.

Mess. Much deserved on his part, and equally remembered by Don Pedro. He hath borne himself beyond the promise of his age, doing in the figure of a lamb the feats of a lion: he hath, indeed, better bettered expectation than you must expect of me to tell you how.

Leon. He hath an uncle here in Messina will be very much glad of it.

Mess. I have already delivered him letters, and there appears much joy in him; even so much, that joy could not show itself modest enough without a badge of bitterness.

Leon. Did he break out into tears?

Mess. In great measure.

Leon. A kind overflow of kindness: there are no faces truer than those that are so washed. How much better is it to weep at joy than to joy at weeping!

Beat. I pray you, is Signior Montanto returned from the wars or no?

Mess. I know none of that name, lady: there was none such in the army of any sort.

Leon. What is he that you ask for, niece?

Hero. My cousin means Signior Benedick of Padua.

Mess. O, he's returned and as pleasant as ever he was.

Beat. He set up his bills here in Messina, and challenged Cupid at the flight; and my uncle's fool, reading the challenge, subscribed for Cupid, and challenged him at the birdbolt.—I pray you, how many hath he killed and eaten in these wars? But how many hath he killed? for, indeed, I promised to eat all of his killing.

Leon. Faith, niece, you tax Signior Benedick too much; but he'll be met with you, I doubt it not.

Mess. He hath done good service, lady, in these wars.

Beat. You had musty victual, and he hath holp to eat it: he is a very valiant trencherman; he hath an excellent stomach.

Mess. And a good soldier too, lady.

Beat. And a good soldier to a lady. But what is he to a lord?

Mess. A lord to a lord, a man to a man; stuffed with all honourable virtues.

Beat. It is so, indeed; he is no less than a stuffed man: but for the stuffing,—well, we are all mortal.

Leon. You must not, sir, mistake my niece. There is a kind of merry war betwixt Signior Benedick and her: they never meet, but there's a skirmish of wit between them.

Beat. Alas, he gets nothing by that. In our last conflict four of his five wits went halting off, and now is the whole man governed with one; so that if he have wit enough to keep himself warm, let him bear it for a difference between himself and his horse; for it is all the wealth that he hath left, to be known a reasonable creature.—Who is his companion now? He hath every month a new sworn brother.

Mess. Is 't possible?

Beat. Very easily possible: he wears his faith but as the fashion of his hat; it ever changes with the next block.

Mess. I see, lady, the gentleman is not in your books.

Beat. No; an he were, I would burn my study. But, I pray you, who is his companion? Is there no young squarer now that will make a voyage with him to the devil?

Mess. He is most in the company of the right noble Claudio.

Beat. O Lord, he will hang upon him like a disease: he is sooner caught than the pestilence, and the taker runs presently mad. God help the noble Claudio! if he have caught the Benedick, it will cost him a thousand pound ere he be cured.

Mess. I will hold friends with you, lady.

Beat. Do, good friend.

Leon. You will never run mad, niece.

Beat. No, not till a hot January.

Mess. Don Pedro is approached.

Enter Don Pedro, Claudio, Benedick, Balthazar, *and* Don John

D. Pedro. Good Signior Leonato, you are come to meet your trouble: the fashion of the world is to avoid cost, and you encounter it.

Leon. Never came trouble to my house in the likeness

of your grace; for trouble being gone, comfort should
remain; but when you depart from me, sorrow abides, and
happiness takes his leave.

D. Pedro. You embrace your charge too willingly.—I
think, this is your daughter.

Leon. Her mother hath many times told me so.

Bene. Were you in doubt, sir, that you asked her?

Leon. Signior Benedick, no; for then were you a child.

D. Pedro. You have it full, Benedick; we may guess
by this what you are, being a man.—Truly, the lady fathers
herself.—Be happy, lady, for you are like an honourable
father.

Bene. If Signior Leonato be her father, she would not
have his head on her shoulders for all Messina, as like him
as she is.

Beat. I wonder that you will still be talking, Signior
Benedick: nobody marks you.

Bene. What, my dear Lady Disdain! are you yet living?

Beat. Is it possible disdain should die while she hath
such meet food to feed it as Signior Benedick? Courtesy
itself must convert to disdain, if you come in her presence.

Bene. Then is courtesy a turncoat.—But it is certain
I am loved of all ladies, only you excepted; and I would
I could find in my heart that I had not a hard heart; for
truly, I love none.

Beat. A dear happiness to women: they would else
have been troubled with a pernicious suitor. I thank God
and my cold blood, I am of your humour for that: I had
rather hear my dog bark at a crow than a man swear he
loves me.

Bene. God keep your ladyship still in that mind; so some
gentleman or other shall scape a predestinate scratched face.

Beat. Scratching could not make it worse, an 't were
such a face as yours were.

Bene. Well, you are a rare parrot-teacher.

Beat. A bird of my tongue is better than a beast of yours.

Bene. I would my horse had the speed of your tongue,
and so good a continuer. But keep your way o' God's
name, I have done.

Beat. You always end with a jade's trick: I know
you of old.

D. Pedro. This is the sum of all: Leonato,—Signior
Claudio and Signior Benedick,—my dear friend Leonato
hath invited you all. I tell him we shall stay here at the
least a month, and he heartily prays some occasion may
detain us longer: I dare swear he is no hypocrite, but
prays from his heart.

Leon. If you swear, my lord, you shall not be forsworn.
—Let me bid you welcome, my lord: being reconciled to
the prince your brother, I owe you all duty.

185

John.   I thank you: I am not of many words, but I thank you.

Leon.   Please it your grace lead on?

D. Pedro.   Your hand, Leonato: we will go together.

[*Exeunt all but Benedick and Claudio*

Claud.   Benedick, didst thou note the daughter of Signior Leonato?

Bene.   I noted her not; but I looked on her.

Claud.   Is she not a modest young lady?

Bene.   Do you question me, as an honest man should do, for my simple true judgment; or would you have me speak after my custom, as being a professed tyrant to their sex?

Claud.   No; I pray thee, speak in sober judgment.

Bene.   Why, i' faith, methinks she's too low for a high praise, too brown for a fair praise, and too little for a great praise; only this commendation I can afford her, that were she other than she is, she were unhandsome; and being no other but as she is, I do not like her.

Claud.   Thou thinkest I am in sport: I pray thee, tell me truly how thou likest her.

Bene.   Would you buy her, that you inquire after her?

Claud.   Can the world buy such a jewel?

Bene.   Yea, and a case to put it into. But speak you this with a sad brow, or do you play the flouting Jack, to tell us Cupid is a good hare-finder, and Vulcan a rare carpenter? Come, in what key shall a man take you, to go in the song?

Claud.   In mine eye she is the sweetest lady that ever I looked on.

Bene.   I can see yet without spectacles, and I see no such matter: there's her cousin, an she were not possessed with a fury, exceeds her as much in beauty as the first of May doth the last of December. But I hope you have no intent to turn husband, have you?

Claud.   I would scarce trust myself, though I had sworn the contrary, if Hero would be my wife.

Bene.   Is't come to this, in faith? Hath not the world one man, but he will wear his cap with suspicion? Shall I never see a bachelor of threescore again? Go to, i' faith; an thou wilt needs thrust thy neck into a yoke, wear the print of it, and sigh away Sundays. Look; Don Pedro is returned to seek you.

Re-enter DON PEDRO

D. Pedro.   What secret hath held you here, that you followed not to Leonato's?

Bene.   I would your grace would constrain me to tell.

D. Pedro.   I charge thee on thy allegiance.

Bene.   You hear, Count Claudio: I can be secret as a dumb man, I would have you think so; but on my allegi-

ance,—mark you this, on my allegiance:—he is in love.
With who?—now that is your grace's part.—Mark, how
short his answer is:—with Hero, Leonato's short daughter.

Claud. If this were so, so were it uttered.

Bene. Like the old tale, my lord: it is not so, nor 't was
not so; but, indeed, God forbid it should be so.

Claud. If my passion change not shortly, God forbid it
should be otherwise.

D. Pedro. Amen, if you love her; for the lady is very
well worthy.

Claud. You speak this to fetch me in, my lord.

D. Pedro. By my troth, I speak my thought.

Claud. And in faith, my lord, I spoke mine.

Bene. And by my two faiths and troths, my lord, I spoke
mine.

Claud. That I love her, I feel.

D. Pedro. That she is worthy, I know.

Bene. That I neither feel how she should be loved, nor
know how she should be worthy, is the opinion that fire
cannot melt out of me: I will die in it at the stake.

D. Pedro. Thou wast ever an obstinate heretic in the
despite of beauty.

Claud. And never could maintain his part but in the
force of his will.

Bene. That a woman conceived me, I thank her; that
she brought me up, I likewise give her most humble thanks:
but that I will have a recheat winded in my forehead, or
hang my bugle in an invisible baldrick, all women shall
pardon me. Because I will not do them the wrong to mistrust any, I will do myself the right to trust none; and the
fine is (for the which I may go the finer), I will live a bachelor.

D. Pedro. I shall see thee, ere I die, look pale with love.

Bene. With anger, with sickness, or with hunger, my
lord; not with love: prove that ever I lose more blood
with love, than I will get again with drinking, pick out mine
eyes with a ballad-maker's pen, and hang me up at the door
of a brothel-house for the sign of blind Cupid.

D. Pedro. Well, if ever thou dost fall from this faith,
thou wilt prove a notable argument.

Bene. If I do, hang me in a bottle like a cat, and shoot
at me; and he that hits me, let him be clapped on the
shoulder, and called Adam.

D. Pedro. Well, as time shall try:
" In time the savage bull doth bear the yoke."

Bene. The savage bull may; but if ever the sensible
Benedick bear it, pluck off the bull's horns, and set them in
my forehead; and let me be vilely painted; and in such
great letters as they write, "Here is good horse to hire,"
let them signify under my sign,—"Here you may see Benedick the married man."

Claud. If this should ever happen, thou wouldst be horn-mad.

D. Pedro. Nay, if Cupid have not spent all his quiver in Venice, thou wilt quake for this shortly.

Bene. I look for an earthquake too, then.

D. Pedro. Well, you will temporise with the hours. In the meantime, good Signior Benedick, repair to Leonato's: commend me to him, and tell him, I will not fail him at supper; for, indeed, he hath made great preparation.

Bene. I have almost matter enough in me for such an embassage; and so I commit you—

Claud. To the tuition of God. From my house, if I had it,—

D. Pedro. The sixth of July: your loving friend, Benedick.

Bene. Nay, mock not, mock not. The body of your discourse is sometime guarded with fragments, and the guards are but slightly basted on neither: ere you flout old ends any further, examine your conscience: and so I leave you.   [*Exit*

Claud. My liege, your highness now may do me good.

D. Pedro. My love is thine to teach: teach it but how, And thou shalt see how apt it is to learn Any hard lesson that may do thee good.

Claud. Hath Leonato any son, my lord?

D. Pedro. No child but Hero, she's his only heir. Dost thou affect her, Claudio?

Claud.   O, my lord, When you went onward on this ended action, I looked upon her with a soldier's eye, That liked, but had a rougher task in hand Than to drive liking to the name of love: But now I am returned, and that war-thoughts Have left their places vacant, in their rooms Come thronging soft and delicate desires, All prompting me how fair young Hero is, Saying, I liked her ere I went to wars.

D. Pedro. Thou wilt be like a lover presently, And tire the hearer with a book of words. If thou dost love fair Hero, cherish it; And I will break with her, and with her father, And thou shalt have her. Was't not to this end, That thou begann'st to twist so fine a story?

Claud. How sweetly do you minister to love, That know love's grief by his complexion! But lest my liking might too sudden seem, I would have salved it with a longer treatise.

D. Pedro. What need the bridge much broader than the flood? The fairest grant is the necessity.

Look, what will serve is fit: 't is once, thou lovest;
And I will fit thee with the remedy.
I know we shall have revelling to-night:
I will assume thy part is some disguise,
And tell fair Hero I am Claudio;
And in her bosom I'll unclasp my heart,
And take her hearing prisoner with the force
And strong encounter of my amorous tale:
Then, after, to her father will I break;
And, the conclusion is, she shall be thine.
In practice let us put it presently.   [*Exeunt*

SCENE II.—A Room in LEONATO's House

Enter LEONATO *and* ANTONIO, *meeting*

Leon.   How now, brother?   Where is my cousin, your
son?   Hath he provided this music?
Ant.   He is very busy about it.   But, brother, I can tell
you strange news that you yet dreamt not of.
Leon.   Are they good?
Ant.   As the event stamps them; they have a good
cover; they show well outward.   The prince and Count
Claudio, walking in a thick-pleached alley in my orchard,
were thus much overheard by a man of mine: the prince
discovered to Claudio that he loved my niece your daughter,
and meant to acknowledge it this night in a dance; and, if
he found her accordant, he meant to take the present time
by the top, and instantly break with you of it.
Leon.   Hath the fellow any wit that told you this?
Ant.   A good sharp fellow: I will send for him; and
question him yourself.
Leon.   No, no; we will hold it as a dream, till it appear
itself: but I will acquaint my daughter withal, that she
may be the better prepared for an answer, if peradventure
this be true.   Go you, and tell her of it.   [*Exit Antonio.*
Several persons cross the stage]   Cousins, you know what
you have to do.—O, I cry you mercy, friend; go you with
me, and I will use your skill.—Good cousin, have a care
this busy time.   [*Exeunt*

SCENE III.—Another Room in LEONATO's House

Enter DON JOHN *and* CONRADE

Con.   What the good year, my lord! why are you thus
out of measure sad?
John.   There is no measure in the occasion that breeds;
therefore the sadness is without limit.
Con.   You should hear reason.

John. And when I have heard it, what blessing brings it?

Con. If not a present remedy, yet a patient sufferance.

John. I wonder, that thou, being (as thou say'st thou art) born under Saturn, goest about to apply a moral medicine to a mortifying mischief. I cannot hide what I am: I must be sad when I have cause, and smile at no man's jests; eat when I have stomach, and wait for no man's leisure; sleep when I am drowsy, and tend on no man's business; laugh when I am merry, and claw no man in his humour.

Con. Yea; but you must not make the full show of this, till you may do it without controlment. You have of late stood out against your brother, and he hath ta'en you newly into his grace; where it is impossible you should take true root, but by the fair weather that you make yourself: it is needful that you frame the season for your own harvest.

John. I had rather be a canker in a hedge than a rose in his grace; and it better fits my blood to be disdained of all than to fashion a carriage to rob love from any: in this, though I cannot be said to be a flattering honest man, it must not be denied but I am a plain-dealing villain. I am trusted with a muzzle, and enfranchised with a clog; therefore I have decreed not to sing in my cage. If I had my mouth, I would bite; if I had my liberty, I would do my liking: in the meantime, let me be that I am, and seek not to alter me.

Con. Can you make no use of your discontent?

John. I make all use of it, for I use it only. Who comes here?

Enter BORACHIO

What news, Borachio?

Bora. I came yonder from a great supper; the prince, your brother, is royally entertained by Leonato, and I can give you intelligence of an intended marriage.

John. Will it serve for any model to build mischief on? What is he for a fool that betroths himself to unquietness?

Bora. Marry, it is your brother's right hand.

John. Who? the most exquisite Claudio?

Bora. Even he.

John. A proper squire! And who and who? which way looks he?

Bora. Marry, on Hero, the daughter and heir of Leonato.

John. A very forward March-chick! How came you to this?

Bora. Being entertained for a perfumer, as I was smoking a musty room, comes me the prince and Claudio, hand in hand, in sad conference: I whipt me behind the arras, and there heard it agreed upon, that the prince should woo Hero for himself, and having obtained her, give her to Count Claudio.

John. Come, come; let us thither: this may prove food to my displeasure. That young start-up hath all the glory of my overthrow: if I can cross him any way, I bless myself every way. You are both sure, and will assist me?

Con. To the death, my lord.

John. Let us to the great supper: their cheer is the greater, that I am subdued. 'Would the cook were of my mind!—Shall we go prove what's to be done?

Bora. We'll wait upon your lordship.   [*Exeunt*

ACT TWO

Scene I.—A Hall in Leonato's House

Enter Leonato, Antonio, Hero, Beatrice, *and others*

Leon. Was not Count John here at supper?

Ant. I saw him not.

Beat. How tartly that gentleman looks: I never can see him, but I am heart-burned an hour after.

Hero. He is of a very melancholy disposition.

Beat. He were an excellent man that were made just in the midway between him and Benedick: the one is too like an image, and says nothing; and the other too like my lady's eldest son, evermore tattling.

Leon. Then, half Signior Benedick's tongue in Count John's mouth, and half Count John's melancholy in Signior Benedick's face,—

Beat. With a good leg, and a good foot, uncle, and money enough in his purse, such a man would win any woman in the world,—if he could get her good will.

Leon. By my troth, niece, thou wilt never get thee a husband, if thou be so shrewd of thy tongue.

Ant. In faith: she's too curst.

Beat. Too curst is more than curst: I shall lessen God's sending that way, for it is said, "God sends a curst cow short horns;" but to a cow too curst he sends none.

Leon. So, by being too curst, God will send you no horns?

Beat. Just, if he send me no husband; for the which blessing I am at him upon my knees every morning and evening. Lord, I could not endure a husband with a beard on his face: I had rather lie in the woollen.

Leon. You may light on a husband that hath no beard.

Beat. What should I do with him? dress him in my apparel, and make him my waiting-gentlewoman? He that hath a beard is more than a youth, and he that hath no beard is less than a man: and he that is more than a youth is not for me; and he that is less than a man, I am not for him: therefore I will even take sixpence in earnest of the bearward, and lead his apes into hell.

Leon. Well, then go you into hell?

Beat. No; but to the gate; and there will the devil meet me, like an old cuckold, with horns on his head, and say, "Get you to heaven, Beatrice, get you to heaven; here's no place for you maids:" so deliver I up my apes, and away to Saint Peter: for the heavens, he shows me where the bachelors sit, and there live we as merry as the day is long.

Ant. [*To Hero*] Well, niece, I trust you will be ruled by your father.

Beat. Yes, faith; it is my cousin's duty to make courtesy, and say, "Father, as it please you:" but yet for all that, cousin, let him be a handsome fellow, or else make another courtesy, and say, "Father, as it please me."

Leon. Well, niece, I hope to see you one day fitted with a husband.

Beat. Not till God make men of some other metal than earth. Would it not grieve a woman to be over-mastered with a piece of valiant dust? to make an account of her life to a clod of wayward marl? No, uncle, I'll none: Adam's sons are my brethren; and, truly, I hold it a sin to match in my kindred.

Leon. Daughter, remember what I told you: if the prince do solicit you in that kind, you know your answer.

Beat. The fault will be in the music, cousin, if you be not wooed in good time: if the prince be too important, tell him there is measure in everything, and so dance out the answer. For hear me, Hero: wooing, wedding, and repenting, is as a Scotch jig, a measure, and a cinque-pace: the first suit is hot and hasty, like a Scotch jig, and full as fantastical; the wedding, mannerly modest, as a measure, full of state and ancientry; and then comes repentance, and with his bad legs falls into the cinque-pace faster and faster, till he sink into his grave.

Leon. Cousin, you apprehend passing shrewdly.

Beat. I have a good eye, uncle; I can see a church by daylight.

Leon. The revellers are entering, brother. Make good room!

Enter DON PEDRO, CLAUDIO, BENEDICK, BALTHAZAR, DON JOHN, BORACHIO, MARGARET, URSULA, *and others, masked*

D. Pedro. Lady, will you walk about with your friend?

Hero. So you walk softly, and look sweetly, and say nothing, I am yours for the walk; and especially when I walk away.

D. Pedro. With me in your company?

Hero. I may say so, when I please.

D. Pedro.   And when please you to say so?

Hero.   When I like your favour; for God defend the lute should be like the case!

D. Pedro.   My visor is Philemon's roof; within the house is Jove.

Hero.   Why, then your visor should be thatched.

D. Pedro.   Speak low, if you speak love.

[Takes her aside

Balth.   Well, I would you did like me.

Marg.   So would not I, for your own sake; for I have many ill qualities.

Balth.   Which is one?

Marg.   I say my prayers aloud.

Balth.   I love you the better; the hearers may cry Amen.

Marg.   God match me with a good dancer!

Balth.   Amen.

Marg.   And God keep him out of my sight, when the dance is done!—Answer, clerk.

Balth.   No more words: the clerk is answered.

Urs.   I know you well enough: you are Signior Antonio.

Ant.   At a word, I am not.

Urs.   I know you by the waggling of your head.

Ant.   To tell you true, I counterfeit him.

Urs.   You could never do him so ill-well, unless you were the very man.   Here's his dry hand up and down: you are he, you are he.

Ant.   At a word, I am not.

Urs.   Come, come, do you think I do not know you by your excellent wit?   Can virtue hide itself?   Go to, mum, you are he: graces will appear, and there's an end.

Beat.   Will you not tell me who told you so?

Bene.   No, you shall pardon me.

Beat.   Nor will you not tell me who you are?

Bene.   Not now.

Beat.   That I was disdainful, and that I had my good wit out of the "Hundred Merry Tales."—Well, this was Signior Benedick that said so.

Bene.   What's he?

Beat.   I am sure you know him well enough.

Bene.   Not I, believe me.

Beat.   Did he never make you laugh?

Bene.   I pray you, what is he?

Beat.   Why, he is the prince's jester: a very dull fool; only his gift is in devising impossible slanders: none but libertines delight in him; and the commendation is not in his wit, but in his villainy, for he both pleases men and angers them, and then they laugh at him and beat him. I am sure, he is in the fleet: I would he had boarded me!

Bene.   When I know the gentleman, I'll tell him what you say.

Beat. Do, do: he'll but break a comparison or two on me; which, peradventure, not marked, or not laughed at, strikes him into melancholy; and then there's a partridge wing saved, for the fool will eat no supper that night. [*Music within*] We must follow the leaders.

Bene. In every good thing.

Beat. Nay, if they lead to any ill, I will leave them at the next turning.

[*Dance. Then exeunt all except Don John,*
Borachio, and Claudio

John. Sure, my brother is amorous on Hero, and hath withdrawn her father to break with him about it. The ladies follow her, and but one visor remains.

Bora. And that is Claudio: I know him by his bearing.

John. Are you not Signior Benedick?

Claud. You know me well; I am he.

John. Signior, you are very near my brother in his love: he is enamoured on Hero. I pray you, dissuade him from her, she is no equal for his birth: you may do the part of an honest man in it.

Claud. How know you he loves her?

John. I heard him swear his affection.

Bora. So did I too; and he swore he would marry her to-night.

John. Come, let us to the banquet.

[*Exeunt Don John and Borachio*

Claud. Thus answer I in name of Benedick,
But hear these ill news with the ears of Claudio.
'T is certain so;—the prince woos for himself.
Friendship is constant in all other things
Save in the office and affairs of love:
Therefore, all hearts in love use their own tongues;
Let every eye negotiate for itself,
And trust no agent; for beauty is a witch,
Against whose charms faith melted into blood.
This is an accident of hourly proof,
Which I mistrusted not. Farewell, then, Hero!

Re-enter BENEDICK

Bene. Count Claudio?

Claud. Yea, the same.

Bene. Come, will you go with me?

Claud. Whither?

Bene. Even to the next willow, about your own business, count. What fashion will you wear the garland of? About your neck, like an usurer's chain, or under your arm, like a lieutenant's scarf? You must wear it one way, for the prince hath got your Hero.

Claud. I wish him joy of her.

Bene. Why, that's spoken like an honest drover: so

they sell bullocks. But did you think, the prince would
have served you thus?

Claud. I pray you, leave me.

Bene. Ho! now you strike like the blind man: 't was
the boy that stole your meat, and you'll beat the post.

Claud. If it will not be, I'll leave you.   [*Exit*

Bene. Alas, poor hurt fowl! Now will he creep into
sedges.—But, that my Lady Beatrice should know me,
and not know me! The prince's fool!—Ha! it may be
I go under that title because I am merry.—Yes; but so
I am apt to do myself wrong: I am not so reputed: it is
the base, though bitter disposition of Beatrice, that puts
the world into her person, and so gives me out. Well, I'll
be revenged as I may.

Re-enter DON PEDRO

D. Pedro. Now, Signior, where's the count? Did you
see him?

Bene. Troth, my lord, I have played the part of Lady
Fame. I found him here as melancholy as a lodge in a
warren. I told him, and I think I told him true, that your
grace had got the good will of this young lady; and I offered
him my company to a willow-tree, either to make him a
garland, as being forsaken, or to bind him up a rod, as being
worthy to be whipped.

D. Pedro. To be whipped! What's his fault?

Bene. The flat transgression of a schoolboy; who,
being overjoyed with finding a birds' nest, shows it his
companion, and he steals it.

D. Pedro. Wilt thou make a trust a transgression?
The transgression is in the stealer.

Bene. Yet it had not been amiss the rod had been made,
and the garland too; for the garland he might have worn
himself, and the rod he might have bestowed on you, who,
as I take it, have stolen his birds' nest.

D. Pedro. I will but teach them to sing, and restore
them to the owner.

Bene. If their singing answer your saying, by my faith,
you say honestly.

D. Pedro. The Lady Beatrice hath a quarrel to you: the
gentleman that danced with her told her she is much
wronged by you.

Bene. O, she misused me past the endurance of a block:
an oak, but with one green leaf on it, would have answered
her: my very visor began to assume life, and scold with
her. She told me, not thinking I had been myself, that I
was the prince's jester; that I was duller than a great
thaw; huddling jest upon jest, with such impossible conveyance, upon me, that I stood like a man at a mark, with
a whole army shooting at me. She speaks poniards, and

every word stabs: if her breath were as terrible as her terminations, there were no living near her; she would infect to the north star. I would not marry her, though she were endowed with all that Adam had left him before he transgressed: she would have made Hercules have turned spit, yea, and have cleft his club to make the fire too. Come, talk not of her; you shall find her the infernal Até in good apparel. I would to God, some scholar would conjure her, for, certainly, while she is here, a man may live as quiet in hell as in a sanctuary; and people sin upon purpose, because they would go thither; so, indeed, all disquiet, horror, and perturbation follow her.

D. Pedro. Look, here she comes.

Enter CLAUDIO, BEATRICE, HERO, *and* LEONATO

Bene. Will your grace command me any service to the world's end? I will go on the slightest errand now to the Antipodes, that you can devise to send me on: I will fetch you a toothpicker now from the farthest inch of Asia; bring you the length of Prester John's foot; fetch you a hair of the Great Cham's beard; do you any embassage to the Pigmies, rather than hold three words' conference with this harpy. You have no employment for me?

D. Pedro. None, but to desire your good company.

Bene. O God, sir, here's a dish I love not: I cannot endure my Lady Tongue.   [*Exit*

D. Pedro. Come, lady, come; you have lost the heart of Signior Benedick.

Beat. Indeed, my lord, he lent it me awhile; and I gave him use for it, a double heart for his single one: marry, once before he won it of me with false dice, therefore your grace may well say I have lost it.

D. Pedro. You have put him down, lady; you have put him down.

Beat. So I would not he should do me, my lord, lest I should prove the mother of fools. I have brought Count Claudio, whom you sent me to seek.

D. Pedro. Why, how now, count? wherefore are you sad?

Claud. Not sad, my lord.

D. Pedro. How then? sick?

Claud. Neither, my lord.

Beat. The count is neither sad nor sick, nor merry, nor well; but civil, count, civil as an orange, and something of that jealous complexion.

D. Pedro. I' faith, lady, I think your blazon to be true; though, I'll be sworn, if he be so, his conceit is false.—Here, Claudio, I have wooed in thy name, and fair Hero is won; I have broke with her father, and his good will obtained; name the day of marriage, and God give thee joy!

Leon. Count, take of me my daughter, and with her my fortunes: his grace hath made the match, and all grace say Amen to it!

Beat. Speak, count, 't is your cue.

Claud. Silence is the perfectest herald of joy: I were but little happy, if I could say how much.—Lady, as you are mine, I am yours: I give away myself for you, and dote upon the exchange.

Beat. Speak, cousin; or, if you cannot, stop his mouth with a kiss, and let him not speak neither.

D. Pedro. In faith, lady, you have a merry heart.

Beat. Yea, my lord; I thank it, poor fool, it keeps on the windy side of care.—My cousin tells him in his ear, that he is in her heart.

Claud. And so she doth, cousin.

Beat. Good Lord, for alliance!—Thus goes every one to the world but I, and I am sunburnt. I may sit in a corner, and cry heigh-ho for a husband!

D. Pedro. Lady Beatrice, I will get you one.

Beat. I would rather have one of your father's getting. Hath your grace ne'er a brother like you? Your father got excellent husbands, if a maid could come by them.

D. Pedro. Will you have me, lady?

Beat. No, my lord, unless I might have another for working-days: your grace is too costly to wear every day. —But, I beseech your grace, pardon me; I was born to speak all mirth, and no matter.

D. Pedro. Your silence most offends me, and to be merry best becomes you; for, out of question, you were born in a merry hour.

Beat. No, sure, my lord, my mother cried; but then there was a star danced, and under that was I born.— Cousins, God give you joy!

Leon. Niece, will you look to those things I told you of?

Beat. I cry you mercy, uncle.—By your grace's pardon.

[Exit

D. Pedro. By my troth, a pleasant-spirited lady.

Leon. There is little of the melancholy element in her, my lord: she is never sad, but when she sleeps; and not ever sad then, for I have heard my daughter say, she hath often dreamed of unhappiness, and waked herself with laughing.

D. Pedro. She cannot endure to hear tell of a husband.

Leon. O, by no means, she mocks all her wooers out of suit.

D. Pedro. She were an excellent wife for Benedick.

Leon. O Lord, my lord, if they were but a week married they would talk themselves mad.

D. Pedro. Count Claudio, when mean you to go to church?

Claud. To-morrow, my lord. Time goes on crutches, till love have all his rites.

Leon. Not till Monday, my dear son, which is hence a just seven-night; and a time too brief too, to have all things answer my mind.

D. Pedro. Come, you shake the head at so long a breathing; but, I warrant thee, Claudio, the time shall not go dully by us. I will, in the interim, undertake one of Hercules' labours; which is, to bring Signior Benedick and the Lady Beatrice into a mountain of affection the one with the other. I would fain have it a match; and I doubt not but to fashion it, if you three will but minister such assistance as I shall give you direction.

Leon. My lord, I am for you, though it cost me ten nights' watchings.

Claud. And I, my lord.

D. Pedro. And you too, gentle Hero?

Hero. I will do any modest office, my lord, to help my cousin to a good husband.

D. Pedro. And Benedick is not the unhopefullest husband that I know. Thus far can I praise him: he is of a noble strain, of approved valour, and confirmed honesty. I will teach you how to humour your cousin, that she shall fall in love with Benedick; and I, with your two helps, will so practise on Benedick, that, in despite of his quick wit and his queasy stomach, he shall fall in love with Beatrice. If we can do this, Cupid is no longer an archer: his glory shall be ours, for we are the only love-gods. Go in with me, and I will tell you my drift.   [*Exeunt*

Scene II.—Another Room in Leonato's House

Enter Don John *and* Borachio

John. It is so: the Count Claudio shall marry the daughter of Leonato.

Bora. Yea, my lord: but I can cross it.

John. Any bar, any cross, any impediment will be medicinable to me: I am sick in displeasure to him, and whatsoever comes athwart his affection ranges evenly with mine. How canst thou cross this marriage?

Bora. Not honestly, my lord; but so covertly that no dishonesty shall appear in me.

John. Show me briefly how.

Bora. I think I told your lordship, a year since, how much I am in the favour of Margaret, the waiting-gentlewoman to Hero.

John. I remember.

Bora. I can, at any unseasonable instant of the night, appoint her to look out at her lady's chamber window.

John. What life is in that, to be the death of this marriage?

Bora. The poison of that lies in you to temper. Go you to the prince your brother: spare not to tell him that he hath wronged his honour in marrying the renowned Claudio (whose estimation do you mightily hold up) to a contaminated stale, such a one as Hero.

John. What proof shall I make of that?

Bora. Proof enough to misuse the prince, to vex Claudio, to undo Hero, and kill Leonato. Look you for any other issue?

John. Only to despite them, I will endeavour anything.

Bora. Go then; find me a meet hour to draw Don Pedro and the Count Claudio alone: tell them, that you know that Hero loves me; intend a kind of zeal both to the prince and Claudio, as—in love of your brother's honour, who hath made this match, and his friend's reputation, who is thus like to be cozened with the semblance of a maid—that you have discovered thus. They will scarcely believe this without trial: offer them instances, which shall bear no less likelihood than to see me at her chamber window, hear me call Margaret Hero; hear Margaret term me Claudio; and bring them to see this the very night before the intended wedding: for in the meantime I will so fashion the matter, that Hero shall be absent, and there shall appear such seeming truth of Hero's disloyalty, that jealousy shall be called assurance, and all the preparation overthrown.

John. Grow this to what adverse issue it can, I will put it in practice. Be cunning in the working this, and thy fee is a thousand ducats.

Bora. Be you constant in the accusation, and my cunning shall not shame me.

John. I will presently go learn their day of marriage.

[Exeunt

Scene III.—Leonato's Orchard

Enter Benedick

Bene. Boy,—

Enter a Boy

Boy. Signior.

Bene. In my chamber window lies a book; bring it hither to me in the orchard.

Boy. I am here already, sir.

Bene. I know that; but I would have thee hence, and here again. [*Exit Boy.*] I do much wonder, that one man, seeing how much another man is a fool when he dedicates his behaviours to love, will, after he hath laughed at such shallow follies in others, become the argument of his own scorn by falling in love: and such a man is Claudio. I have known when there was no music with him but the drum and the fife; and now had he rather hear the tabor and the pipe: I have known, when he would have walked ten mile afoot to see a good armour; and now will he lie ten nights awake, carving the fashion of a new doublet. He was wont to speak plain and to the purpose, like an honest man and a soldier; and now is he turned orthographer: his words are a very fantastical banquet, just so many strange dishes. May I be so converted, and see with these eyes? I cannot tell; I think not: I will not be sworn but love may transform me to an oyster; but I'll take my oath on it, till he have made an oyster of me, he shall never make me such a fool. One woman is fair,—yet I am well; another is wise,—yet I am well; another virtuous,—yet I am well; but till all graces be in one woman, one woman shall not come in my grace. Rich she shall be, that's certain; wise, or I'll none; virtuous, or I'll never cheapen her; fair, or I'll never look on her; mild, or come not near me; noble, or not I for an angel; of good discourse, an excellent musician, and her hair shall be of what colour it please God. Ha, the prince and Monsieur Love! I will hide me in the arbour.   [*Withdraws*

Enter DON PEDRO, LEONATO, *and* CLAUDIO, *followed by*
BALTHAZAR *and Musicians*

D. Pedro.   Come, shall we hear this music?
Claud.   Yea, my good lord. How still the evening is,
As hushed on purpose to grace harmony!—
D. Pedro.   See you where Benedick hath hid himself?
Claud.   O, very well, my lord: the music ended,
We'll fit the kid-fox with a pennyworth.
D. Pedro.   Come, Balthazar, we'll hear that song again.
Balth.   O, good my lord, tax not so bad a voice
To slander music any more than once.
D. Pedro.   It is the witness still of excellency,
To put a strange face on its own perfection.—
I pray thee, sing, and let we woo no more.
Balth.   Because you talk of wooing, I will sing;
Since many a wooer doth commence his suit
To her he thinks not worthy; yet he wooes,
Yet will he swear he loves.
D. Pedro.   Nay, pray thee, come:
Or, if thou wilt hold longer argument,
Do it in notes.
Balth.   Note this before my notes;
There's not a note of mine that's worth the noting.
D. Pedro.   Why, these are very crotchets that he speaks;
Notes, notes, forsooth, and noting!   [*Music*
Bene.   [*Aside*] Now, divine air! now is his soul ravished!

—Is it not strange, that sheep's guts should hale souls out of men's bodies?—Well, a horn for my money, when all's done.

Balth.   *Sings*

     Sigh no more, ladies, sigh no more,
       Men were deceivers ever;
     One foot in sea, and one on shore:
       To one thing constant never.
         Then sigh not so,
         But let them go,
     And be you blithe and bonny,
     Converting all your sounds of woe
     Into, Hey nonny, nonny.

     Sing no more ditties, sing no more
     Of dumps so dull and heavy;
     The fraud of men was ever so,
       Since summer first was leavy.
       Then sigh not so, etc.

D. Pedro.   By my troth, a good song.

Balth.   And an ill singer, my lord.

D. Pedro.   Ha? no, no; faith, thou singest well enough for a shift.

Bene.   [*Aside*] An he had been a dog that should have howled thus, they would have hanged him; and I pray God, his bad voice bode no mischief!   I had as lief have heard the night-raven, come what plague could have come after it.

D. Pedro.   Yea, marry; dost thou hear, Balthazar?   I pray thee, get us some excellent music, for to-morrow night we would have it at the Lady Hero's chamber window.

Balth.   The best I can, my lord.

D. Pedro.   Do so: farewell.   [*Exeunt Balthazar and Musicians.*]   Come hither Leonato: what was it you told me of to-day? that your niece Beatrice was in love with Signior Benedick?

Claud.   O, ay.—[*Aside to Pedro*] Stalk on, stalk on; the fowl sits.—I did never think that lady would have loved any man.

Leon.   No, nor I neither; but most wonderful, that she should so dote on Signior Benedick, whom she hath in all outward behaviours seemed ever to abhor.

Bene.   [*Aside*] Is 't possible? Sits the wind in that corner?

Leon.   By my troth, my lord, I cannot tell what to think of it, but that she loves him with an enraged affection,—it is past the infinite of thought.

D. Pedro.   May be she doth but counterfeit.

Claud.   'Faith, like enough.

Leon.   O God, counterfeit!   There was never counterfeit of passion came so near the life of passion as she discovers it.

D. Pedro. Why, what effects of passion shows she?—

Claud. [*Aside*] Bait the hook well: this fish will bite.—

Leon. What effects, my lord? She will sit you,—you heard my daughter tell you how.

Claud. She did indeed.

D. Pedro. How, how, I pray you? You amaze me: I would have thought her spirit had been invincible against all assaults of affection.

Leon. I would have sworn it had, my lord; especially against Benedick.—

Bene. [*Aside*] I should think this a gull, but that the white-bearded fellow speaks it: knavery cannot, sure, hide himself in such reverence.—

Claud. [*Aside*] He hath ta'en the infection: hold it up.—

D. Pedro. Hath she made her affection known to Benedick?

Leon. No, and swears she never will: that's her torment.

Claud. 'T is true, indeed; so your daughter says: "Shall I," says she, "that have so oft encountered him with scorn, write to him that I love him?"

Leon. This says she, now, when she is beginning to write to him; for she'll be up twenty times a night, and there will she sit in her smock, till she have writ a sheet of paper.—My daughter tells us all.

Claud. Now you talk of a sheet of paper, I remember a pretty jest your daughter told us of.

Leon. O,—when she had writ it, and was reading it over, she found Benedick and Beatrice between the sheet?—

Claud. That.

Leon. O, she tore the letter into a thousand halfpence, railed at herself, that she should be so immodest to write to one that she knew would flout her:—"I measure him," says she, "by my own spirit; for I should flout him, if he writ to me; yea, though I love him, I should."

Claud. Then down upon her knees she falls, weeps, sobs, beats her heart, tears her hair, prays, curses;—"O sweet Benedick! God give me patience!"

Leon. She doth indeed: my daughter says so; and the ecstasy hath so much overborne her, that my daughter is sometimes afeard she will do a desperate outrage to herself. It is very true.

D. Pedro. It were good that Benedick knew of it by some other, if she will not discover it.

Claud. To what end? He would but make a sport of it, and torment the poor lady worse.

D. Pedro. An he should, it were an alms to hang him.

She's an excellent sweet lady, and, out of all suspicion, she is virtuous.

Claud. And she is exceeding wise.

D. Pedro. In everything, but in loving Benedick.

Leon. O! my lord, wisdom and blood combating in so tender a body, we have ten proofs to one, that blood hath the victory. I am sorry for her, as I have just cause, being her uncle and her guardian.

D. Pedro. I would she had bestowed this dotage on me; I would have daffed all other respects, and made her half myself. I pray you, tell Benedick of it, and hear what a' will say.

Leon. Were it good, think you?

Claud. Hero, thinks surely, she will die: for she says, she will die if he love her not, and she will die ere she make her love known, and she will die if he woo her, rather than she will bate one breath of her accustomed crossness.

D. Pedro. She doth well: if she should make tender of her love, 't is very possible he'll scorn it; for the man, as you know all, hath a contemptible spirit.

Claud. He is a very proper man.

D. Pedro. He hath, indeed, a good outward happiness.

Claud. Before God, and in my mind, very wise.

D. Pedro. He doth, indeed, show some sparks that are like wit.

Leon. And I take him to be valiant.

D. Pedro. As Hector, I assure you: and in the managing of quarrels you may say he is wise; for either he avoids them with great discretion, or undertakes them with a most Christian-like fear.

Leon. If he do fear God, he must necessarily keep peace: if he break the peace, he ought to enter into a quarrel with fear and trembling.

D. Pedro. And so will he do; for the man doth fear God, howsoever it seems not in him by some large jests he will make. Well, I am sorry for your niece. Shall we go seek Benedick, and tell him of her love?

Claud. Never tell him, my lord: let her wear it out with good counsel.

Leon. Nay, that's impossible: she may wear her heart out first.

D. Pedro. Well, we will hear further of it by your daughter: let it cool the while. I love Benedick well, and I could wish he would modestly examine himself, to see how much he is unworthy to have so good a lady.

Leon. My lord, will you walk? dinner is ready.—

Claud. [*Aside*] If he do not dote on her upon this, I will never trust my expectation.

D. Pedro. [*Aside*] Let there be the same net spread for her; and that must your daughter and her gentlewoman carry.   The sport will be, when they hold one an opinion of another's dotage, and no such matter: that's the scene that I would see, which will be merely a dumb-show.   Let us send her to call him in to dinner.

[*Exeunt Don Pedro, Claudio, and Leonato*

Bene.   [Advancing from the arbour] This can be no trick: the conference was sadly borne.—They have the truth of this from Hero.   They seem to pity the lady: it seems, her affections have their full bent.   Love me! why, it must be requited.   I hear how I am censured: they say, I will bear myself proudly, if I perceive the love come from her; they say, too, that she will rather die than give any sign of affection.—I did never think to marry.—I must not seem proud.—Happy are they that hear their detractions, and can put them to mending.   They say, the lady is fair: 't is a truth, I can bear them witness; and virtuous: 't is so, I cannot reprove it; and wise, but for loving me.   By my troth, it is no addition to her wit, nor no great argument of her folly, for I will be horribly in love with her.   I may chance have some odd quirks and remnants of wit broken on me, because I have railed so long against marriage; but doth not the appetite alter?   A man loves the meat in his youth, that he cannot endure in his age.   Shall quips, and sentences, and these paper bullets of the brain, awe a man from the career of his humour?   No; the world must be peopled.   When I said I would die a bachelor, I did not think I should live till I were married.—Here comes Beatrice.   By this day, she's a fair lady; I do spy some marks of love in her.

Enter BEATRICE

Beat.   Against my will I am sent to bid you come in to dinner.

Bene.   Fair Beatrice, I thank you for your pains.

Beat.   I took no more pains for those thanks, than you take pains to thank me: if it had been painful, I would not have come.

Bene.   You take pleasure then in the message?

Beat.   Yea, just so much as you may take upon a knife's point, and choke a daw withal.—You have no stomach, signior: fare you well.   [*Exit*

Bene.   Ha! "Against my will I am sent to bid you come in to dinner;"—there's a double meaning in that.   "I took no more pains for those thanks, than you took pains to thank me;"—that's as much as to say, any pains that I take for you is as easy as thanks.—If I do not take pity on her, I am a villain; if I do not love her, I am a Jew.   I will go get her picture.   [*Exit*

ACT THREE

SCENE I.—LEONATO's Garden

Enter HERO, MARGARET, *and* URSULA

Hero. Good Margaret, run thee to the parlour;
There shalt thou find my cousin Beatrice
Proposing with the prince and Claudio:
Whisper her ear, and tell her, I and Ursula
Walk in the orchard, and our whole discourse
Is all of her; say, that thou overheardst us,
And bid her steal into the pleachéd bower,
Where honeysuckles, ripened by the sun,
Forbid the sun to enter; like favourites,
Made proud by princes, that advance their pride
Against that power that bred it.—There will she hide her,
To listen our propose. This is thy office;
Bear thee well in it, and leave us alone.
Marg. I'll make her come, I warrant you, presently.
                                                    [*Exit*

Hero. Now, Ursula, when Beatrice doth come,
As we do trace this alley up and down,
Our talk must only be of Benedick:
When I do name him, let it be thy part
To praise him more than ever man did merit.
My talk to thee must be, how Benedick
Is sick in love with Beatrice: of this matter
Is little Cupid's crafty arrow made,
That only wounds by hearsay. Now begin;

Enter BEATRICE, *behind*

For look where Beatrice, like a lapwing, runs
Close by the ground, to hear our conference.
Urs. The pleasant'st angling is to see the fish
Cut with her golden oars the silver stream,
And greedily devour the treacherous bait:
So angle we for Beatrice; who even now
Is couchéd in the woodbine coverture.
Fear you not my part of the dialogue.
Hero. Then go we near her, that her ear lose nothing
of the false sweet bait that we lay for it.—
No, truly, Ursula, she is too disdainful;
I know, her spirits are as coy and wild
As haggards of the rock.
Urs.   But are you sure
That Benedick loves Beatrice so entirely?
Hero. So says the prince, and my new-trothéd lord.

Urs.   And did they bid you tell her of it, madam?
Hero.   They did entreat me to acquaint her of it;
But I persuaded them, if they loved Benedick,
To wish him wrestle with affection,
And never to let Beatrice know of it.
Urs.   Why did you so? Doth not the gentleman
Deserve as full as fortunate a bed
As ever Beatrice shall couch upon?
Hero.   O God of love! I know, he doth deserve
As much as may be yielded to a man;
But Nature never framed a woman's heart
Of prouder stuff than that of Beatrice:
Disdain and scorn ride sparkling in her eyes,
Misprising what they look on; and her wit
Values itself so highly, that to her
All matter else seems weak. She cannot love,
Nor take no shape nor project of affection,
She is so self-endeared.
Urs.   Sure, I think so;
And therefore, certainly it were not good
She knew his love, lest she make sport at it.
Hero.   Why, you speak truth. I never yet saw man,
How wise, how noble, young, how rarely featured,
But she would spell him backward: if fair-faced,
She would swear the gentleman should be her sister:
If black, why, Nature, drawing of an antick,
Made a foul blot; if tall, a lance ill-headed;
If low, an agate very vilely cut;
If speaking, why, a vane blown with all winds;
If silent, why, a block movéd with none.
So turns she every man the wrong side out,
And never gives to truth and virtue that
Which simpleness and merit purchaseth.
Urs.   Sure, sure, such carping is not commendable.
Hero.   No; not to be so odd, and from all fashions,
As Beatrice is, cannot be commendable.
But who dare tell her so? If I should speak,
She'd mock me into air: O, she would laugh me
Out of myself, press me to death with wit.
Therefore let Benedick, like covered fire,
Consume away in sighs, waste inwardly:
It were a better death than die with mocks,
Which is as bad as die with tickling.
Urs.   Yet tell her of it: hear what she will say.
Hero.   No; rather I will go to Benedick,
And counsel him to fight against his passion,
And, truly, I'll devise some honest slanders
To stain my cousin with. One doth not know,
How much an ill word may empoison liking.
Urs.   O, do not do your cousin such a wrong.

She cannot be so much without true judgment—
Having so swift and excellent a wit
As she is prized to have—as to refuse
So rare a gentleman as Signior Benedick.
    Hero. He is the only man of Italy,
Always excepted my dear Claudio.
    Urs. I pray you, be not angry with me, madam.
Speaking my fancy: Signior Benedick,
For shape, for bearing, argument, and valour,
Goes foremost in report through Italy.
    Hero. Indeed, he hath an excellent good name.
    Urs. His excellence did earn it, ere he had it.—
When are you married, madam?
    Hero. Why, every day;—to-morrow. Come, go in:
I'll show thee some attires, and have thy counsel,
Which is the best to furnish me to-morrow.—
    Urs. [*Aside*] She's limed, I warrant you: we have
caught her, madam.
    Hero. [*Aside*] If it prove so, then loving goes by haps:
Some Cupid kills with arrows, some with traps.
                        [*Exeunt Hero and Ursula*
    Beat. [*Advancing*] What fire is in mine ears? Can
      this be true?
Stand I condemned for pride and scorn so much?
Contempt, farewell! and maiden pride, adieu!
No glory lives behind the back of such.
And, Benedick, love on; I will requite thee,
Taming my wild heart to thy loving hand.
If thou dost love, my kindness shall incite thee
To bind our loves up in a holy band;
For others say thou dost deserve, and I
Believe it better than reportingly.   [*Exit*

SCENE II.—A Room in LEONATO's House

Enter DON PEDRO, CLAUDIO, BENEDICK, *and* LEONATO

    D. Pedro. I do but stay till your marriage be consummate, and then go I toward Aragon.
    Claud. I'll bring you thither, my lord, if you'll vouchsafe me.
    D. Pedro. Nay; that would be as great a soil in the new gloss of your marriage, as to show a child his new coat, and forbid him to wear it. I will only be bold with Benedick for his company; for, from the crown of his head to the sole of his foot, he is all mirth: he hath twice or thrice cut Cupid's bowstring, and the little hangman dare not shoot at him. He hath a heart as sound as a bell, and his tongue is the clapper,—for what his heart thinks, his tongue speaks.
    Bene. Gallants, I am not as I have been.

Leon. So say I: methinks you are sadder.

Claud. I hope he be in love.

D. Pedro. Hang him, truant! there's no true drop of blood in him, to be truly touched with love. If he be sad, he wants money.

Bene. I have the toothache.

D. Pedro. Draw it.

Bene. Hang it!

Claud. You must hang it first, and draw it afterwards.

D. Pedro. What! sigh for the toothache?

Leon. Where is but a humour, or a worm?

Bene. Well, every one can master a grief, but he that has it.

Claud. Yet say I, he is in love.

D. Pedro. There is no appearance of fancy in him, unless it be a fancy that he hath to strange disguises; as to be a Dutchman to-day, a Frenchman to-morrow, or in the shape of two countries at once, as a German from the waist downwards, all slops, and a Spaniard from the hip upward, no doublet. Unless he have a fancy to this foolery, as it appears he hath, he is no fool for fancy, as you would have it appear he is.

Claud. If he be not in love with some woman, there is no believing old signs. He brushes his hat o' mornings: what should that bode?

D. Pedro. Hath any man seen him at the barber's?

Claud. No, but the barber's man hath been seen with him, and the old ornament of his cheek hath already stuffed tennis-balls.

Leon. Indeed, he looks younger than he did, by the loss of a beard.

D. Pedro. Nay, he rubs himself with civet: can you smell him out by that?

Claud. That's as much as to say, the sweet youth's in love.

D. Pedro. The greatest note of it is his melancholy.

Claud. And when was he wont to wash his face?

D. Pedro. Yea, or to paint himself? for the which, I hear what they say of him.

Claud. Nay, but his jesting spirit, which is now crept into a lute-string, and now governed by stops.

D. Pedro. Indeed, that tells a heavy tale for him. Conclude, conclude, he is in love.

Claud. Nay, but I know who loves him.

D. Pedro. That would I know too: I warrant, one that knows him not.

Claud. Yes, and all his ill conditions; and, in despite of all, dies for him.

D. Pedro. She shall be buried with her face upwards.

Bene. Yet it is no charm for the toothache.—Old signior,

walk aside with me: I have studied eight or nine wise words to speak to you, which these hobby-horses must not hear.   [*Exeunt Benedick and Leonato*

D. Pedro.   For my life, to break with him about Beatrice.

Claud.   'T is even so.   Hero and Margaret have by this played their parts with Beatrice, and then the two bears will not bite one another when they meet.

Enter JOHN

John.   My lord and brother, God save you.

D. Pedro.   Good den, brother.

John.   If your leisure served, I would speak with you.

D. Pedro.   In private?

John.   If it please you; yet Count Claudio may hear, for what I would speak of concerns him.

D. Pedro.   What's the matter?

John.   [*To Claud.*]   Means your lordship to be married to-morrow?

D. Pedro.   You know he does.

John.   I know not that, when he knows what I know.

Claud.   If there be any impediment, I pray you, discover it.

John.   You may think, I love you not: let that appear hereafter, and aim better at me by that I now will manifest. For my brother, I think, he holds you well, and in dearness of heart hath holp to effect your ensuing marriage; surely, suit ill spent, and labour ill bestowed!

D. Pedro.   Why, what's the matter?

John.   I came hither to tell you: and circumstances shortened—for she has been too long a talking of—the lady is disloyal.

Claud.   Who?   Hero?

John.   Even she: Leonato's Hero, your Hero, every man's Hero.

Claud.   Disloyal?

John.   The word is too good to paint out her wickedness; I could say, she were worse: think you of a worse title, and I will fit her to it.   Wonder not till further warrant: go but with me to-night, you shall see her chamber-window entered, even the night before her wedding-day: if you love her then, to-morrow wed her; but it would better fit your honour to change your mind.

Claud.   May this be so?

D. Pedro.   I will not think it.

John.   If you dare not trust that you see, confess not that you know.   If you will follow me, I will show you enough; and when you have seen more, and heard more, proceed accordingly.

Claud.   If I see anything to-night why I should not marry her to-morrow: in the congregation, where I should wed, there will I shame her.

D. Pedro. And, as I wooed for thee to obtain her, I will join with thee to disgrace her.

John. I will disparage her no further, till you are my witnesses: bear it coldly but till midnight, and let the issue show itself?

D. Pedro. O day untowardly turned!

Claud. O mischief strangely thwarting!

John. O plague right well prevented! So will you say, when you have seen the sequel.   [*Exeunt*

Scene III.—A Street

Enter Dogberry *and* Verges, *with the Watch*

Dogb. Are you good men and true?

Verg. Yea, or else it were pity but they should suffer salvation, body and soul.

Dogb. Nay, that were a punishment too good for them, if they should have any allegiance in them, being chosen for the prince's watch.

Verg. Well, give them their charge, neighbour Dogberry.

Dogb. First, who think you the most desartless man to be constable?

First Watch. Hugh Oatcake, sir, or George Seacoal, for they can write and read.

Dogb. Come hither, neighbour Seacoal. God hath blessed you with a good name: to be a well-favoured man is the gift of fortune, but to write and read comes by nature.

Sec. Watch. Both which, master constable,—

Dogb. You have: I knew it would be your answer. Well, for your favour, sir, why, give God thanks, and make no boast of it; and for your writing and reading, let that appear when there is no need of such vanity. You are thought here to be the most senseless and fit man for the constable of the watch; therefore bear you the lantern. This is your charge:—You shall comprehend all vagrom men; you are to bid any man stand, in the prince's name.

Sec. Watch. How, if a' will not stand?

Dogb. Why, then take no note of him, but let him go; and presently call the rest of the watch together, and thank God you are rid of a knave.

Verg. If he will not stand when he is bidden, he is none of the prince's subjects.

Dogb. True, and they are to meddle with none but the prince's subjects.—You shall also make no noise in the streets; for, for the watch to babble and talk is most tolerable, and not to be endured.

Sec. Watch. We will rather sleep than talk: we know what belongs to a watch.

Dogb. Why, you speak like an ancient and most quiet watchman, for I cannot see how sleeping should offend; only, have a care that your bills be not stolen. Well, you are to call at all the ale-houses, and bid those that are drunk get them to bed.

Sec. Watch. How, if they will not?

Dogb. Why, then let them alone till they are sober: if they make you not then the better answer, you may say, they are not the men you took them for.

Sec. Watch. Well, sir.

Dogb. If you meet a thief, you may suspect him, by virtue of your office, to be no true man; and, for such kind of men, the less you meddle or make with them, why, the more is for your honesty.

Sec. Watch. If we know him to be a thief, shall we not lay hands on him?

Dogb. Truly, by your office you may; but, I think, they that touch pitch will be defiled. The most peaceable way for you, if you do take a thief, is, to let him show himself what he is, and steal out of your company.   [partner.

Verg. You have been always called a merciful man,

Dogb. Truly, I would not hang a dog by my will, much more a man who hath any honesty in him.

Verg. If you hear a child cry in the night, you must call to the nurse, and bid her still it.

Sec. Watch. How, if the nurse be asleep, and will not hear us?

Dogb. Why, then depart in peace, and let the child wake her with crying; for the ewe that will not bear her lamb when it baes, will never answer a calf when he bleats.

Verg. 'T is very true.

Dogb. This is the end of the charge. You, constable, are to present the prince's own person: if you meet the prince in the night, you may stay him.

Verg. Nay, by 'r lady, that, I think, a' cannot.

Dogb. Five shillings to one on 't, with any man that knows the statues, he may stay him: marry, not without the prince be willing; for, indeed, the watch ought to offend no man, and it is an offence to stay a man against his will.

Verg. By 'r lady, I think it be so.

Dogb. Ha, ah-ha! Well, masters, good night: an there be any matter of weight chances, call up me. Keep your fellows' counsels and your own, and good night. Come, neighbour.

Sec. Watch. Well, masters, we hear our charge: let us go sit here upon the church-bench till two, and then all to bed.

Dogb. One more word, honest neighbours. I pray you, watch about Signior Leonato's door; for the wedding being there to-morrow, there is a great coil to-night. Adieu, be vigitant, I beseech you.   [*Exeunt Dogberry and Verges*

Enter BORACHIO *and* CONRADE

Bora.   What, Conrade!—
Watch.   [*Aside*] Peace! stir not.—
Bora.   Conrade, I say!
Con.   Here, man, I am at thy elbow.
Bora.   Mass, and my elbow itched; I thought, there would a scab follow.
Con.   I will owe thee an answer for that; and now forward with thy tale.
Bora.   Stand thee close then under this penthouse, for it drizzles rain, and I will, like a true drunkard, utter all to thee.—
Watch.   [*Aside*] Some treason, masters; yet stand close.
Bora.   Therefore know, I have earned of Don John a thousand ducats.
Con.   Is it possible that any villainy should be so dear?
Bora.   Thou shouldst rather ask, if it were possible any villainy should be so rich; for when rich villains have need of poor ones, poor ones may make what price they will.
Con.   I wonder at it.
Bora.   That shows thou art unconfirmed. Thou knowest that the fashion of a doublet, or a hat, or a cloak, is nothing to a man.
Con.   Yes, it is apparel.
Bora.   I mean, the fashion.
Con.   Yes, the fashion is the fashion.
Bora.   Tush: I may as well say, the fool's the fool. But seest thou not what a deformed thief this fashion is?—
Watch.   [*Aside*] I know that Deformed; a' has been a vile thief this seven year; a' goes up and down like a gentleman. I remember his name.
Bora.   Didst thou not hear somebody?
Con.   No: 't was the vane on the house.
Bora.   Seest thou not, I say, what a deformed thief this fashion is? how giddily a' turns about all the hot bloods between fourteen and five-and-thirty? sometime, fashioning them like Pharaoh's soldiers in the reechy painting; sometime, like god Bel's priests in the old church-window; sometime, like the shaven Hercules in the smirched worm-eaten tapestry, where his codpiece seems as massy as his club?
Con.   All this I see, and I see that the fashion wears out more apparel than the man.   But art not thou thyself giddy with the fashion too, that thou hast shifted out of thy tale into telling me of the fashion?
Bora.   Not so neither; but know, that I have to-night wooed Margaret, the Lady Hero's gentlewoman, by the name of Hero: she leans me out at her mistress' chamber window, bids me a thousand times good night,—I tell this tale vilely:—I should first tell thee, how the prince, Claudio,

and my master, planted, and placed, and possessed by my master Don John, saw afar off in the orchard this amiable encounter.

Con. And thought they Margaret was Hero?

Bora. Two of them did, the prince and Claudio; but the devil my master knew she was Margaret; and partly by his oaths, which first possessed them, partly by the dark night, which did deceive them, but chiefly by my villainy, which did confirm any slander that Don John had made, away went Claudio enraged; swore he would meet her, as he was appointed, next morning at the temple, and there, before the whole congregation, shame her with what he saw over-night, and send her home again without a husband.

First Watch. We charge you in the prince's name, stand.

Sec. Watch. Call up the right master constable. We have here recovered the most dangerous piece of lechery, that ever was known in the commonwealth.

First Watch. And one Deformed is one of them: I know him, a' wears a lock.

Con. Masters, masters,—

Sec. Watch. You'll be made bring Deformed forth, I warrant you.

Con. Masters,—

First Watch. Never speak: we charge you, let us obey you to go with us.

Bora. We are like to prove a goodly commodity, being taken up of these men's bills.

Con. A commodity in question, I warrant you. *Come,* we'll obey you.   [*Exeunt*

Scene IV.—A Room in Leonato's House

Enter Hero, Margaret, *and* Ursula

Hero. Good Ursula, wake my cousin Beatrice, and desire her to rise.

Urs. I will, lady.

Hero. And bid her come hither.

Urs. Well.   [*Exit*

Marg. Troth, I think, your other rabato were better.

Hero. No, pray thee, good Meg, I'll wear this.

Marg. By my troth's not so good; and I warrant, your cousin will say so.

Hero. My cousin's a fool, and thou art another. I'll wear none but this.

Marg. I like the new tire within excellently, if the hair were a thought browner; and your gown's a most rare fashion, i' faith. I saw the Duchess of Milan's gown, that they praise so.

Hero. O, that exceeds, they say.

Marg. By my troth's but a night-gown in respect of

yours,—cloth o' gold, and cuts, and laced with silver, set with pearls down sleeves, side sleeves, and skirts round, underborne with a bluish tinsel; but for a fine, quaint, graceful, and excellent fashion, yours is worth ten on 't.

Hero. God give me joy to wear it, for my heart is exceeding heavy!

Marg. 'T will be heavier soon by the weight of a man.

Hero. Fie upon thee! art not ashamed?

Marg. Of what, lady? of speaking honourably? Is not marriage honourable in a beggar? Is not your lord honourable without marriage? I think, you would have me say, saving your reverence,—a husband: an' bad thinking do not wrest true speaking, I'll offend nobody. Is there any harm in—the heavier for a husband? None, I think, an it be the right husband, and the right wife; otherwise 't is light, and not heavy: ask my Lady Beatrice else: here she comes.

Enter BEATRICE

Hero. Good morning, coz.

Beat. Good morrow, sweet Hero.

Hero. Why, how now? do you speak in the sick tune?

Beat. I am out of all other tune, methinks.

Marg. Clap's into "Light o' love;" that goes without a burden: do you sing it, and I'll dance it.

Beat. Yea, "Light o' love," with your heels!—then, if your husband have stables enough, you'll see he shall lack no barns.

Marg. O illegitimate construction! I scorn that with my heels.

Beat. 'T is almost five o'clock, cousin: 't is time you were ready. By my troth, I am exceeding ill—heigh-ho!

Marg. For a hawk, a horse, or a husband?

Beat. For the letter that begins them all, H.

Marg. Well, an you be not turned Turk, there's no more sailing by the star.

Beat. What means the fool, trow?

Marg. Nothing I; but God send every one their heart's desire!

Hero. These gloves the count sent me, they are an excellent perfume.

Beat. I am stuffed, cousin, I cannot smell.

Marg. A maid, and stuffed! there's goodly catching of cold.

Beat. O, God help me, God help me! how long have you professed apprehension?

Marg. Ever since you left it. Doth not my wit become me rarely?

Beat. It is not seen enough, you should wear it in your cap.—By my troth, I am sick.

Marg. Get you some of this distilled Carduus Benedictus, and lay it to your heart: it is the only thing for a qualm.

Hero. There thou prick'st her with a thistle.

Beat. Benedictus! Why Benedictus? you have some moral in this Benedictus.

Marg. Moral? no, by my troth, I have no moral meaning; I meant, plain holy-thistle. You may think, perchance, that I think you are in love: nay, by 'r lady, I am not such a fool to think what I list; nor I list not to think what I can; nor indeed, I cannot think, if I would think my heart out of thinking, that you are in love, or that you will be in love, or that you can be in love. Yet Benedick was such another, and now is he become a man: he swore he would never marry; and yet now, in despite of his heart, he eats his meat without grudging: and how you may be converted, I know not, but, methinks, you look with your eyes as other women do.

Beat. What pace is this that thy tongue keeps?

Marg. Not a false gallop.

Re-enter URSULA

Urs. Madam, withdraw: the prince, the count, Signior Benedick, Don John, and all the gallants of the town, are come to fetch you to church.

Hero. Help to dress me, good coz, good Meg, good Ursula.   [*Exeunt*

SCENE V.—Another Room in LEONATO's House

Enter LEONATO, with DOGBERRY and VERGES

Leon. What would you with me, honest neighbour?

Dogb. Marry, sir, I would have some confidence with you, that decerns you nearly.

Leon. Brief, I pray you; for you see, it is a busy time with me.

Dogb. Marry, this it is, sir,—

Verg. Yes, in truth it is, sir.

Leon. What is it, my good friends?

Dogb. Goodman Verges, sir, speaks a little off the matter: an old man, sir, and his wits are not so blunt, as, God help, I would desire they were; but, in faith, honest as the skin between his brows.

Verg. Yes, I thank God, I am as honest as any man living, that is an old man, and no honester than I.

Dogb. Comparisons are odorous: *palabras*, neighbour Verges.

Leon. Neighbours, you are tedious.

Dogb. It pleases your worship to say so, but we are the poor duke's officers; but, truly, for mine own part, if I were as tedious as a king, I could find in my heart to bestow it all on your worship.

215

Leon. All thy tediousness on me, ha!

Dogb. Yea, an 't were a thousand pound more than 't is; for I hear as good exclamation on your worship as of any man in the city; and though I be but a poor man, I am glad to hear it.

Verg. And so am I.

Leon. I would fain know what you have to say.

Verg. Marry, sir, our watch to-night, excepting your worship's presence, have ta'en a couple of as arrant knaves as any in Messina.

Dogb. A good old man, sir; he will be talking: as they say, when the age is in, the wit is out. God help us! it is a world to see!—Well, said, i' faith, neighbour Verges:— well, God's a good man; and two men ride of a horse, one must ride behind.—An honest soul, i' faith, sir: by my troth he is, as ever broke bread; but, God is to be worshipped: all men are not alike,—alas, good neighbour!

Leon. Indeed, neighbour, he comes too short of you.

Dogb. Gifts that God gives.

Leon. I must leave you.

Dogb. One word, sir. Our watch, sir, have, indeed, comprehended two auspicious persons, and we would have them this morning examined before your worship.

Leon. Take their examination yourself, and bring it me: I am now in great haste, as may appear unto you.

Dogb. It shall be suffigance.

Leon. Drink some wine ere you go. Fare you well.

Enter a Messenger

Mess. My lord, they stay for you to give your daughter to her husband.

Leon. I'll wait upon them: I am ready.

[Exeunt Leonato and Messenger

Dogb. Go, good partner, go; get you to Francis Seacoal; bid him bring his pen and inkhorn to the gaol: we are now to examination these men.

Verg. And we must do it wisely.

Dogb. We will spare for no wit, I warrant you; here's that shall drive some of them to a *non-come:* only get the learned writer to set down our excommunication, and meet me at the gaol.   *[Exeunt*

ACT FOUR

Scene I.—The Inside of a Church

Enter Don Pedro, Don John, Leonato, Friar Francis, Claudio, Benedick, Hero, Beatrice, *and Attendants*

Leon. Come, Friar Francis, be brief: only to the plain form of marriage, and you shall recount their particular duties afterwards.

216

Fri. You come hither, my lord, to marry this lady?
Claud. No.
Leon. To be married to her:—friar, you come to marry her.
Fri. Lady, you come hither to be married to this count?
Hero. I do.
Fri. If either of you know any inward inpediment, why
you should not be conjoined, I charge you on your souls to
utter it.
Claud. Know you any, Hero?
Hero. None, my lord.
Fri. Know you any, count?
Leon. I dare make his answer; none.
Claud. O, what men dare do! what men may do! what
men daily do, not knowing what they do!
Bene. How now! Interjections? Why then, some be
of laughing, as, ha! ha! he!
Claud. Stand thee by, friar.—Father, by your leave:
Will you with free and unconstrainéd soul
Give me this maid, your daughter?
Leon. As freely, son, as God did give her me,
Claud. And what have I to give you back, whose worth
May counterpoise this rich and precious gift?
D. Pedro. Nothing, unless you render her again.
Claud. Sweet prince, you learn me noble thankfulness.—
There, Leonata, take her back again:
Give not this rotten orange to your friend;
She's but the sign and semblance of her honour.—
Behold, how like a maid she blushes here:
O, what authority and show of truth
Can cunning sin cover itself withal!
Comes not that blood, as modest evidence,
To witness simple virtue? Would you not swear,
All you that see her, that she were a maid,
By these exterior shows? But she is none:
She knows the heat of a luxurious bed;
Her blush is guiltiness, not modesty.
Leon. What do you mean, my lord?
Claud.   Not to be married,
Not to knit my soul to an approvéd wanton.
Leon. Dear my lord, if you, in your own proof,
Have vanquished the resistance of her youth,
And made defeat of her virginity,—
Claud. I know what you would say: if I have known her,
You'll say, she did embrace me as a husband,
And so extenuate the 'forehand sin:
No, Leonato,
I never tempted her with word too large;
But, as a brother to his sister, showed
Bashful sincerity, and comely love.
Hero. And seemed I ever otherwise to you?

   Claud. Out on thee, seeming! I will write against it:
You seem to me as Dian in her orb,
As chaste as is the bud ere it be blown;
But you are more intemperate in your blood
Than Venus, or those pampered animals
That rage in savage sensuality.
   Hero. Is my lord well, that he doth speak so wide?
   Claud. Sweet prince, why speak not you?
   D. Pedro.   What should I speak?
I stand dishonoured, that have gone about
To link my dear friend to a common stale.
   Leon. Are these things spoken, or do I but dream?
   John. Sir, they are spoken, and these things are true.
   Bene. This looks not like a nuptial.
   Hero.   True! O God!
   Claud. Leonato, stand I here?
Is this the prince? Is this the prince's brother?
Is this face Hero's? Are our eyes our own?
   Leon. All this is so; but what of this, my lord?
   Claud. Let me but move one question to your daughter.
And, by that fatherly and kindly power
That you have in her, bid her answer truly.
   Leon. I charge thee do so, as thou art my child.
   Hero. O God, defend me! how am I beset!—
What kind of catechising call you this?
   Claud. To make you answer truly to your name.
   Hero. Is it not Hero? Who can blot that name
With any just reproach?
   Claud.   Marry, that can Hero:
Hero itself can blot out Hero's virtue.
What man was he talked with you yesternight
Out of your window, betwixt twelve and one?
Now, if you are a maid, answer to this.
   Hero. I talked with no man at that hour, my lord.
   D. Pedro. Why, then are you no maiden.—Leonato,
I am sorry you must hear: upon mine honour,
Myself, my brother, and this grievéd count,
Did see her, hear her, at that hour last night,
Talk with a ruffian at her chamber window,
Who hath, indeed, most like a liberal villain,
Confessed the vile encounters they have had
A thousand times in secret.
   John. Fie, fie: they are not to be named, my lord,
Not to be spoke of;
There is not chastity enough in language,
Without offence to utter them.—Thus, pretty lady,
I am sorry for thy much misgovernment.
   Claud. O Hero! what a Hero hadst thou been,
If half thy outward graces had been placed
About the thoughts and counsels of thy heart!

But, fare thee well, most foul, most fair! farewell,
Thou pure impiety, and impious purity!
For thee I'll lock up all the gates of love,
And on my eyelids shall conjecture hang,
To turn all beauty into thoughts of harm,
And never shall it more be gracious.
    Leon. Hath no man's dagger here a point for me?
                                   [Hero swoons
    Beat. Why, how now, cousin! wherefore sink you down?
    John. Come, let us go. These things, come thus to light,
Smother her spirits up.
                [Exeunt Don Pedro, John, and Claudio
    Bene. How doth the lady?
    Beat.   Dead, I think:—help, uncle!
Hero! why, Hero!—Uncle!—Signior Benedick!—Friar!
    Leon. O fate, take not away thy heavy hand!
Death is the fairest cover for her shame
That may be wished for.
    Beat.   How now, cousin Hero?
    Fri. Have comfort, lady.
    Leon. Dost thou look up?
    Fri.   Yea; wherefore should she not?
    Leon. Wherefore? Why, doth not every earthly thing
Cry shame upon her? Could she here deny
The story that is printed in her blood?—
Do not live, Hero; do not ope thine eyes;
For did I think thou wouldst not quickly die,
Thought I thy spirits were stronger than thy shames,
Myself would, on the rearward of reproaches,
Strike at thy life. Grieved I, I had but one?
Chid I for that at frugal Nature's frame?
O, one too much by thee! Why had I one?
Why ever wast thou lovely in my eyes?
Why had I not with charitable hand
Took up a beggar's issue at my gates;
Who smirchéd thus, and mired with infamy,
I might have said, "No part of it is mine,
This shame derives itself from unknown loins?"
But mine, and mine I loved, and mine I praised,
And mine that I was proud on; mine so much,
That I myself was to myself not mine,
Valuing of her; why, she—O, she is fallen
Into a pit of ink, that the wide sea
Hath drops too few to wash her clean again,
And salt too little, which may season give
To her foul-tainted flesh!
    Bene.   Sir, sir, be patient,
For my part, I am so attired in wonder,
I know not what to say.
    Beat. O, on my soul, my cousin is belied!

   Bene. Lady, were you her bedfellow last night?
   Beat. No, truly, not; although, until last night,
I have this twelvemonth been her bedfellow.
   Leon. Confirmed, confirmed! O, that is stronger
      made,
Which was before barred up with ribs of iron!
Would the two princes lie? and Claudio lie,
Who loved her so, that, speaking of her foulness,
Washed it with tears?   Hence from her, let her die.
   Fri. Hear me a little;
For I have only been silent so long,
And given way unto this course of fortune,
By noting of the lady: I have marked
A thousand blushing apparitions
To start into her face; a thousand innocent shames
In angel whiteness beat away those blushes;
And in her eye there hath appeared a fire,
To burn the errors that these princes hold
Against her maiden truth.—Call me a fool;
Trust not my reading, nor my observation,
Which with experimental seal doth warrant
The tenor of my book; trust not my age,
My reverence, calling, nor divinity,
If this sweet lady lie not guiltless here
Under some biting error.
   Leon.   Friar, it cannot be.
Thou seest, that all the grace that she hath left,
Is, that she will not add to her damnation
A sin of perjury: she not denies it.
Why seek'st thou then to cover with excuse
That which appears in proper nakedness?
   Fri. Lady, what man is he you are accused of?
   Hero. They know that do accuse me, I know none.
If I know more of any man alive
Than that which maiden modesty doth warrant,
Let all my sins lack mercy!—O my father!
Prove you that any man with me conversed
At hours unmeet, or that I yesternight
Maintained the change of words with any creature,
Refuse me, hate me, torture me to death.
   Fri. There is some strange misprision in the princes.
   Bene. Two of them have the very bent of honour;
And if their wisdoms be misled in this,
The practice of it lives in John the bastard,
Whose spirits toil in frame of villainies.
   Leon. I know not. If they speak but truth of her,
These hands shall tear her; if they wrong her honour,
The proudest of them shall well hear of it.
Time hath not yet so dried this blood of mine,
Nor age so eat up my invention,

Nor fortune made such havoc of my means,
Nor my bad life reft me so much of friends,
But they shall find, awaked in such a kind,
Both strength of limb, and policy of mind,
Ability in means, and choice of friends,
To quit me of them throughly.
    Fri.   Pause awhile,
And let my counsel sway you in this case.
Your daughter here the princes left for dead;
Let her awhile be secretly kept in,
And publish it that she is dead indeed;
Maintain a mourning ostentation;
And on your family's old monument
Hang mournful epitaphs, and do all rites
That appertain unto a burial.
    Leon.   What shall become of this? what will this do?
    Fri.   Marry, this, well carried, shall on her behalf
Change slander to remorse;—that is some good:
But not for that dream I on this strange course,
But on this travail look for greater birth.
She dying, as it must be so maintained,
Upon the instant that she was accused,
Shall be lamented, pitied and excused
Of every hearer; for it so falls out,
That what we have we prize not to the worth
Whiles we enjoy it, but being lacked and lost,
Why, then we rack the value, then we find
The virtue, that possession would not show us
Whiles it was ours.—So will it fare with Claudio:
When we shall hear she died upon his words,
The idea of her life shall sweetly creep
Into his study of imagination,
And every lovely organ of her life
Shall come apparelled in more precious habit,
More moving, delicate, and full of life,
Into the eye and prospect of his soul,
Than when she lived indeed; then shall he mourn,—
If ever love had interest in his liver—
And wish he had not so accuséd her;
No, though he thought his accusation true.
Let this be so, and doubt not but success
Will fashion the event in better shape
Than I can lay it down in likelihood.
But if all aim but this be levelled false,
The supposition of the lady's death
Will quench this wonder of her infamy:
And, if it sort not well, you may conceal her,
As best befits her wounded reputation,
In some reclusive and religious life,
Out of all eyes, tongues, minds, and injuries.

Bene.   Signior Leonato, let the friar advise you:
And though you know my inwardness and love
Is very much unto the prince and Claudio,
Yet, by mine honour, I will deal in this
As secretly and justly as your soul
Should with your body.
          Leon.   Being that I flow in grief,
The smallest twine may lead me.
     Fri.   'T is well consented: presently away;
For to strange sores strangely they strain the cure.—
Come, lady, die to live: this wedding-day,
Perhaps is but prolonged: have patience, and endure.

                    [*Exeunt Friar, Hero, and Leonato*

     Bene.   Lady Beatrice, have you wept all this while?
     Beat.   Yea, and I will weep a while longer.
     Bene.   I will not desire that.
     Beat.   You have no reason: I do it freely.
     Bene.   Surely, I do believe your fair cousin is wronged.
     Beat.   Ah, how much might the man deserve of me that
would right her!
     Bene.   Is there any way to show such friendship?
     Beat.   A very even way, but no such friend.
     Bene.   May a man do it?
     Beat.   It is a man's office, but not yours.
     Bene.   I do love nothing in the world so well as you.   Is
not that strange?
     Beat.   As strange as the thing I know not.   It were as
possible for me to say, I loved nothing so well as you; but
believe me not, and yet I lie not: I confess nothing, nor I
deny nothing.—I am sorry for my cousin.
     Bene.   By my sword, Beatrice, thou lovest me.
     Beat.   Do not swear by it, and eat it.
     Bene.   I will swear by it, that you love me; and I will
make him eat it, that says I love you not.
     Beat.   Will you not eat your word?
     Bene.   With no sauce that can be devised to it.   I pro-
test, I love thee.
     Beat.   Why then, God forgive me!
     Bene.   What offence, sweet Beatrice?
     Beat.   You have stayed me in a happy hour: I was
about to protest I loved you.
     Bene.   And do it with all thy heart.
     Beat.   I love you with so much of my heart, that none
is left to protest.
     Bene.   Come, bid me do anything for thee.
     Beat.   Kill Claudio.
     Bene.   Ha! not for the wide world.
     Beat.   You kill me to deny it.   Farewell.
     Bene.   Tarry, sweet Beatrice.

Beat. I am gone, though I am here.—There is no love in you.—Nay, I pray you, let me go.

Bene. Beatrice,—

Beat. In faith, I will go.

Bene. We'll be friends first.

Beat. You dare easier be friends with me, than fight with mine enemy.

Bene. Is Claudio thine enemy?

Beat. Is he not approved in the height a villain, that hath slandered, scorned, dishonoured my kinswoman?—O, that I were a man!—What! bear her in hand until they come to take hands, and then with public accusation, uncovered slander, unmitigated rancour,—O God, that I were a man! I would eat his heart in the market-place.

Bene. Hear me, Beatrice,—

Beat. Talk with a man out at a window!—a proper saying.

Bene. Nay, but, Beatrice,—

Beat. Sweet Hero!—she is wronged, she is slandered, she is undone.

Bene. Beat—

Beat. Princes and counties! Surely, a princely testimony, a goodly count, count confect; a sweet gallant, surely! O, that I were a man for his sake! or that I had any friend would be a man for my sake! but manhood is melted into courtesies, valour into compliment, and men are only turned into tongue, and trim ones too: he is now as valiant as Hercules, that only tells a lie, and swears it.—I cannot be a man with wishing, therefore I will die a woman with grieving.

Bene. Tarry, good Beatrice. By this hand, I love thee.

Beat. Use it for my love some other way than swearing by it.

Bene. Think you in your soul the Count Claudio hath wronged Hero?

Beat. Yea, as sure as I have a thought or a soul.

Bene. Enough! I am engaged, I will challenge him. I will kiss your hand, and so I leave you. By this hand, Claudio shall render me a dear account. As you hear of me, so think of me. Go, comfort your cousin; I must say she is dead; and so, farewell.   [*Exeunt*

SCENE II.—A Prison

Enter DOGBERRY, VERGES, *and Sexton, in gowns; and the Watch, with* CONRADE *and* BORACHIO

Dogb. Is our whole dissembly appeared?

Verg. O, a stool and a cushion for the sexton.

Sexton. Which be the malefactors?

Dogb. Marry, that am I and my partner.

Verg. Nay, that's certain: we have the exhibition to examine.

Sexton. But which are the offenders that are to be examined? let them come before master constable.

Dogb. Yea, marry, let them come before me.—What is your name, friend?

Bora. Borachio.

Dogb. Pray, write down—Borachio.—Yours, sirrah?

Con. I am a gentleman, sir, and my name is Conrade.

Dogb. Write down—master gentleman Conrade.— Masters, do you serve God?

Con. } Yea, sir, we hope.
Bora. }

Dogb. Write down—that they hope they serve God: —and write God first; for God defend but God should go before such villains!—Masters, it is proved already that you are little better than false knaves, and it will go near to be thought so shortly. How answer you for yourselves?

Con. Marry, sir, we say we are none.

Dogb. A marvellous witty fellow, I assure you; but I will go about with him.—Come you hither, sirrah; a word in your ear, sir: I say to you, it is thought you are false knaves.

Bora. Sir, I say to you, we are none.

Dogb. Well, stand aside.—'Fore God, they are both in a tale. Have you writ down—that they are none?

Sexton. Master constable, you go not the way to examine: you must call forth the watch that are their accusers.

Dogb. Yea, marry, that's the eftest way.—Let the watch come forth.—Masters, I charge you, in the prince's name, accuse these men.

First Watch. This man said, sir, that Don John, the prince's brother, was a villain.

Dogb. Write down—Prince John a villain.—Why, this is flat perjury, to call a prince's brother villain.

Bora. Master constable.—

Dogb. Pray thee, fellow, peace: I do not like thy look, I promise thee.

Sexton. What heard you him say else?

Sec. Watch. Marry, that he had received a thousand ducats of Don John, for accusing the Lady Hero wrongfully.

Dogb. Flat burglary as ever was committed.

Verg. Yea, by the mass, that it is.

Sexton. What else, fellow?

First Watch. And that Count Claudio did mean, upon his words, to disgrace Hero before the whole assembly, and not marry her.

Dogb. O villain! thou wilt be condemned into everlasting redemption for this.

Sexton. What else?

Sec. Watch. This is all.

Sexton. And this is more, masters, than you can deny.
Prince John is this morning secretly stolen away; Hero
was in this manner accused, in this very manner refused,
and, upon the grief of this, suddenly died.—Master constable, let these men be bound, and brought to Leonato's:
I will go before, and show him their examination.   [*Exit*

Dogb. Come, let them be opinioned.

Verg. Let them be in the hands—

Con. Off, coxcomb!

Dogb. God's my life! where's the sexton? let him
write down—the prince's officer, coxcomb.—Come, bind
them.—Thou naughty varlet!

Con. Away! you are an ass; you are an ass.

Dogb. Dost thou not suspect my place? Dost thou
not suspect my years?—O, that he were here to write
me down an ass!—but, masters, remember, that I am
an ass; though it be not written down, yet forget not
that I am an ass.—No, thou villain, thou art full of piety,
as shall be proved upon thee by good witness. I am
a wise fellow; and, which is more, an officer; and, which
is more, a householder; and, which is more, as pretty
a piece of flesh as any in Messina; and one that knows
the law, go to; and a rich fellow enough, go to; and a
fellow that hath had losses; and one that hath two gowns,
and everything handsome about him.—Bring him away.
—O, that I had been writ down an ass!   [*Exeunt*

ACT FIVE

SCENE I.—Before LEONATO's House

Enter LEONATO *and* ANTONIO

Ant.   If you go on thus, you will kill yourself;
And 't is not wisdom thus to second grief
Against yourself.

Leon.   I pray thee, cease thy counsel,
Which falls into mine ears as profitless
As water in a sieve.   Give not me counsel;
Nor let no comforter delight mine ear
But such a one whose wrongs do suit with mine:
Bring me a father that so loved his child,
Whose joy of her is overwhelmed like mine,
And bid him speak of patience:
Measure his woe the length and breadth of mine,
And let it answer every strain for strain;

As thus for thus, and such a grief for such,
In every lineament, branch, shape, and form:
If such a one will smile, and stroke his beard,
Bid sorrow wag, cry hem when he should groan;
Patch grief with proverbs; make misfortune drunk
With candle-wasters: bring him yet to me,
And I of him will gather patience.
But there is no such man; for, brother, men
Can counsel, and speak comfort to that grief
Which they themselves not feel; but, tasting it,
Their counsel turns to passion, which before
Would give preceptial medicine to rage,
Fetter strong madness in a silken thread,
Charm ache with air, and agony with words.
No, no; 't is all men's office to speak patience
To those that wring under the load of sorrow,
But no man's virtue nor sufficiency
To be so moral when he shall endure
The like himself.   Therefore give me no counsel:
My griefs cry louder than advertisement.
    Ant.   Therein do men from children nothing differ.
    Leon.   I pray thee, peace! I will be flesh and blood;
For there was never yet philosopher
That could endure the toothache patiently,
However they have writ the style of gods
And made a push at chance and sufferance.
    Ant.   Yet bend not all the harm upon yourself;
Make those that do offend you suffer too.
    Leon.   There thou speak'st reason: nay, I will do so.
My soul doth tell me Hero is belied;
And that shall Claudio know; so shall the prince,
And all of them that thus dishonour her.

Enter DON PEDRO *and* CLAUDIO

    Ant.   Here comes the prince and Claudio hastily.
    D. Pedro.   Good den, good den.
    Claud.   Good day to both of you.
    Leon.   Hear you, my lords,—
    D. Pedro.   We have some haste, Leonato.
    Leon.   Some haste, my lord!—well, fare you well, my
      lord:—
Are you so hasty now?—well, all is one.
    D. Pedro.   Nay, do not quarrel with us, good old man.
    Ant.   If he could right himself with quarrelling,
Some of us would lie low.
    Claud.   Who wrongs him?
    Leon.   Marry, thou dost wrong me; thou, dissembler,
      thou.—
Nay, never lay thy hand upon thy sword;
I fear thee not.

Claud.   Marry, beshrew my hand
If it should give your age such cause of fear.
In faith, my hand meant nothing to my sword.
  Leon.   Tush, tush, man! never fleer and jest at me:
I speak not like a dotard, nor a fool,
As, under privilege of age, to brag
What I have done being young, or what would do
Were I not old. Know, Claudio, to thy head,
Thou hast so wronged mine innocent child and me,
That I am forced to lay my reverence by,
And, with grey hairs, and bruise of many days,
Do challenge thee to trial of a man.
I say, thou hast belied mine innocent child:
Thy slander hath gone through and through her heart,
And she lies buried with her ancestors,
O, in a tomb where never scandal slept,
Save this of hers, framed by thy villainy.
  Claud. My villainy?
  Leon.   Thine, Claudio; thine, I say.
  D. Pedro. You say not right, old man.
  Leon.   My lord, my lord,
I'll prove it on his body, if he dare,
Despite his nice fence and his active practice,
His May of youth and bloom of lustihood.
  Claud. Away! I will not have to do with you.
  Leon. Canst thou so daff me? Thou hast killed my
      child:
If thou kill'st me, boy, thou shalt kill a man.
  Ant. He shall kill two of us, and men indeed:
But that's no matter; let him kill one first;—
Win me and wear me,—let him answer me.—
Come, follow me, boy! come, sir boy, come, follow me.
Sir boy, I'll whip you from your foining fence;
Nay, as I am a gentleman, I will.
  Leon. Brother,—
  Ant. Content yourself. God knows, I loved my niece;
And she is dead; slandered to death by villains,
That dare as well answer a man indeed
As I dare take a serpent by the tongue.
Boys, apes, braggarts, Jacks, milksops!—
  Leon.   Brother Antony,—
  Ant. Hold you content. What, man, I know them
      yea,
And what they weigh, even to the utmost scruple:
Scrambling, outfacing, fashion-monging boys,
That lie, and cog, and flout, deprave and slander,
Go antickly, show outward hideousness,
And speak off half a dozen dangerous words,
How they might hurt their enemies, if they durst;
And this is all!

Leon. But, brother Antony,—

Ant.   Come, 't is no matter;
Do not you meddle, let me deal in this.

D. Pedro. Gentlemen both, we will not wake your
patience.
My heart is sorry for your daughter's death;
But, on my honour, she was charged with nothing
But what was true, and very full of proof.

Leon. My lord, my lord—

D. Pedro.   I will not hear you.

Leon.   No?
Come, brother, away.—I will be heard.—

Ant. And shall, or some of us will smart for it.

[Exeunt Leonato and Antonio

Enter BENEDICK

D. Pedro. See, see: here comes the man we went to
seek.

Claud. Now, signior, what news?

Bene. Good day, my lord.

D. Pedro. Welcome, signior: you are almost come to
part almost a fray.

Claud. We had like to have had our two noses snapped
off with two old men without teeth.

D. Pedro. Leonato and his brother. What think'st
thou? Had we fought, I doubt we should have been
too young for them.

Bene. In a false quarrel there is no true valour. I
came to seek you both.

Claud. We have been up and down to seek thee; for
we are high-proof melancholy, and would fain have it
beaten away. Wilt thou use thy wit?

Bene. It is in my scabbard; shall I draw it?

D. Pedro. Dost thou wear thy wit by thy side?

Claud. Never any did so, though very many have been
beside their wit.—I will bid thee draw, as we do the min-
strels; draw to pleasure us.

D. Pedro. As I am an honest man, he looks pale.—Art
thou sick, or angry?

Claud. What, courage, man! What though care killed
a cat, thou hast mettle enough in thee to kill care.

Bene. Sir, I shall meet your wit in the career, an you
charge it against me. I pray you, choose another subject.

Claud. Nay, then give him another staff: this last
was broke cross.

D. Pedro. By this light, he changes more and more.
I think he be angry indeed.

Claud. If he be, he knows how to turn his girdle.

Bene. Shall I speak a word in your ear?

Claud. God bless me from a challenge!

Bene. You are a villain.—I jest not.—I will make it good how you dare, with what you dare, and when you dare.—Do me right, or I will protest your cowardice. You have killed a sweet lady, and her death shall fall heavy on you. Let me hear from you.

Claud. Well, I will meet you, so I may have good cheer.

D. Pedro. What, a feast? a feast?

Claud. I' faith, I thank him; he hath bid me to a calf's head and a capon, the which if I do not carve most curiously, say my knife's naught.—Shall I not find a woodcock too?

Bene. Sir, your wit ambles well: it goes easily.

D. Pedro. I'll tell thee how Beatrice praised thy wit the other day. I said, thou hadst a fine wit. "True," said she, "a fine little one." "No," said I, "a great wit," "Right," says she, "a great gross one." "Nay," said I, "a good wit." "Just," said she, "it hurts nobody." "Nay," said I, "the gentleman is wise." "Certain," said she, "a wise gentleman." "Nay," said I, "he hath the tongues." "That I believe," said she, "for he swore a thing to me on Monday night, which he forswore on Tuesday morning: there's a double tongue; there's two tongues." Thus did she, an hour together, trans-shape thy particular virtues; yet at last she concluded with a sigh, thou wast the properest man in Italy.

Claud. For the which she wept heartily, and said she cared not.

D. Pedro. Yea, that she did; but yet, for all that, an if she did not hate him deadly, she would love him dearly. The old man's daughter told us all.

Claud. All, all; and moreover, God saw him when he was hid in the garden.

D. Pedro. But when shall we set the savage bull's horns on the sensible Benedick's head?

Claud. Yea, and text underneath, "Here dwells Benedick the married man!"

Bene. Fare you well, boy: you know my mind. I will leave you now to your gossip-like humour: you break jests as braggarts do their blades, which, God be thanked, hurt not.—My lord, for your many courtesies I thank you: I must discontinue your company. Your brother, the bastard, is fled from Messina: you have, among you, killed a sweet and innocent lady. For my Lord Lackbeard there, he and I shall meet; and till then, peace be with him.   [*Exit*

D. Pedro. He is in earnest.

Claud. In most profound earnest; and, I'll warrant you, for the love of Beatrice.

D. Pedro. And hath challenged thee?

Claud. Most sincerely.

D. Pedro. What a pretty thing man is, when he goes in his doublet and hose, and leaves off his wit!

Claud. He is then a giant to an ape; but then is an ape a doctor to such a man.

D. Pedro. But, soft you; let me be: pluck up, my heart, and be sad! Did he not say, my brother was fled?

Enter DOGBERRY, VERGES, *and the Watch, with* CONRADE *and* BORACHIO

Dogb. Come you, sir: if justice cannot tame you, she shall ne'er weigh more reasons in her balance. Nay, an you be a cursing hypocrite once, you must be looked to.

D. Pedro. How now! two of my brother's men bound! Borachio one!

Claud. Hearken after their offence, my lord!

D. Pedro. Officers, what offence have these men done?

Dogb. Marry, sir, they have committed false report; moreover, they have spoken untruths; secondarily, they are slanders; sixth and lastly, they have belied a lady; thirdly, they have verified unjust things; and, to conclude, they are lying knaves.

D. Pedro. First, I ask thee what they have done; thirdly, I ask thee what's their offence; sixth and lastly, why they are committed; and, to conclude, what you lay to their charge.

Claud. Rightly reasoned, and in his own division; and, by my troth, there's one meaning well suited.

D. Pedro. Who have you offended, masters, that you are thus bound to your answer? this learned constable is too cunning to be understood. What's your offence?

Bora. Sweet prince, let me go no further to mine answer: do you hear me, and let this count kill me. I have deceived even your very eyes: what your wisdoms could not discover, these shallow fools have brought to light; who, in the night, overheard me confessing to this man, how Don John your brother incensed me to slander the Lady Hero; how you were brought into the orchard, and saw me court Margaret in Hero's garments; how you disgraced her, when you should marry her. My villainy they have upon record, which I had rather seal with my death, than repeat over to my shame. The lady is dead upon mine and my master's false accusation; and, briefly, I desire nothing but the reward of a villain.

D. Pedro. Runs not this speech like iron through your blood?

Claud. I have drunk poison whiles he uttered it.

D. Pedro. But did my brother set thee on to this?

Bora. Yea; and paid me richly for the practice of it.

D. Pedro. He is composed and framed of treachery.— And fled he is upon this villainy.

Claud. Sweet Hero! now thy image doth appear In the rare semblance that I loved it first.

Dogb. Come, bring away the plaintiffs: by this time
our sexton hath reformed Signior Leonato of the matter.
And, masters, do not forget to specify, when time and
place shall serve, that I am an ass.

Verg. Here, here comes master Signior Leonato, and
the sexton too.

Re-enter LEONATO, ANTONIO, *and the Sexton*

Leon. Which is the villain?   Let me see his eyes,
That when I note another man like him,
I may avoid him.   Which of these is he?

Bora. If you would know your wronger, look on me.

Leon. Art thou the slave, that with thy breath hast
                   killed
Mine innocent child?

Bora.   Yea, even I alone.

Leon. No, not so, villain; thou beliest thyself:
Here stand a pair of honourable men,
A third is fled, that had a hand in it.—
I thank you, princes, for my daughter's death:
Record it with your high and worthy deeds.
'T was bravely done, if you bethink you of it.

Claud. I know not how to pray your patience,
Yet I must speak.   Choose your revenge yourself;
Impose me to what penance your invention
Can lay upon my sin: yet sinned I not,
But in mistaking.

D. Pedro.   By my soul, nor I;
And yet, to satisfy this good old man,
I would bend under any heavy weight
That he'll enjoin me to.

Leon. I cannot bid you bid my daughter live,
That were impossible; but, I pray you both,
Possess the people in Messina here
How innocent she died; and, if your love
Can labour aught in sad invention,
Hang her an epitaph upon her tomb,
And sing it to her bones—sing it to-night.—
To-morrow morning come you to my house,
And since you could not be my son-in-law,
Be yet my nephew.   My brother hath a daughter,
Almost the copy of my child that's dead,
And she alone is heir to both of us:
Give her the right you should have given her cousin,
And so dies my revenge.

Claud.   O noble sir,
Your over-kindness doth wring tears from me.
I do embrace your offer; and dispose
From henceforth of poor Claudio.

Leon. To-morrow then I will expect your coming;

To-night I take my leave.—This naughty man
Shall face to face be brought to Margaret,
Who, I believe, was packed in all this wrong,
Hired to it by your brother.

Bora. No, by my soul she was not;
Nor knew not what she did, when she spoke to me;
But always hath been just and virtuous
In anything that I do know by her.

Dogb. Moreover, sir, which, indeed, is not under white
and black, this plaintiff here, the offender, did call me
ass: I beseech you, let it be remembered in his punish-
ment. And also, the watch heard them talk of one Deformed: they say, he wears a key in his ear, and a lock
hanging by it, and borrows money in God's name, the
which he hath used so long, and never paid, that now men
grow hard-hearted, and will lend nothing for God's sake.
Pray you, examine him upon that point.

Leon. I thank thee for thy care and honest pains.

Dogb. Your worship speaks like a most thankful and
reverend youth; and I praise God for you.

Leon. There's for thy pains.

Dogb. God save the foundation.

Leon. Go, I discharge thee of thy prisoner, and I thank
thee.

Dogb. I leave an arrant knave with your worship;
which I beseech your worship to correct yourself for the
example of others. God keep your worship; I wish your
worship well; God restore you to health. I humbly give
you leave to depart, and if a merry meeting may be wished,
God prohibit it!—Come, neighbour.

[Exeunt Dogberry, Verges, and Watch

Leon. Until to-morrow morning, lords, farewell.

Ant. Farewell, my lords: we look for you to-morrow.

D. Pedro We will not fail.

Claud. To-night I'll mourn with Hero.

[Exeunt Don Pedro and Claudio

Leon. Bring you these fellows on. We'll talk with
Margaret,
How her acquaintance grew with this lewd fellow.

[Exeunt

SCENE II.—Leonato's Garden

Enter BENEDICK *and* MARGARET, *meeting*

Bene. Pray thee, sweet Mistress Margaret, deserve
well at my hands by helping me to the speech of Beatrice.

Marg. Will you then write me a sonnet in praise of
my beauty?

Bene. In so high a style, Margaret, that no man living

232

shall come over it; for, in most comely truth, thou deservest it.

Marg. To have no man come over me? why, shall I always keep below stairs?

Bene. Thy wit is as quick as the greyhound's mouth: it catches.

Marg. And yours as blunt as the fencer's foils, which hit, but hurt not.

Bene. A most manly wit, Margaret; it will not hurt a woman; and so, I pray thee, call Beatrice. I give thee the bucklers.

Marg. Give us the swords, we have bucklers of our own.

Bene. If you use them, Margaret, you must put in the pikes with a vice; and they are dangerous weapons for maids.

Marg. Well, I will call Beatrice to you, who, I think, hath legs.

Bene. And therefore will come.   [*Exit Marg.*

[*Singing*]   *The god of love,*
                That sits above,
          And knows me, and knows me,
               How pitiful I deserve,—

I mean, in singing; but in loving, Leander the good swimmer, Troilus the first employer of panders, and a whole bookful of these quondam carpet-mongers, whose names yet run smoothly in the even road of a blank verse, why, they were never so truly turned over and over as my poor self in love. Marry, I cannot show it in rhyme; I have tried: I can find out no rhyme to "lady" but "baby," an innocent rhyme; for "scorn," "horn," a hard rhyme; for "school," "fool," a babbling rhyme—very ominous endings. No, I was not born under a rhyming planet, nor I cannot woo in festival terms.—

Enter BEATRICE

Sweet Beatrice, wouldst thou come when I called thee?

Beat. Yea, signior; and depart when you bid me.

Bene. O, stay but till then!

Beat. "Then" is spoken; fare you well now:—and yet, ere I go, let me go with that I came; which is, with knowing what hath passed between you and Claudio.

Bene. Only foul words; and thereupon I will kiss thee.

Beat. Foul words is but foul wind, and foul wind is but foul breath, and foul breath is noisome; therefore I will depart unkissed.

Bene. Thou hast frighted the word out of his right sense, so forcible is thy wit. But, I must tell thee plainly, Claudio undergoes my challenge, and either I must shortly hear from him, or I will subscribe him a coward. And,

I pray thee now, tell me, for which of my bad parts didst thou first fall in love with me?

Beat. For them all together; which maintained so politic a state of evil, that they will not admit any good parts to intermingle with them. But for which of my good parts did you first suffer love for me?

Bene. Suffer love—a good epithet. I do suffer love, indeed, for I love thee against my will.

Beat. In spite of your heart, I think. Alas, poor heart! If you spite it for my sake, I will spite it for yours; for I will never love that which my friend hates.

Bene. Thou and I are too wise to woo peaceably.

Beat. It appears not in this confession: there 's not one wise man among twenty that will praise himself.

Bene. An old, an old instance, Beatrice, that lived in the time of good neighbours. If a man do not erect, in this age, his own tomb ere he dies, he shall live no longer in monument than the bell rings and the widow weeps.

Beat. And how long is that, think you?

Bene. Question:—why, an hour in clamour, and a quarter in rheum: therefore is it most expedient for the wise—if Don Worm, his conscience, find no impediment to the contrary—to be the trumpet of his own virtues, as I am to myself. So much for praising myself, who, I myself will bear witness, is praiseworthy. And now tell me, how doth your cousin?

Beat. Very ill.

Bene. And how do you?

Beat. Very ill too.

Bene. Serve God, love me, and mend. There will I leave you too, for here comes one in haste.

Enter URSULA

Urs. Madam, you must come to your uncle. Yonder 's old coil at home: it is proved, my Lady Hero hath been falsely accused; and the prince and Claudio mightily abused; and Don John is the author of all, who is fled and gone. Will you come presently?

Beat. Will you go hear this news, signior?

Bene. I will live in thy heart, die in thy lap, and be buried in thy eyes; and, moreover, I will go with thee to thy uncle's.   [*Exeunt*

SCENE III.—The Inside of a Church

Enter DON PEDRO, CLAUDIO, *and Attendants, with music and tapers*

Claud. Is this the monument of Leonato?

Atten. It is, my lord.

Claud. [*Reads from a scroll*]
    " *Done to death by slanderous tongues*
      Was the Hero that here lies :
    Death, in guerdon of her wrongs,
      Gives her fame which never dies.
    So the life, that died with shame,
      Lives in death with glorious fame."

Hang thou there upon the tomb,
Praising her when I am dumb.—
Now, music, sound, and sing your solemn hymn.

SONG

    Pardon, goddess of the night,
    Those that slew thy virgin knight ;
    For the which, with songs of woe,
    Round about her tomb they go.
      Midnight, assist our moan ;
      Help us to sigh and groan,
        Heavily, heavily :
      Graves, yawn and yield your dead,
      Till death be utteréd,
        Heavily, heavily.

Claud. Now, unto thy bones good night!
Yearly will I do this rite.
    D. Pedro. Good morrow, masters: put your torches
      out.
The wolves have preyed; and look, the gentle day,
Before the wheels of Phœbus, round about
Dapples the drowsy east with spots of grey.
Thanks to you all, and leave us: fare you well.
    Claud. Good morrow, masters: each his several way.
    D. Pedro. Come, let us hence, and put on other weeds;
And then to Leonato's we will go.
    Claud. And Hymen now with luckier issue speeds,
Than this, for whom we rendered up this woe!   [*Exeunt*

SCENE IV.—A Room in LEONATO's House

Enter LEONATO, ANTONIO, BENEDICK, MARGARET,
BEATRICE, URSULA, FRIAR FRANCIS, *and* HERO

Fri. Did I not tell you she was innocent?
    Leon. So are the prince and Claudio, who accused her
Upon the error that you heard debated:
But Margaret was in some fault for this,
Although against her will, as it appears
In the true course of all the question.
    Ant. Well, I am glad that all things sort so well.

Bene.   And so am I, being else by faith enforced
To call young Claudio to a reckoning for it.
  Leon.   Well, daughter, and you gentlewomen all,
Withdraw into a chamber by yourselves,
And, when I send for you, come hither masked:
The prince and Claudio promised by this hour
To visit me. [*Exeunt Ladies.*]—You know your office,
            brother:
You must be father to your brother's daughter,
And give her to young Claudio.
  Ant.   Which I will do with confirmed countenance.
  Bene.   Friar, I must entreat your pains, I think.
  Fri.   To do what, signior?
  Bene.   To bind me, or undo me; one of them.—
Signior Leonato, truth it is, good signior,
Your niece regards me with an eye of favour.
  Leon.   That eye my daughter lent her: 't is most true.
  Bene.   And I do with an eye of love requite her.
  Leon.   The sight whereof, I think, you had from me,
From Claudio, and the prince. But what's your will?
  Bene.   Your answer, sir, is enigmatical:
But, for my will, my will is, your good will
May stand with ours, this day to be conjoined
In the state of honourable marriage:—
In which, good friar, I shall desire your help.
  Leon.   My heart is with your liking.
  Fri.   And my help.
Here come the prince and Claudio.

        Enter DON PEDRO *and* CLAUDIO, *with Attendants*

  D. Pedro.   Good morrow to this fair assembly.
  Leon.   Good morrow, prince; good morrow, Claudio:
We here attend you. Are you yet determined
To-day to marry with my brother's daughter?
  Claud.   I'll hold my mind, were she an Ethiop.
  Leon.   Call her forth, brother: here's the friar ready.
                                       [*Exit Antonio*
  D. Pedro.   Good morrow, Benedick. Why, what's the
            matter,
That you have such a February face,
So full of frost, of storm, and cloudiness?
  Claud.   I think, he thinks upon the savage bull.—
Tush! fear not, man, we'll tip thy horns with gold,
And all Europa shall rejoice at thee,
As once Europa did at lusty Jove,
When he would play the noble beast in love.
  Bene.   Bull Jove, sir, had an amiable low:
And some such strange bull leaped your father's cow,
And got a calf in that same noble feat,
Much like to you, for you have just his bleat.

Re-enter ANTONIO, *with the Ladies masked*

Claud.   For this I owe you: here come other reckonings.
Which is the lady I must seize upon?
    Ant.   This same is she, and I do give you her.
    Claud.   Why, then she's mine.—Sweet, let me see your
            face.
    Leon.   No, that you shall not, till you take her hand
Before this friar, and swear to marry her.
    Claud.   Give me your hand before this holy friar:
I am your husband, if you like of me.
    Hero.   And when I lived, I was your other wife:
                                            [*Unmasking*
And when you loved, you were my other husband.
    Claud.   Another Hero?
    Hero.   Nothing certainer.
One Hero died defiled; but I do live,
And, surely, as I live, I am a maid.
    D. Pedro.   The former Hero! Hero that is dead!
    Leon.   She died, my lord, but whiles her slander lived.
    Fri.   All this amazement can I qualify:
When after that the holy rites are ended,
I'll tell you largely of fair Hero's death:
Meantime, let wonder seem familiar,
And to the chapel let us presently.
    Bene.   Soft and fair, friar.—Which is Beatrice?
    Beat.   I answer to that name. [*Unmasking*] What is
            your will?
    Bene.   Do not you love me?
    Beat.   Why, no; no more than reason.
    Bene.   Why, then, your uncle, and the prince, and
Claudio, have been deceived: they swore you did.
    Beat.   Do not you love me?
    Bene.   Troth, no; no more than reason.
    Beat.   Why, then my cousin, Margaret, and Ursula
Are much deceived; for they did swear you did.
    Bene.   They swore that you were almost sick for me.
    Beat.   They swore that you were well-nigh dead for me.
    Bene.   'T is no such matter.—Then, you do not love
            me?
    Beat.   No, truly, but in friendly recompense.
    Leon.   Come, cousin, I am sure you love the gentleman.
    Claud.   And I'll be sworn upon 't, that he loves her;
For here's a paper written in his hand,
A halting sonnet of his own pure brain,
Fashioned to Beatrice.
    Hero.   And here's another,
Writ in my cousin's hand, stol'n from her pocket,
Containing her affection unto Benedick.
    Bene.   A miracle! here's our own hands against our

hearts.—Come, I will have thee; but, by this light, I take thee for pity.

Beat. I would not deny you;—but, by this good day, I yield upon great persuasion, and, partly, to save your life, for I was told you were in a consumption.

Bene. Peace! I will stop your mouth.

D. Pedro. How dost thou, Benedick, the married man?

Bene. I'll tell thee what, prince: a college of wit-crackers cannot flout me out of my humour. Dost thou think: I care for a satire or an epigram? No: if a man will be beaten with brains, a' shall wear nothing handsome about him. In brief, since I do purpose to marry, I will think nothing to any purpose that the world can say against it; and therefore never flout at me for what I have said against it, for man is a giddy thing, and this is my conclusion.—For thy part, Claudio, I did think to have beaten thee; but in that thou art like to be my kinsman, live unbruised, and love my cousin.

Claud. I had well hoped thou wouldst have denied Beatrice, that I might have cudgelled thee out of thy single life, to make thee a double-dealer; which, out of question, thou wilt be, if my cousin do not look exceeding narrowly to thee.

Bene. Come, come, we are friends. Let's have a dance ere we are married, that we may lighten our own hearts and our wives' heels.

Leon. We'll have dancing afterward.

Bene. First, of my word; therefore play, music!—Prince, thou art sad; get thee a wife, get thee a wife: there is no staff more reverend than one tipped with horn.

Enter a Messenger

Mess. My lord, your brother John is ta'en in flight, And brought with arméd men back to Messina.

Bene. Think not on him till to-morrow: I'll devise thee brave punishments for him.—Strike up, pipers.

[Dance. Exeunt

OTHELLO, THE MOOR OF VENICE

DRAMATIS PERSONÆ

DUKE OF VENICE

BRABANTIO, *a senator*
Other Senators
GRATIANO, *brother to Brabantio*
LODOVICO, *kinsman to Brabantio*
OTHELLO, *a noble Moor in the service of the Venetian state*
CASSIO, *his lieutenant*
IAGO, *his ancient*
RODERIGO, *a Venetian gentleman*
MONTANO, *Othello's predecessor in the government of Cyprus*
Clown, servant to Othello

DESDEMONA, *daughter to Brabantio and wife to Othello*
EMILIA, *wife to Iago*
BIANCA, *mistress to Cassio*

Sailor, Messenger, Herald, Officers, Gentlemen, Musicians, and Attendants

SCENE—*For the First Act in Venice: during the rest of the play at a seaport in Cyprus*

OTHELLO, THE MOOR OF VENICE

ACT ONE

Scene I.—Venice.   A Street

Enter Roderigo *and* Iago

Rod.   Tush, never tell me; I take it much unkindly
That thou, Iago, who hast had my purse
As if the strings were thine, shouldst know of this.
   Iago.   'Sblood, but you will not hear me:—
If ever I did dream of such a matter,
Abhor me.
   Rod.   Thou told'st me, thou didst hold him in thy hate.
   Iago.   Despise me, if I do not.   Three great ones of the city,
In personal suit to make me his lieutenant,
Off capped to him;—and, by the faith of man,
I know my price, I'm worth no worse a place;—
But he, as loving his own pride and purposes,
Evades them with a bombast circumstance
Horribly stuffed with epithets of war;
And, in conclusion,
Nonsuits my mediators; for, "Certes," says he,
"I have already chose my officer."
And what was he?
Forsooth, a great arithmetician,
One Michael Cassio, a Florentine,
A fellow almost damned in a fair wife
That never set a squadron in the field,
Nor the division of a battle knows
More than a spinster, unless the bookish theoric,
Wherein the togéd consuls can purpose
As masterly as he: mere prattle, without practice,
Is all his soldiership.   But he, sir, had the election:
And I—of whom his eyes had seen the proof
At Rhodes, at Cyprus, and on other grounds,
Christian and heathen,—must be lee'd and calmed
By debitor-and-creditor, this counter-caster;
He, in good time, must his lieutenant be,
And I—God bless the mark!—his Moorship's ancient.
   Rod.   By Heaven, I rather would have been his hangman.
   Iago.   But there's no remedy; 't is the curse of service,
Preferment goes by letter and affection,
Not by the old gradation, where each second
Stood heir to the first.   Now, sir, be judge yourself,
Whether I in any just term am affined
To love the Moor.

Rod.   I would not follow him then.
  Iago.   O, sir, content you;
I follow him to serve my turn upon him:
We cannot all be masters, nor all masters
Cannot be truly followed.   You shall mark
Many a duteous and knee-crooking knave,
That, doting on his own obsequious bondage,
Wears out his time, much like his master's ass,
For nought but provender; and when he 's old, cashiered:
Whip me such honest knaves.   Others there are,
Who, trimmed in forms and visages of duty,
Keep yet their hearts attending on themselves;
And, throwing but shows of service on their lords,
Do well thrive by 'em, and, when they've lined their coats,
Do themselves homage: these fellows have some soul;
And such a one do I profess myself.
For, sir,
It is as sure as you are Roderigo,
Were I the Moor, I would not be Iago:
In following him, I follow but myself;
Heaven is my judge, not I for love and duty,
But seeming so, for my peculiar end:
For when my outward action doth demonstrate
The native act and figure of my heart
In complement extern, 't is not long after
But I will wear my heart upon my sleeve
For daws to peck at: I am not what I am.
  Rod.   What a full fortune does the thick-lip owe,
If he can carry 't thus!
  Iago.   Call up her father;
Rouse him:—make after him, poison his delight,
Proclaim him in the streets: incense her kinsmen:
And, though he in a fertile climate dwell,
Plague him with flies: though that his joy be joy,
Yet throw such chances of vexation on 't,
As it may lose some colour.
  Rod.   Here is her father's house; I 'll call aloud.
  Iago.   Do; with like timorous accent, and dire yell,
As when, by night and negligence, the fire
Is spied in populous cities.
  Rod.   What, ho! Brabantio! Signior Brabantio, ho!
  Iago.   Awake! what ho! Brabantio! thieves! thieves!
        thieves!
Look to your house, your daughter, and your bags!
Thieves! thieves!

           BRABANTIO *appears above, at a window*

  Bra.   What is the reason of this terrible summons?
What is the matter there?
  Rod.   Signior, is all your family within?
                           242

Iago.   Are your doors locked?
Bra.   Why, wherefore ask you this?
Iago.   Zounds, sir! you are robbed; for shame, put on
    your gown;
Your heart is burst, you have lost half your soul;
Even now, now, very now, an old black ram
Is tupping your white ewe.   Arise, arise!
Awake the snorting citizens with the bell,
Or else the devil will make a grandsire of you.
Arise, I say.
Bra.   What, have you lost your wits?
Rod.   Most reverend signior, do you know my voice?
Bra.   Not I: what are you?
Rod.   My name is Roderigo.
Bra.   The worser welcome:
I've charged thee not to haunt about my doors.
In honest plainness thou hast heard me say
My daughter's not for thee; and now, in madness,
Being full of supper and distempering draughts,
Upon malicious bravery dost thou come
To start my quiet.
Rod.   Sir, sir, sir,—
Bra.   But thou must needs be sure
My spirit and my place have in them power
To make this bitter to thee.
Rod.   Patience, good sir.
Bra.   What tell'st thou me of robbing? this is Venice;
My house is not a grange.
Rod.   Most grave Brabantio,
In simple and pure soul I come to you.
Iago.   Zounds, sir! you are one of those that will not
serve God, if the devil bid you.   Because we come to do
you service, and you think we are ruffians, you 'll have your
daughter covered with a Barbary horse; you 'll have your
nephews neigh to you; you'll have coursers for cousins, and
gennets for germans.
Bra.   What profane wretch art thou?
Iago.   I am one, sir, that comes to tell you, your daughter
and the Moor are now making the beast with two backs.
Bra.   Thou art a villain.
Iago.   You are—a senator.
Bra.   This thou shalt answer: I know thee, Roderigo.
Rod.   Sir, I will answer anything.   But I beseech you,
If 't be your pleasure, and most wise consent,—
As partly, I find, it is,—that your fair daughter,
At this odd-even and dull watch o' the night,
Transported with no worse nor better guard
But with a knave of common hire, a gondolier,
To the gross clasps of a lascivious Moor,—
If this be known to you, and your allowance,

We then have done you bold and saucy wrongs;
But if you know not this, my manners tell me
We have your wrong rebuke.   Do not believe
That, from the sense of all civility,
I thus would play and trifle with your reverence:
Your daughter,—if you have not given her leave,—
I say again, hath made a gross revolt;
Tying her duty, beauty, wit and fortunes,
In an extravagant and wheeling stranger,
Of here and everywhere.   Straight satisfy yourself:
If she be in her chamber or your house,
Let loose on me the justice of the state
For thus deluding you.
    Bra.   Strike on the tinder, ho!
Give me a taper!—call up all my people!—
This accident is not unlike my dream:
Belief of it oppresses me already.—
Light, I say! light!   *[Exit from above*
    Iago.   Farewell; for I must leave you;
It seems not meet, nor wholesome to my place,
To be produced—as, if I stay, I shall—
Against the Moor; for I do know, the state—
However this may gall him with some check—
Cannot with safety cast him; for he's embarked
With such loud reason to the Cyprus wars,
Which even now stands in act, that, for their souls,
Another of his fathom they have none,
To lead their business: in which regard,
Though I do hate him as I do hell-pains,
Yet, for necessity of present life,
I must show out a flag and sign of love,
Which is indeed but sign.   That you shall surely find him,
Lead to the Sagittary the raiséd search;
And there will I be with him.   So, farewell.   *[Exit*

    Enter, below, BRABANTIO, *and Servants with torches*

    Bra. It is too true an evil: gone she is;
And what's to come of my despiséd time
Is nought but bitterness.—Now, Roderigo,
Where didst thou see her?—O unhappy girl!—
With the Moor, say'st thou?—Who would be a father?—
How didst thou know 't was she?—O, she deceives me
Past thought!—What said she to you?—Get more tapers!
Raise all my kindred!—Are they married, think you?
    Rod. Truly, I think they are.
    Bra. O Heaven!—How got she out?—O, treason of the
        blood!—
Fathers, from hence trust not your daughters' minds
By what you see them act.—Is there not charms
By which the property of youth and maidhood

May be abused?   Have you not read, Roderigo,
Of some such thing?
   Rod.   Yes, sir; I have, indeed.
   Bra.   Call up my brother.—O, would you had had her!
Some one way, some another.—Do you know
Where we may apprehend her and the Moor?
   Rod.   I think, I can discover him, if you please
To get good guard, and go along with me.
   Bra.   Pray you, lead on.   At every house I'll call;
I may command at most.—Get weapons, ho!
And raise some special officers of night.—
On, good Roderigo;—I'll deserve your pains.   [*Exeunt*

SCENE II.—Venice.   Another Street

Enter OTHELLO, IAGO, *and Attendants, with torches*

   Iago.   Though in the trade of war I have slain men,
Yet do I hold it very stuff o' the conscience
To do no contrivéd murder: I lack iniquity
Sometimes to do me service.   Nine or ten times
I had thought to have yerked him here under the ribs.
   Oth.   'T is better as it is.
   Iago.   Nay, but he prated,
And spoke with such scurvy and provoking terms
Against your honour,
That, with the little godliness I have,
I did full hard forbear him.   But, I pray you, sir,
Are you fast married!   Be assured of this,
That the magnifico is much beloved;
And hath, in his effect, a voice potential
As double as the duke's: he will divorce you;
Or put upon you what restraint and grievance
The law—with all his might to enforce it on—
Will give him cable.
   Oth.   Let him do his spite:
My services which I have done the signiory
Shall out-tongue his complaints.   'T is yet to know,—
Which, when I know that boasting is an honour,
I shall promulgate,—I fetch my life and being
From men of royal siege; and my demerits
May speak, unbonneted, to as proud a fortune
As this that I have reached: for know, Iago,
But that I love the gentle Desdemona,
I would not my unhouséd free condition
Put into circumscription and confine
For the sea's worth.   But, look, what lights come yond?
   Iago.   Those are the raiséd father, and his friends:
You were best go in.
   Oth.   Not I; I must be found:

My parts, my title, and my perfect soul,
Shall manifest me rightly.   Is it they?
   Iago.   By Janus, I think no.

     Enter Cassio *and certain Officers with torches*

   Oth.   The servants of the duke, and my lieutenant.
The goodness of the night upon you, friends!
What is the news?
   Cas.   The duke doth greet you, general;
And he requires your haste-post-haste appearance,
Even on the instant.
   Oth.   What is the matter, think you?
   Cas.   Something from Cyprus, as I may divine.
It is a business of some heat; the galleys
Have sent a dozen sequent messengers
This very night at one another's heels;
And many of the consuls, raised and met,
Are at the duke's already. You have been hotly called for:
When, being not at your lodging to be found,
The senate hath sent about three several quests
To search you out.
   Oth.   'T is well I am found by you.
I will but spend a word here in the house,
And go with you.   [*Exit*
   Cas.   Ancient, what makes he here?
   Iago.   Faith, he to-night hath boarded a land-carack;
If it prove lawful prize, he's made for ever.
   Cas.   I do not understand.
   Iago.   He's married.
   Cas.   To who?

     Re-enter Othello

   Iago.   Marry, to—Come, captain, will you go?
   Oth.   Have with you.
   Cas.   Here comes another troop to seek for you.
   Iago.   It is Brabantio.—General, be advised;
He comes to bad intent.

Enter Brabantio, Roderigo, *and Officers, with torches and
weapons*

   Oth.   Holla! stand there!
   Rod.   Signior, it is the Moor.
   Bra.   Down with him, thief!
     [*They draw on both sides*
   Iago.   You, Roderigo! come, sir, I am for you.
   Oth.   Keep up your bright swords, for the dew will rust
    them.—
Good signior, you shall more command with years
Than with your weapons.
   Bra.   O thou foul thief, where hast thou stowed my
    daughter?—

Damned as thou art, thou hast enchanted her;
For I'll refer me to all things of sense,
If she in chains of magic were not bound,
Whether a maid so tender, fair, and happy,
So opposite to marriage that she shunned
The wealthy curléd darlings of our nation,
Would ever have, to incur a general mock,
Run from her guardage to the sooty bosom
Of such a thing as thou,—to fear, not to delight.
Judge me the world, if 't is not gross in sense,
That thou hast practised on her with foul charms;
Abused her delicate youth with drugs or minerals
That weaken motion.—I'll have 't disputed on;
'T is probable, and palpable to thinking.
I therefore apprehend and do attach thee
For an abuser of the world, a practiser
Of arts inhibited and out of warrant,—
Lay hold upon him: if he do resist,
Subdue him at his peril
    Oth.   Hold your hands,
Both you of my inclining, and the rest:
Were it my cue to fight, I should have known it
Without a prompter.—Where will you that I go
To answer this your charge?
    Bra.   To prison; till fit time
Of law, and course of direct session,
Call thee to answer.
    Oth.   What if I do obey?
How may the duke be therewith satisfied,
Whose messengers are here about my side,
Upon some present business of the state,
To bring me to him?
    Off.   'T is true, most worthy signior:
The duke's in council, and your noble self,
I am sure, is sent for.
    Bra.   How! the duke in council!
In this time of the night!—Bring him away.
Mine's not an idle cause: the duke himself,
Or any of my brothers of the state,
Cannot but feel this wrong as 't were their own;
For if such actions may have passage free,
Bond-slaves and pagans shall our statesman be.   [*Exeunt*

SCENE III.—The Same.   A Council Chamber

The DUKE, *and Senators, sitting at a table ; Officers
attending*

    Duke.   There is no composition in these news,
That gives them credit.

First Sen. Indeed, they're disproportioned:
My letters say, a hundred and seven galleys.
   Duke. And mine, a hundred and forty.
   Sec. Sen.   And mine, two hundred:
But though they jump not on a just account,—
As in these cases where the aim reports
'T is oft with difference,—yet do they all confirm
A Turkish fleet, and bearing up to Cyprus.
   Duke. Nay, it is possible enough to judgment:
I do not so secure me in the error,
But the main article I do approve
In fearful sense.
   Sailor. [*Within*] What, ho! what, ho! what, ho!
   Off. A messenger from the galleys.

Enter a Sailor

   Duke.   Now, what's the business?
   Sail. The Turkish preparation makes for Rhodes:
So I was bid report here to the state
By Signior Angelo.
   Duke. How say you by this change?
   First Sen.   This cannot be,
By no assay of reason: 't is a pageant,
To keep us in false gaze. When we consider
The importancy of Cyprus to the Turk;
And let ourselves again but understand
That, as it more concerns the Turk than Rhodes,
So may he with more facile question bear it,
For that it stands not in such warlike brace,
But altogether lacks the abilities
That Rhodes is dressed in:—If we make thought of this,
We must not think the Turk is so unskilful,
To leave that latest which concerns him first,
Neglecting an attempt of ease and gain
To wake and wage a danger profitless.
   Duke. Nay, in all confidence, he's not for Rhodes.
   First Off. Here is more news.

Enter a Messenger

   Mess. The Ottomites, reverend and gracious,
Steering with due course toward the isle of Rhodes,
Have there injointed them with an after fleet.
   First Sen. Ay, so I thought.—How many, as you guess?
   Mess. Of thirty sail; and now do they re-stem
Their backward course, bearing with frank appearance
Their purposes towards Cyprus.—Signior Montano,
Your trusty and most valiant servitor
With his free duty, recommends you thus,
And prays you to believe him.
   Duke. 'T is certain then for Cyprus.—
Marcus Luccicos, is not he in town?

First Sen.   He's now in Florence.
Duke.   Write from us to him; post-post-haste despatch.
First Sen.   Here comes Brabantio and the valiant Moor.

Enter BRABANTIO, OTHELLO, IAGO, RODERIGO, *and*
Officers

Duke.   Valiant Othello, we must straight employ you
Against the general enemy Ottoman.—
[*To Brabantio*] I did not see you; welcome, gentle
    signior;
We lacked your counsel and your help to-night.
    Bra.   So did I yours.   Good your grace, pardon me;
Neither my place, nor aught I heard of business
Hath raised me from my bed; nor doth the general care
Take hold on me, for my particular grief
Is of so flood-gate and o'erbearing nature
That it engluts and swallows other sorrows,
And it is still itself.
    Duke.   Why, what's the matter?
    Bra.   My daughter! O, my daughter!
    Sen.   Dead?
    Bra.   Ay, to me;
She is abused, stolen from me, and corrupted
By spells and medicines bought of mountebanks;
For nature so preposterously to err,
Being not deficient, blind, or lame of sense,
Sans witchcraft could not.
    Duke.   Whoe'er he be that, in this foul proceeding,
Hath thus beguiled your daughter of herself,
And you of her, the bloody book of law
You shall yourself read in the bitter letter,
After your own sense; yea, though our proper son
Stood in your action.
    Bra.   Humbly I thank your grace.
Here is the man, this Moor; whom now, it seems,
Your special mandate, for the state affairs,
Hath hither brought.
    Duke and Sen.   We are very sorry for it.
    Duke. [*To Othello*] What, in your own part, can you say
        to this?
    Bra.   Nothing, but this is so.
    Oth.   Most potent, grave, and reverend signiors,
My very noble and approved good masters,
That I have ta'en away this old man's daughter,
It is most true; true, I have married her:
The very head and front of my offending
Hath this extent, no more. Rude am I in my speech,
And little blessed with the soft phrase of peace;
For since these arms of mine had seven years' pith,
Till now some nine moons wasted, they have used

Their dearest action in the tented field;
And little of this great world can I speak
More than pertains to feats of broil and battle;
And, therefore, little shall I grace my cause
In speaking for myself.   Yet, by your gracious patience.
I will a round unvarnished tale deliver
Of my whole course of love: what drugs, what charms,
What conjuration, and what mighty magic,—
For such proceeding I am charg'd withal,—
I won his daughter.
    Bra.   A maiden never bold;
Of spirit so still and quiet, that her motion
Blushed at herself; and she—in spite of nature,
Of years, of country, credit, everything—
To fall in love with what she feared to look on!
It is a judgment maimed and most imperfect
That will confess, perfection so could err
Against all rules of nature; and must be driven
To find out practices of cunning hell,
Why this should be.   I, therefore, vouch again,
That with some mixtures powerful o'er the blood,
Or with some dram conjured to this effect,
He wrought upon her.
    Duke.   To vouch this is no proof,
Without more wider and more overt test
Than these thin habits and poor likelihoods
Of modern seeming do prefer against him.
    First Sen.   But, Othello, speak:
Did you by indirect and forcéd courses
Subdue and poison this young maid's affections;
Or came it by request, and such fair question
As soul to soul affordeth?
    Oth.   I do beseech you,
Send for the lady to the Sagittary,
And let her speak of me before her father:
If you do find me foul in her report,
The trust, the office, I do hold of you,
Not only take away, but let your sentence
Even fall upon my life.
    Duke.   Fetch Desdemona hither.
    Oth.   Ancient, conduct them; you best know the
         place.—   [*Exeunt Iago and Attendants*
And, till she come, as truly as to Heaven
I do confess the vices of my blood,
So justly to your grave ears I'll present
How I did thrive in this fair lady's love,
And she in mine.
    Duke.   Say it, Othello.
    Oth.   Her father loved me; oft invited me;
Still questioned me the story of my life,

From year to year,—the battles, sieges, fortunes,
That I have passed.
I ran it through, even from my boyish days
To the very moment that he bade me tell it:
Wherein I spake of most disastrous chances,
Of moving accidents by flood and field;
Of hair-breadth 'scapes i' the imminent deadly breach;
Of being taken by the insolent foe,
And sold to slavery; of my redemption thence,
And portance in my travel's history;
Wherein of antres vast and deserts idle,
Rough quarries, rocks, and hills whose heads touch heaven,
It was my hint to speak,—such was the process;—
And of the Cannibals that each other eat,
The Anthropophagi, and men whose heads
Do grow beneath their shoulders.   This, to hear,
Would Desdemona seriously incline:
But still the house-affairs would draw her thence;
Which ever as she could with haste despatch,
She'd come again, and with a greedy ear
Devour up my discourse.   Which I observing,
Took once a pliant hour; and found good means
To draw from her a prayer of earnest heart
That I would all my pilgrimage dilate,
Whereof by parcels she had something heard,
But not intentively: I did consent,
And often did beguile her of her tears,
When I did speak of some distressful stroke
That my youth suffered.   My story being done,
She gave me for my pains a world of sighs:
She swore,—in faith, 't was strange, 't was passing strange;
'T was pitiful, 't was wondrous pitiful:
She wished she had not heard it; yet she wished
That Heaven had made her such a man: she thanked
            me;
And bade me, if I had a friend that loved her,
I should but teach him how to tell my story,
And that would woo her.   Upon this hint I spake.
She loved me for the dangers I had passed,
And I loved her that she did pity them.
This only is the witchcraft I have used:
Here comes the lady; let her witness it.

Enter DESDEMONA *with* IAGO, *and Attendants*

Duke.   I think, this tale would win my daughter, too.—
Good Brabantio,
Take up this mangled matter at the best:
Men do their broken weapons rather use
Than their bare hands.
    Bra.   I pray you, hear her speak:

If she confess that she was half the wooer
Destruction on my head, if my bad blame
Light on the man!—Come hither, gentle mistress:
Do you perceive in all this noble company
Where most you owe obedience?

    Des.   My noble father,
I do perceive here a divided duty:
To you I am bound for life and education:
My life and education both do learn me
How to respect you; you're the lord of duty,—
I'm hitherto your daughter: but here's my husband;
And so much duty as my mother showed
To you, preferring you before her father,
So much I challenge that I may profess
Due to the Moor my lord.

    Bra.   God be with you!—I have done.—
Please it your grace, on to the state affairs:
I had rather to adopt a child than get it.—
Come hither, Moor:
I here do give thee that with all my heart,
Which, but thou hast already, with all my heart
I would keep from thee.—For your sake, jewel,
I'm glad at soul I have no other child;
For thy escape would teach me tyranny,
To hang clogs on them.—I have done, my lord.

    Duke. Let me speak like yourself; and lay a sentence,
Which, as a grise or step, may help these lovers
Into your favour.
When remedies are past, the griefs are ended
By seeing the worst, which late on hopes depended.
To mourn a mischief that is past and gone
Is the next way to draw new mischief on.
What cannot be preserved when fortune takes,
Patience her injury a mockery makes.
The robbed that smiles, steals something from the thief:
He robs himself that spends a bootless grief.

    Bra. So let the Turk of Cyprus us beguile;
We lose it not, so long as we can smile.
He bears the sentence well that nothing bears
But the free comfort which from thence he hears;
But he bears both the sentence and the sorrow
That to pay grief must of poor patience borrow.
These sentences, to sugar, or to gall,
Being strong on both sides, are equivocal:
But words are words; I never yet did hear,
That the bruised heart was pierced through the ear.
I humbly beseech you, proceed to the affairs of state.

    Duke. The Turk with a most mighty preparation makes
for Cyprus:—Othello, the fortitude of the place is best
known to you; and though we have there a substitute of

most allowed sufficiency, yet opinion, a sovereign mistress
of effects, throws a more safer voice on you: you must
therefore be content to slubber the gloss of your new fortunes with this more stubborn and boisterous expedition.

Oth.   The tyrant custom, most grave senators,
Hath made the flinty and steel couch of war
My thrice-driven bed of down: I do agnize
A natural and prompt alacrity
I find in hardness; and do undertake
These present wars against the Ottomites.
Most humbly, therefore, bending to your state,
I crave fit disposition for my wife;
Due reference of place, and exhibition;
With such accommodation and besort
As levels with her breeding.

Duke.   If you please, be 't at her father's.
Bra.   I'll not have it so.
Oth.   Nor I.
Des.   Nor I; I would not there reside,
To put my father in impatient thoughts,
By being in his eye.   Most gracious duke,
To my unfolding lend your prosperous ear;
And let me find a charter in your voice,
To assist my simpleness.

Duke.   What would you, Desdemona?
Des.   That I did love the Moor to live with him,
My downright violence and storm of fortunes
May trumpet to the world: my heart's subdued
Even to the very quality of my lord:
I saw Othello's visage in his mind;
And to his honours and his valiant parts
Did I my soul and fortunes consecrate.
So that, dear lords, if I be left behind,
A moth of peace, and he go to the war,
The rites for which I love him are bereft me,
And I a heavy interim shall support
By his dear absence.   Let me go with him.

Oth.   Let her have your voice.
Vouch with me, Heaven, I therefore beg it not,
To please the palate of my appetite,
Nor to comply with heat,—the young affects,
In me defunct,—and proper satisfaction;
But to be free and bounteous to her mind:
And Heaven defend your good souls, that you think
I will your serious and great business scant
For she is with me.   No, when light-winged toys
Of feathered Cupid seel with wanton dullness
My speculative and officed instruments,
That my disports corrupt and taint my business,
Let housewives make a skillet of my helm,

And all indign and base adversities
Make head against my estimation.
    Duke. Be it as you shall privately determine.
Either for her stay or going. The affair cries haste,
And speed must answer it.
    First Sen. You must away to-night.
    Oth.   With all my heart.
    Duke. At nine i' the morning here we'll meet again.—
Othello, leave some officer behind,
And he shall our commission bring to you,
With such things else of quality and respect
As doth import you.
    Oth.   So please your grace, my ancient;
A man he is of honesty and trust:
To his conveyance I assign my wife,
With what else needful your good grace shall think
To be sent after me.
    Duke.   Let it be so.—
Good night to every one.—[*To Brabantio*] And, noble signior,
If virtue no delighted beauty lack,
Your son-in-law is far more fair than black.
    First Sen. Adieu, brave Moor; use Desdemona well.
    Bra. Look to her, Moor, if thou hast eyes to see:
She has deceived her father, and may thee.
             [*Exeunt Duke, Senators, Officers, etc.*
    Oth. My life upon her faith!—Honest Iago,
My Desdemona must I leave to thee:
I pr'ythee, let thy wife attend on her
And bring them after in the best advantage.
Come, Desdemona; I have but an hour
Of love, of worldly matters and direction,
To spend with thee: we must obey the time.
          [*Exeunt Othello and Desdemona*
    Rod. Iago!
    Iago. What say'st thou, noble heart?
    Rod. What will I do, thinkest thou?
    Iago. Why, go to bed, and sleep.
    Rod. I will incontinently drown myself.
    Iago. Well, if thou dost, I shall never love thee after it.
Why, thou silly gentleman!
    Rod. It is silliness to live when to live is torment; and
then have we a prescription to die when death is our physician.
    Iago. O, villainous! I have looked upon the world for
four times seven years, and since I could distinguish betwixt
a benefit and an injury, I never found a man that knew how
to love himself. Ere I would say I would drown myself
for the love of a guinea-hen, I would change my humanity
with a baboon.
    Rod. What should I do? I confess, it is my shame
to be so fond; but it is not in my virtue to amend it.

Iago. Virtue? a fig! 't is in ourselves that we are thus, or thus. Our bodies are our gardens, to which our wills are gardeners; so that if we will plant nettles, or sow lettuce; set hyssop, and weed up thyme; supply it with one gender of herbs, or distract it with many; either to have it sterile with idleness, or manured with industry; why, the power and corrigible authority of this lies in our wills. If the balance of our lives had not one scale of reason to poise another of sensuality, the blood and baseness of our natures would conduct us to most preposterous conclusions: but we have reason to cool our raging motions, our carnal stings, our unbitted lusts; whereof I take this that you call love to be a sect or scion.

Rod. It cannot be.

Iago. It is merely a lust of the blood and a permission of the will. Come, be a man: drown thyself? drown cats, and blind puppies. I have professed me thy friend, and I confess me knit to thy deserving with cables of perdurable toughness; I could never better stead thee than now. Put money in thy purse; follow these wars; defeat thy favour with an usurped beard; I say, put money in thy purse. It cannot be that Desdemona should long continue her love to the Moor,—put money in thy purse,—nor he his to her: it was a violent commencement in her, and thou shalt see an answerable sequestration;—put but money in thy purse.—These Moors are changeable in their wills;—fill thy purse with money:—the food that to him now is as luscious as locusts, shall be to him shortly as bitter as coloquintida. She must change for youth: when she is sated with his body, she will find the error of her choice.—She must have change, she must: therefore, put money in thy purse.— If thou wilt needs damn thyself, do it a more delicate way than drowning. Make all the money thou canst; if sanctimony and a frail vow betwixt an erring barbarian and a super-subtle Venetian be not too hard for my wits and all the tribe of hell, thou shalt enjoy her; therefore, make money. A pox of drowning thyself! it is clean out of the way: seek thou rather to be hanged in compassing thy joy than to be drowned and go without her.

Rod. Wilt thou be fast to my hopes, if I depend on the issue?

Iago. Thou art sure of me.—Go, make money.—I have told thee often, and I re-tell thee again and again, I hate the Moor: my cause is hearted; thine hath no less reason. Let us be conjunctive in our revenge against him: if thou canst cuckold him, thou dost thyself a pleasure, me a sport. There are many events in the womb of time, which will be delivered. Traverse; go: provide thy money. We will have more of this to-morrow. Adieu.

Rod. Where shall we meet i' the morning?

Iago. At my lodging.
Rod. I'll be with thee betimes.
Iago. Go to; farewell.—Do you hear, Roderigo?
Rod. What say you?
Iago. No more of drowning, do you hear?
Rod. I am changed. I'll go sell all my land.
Iago. Go to; farewell! put money enough in your
    purse.   [*Exit Roderigo*

Thus do I ever make my fool my purse;
For I mine own gained knowledge should profane
If I would time expend with such a snipe
But for my sport and profit. I hate the Moor;
And it is thought abroad that 'twixt my sheets
He has done my office: I know not if 't be true;
Yet I, for mere suspicion in that kind,
Will do as if for surety. He holds me well;
The better shall my purpose work on him.
Cassio's a proper man: let me see now;
To get his place, and to plume up my will
In double knavery,—How, how?—Let's see:
After some time, to abuse Othello's ear
That he is too familiar with his wife:—
He hath a person, and a smooth dispose;
To be suspected; framed to make women false.
The Moor is of a free and open nature,
That thinks men honest that but seem to be so,
And will as tenderly be led by the nose
As asses are.—
I have 't. It is engendered. Hell and night
Must bring this monstrous birth to the world's light. [*Exit*

ACT TWO

SCENE I.—A Seaport Town in Cyprus.   A Platform

Enter MONTANO *and two Gentlemen*

Mon. What from the cape can you discern at sea?
First Gent. Nothing at all: it is a high-wrought flood;
I cannot, 'twixt the heaven and the main
Descry a sail.
Mon. Methinks the wind hath spoke aloud at land;
A fuller blast ne'er shook out battlements;
If it hath ruffianed so upon the sea,
What ribs of oak, when mountains melt on them,
Can hold the mortise? What shall we hear of this?
Sec. Gent. A segregation of the Turkish fleet:
For do but stand upon the foaming shore,
The chidden billow seems to pelt the clouds;
The wind-shaked surge, with high and monstrous mane,

Seems to cast water on the burning bear,
And quench the guards of the ever-fixéd pole:
I never did like molestation view
On the enchaféd flood.
   Mon.   If that the Turkish fleet
Be not ensheltered and embayed, they are drowned;
It is impossible to bear it out.

Enter a third Gentleman

   Third Gent.   News, lads! our wars are done.
The desperate tempest hath so banged the Turks,
That their designment halts: a noble ship of Venice
Hath seen a grievous wrack and sufferance
On most part of their fleet.
   Mon.   How! is this true?
   Third Gent.   The ship is here put in,
A Veronesa; Michael Cassio,
Lieutenant to the warlike Moor, Othello,
Is come on shore: the Moor himself's at sea,
And is in full commission here for Cyprus.
   Mon.   I am glad on 't; 't is a worthy governor.
   Third Gent.   But this same Cassio, though he speak of
      comfort,
Touching the Turkish loss, yet he looks sadly,
And prays the Moor be safe; for they were parted
With foul and violent tempest.
   Mon.   Pray heavens he be;
For I have served him, and the man commands
Like a full soldier. Let's to the sea-side, ho!
As well to see the vessel that's come in
As to throw out our eyes for brave Othello,
Even till we make the main and the aerial blue
An indistinct regard.
   Third Gent.   Come, let's do so;
For every minute is expectancy
Of more arrivance.

Enter CASSIO

   Cas.   Thanks, you the valiant of this warlike isle,
That so approve the Moor.—O, let the heavens
Give him defence against the elements,
For I have lost him on a dangerous sea.
   Mon.   Is he well shipped?
   Cas.   His bark is stoutly timbered, and his pilot
Of very expert and approved allowance;
Therefore my hopes, not surfeited to death,
Stand in bold cure.
   Within]   A sail, a sail, a sail!

Enter a fourth Gentleman

   Cas.   What noise?

257

Fourth Gent. The town is empty; on the brow o' the sea
Stand ranks of people, and they cry "A sail!"
  Cas. My hopes do shape him for the governor.

                                                    [*Guns heard*
  Sec. Gent. They do discharge their shot of courtesy:
Our friends, at least.
  Cas.   I pray you, sir, go forth,
And give us truth who 't is that is arrived.
  Sec. Gent. I shall.   [*Exit*
  Mon. But, good lieutenant, is your general wived?
  Cas. Most fortunately: he hath achieved a maid
That paragons description and wild fame;
One that excels the quirks of blazoning pens,
And, in the essential vesture of creation
Does tire the ingener.

                 Re-enter second Gentleman

                              How now! who has put in!
  Sec. Gent. 'T is one Iago, ancient to the general.
  Cas. He has had most favourable and happy speed:
Tempests themselves, high seas, and howling winds,
The guttered rocks, and congregated sands,—
Traitors ensteeped to clog the guiltless keel,—
As having sense of beauty, do omit
Their mortal natures, letting go safely by
The divine Desdemona.
  Mon.   What is she?
  Cas. She that I spake of, our great captain's captain,
Left in the conduct of the bold Iago;
Whose footing here anticipates our thoughts
A se'nnight's speed.—Great Jove, Othello guard,
And swell his sail with thine own powerful breath,
That he may bless this bay with his tall ship,
Make love's quick pants in Desdemona's arms,
Give renewed fire to our extincted spirits,
And bring all Cyprus comfort?—

       Enter DESDEMONA, EMILIA, IAGO, RODERIGO, *and*
                          Attendants

                              O, behold,
The riches of the ship is come on shore!
Ye men of Cyprus let her have your knees.—
Hail to thee, lady! and the grace of Heaven,
Before, behind thee, and on every hand,
Enwheel thee round!
  Des.   I thank you, valiant Cassio.
What tidings can you tell me of my lord?
  Cas. He is not yet arrived: nor know I aught
But that he's well, and will be shortly here.
  Des. O, but I fear—How lost you company?

                             258

Cas.   The great contention of the sea and skies
Parted our fellowship: but, hark! a sail.
    [*Within*]   A sail, a sail!   [*Guns heard*
Sec. Gent.   They give their greeting to the citadel:
This likewise is a friend.
Cas.   See, for the news!—
                                        [*Exit Gentlemen*
Good ancient, you are welcome:—[*To Emilia*] welcome,
        mistress:
Let it not gall your patience, good Iago,
That I extend my manners: 't is my breeding
That gives me this bold show of courtesy.   [*Kissing her*
    Iago.   Sir, would she give you so much of her lips
As of her tongue she oft bestows on me,
You 'd have enough.
    Des.   Alas, she has no speech.
    Iago.   In faith, too much;
I find it still, when I have list to sleep:
Marry, before your ladyship, I grant,
She puts her tongue a little in her heart,
And chides with thinking.
    Emil.   You have little cause to say so.
    Iago.   Come on, come on: you 're pictures out of doors,
Bells in your parlours, wild cats in your kitchens,
Saint in your injuries, devils being offended,
Players in your housewifery, and housewives in your beds.
    Des.   O, fie upon thee, slanderer!
    Iago.   Nay, it is true, or else I am a Turk:
You rise to play, and go to bed to work.
    Emil.   You shall not write my praise.
    Iago.   No, let me not.
    Des.   What wouldst thou write of me, if thou shouldst
        praise me?
    Iago.   O gentle lady, do not put me to 't;
For I am nothing, if not critical.
    Des.   Come on; assay.—There 's one gone to the harbour?
    Iago.   Ay, madam.
    Des.   I am not merry; but I do beguile
The thing I am, by seeming otherwise.—
Come, how wouldst thou praise me?
    Iago.   I am about it; but, indeed, my invention
Comes from my pate as birdlime does from frize,—
It plucks out brains and all: but my Muse labours,
And thus she is delivered.
If she be fair and wise,—fairness, and wit,
The one 's for use, the other useth it.
    Des.   Well praised!   How, if she be black and witty?
    Iago.   If she be black, and thereto have a wit,
She 'll find a white that shall her blackness fit.
    Des.   Worse and worse.

Iago..   How, if fair and foolish?
Emil   She never yet was foolish that was fair;
For even her folly helped her to an heir.
  Des.   These are old fond paradoxes, to make fools laugh
i' the ale-house.   What miserable praise hast thou for her
that's foul and foolish?
  Iago.   There's none so foul, and foolish thereunto,
But does foul pranks which fair and wise ones do.
  Des.   O heavy ignorance! thou praisest the worst
best.   But what praise couldst thou bestow on a deserving
woman indeed? one that, in the authority of her merit,
did justly put on the vouch of very malice itself?
  Iago.   She that was ever fair, and never proud;
Had tongue at will, and yet was never loud;
Never lacked gold, and yet went never gay;
Fled from her wish, and yet said, "Now I may;"
She that, being angered, her revenge being nigh,
Bade her wrong stay, and her displeasure fly;
She that in wisdom never was so frail
To change the cod's head for the salmon's tail;
She that could think, and ne'er disclose her mind,
See suitors following, and not look behind:
She was a wight, if ever such wights were,—
  Des.   To do what?
  Iago.   To suckle fools, and chronicle small beer.
  Des.   O most lame and impotent conclusion!—Do not
learn of him, Emilia, though he be thy husband.—How say
you, Cassio? is he not a most profane and liberal counseller?
  Cas.   He speaks home, madam: you may relish him
more in the soldier than in the scholar.
  Iago.   [*Aside*] He takes her by the palm: ay, well said,
whisper: with as little a web as this will I ensnare as great
a fly as Cassio.   Ay, smile upon her, do; I will gyve thee
in thine own courtship.   You say true, 't is so, indeed:
if such tricks as these strip you out of your lieutenantry,
it had better you had not kissed your three fingers so
oft, which now again you are most apt to play the sir in.
Very good; well kissed, an excellent courtesy! 't is so,
indeed.   Yet again your fingers to your lips? would they
were clyster-pipes for your sake!—[*A trumpet heard*] The
Moor!   I know his trumpet.
  Cas.   'T is truly he.
  Des.   Let's meet him, and receive him.
  Cas.   Lo, where he comes!

Enter OTHELLO *and Attendants*

  Oth.   O my fair warrior!
  Des.   My dear Othello!
  Oth.   It gives me wonder great as my content,
To see you here before me.   O my soul's joy!

If after every tempest came such calms,
May the winds blow till they have wakened death;
And let the labouring bark climb hills of seas,
Olympus-high, and duck again as low
As hell's from heaven!   If it were now to die,
'T were now to be most happy; for, I fear,
My soul hath her content so absolute,
That not another comfort like to this
Succeeds in unknown fate.
   Des.   The heavens forbid
But that our loves and comforts should increase,
Even as our days do grow!
   Oth.   Amen to that, sweet powers!
I cannot speak enough to this content;
It stops me here; it is too much of joy:
And this, and this, the greatest discords be   [*Kissing her*
That e'er our hearts shall make!
   Iago. [*Aside*]   O, you are well tuned now;
But I 'll set down the pegs that make this music,
As honest as I am.
   Oth.   Come, let us to the castle.—
News, friends: our wars are done, the Turks are drowned.
How does my old acquaintance of this isle?—
Honey, you shall be well-desired in Cyprus;
I've found great love amongst them.   O my sweet,
I prattle out of fashion, and I dote
In mine own comforts.—I pr'ythee, good Iago,
Go to the bay, and disembark my coffers.
Bring thou the master to the citadel;
He is a good one, and his worthiness
Does challenge much respect.—Come, Desdemona,
Once more well met at Cyprus.
           [*Exeunt Othello, Desdemona, and Attendants*
   Iago.   Do thou meet me presently at the harbour.   Come
hither.   If thou be'st valiant,—as they say, base men being
in love have then a nobility in their natures more than is
native to them,—list me.   The lieutenant to-night watches
on the court of guard:—first, I must tell thee this—
Desdemona is directly in love with him.
   Rod.   With him!   why, 't is not possible.
   Iago.   Lay thy fingers thus, and let thy soul be instructed.
Mark me with what violence she first loved the Moor, but
for bragging, and telling her fantastical lies; and will she
love him still for prating? let not thy discreet heart think
it.   Her eye must be fed; and what delight shall she have
to look on the devil? when the blood is made dull with the
act of sport, there should be—again to inflame it, and to give
satiety a fresh appetite—loveliness in favour, sympathy in
years, manners, and beauties; all which the Moor is de-
fective in.   Now, for the want of these required conveniences,

261

her delicate tenderness will find itself abused, begin to heave the gorge, disrelish and abhor the Moor; very nature will instruct her in it, and compel her to some second choice. Now, sir, this granted,—as it is a most pregnant and unforced position,—who stands so eminent in the degree of this fortune, as Cassio does? a knave very voluble, no further conscionable than in putting on the mere form of civil and humane seeming, for the better compassing of his salt and most hidden-loose affection? why, none; why none: a slipper and subtle knave; a finder-out of occasions; that has an eye can stamp and counterfeit advantages, though true advantage never present itself: a devilish knave! Besides, the knave is handsome, young, and hath all those requisites in him that folly and green minds look after; a pestilent complete knave: and the woman hath found him already.

Rod. I cannot believe that in her: she is full of most blessed condition.

Iago. Blessed fig's end! the wine she drinks is made of grapes: if she had been blessed, she would never have loved the Moor: blessed pudding! Didst thou not see her paddle with the palm of his hand? didst not mark that?

Rod. Yes, that I did; but that was but courtesy.

Iago. Lechery, by this hand! an index, and obscure prologue to the history of lust and foul thoughts. They met so near with their lips, that their breaths embraced together. Villainous thoughts, Roderigo! when these mutualities so marshal the way, hard at hand comes the master and main exercise, the incorporate conclusion: pish!—But, sir, be you ruled by me: I have brought you from Venice. Watch you to-night; for the command, I'll lay 't upon you: Cassio knows you not:—I'll not be far from you: do you find some occasion to anger Cassio, either by speaking too loud, or tainting his discipline; or from what other course you please, which the time shall more favourably minister.

Rod. Well.

Iago. Sir, he is rash, and very sudden in choler, and, haply, may strike at you: provoke him, that he may; for even out of that will I cause these of Cyprus to mutiny, whose qualification shall come into no true taste but by the displanting of Cassio. So shall you have a shorter journey to your desires, by the means I shall then have to prefer them; and the impediment most profitably removed, without the which there were no expectation of our prosperity.

Rod. I will do this, if I can bring it to any opportunity.

Iago. I warrant thee. Meet me by-and-by at the citadel: I must fetch his necessaries ashore. Farewell.

Rod. Adieu.   [*Exit*

Iago. That Cassio loves her, I do well believe it;

That she loves him, 't is apt, and of great credit;
The Moor—howbeit that I endure him not—
Is of a constant, loving, noble nature;
And, I dare think he'll prove to Desdemona
A most dear husband.   Now, I do love her too;
Not out of absolute lust—though, peradventure
I stand accountant for as great a sin—
But partly led to diet my revenge,
For that I do suspect the lusty Moor
Hath leaped into my seat; the thought whereof
Doth like a poisonous mineral gnaw my inwards
And nothing can or shall content my soul,
Till I am evened with him, wife for wife;
Or failing so, yet that I put the Moor
At least into a jealousy so strong
That judgment cannot cure.   Which thing to do
If this poor trash of Venice, whom I trash
For his quick hunting, stand the putting-on,
I'll have our Michael Cassio on the hip;
Abuse him to the Moor in the rank garb,
For I fear Cassio with my night-cap too;
Make the Moor thank me, love me, and reward me,
For making him egregiously an ass,
And practising upon his peace and quiet
Even to madness.   'T is here, but yet confused:
Knavery's plain face is never seen till used.   [*Exit*

SCENE II.—A Street

Enter a Herald, with a proclamation ; people following

Her.   It is Othello's pleasure, our noble and valiant
general, that, upon certain tidings now arrived, importing
the mere perdition of the Turkish fleet, every man put
himself into triumph; some to dance, some to make bon-
fires, each man to what sport and revels his addiction leads
him; for, besides these beneficial news, it is the celebration
of his nuptial.   So much was his pleasure should be pro-
claimed.   All offices are open; and there is full liberty of
feasting, from this present hour of five till the bell have
told eleven.   Heaven bless the isle of Cyprus, and our
noble general, Othello!   [*Exeunt*

SCENE III.—A Hall in the Castle

Enter OTHELLO, DESDEMONA, CASSIO, *and Attendants*

Oth.   Good Michael, look you to the guard to-night:
Let's teach ourselves that honourable stop,
Not to out-sport discretion.
   Cas.   Iago hath direction what to do;

But, notwithstanding, with my personal eye
Will I look to 't.
    Oth.   Iago is most honest.
Michael, good night: to-morrow with your earliest
Let me have speech with you.—[*To Desdemona*] Come,
    my dear love:
The purchase made, the fruits are to ensue;
That profit's yet to come 'twixt me and you.—
Good night.   [*Exeunt Othello, Desdemona, and Attendants*

Enter IAGO

    Cas. Welcome, Iago: we must to the watch.
    Iago. Not this hour, lieutenant; 'tis not yet ten
o'clock. Our general cast us thus early for the love of his
Desdemona, who let us not therefore blame: he hath not yet
made wanton the night with her, and she is sport for Jove.
    Cas. She's a most exquisite lady.
    Iago. And, I'll warrant her, full of game.
    Cas. Indeed, she's a most fresh and delicate creature.
    Iago. What an eye she has! methinks it sounds a parley
to provocation.
    Cas. An inviting eye, and yet methinks right modest.
    Iago. And, when she speaks, is it not an alarum to love?
    Cas. She is, indeed, perfection.
    Iago. Well, happiness to their sheets! Come, lieuten-
ant, I have a stoop of wine; and here without are a brace of
Cyprus gallants that would fain have a measure to the
health of black Othello.
    Cas. Not to-night, good Iago. I have very poor and
unhappy brains for drinking. I could well wish courtesy
would invent some other custom of entertainment.
    Iago. O, they are our friends; but one cup; I'll drink
for you.
    Cas. I have drunk but one cup to-night, and that was
craftily qualified too, and, behold, what innovation it
makes here. I am unfortunate in the infirmity, and dare
not task my weakness with any more.
    Iago. What, man! 't is a night of revels: the gallants
desire it.
    Cas. Where are they?
    Iago. Here at the door; I pray you, call them in.
    Cas. I'll do 't; but it dislikes me.   [*Exit*
    Iago. If I can fasten but one cup upon him,
With that which he hath drunk to-night already,
He'll be as full of quarrel and offence
As my young mistress' dog. Now, my sick fool, Roderigo,
Whom love has turned almost the wrong side out,
To Desdemona hath to-night caroused
Potations pottle-deep; and he's to watch.
Three lads of Cyprus—noble, swelling spirits,

That hold their honours in a wary distance,
The very elements of this warlike isle—
Have I to-night flustered with flowing cups,
And they watch too. Now, 'mongst this flock of drunkards,
Am I to put our Cassio in some action
That may offend the isle:—but here they come.
If consequence do but approve my dream,
My boat sails freely, both with wind and stream.

Re-enter CASSIO, *with him* MONTANO, *Gentlemen, and*
Servant with wine

Cas. 'Fore God, they have given me a rouse already.
Mon. Good faith, a little one; not past a pint, as I
am a soldier.
Iago. Some wine, ho!
[*Sings*]   *And let me the canakin clink, clink;*
            And let me the canakin clink:
               A soldier's a man;
               A life's but a span;
            Why then let a soldier drink.
Some wine, boys!
Cas. 'Fore God, an excellent song.
Iago. I learned it in England, where, indeed, they are
most potent in potting: your Dane, your German, and
your swag-bellied Hollander,—Drink, ho!—are nothing
to your English.
Cas. Is your Englishman so expert in his drinking?
Iago Why, he drinks you, with facility, your Dane dead
drunk; he sweats not to overthrow your Almain; he gives
your Hollander a vomit, ere the next pottle can be filled.
Cas. To the health of our general!
Mon. I am for it, lieutenant; and I'll do you justice.
Iago. O sweet England!

            King Stephen was a worthy peer,
               His breeches cost him but a crown;
            He held them sixpence all too dear,
               With that he called the tailor lown.

            He was a wight of high renown,
               And thou art but of low degree:
            'T is pride that pulls the country down;
               Then take thine auld cloak about thee.

Some wine, ho!
Cas. Why, this is a more exquisite song than the other.
Iago. Will you hear 't again?
Cas. No; for I hold him to be unworthy of his place
that does those things.—Well, God 's above all; and there
be souls must be saved, and there be souls must not be saved.
Iago. It's true, good lieutenant.

Cas. For mine own part,—no offence to the general, nor any man of quality,—I hope to be saved.

Iago. And so do I too, lieutenant.

Cas. Ay, but, by your leave, not before me: the lieutenant is to be saved before the ancient. Let's have no more of this; let's to our affairs.—God forgive us our sins!—Gentleman, let's look to our business. Do not think, gentleman, I am drunk: this is my ancient;—this is my right hand, and this is my left hand.—I am not drunk now; I can stand well enough, and speak well enough.

All. Excellent well.

Cas. Why, very well then; you must not think then, that I am drunk.   [*Exit*

Mon. To the platform, masters: come, let's set the watch.

Iago. You see this fellow, that is gone before:
He is a soldier, fit to stand by Cæsar
And give direction; and do but see his vice.
'T is to his virtue a just equinox,
The one as long as the other: 't is pity of him.
I fear the trust Othello puts him in,
On some odd time of his infirmity,
Will shake this island.

Mon.   But is he often thus?

Iago. 'T is evermore the prologue to his sleep:
He'll watch the horologe a double set,
If drink rock not his cradle.

Mon.   It were well
The general were put in mind of it.
Perhaps, he sees it not; or his good nature
Prizes the virtue that appears in Cassio,
And looks not on his evils.   Is not this true?

Enter RODERIGO

Iago. [*Aside to him*] How now, Roderigo?
I pray you, after the lieutenant; go.   [*Exit Roderigo*

Mon. And 't is great pity that the noble Moor
Should hazard such a place as his own second
With one of an ingraft infirmity.
It were an honest action to say
So to the Moor.

Iago.   Not I, for this fair island:
I do love Cassio well; and would do much
To cure him of this evil.—But hark! what noise?
                        [*Cry within :* "Help! Help!'

Re-enter CASSIO, *pursuing* RODERIGO

Cas. You rogue! you rascal!

Mon.   What's the matter, lieutenant?

Cas. A knave teach me my duty!
I'll beat the knave into a twiggen bottle.

Rod. Beat me!
Cas. Dost thou prate, rogue?   [*Striking Roderigo*
Mon.   Nay, good lieutenant
                                        [*Staying him*
I pray you sir, hold your hand.
Cas.   Let me go, sir,
Or I'll knock you o'er the mazzard.
Mon.   Come, come; you're drunk,
Cas. Drunk!   [*They fight*
Iago. [*Aside to Roderigo*] Away, I say! go out, and
   cry a mutiny.   [*Exit Roderigo*
Nay, good lieutenant,—God's will, gentleman!
Help, ho!—Lieutenant,—sir—Montano,—sir;—
Help, masters!—Here's a goodly watch, indeed!
                                        [*Bell rings*
Who's that which rings the bell?—*Diablo*, ho!
The town will rise: God's will, lieutenant, hold!
You will be shamed for ever.

Enter OTHELLO *and Attendants*

Oth.   What is the matter here?
Mon. I bleed still: I am hurt to the death.
Oth. Hold, for your lives!
Iago. Hold, ho! Lieutenant,—sir,—Montano,—gentle-
   men!—
Have you forgot all sense of place and duty?
Hold! the general speaks to you; hold, for shame!
Oth. Why, how now, ho! from whence ariseth this?
Are we turned Turks, and to ourselves do that
Which Heaven hath forbid the Ottomites?
For Christian shame, put by this barbarous brawl:
He that stirs next to carve for his own rage
Holds his soul light; he dies upon his motion.—
Silence that dreadful bell! it frights the isle
From her propriety.—What is the matter, masters?—
Honest Iago, that look'st dead with grieving,
Speak, who began this? on thy love, I charge thee.
Iago. I do not know:—friends all but now, even now,
In quarter, and in terms like bride and groom
Devesting them for bed; and then, but now—
As if some planet had unwitted men—
Swords out, and tilting one at other's breast,
In opposition bloody. I cannot speak
Any beginning to this peevish odds;
And would in action glorious I had lost
Those legs that brought me to a part of it!
Oth. How came it, Michael, you are thus forgot?
Cas. I pray you, pardon me; I cannot speak.
Oth. Worthy Montano, you were wont be civil;
The gravity and stillness of your youth

The world hath noted, and your name is great
In mouths of wisest censure: what's the matter,
That you unlace your reputation thus,
And spend your rich opinion for the name
Of a night-brawler? give me answer to it.
    Mon. Worthy Othello, I am hurt to danger:
Your officer, Iago, can inform you—
While I spare speech, which something now offends me,—
Of all that I do know; nor know I aught
By me that's said or done amiss this night,
Unless self-charity be sometime a vice,
And to defend ourselves it be a sin
When violence assails us.
    Oth.   Now, by Heaven,
My blood begins my safer guides to rule;
And passion, having my best judgment collied,
Assays to lead the way. If I once stir,
Or do but lift this arm, the best of you
Shall sink in my rebuke. Give me to know
How this foul rout began, who set it on;
And he that is approved in this offence,
Though he had twinned with me, both at a birth,
Shall lose me.—What! in a town of war,
Yet wild, the people's hearts brimful of fear,
To manage private and domestic quarrel,
In night, and on the court and guard of safety!
'T is monstrous.—Iago, who began it?
    Mon. If partially affined, or leagued in office
Thou dost deliver more or less than truth,
Thou art no soldier.
    Iago.   Touch me not so near:
I had rather have this tongue cut from my mouth
Than it should do offence to Michael Cassio;
Yet, I persuade myself, to speak the truth
Shall nothing wrong him.—Thus it is, general.
Montano and myself being in speech,
There comes a fellow crying out for help,
And Cassio following him with determined sword
To execute upon him. Sir, this gentleman
Steps in to Cassio, and entreats his pause:
Myself the crying fellow did pursue,
Lest by his clamour—as it so fell out—
The town might fall in fright: he, swift of foot,
Outran my purpose; and I returned the rather
For that I heard the clink and fall of swords,
And Cassio high in oath, which till to-night
I ne'er might say before. When I came back—
For this was brief—I found them close together,
At blow and thrust, even as again they were
When you yourself did part them.

More of this matter can I not report:—
But men are men: the best sometimes forget:—
Though Cassio did some little wrong to him,
As men in rage strike those that wish them best,
Yet surely Cassio, I believe, received
From him that fled some strange indignity,
Which patience could not pass.
Oth.   I know, Iago,
Thy honesty and love doth mince this matter,
Making it light to Cassio.—Cassio, I love thee,
But never more be officer of mine.—

Re-enter DESDEMONA, *attended*

Look, if my gentle love be not raised up!
I'll make thee an example.
Des.   What's the matter?
Oth.   All's well now, sweeting; come away to bed.—
Sir, for your hurts, myself will be your surgeon:—
Lead him off.—   [*Montana is led off*
Iago, look with care about the town,
And silence those whom this vile brawl distracted.—
Come, Desdemona; 't is the soldiers' life,
To have their balmy slumbers waked with strife.
                           [*Exeunt all but Iago and Cassio*

Iago.   What, are you hurt, lieutenant?
Cas.   Ay; past all surgery.
Iago.   Marry, heaven forbid!
Cas.   Reputation, reputation, reputation! O, I have
lost my reputation. I have lost the immortal part of
myself, and what remains is bestial.—My reputation,
Iago, my reputation!
Iago.   As I am an honest man, I thought you had received some bodily wound; there is more sense in that
than in reputation. Reputation is an idle and most false
imposition; oft got without merit, and lost without deserving: you have lost no reputation at all, unless you repute
yourself such a loser. What, man! there are ways to
recover the general again: you are but now cast in his
mood, a punishment more in policy than in malice; even
so as one would beat his offenceless dog to affright an im-
perious lion. Sue to him again, and he's yours.
Cas.   I will rather sue to be despised, than to deceive
so good a commander with so slight, so drunken, and so
indiscreet an officer. Drunk? and speak parrot? and
squabble? swagger? swear? and discourse fustian with
one's own shadow?—O thou invisible spirit of wine, if thou
hast no name to be known by, let us call thee devil.
Iago.   What was he that you followed with your sword?
What had he done to you?
Cas.   I know not.

Iago. Is 't possible?

Cas. I remember a mass of things, but nothing distinctly; a quarrel, but nothing wherefore.—O God, that men should put an enemy in their mouths to steal away their brains! that we should, with joy, pleasance, revel, and applause, transform ourselves into beasts!

Iago. Why, but you are now well enough: how came you thus recovered?

Cas. It hath pleased the devil drunkenness, to give place to the devil wrath: one unperfectness shows me another, to make me frankly despise myself.

Iago. Come, you are too severe a moraler. As the time, the place, and the condition of this country stands, I could heartily wish this had not befallen; but, since it is as it is, mend it for your own good.

Cas. I will ask him for my place again,—he shall tell me, I am a drunkard. Had I as many mouths as Hydra, such an answer would stop them all. To be now a sensible man, by-and-by a fool, and presently a beast! O, strange! —Every inordinate cup is unblessed, and the ingredient is a devil.

Iago. Come, come, good wine is a good familiar creature, if it be well-used: exclaim no more against it. And, good lieutenant, I think you think I love you.

Cas. I have well approved it, sir.—I drunk!

Iago. You or any man living may be drunk at a time, man. I'll tell you what you shall do. Our general's wife is now the general:—I may say so in this respect, for that he hath devoted and given up himself to the contemplation, mark, and denotement of her parts and graces:—confess yourself freely to her; importune her: she'll help to put you in your place again. She is of so free, so kind, so apt, so blessed a disposition, that she holds it a vice in her goodness, not to do more than she is requested. This broken joint, between you and her husband, entreat her to splinter; and my fortunes against any lay worth naming, this crack of your love shall grow stronger than it was before.

Cas. You advise me well.

Iago. I protest, in the sincerity of love and honest kindness.

Cas. I think it freely; and betimes in the morning I will beseech the virtuous Desdemona to undertake for me. I am desperate of my fortunes if they check me here.

Iago. You are in the right. Good night, lieutenant; I must to the watch.

Cas. Good night, honest Iago.   [*Exit*

Iago. And what's he then, that says I play the villain?
When this advice is free I give and honest,
Probal to thinking, and, indeed, the course
To win the Moor again? For 't is most easy

The inclining Desdemona to subdue
In any honest suit: she's framed as fruitful
As the free elements.   And then for her
To win the Moor,—were 't to renounce his baptism,
All seals and symbols of redeeméd sin,—
His soul is so enfettered to her love
That she may make, unmake, do what she list,
Even as her appetite shall play the god
With his weak function.   How am I then a villain,
To counsel Cassio to this parallel course,
Directly to his good?   Divinity of hell!
When devils will their blackest sins put on
They do suggest at first with heavenly shows,
As I do now; for whiles this honest fool
Plies Desdemona to repair his fortunes,
And she for him pleads strongly to the Moor,
I'll pour this pestilence into his ear,—
That she repeals him for her body's lust;
And, by how much she strives to do him good,
She shall undo her credit with the Moor.
So will I turn her virtue into pitch;
And out of her own goodness make the net
That shall enmesh them all.

Re-enter RODERIGO

How now, Roderigo?
    Rod. I do follow here in the chase, not like a hound that
hunts, but one that fills up the cry.   My money is almost
spent: I have been to-night exceedingly well cudgelled;
and, I think, the issue will be, I shall have so much ex-
perience for my pains; and so, with no money at all, and
a little more wit, return again to Venice.
    Iago. How poor are they that have not patience!
What wound did ever heal but by degrees?
Thou know'st we work by wit, and not by witchcraft;
And wit depends on dilatory time.
Does 't not go well?   Cassio hath beaten thee,
And thou, by that small hurt, has cashiered Cassio.
Though other things grow fair against the sun,
Yet fruits that blossom first will first be ripe:
Content thyself awhile.—By the mass, 't is morning;
Pleasure and action make the hours seem short.
Retire thee; go where thou art billeted:
Away, I say; thou shalt know more hereafter:
Nay, get thee gone. [*Exit Roderigo*] Two things are
          to be done,—
My wife must move for Cassio to her mistress;
I'll set her on;
Myself the while to draw the Moor apart,
And bring him jump when he may Cassio find

Soliciting his wife:—ay, that's the way;
Dull not device by coldness and delay.   [*Exit*

ACT THREE

Scene I.—Before the Castle

Enter Cassio, *and some Musicians*

Cas. Masters, play here,—I will content your pains,—
Something that's brief; and bid, "Good-morrow,
general."   [*Music*

Enter Clown

Clo. Why, masters, have your instruments been in
Naples, that they speak i' the nose thus?
First Mus. How, sir, how?
Clo. Are these, I pray you, called wind-instruments?
First Mus. Ay, marry, are they, sir.
Clo. O, thereby hangs a tail.
First Mus. Whereby hangs a tale, sir?
Clo. Marry, sir, by many a wind-instrument that I
know. But, masters, here's money for you; and the
general so likes your music, that he desires you, for love's
sake, to make no more noise with it.
First Mus. Well, sir, we will not.
Clo. If you have any music that may not be heard,
to 't again; but, as they say, to hear music the general does
not greatly care.
First Mus. We have none such, sir.
Clo. Then put up your pipes in your bag, for I'll away.
Go; vanish into air, away!
                                              [*Exeunt Musicians*
Cas. Dost thou hear, mine honest friend?
Clo. No, I hear not your honest friend; I hear you.
Cas. Pr'ythee, keep up thy quillets. There 's a poor
piece of gold for thee. If the gentlewoman that attends
the general's wife be stirring, tell her there's one Cassio
entreats her a little favour of speech: wilt thou do this?
Clo. She is stirring, sir: if she will stir hither, I shall
seem to notify unto her.
Cas. Do, good my friend.   [*Exit Clown*

Enter Iago

In happy time, Iago.
Iago. You have not been a-bed, then?
Cas. Why, no; the day had broke
Before we parted. I have made bold, Iago,
To send in to your wife: my suit to her
Is, that she will to virtuous Desdemona
Procure me some access.

Iago.   I'll send her to you presently;
And I'll devise a mean to draw the Moor
Out of the way, that your converse and business
May be more free.
   Cas.   I humbly thank you for 't.   [*Exit Iago*
I never knew
A Florentine more kind and honest.

Enter EMILIA

   Emil.   Good morrow, good lieutenant: I am sorry
For your displeasure; but all will sure be well.
The general and his wife are talking of it,
And she speaks for you stoutly: The Moor replies,
That he you hurt is of great fame in Cyprus
And great affinity, and that in wholesome wisdom
He might not but refuse you; but he protests he loves you,
And needs no other suitor but his likings
To take the saf'st occasion by the front
To bring you in again.
   Cas.   Yet, I beseech you,—
If you think fit, or that it may be done,—
Give me advantage of some brief discourse
With Desdemona alone.
   Emil.   Pray you, come in:
I will bestow you where you shall have time
To speak your bosom freely.
   Cas.   I am much bound to you.
                                              [*Exeunt*

SCENE II.—A Room in the Castle

Enter OTHELLO, IAGO, *and Gentlemen*

   Oth.   These letters give, Iago, to the pilot,
And by him do my duties to the senate:
That done, I will be walking on the works;
Repair there to me.
   Iago.   Well, my good lord; I'll do 't.
   Oth.   This fortification, gentlemen,—shall we see 't?
   Gent.   We 'll wait upon your lordship.   [*Exeunt*

SCENE III.—The Garden of the Castle

Enter DESDEMONA, CASSIO, *and* EMILIA

   Des.   Be thou assured, good Cassio, I will do
All my abilities in thy behalf.
   Emil.   Good madam, do: I warrant it grieves my
                  husband
As if the cause were his.
   Des.   O, that's an honest fellow.—Do not doubt, Cassio,
But I will have my lord and you again
As friendly as you were.

273

Cas.   Bounteous madam,
Whatever shall become of Michael Cassio,
He's never anything but your true servant.
   Des. I know't: I thank you.   You do love my lord;
You have known him long: and be you well assured,
He shall in strangeness stand no further off
Than in a politic distance.
   Cas.   Ay, but, lady,
That policy may either last so long,
Or feed upon such nice and waterish diet,
Or breed itself so out of circumstance,
That, I being absent and my place supplied,
My general will forget my love and service.
   Des. Do not doubt that: before Emilia here,
I give thee warrant of thy place.   Assure thee
If I do vow a friendship I'll perform it
To the last article: my lord shall never rest;
I'll watch him tame, and talk him out of patience;
His bed shall seem a school, his board a shrift;
I'll intermingle everything he does
With Cassio's suit.   Therefore, be merry, Cassio;
For thy solicitor shall rather die
Than give thy cause away.

Enter OTHELLO *and* IAGO, *at a distance*

   Emil. Madam, here comes my lord.
   Cas. Madam, I'll take my leave.
   Des. Why, stay, and hear me speak.
   Cas. Madam, not now: I am very ill at ease,
Unfit for mine own purposes.
   Des. Well, do your discretion.   [*Exit Cassio*
   Iago. Ha! I like not that.
   Oth. What dost thou say?
   Iago. Nothing, my lord: or if—I know not what.
   Oth. Was not that Cassio, parted from my wife?
   Iago. Cassio, my lord? No, sure, I cannot think it,
That he would steal away so guilty-like,
Seeing you coming.
   Oth.   I do believe 't was he.
   Des. How now, my lord?
I have been talking with a suitor here,
A man that languishes in your displeasure.
   Oth. Who is 't you mean?
   Des. Why, your lieutenant Cassio.   Good my lord,
If I have any grace, or power to move you,
His present reconciliation take;
For, if he be not one that truly loves you,
That errs in ignorance and not in cunning,
I have no judgment in an honest face.
I pr'ythee, call him back.

274

Oth.   Went he hence now?
Des.   Ay, sooth; so humbled,
That he hath left part of his grief with me,
To suffer with him.   Good love, call him back.
   Oth.   Not now, sweet Desdemon; some other time.
   Des.   But shall 't be shortly?
   Oth.   The sooner, sweet, for you.
   Des.   Shall 't be to-night at supper?
   Oth.   No, not to-night.
   Des.   To-morrow dinner then?
   Oth.   I shall not dine at home;
I meet the captains at the citadel.
   Des.   Why then, to-morrow night; or Tuesday morn;
On Tuesday noon, or night; on Wednesday morn:—
I pr'ythee, name the time, but let it not
Exceed three days; in faith, he's penitent;
And yet his trespass, in our common reason,—
Save that, they say, the wars must make examples
Out of her best,—is not almost a fault
To incur a private check.   When shall he come?
Tell, me, Othello.   I wonder in my soul,
What you could me that I should deny,
Or stand so mammering on.   What! Michael Cassio,
That came a-wooing with you, and so many a time,
When I have spoke of you dispraisingly,
Hath ta'en your part; to have so much to do
To bring him in!   Trust me, I could do much,—
   Oth.   Pr'ythee, no more: let him come when he will;
I will deny thee nothing.
   Des.   Why, this is not a boon;
'T is as I should entreat you wear your gloves,
Or feed on nourishing dishes, or keep you warm,
Or sue to you to do peculiar profit
To your own person: nay, when I have a suit
Wherein I mean to touch your love indeed,
It shall be full of poise and difficult weight,
And fearful to be granted.
   Oth.   I will deny thee nothing:
Whereon, I do beseech thee, grant me this,
To leave me but a little to myself.
   Des.   Shall I deny you? no.   Farewell, my lord.
   Oth.   Farewell, my Desdemona: I'll come to thee
      straight.
   Des.   Emilia, come.—Be as your fancies teach you;
Whate'er you be, I am obedient.   [*Exit, with Emilia*
   Oth.   Excellent wretch!   Perdition catch my soul,
But I do love thee! and when I love thee not,
Chaos is come again.
   Iago.   My noble lord,—
   Oth.   What dost thou say, Iago?

Iago.   Did Michael Cassio, when you woo'd my lady,
Know of your love?
   Oth.   He did, from first to last: why dost thou ask?
   Iago.   But for a satisfaction of my thought;
No further harm.
   Oth.   Why of thy thought, Iago?
   Iago.   I did not think he had been acquainted with her.
   Oth.   O, yes; and went between us very oft.
   Iago.   Indeed?
   Oth.   Indeed! ay, indeed: discern'st thou aught in
      that?
Is he not honest?
   Iago.   Honest, my lord?
   Oth.   Honest! ay, honest.
   Iago.   My lord, for aught I know.
   Oth.   What dost thou think?
   Iago.   Think, my lord?
   Oth.   Think, my lord!
By Heaven, he echoes me,
As if there were some monster in his thought
Too hideous to be shown.—Thou dost mean something.
I heard thee say even now,—thou lik'dst not that,
When Cassio left my wife: what didst not like?
And, when I told thee he was of my counsel
In my whole course of wooing, thou criedst, "Indeed!"
And didst contract and purse thy brow together
As if thou then hadst shut up in thy brain
Some horrible conceit.   If thou dost love me,
Show me thy thought.
   Iago.   My lord, you know I love you.
   Oth.   I think thou dost;
And,—for I know thou art full of love and honesty,
And weigh'st thy words before thou giv'st them breath,
Therefore, these stops of thine fright me the more:
For such things in a false disloyal knave
Are tricks of custom; but in a man that's just
They're close delations, working from the heart,
That passion cannot rule.
   Iago.   For Michael Cassio,
I dare be sworn I think that he is honest.
   Oth.   I think so too.
   Iago.   Men should be what they seem;
Or, those that be not, would they might seem none!
   Oth.   Certain, men should be what they seem.
   Iago.   Why then, I think Cassio's an honest man.
   Oth.   Nay, yet there's more in this.
I pray thee speak to me as to thy thinkings,
As thou dost ruminate; and give thy worst of thoughts
The worst of words.
   Iago.   Good my lord, pardon me:

Though I am bound to every act of duty,
I am not bound to that all slaves are free to.
Utter my thoughts! Why, say they are vile and false,—
As where's that palace, whereinto foul things
Sometimes intrude not? who has a breast so pure,
But some uncleanly apprehensions
Keep leets and law-days, and in session sit
With meditations lawful?
   Oth.   Thou dost conspire against thy friend, Iago,
If thou but think'st him wronged, and mak'st his ear
A stranger to thy thoughts.
   Iago.   I do beseech you—
Though I, perchance, am vicious in my guess,
As, I confess, it is my nature's plague
To spy into abuses, and oft my jealousy
Shapes faults that are not,—that your wisdom yet,
From one that so imperfectly conceits,
Would take no notice; nor build yourself a trouble
Out of his scattering and unsure observance.
It were not for your quiet, nor your good,
Nor for my manhood, honesty, or wisdom,
To let you know my thoughts.
   Oth.   What dost thou mean?
   Iago.   Good name in man and woman, dear my lord,
Is the immediate jewel of their souls:
Who steals my purse, steals trash; 't is something, nothing;
'T was mine, 't is his, and has been slave to thousands;
But he that filches from me my good name
Robs me of that which not enriches him,
And makes me poor indeed.
   Oth.   By Heaven, I'll know thy thoughts.
   Iago.   You cannot, if my heart were in your hand;
Nor shall not, whilst 't is in my custody.
   Oth.   Ha!
   Iago.   O! beware my lord, of jealousy;
It is the green-eyed monster, which doth mock
The meat it feeds on: that cuckold lives in bliss,
Who, certain of his fate, loves not his wronger;
But, O, what damnéd minutes tells he o'er
Who dotes, yet doubts; suspects, yet soundly loves!
   Oth.   O misery!
   Iago.   Poor and content is rich, and rich enough;
But riches fineless is as poor as winter
To him that ever fears he shall be poor:—
Good Heaven, the souls of all my tribe defend
From jealousy!
   Oth.   Why, why is this?
Think'st thou, I'd make a life of jealousy,
To follow still the changes of the moon
With fresh suspicions? No; to be once in doubt

Is once to be resolved.   Exchange me for a goat,
When I shall turn the business of my soul
To such exsufflicate and blown surmises,
Matching thy inference.   'T is not to make me jealous
To say—my wife is fair, feeds well, loves company,
Is free of speech, sings, plays, and dances well;
Where virtue is, these are more virtuous:
Nor from mine own weak merits will I draw
The smallest fear or doubt of her revolt;
For she had eyes, and chose me.   No, Iago;
I'll see before I doubt; when I doubt, prove;
And, on the proof, there is no more but this,—
Away at once with love or jealousy.
    Iago.   I am glad of it: for now I shall have reason
To show the love and duty that I bear you
With franker spirit; therefore, as I am bound,
Receive it from me—I speak not yet of proof.
Look to your wife: observe her well with Cassio;
Wear your eye thus, not jealous nor secure;
I would not have your free and noble nature,
Out of self-bounty, be abused: look to 't.
I know our country disposition well;
In Venice they do let Heaven see the prank
They dare not show their husbands; their best conscience
Is—not to leave 't undone, but keep 't unknown.
    Oth.   Dost thou say so?
    Iago.   She did deceive her father, marrying you;
And, when she seemed to shake and fear your looks,
She loved them most.
    Oth.   And so she did.
    Iago.   Why, go to, then;
She that, so young, could give out such a seeming,
To seel her father's eyes up close as oak,—
He thought 't was witchcraft:—But I'm much to blame;
I humbly do beseech you of your pardon
For too much loving you.
    Oth.   I am bound to thee for ever.
    Iago.   I see this hath a little dashed your spirits.
    Oth.   Not a jot, not a jot.
    Iago.   Trust me, I fear it has.
I hope you will consider what is spoke
Comes from my love.—But I do see you're moved;
I am to pray you not to strain my speech
To grosser issues nor to larger reach
Than to suspicion.
    Oth.   I will not.
    Iago.   Should you do so, my lord,
My speech should fall into such vile success
As my thoughts aim not at.   Cassio's my worthy friend—
My lord, I see you're moved.

Oth.   No, not much moved.—
I do not think but Desdemona's honest.
   Iago. Long live she so! and long live you to think so!
   Oth. And yet, how nature erring from itself,—
   Iago. Ay, there's the point:—as—to be bold with you—
Not to affect many proposéd matches
Of her own clime, complexion, and degree,
Whereto, we see, in all things nature tends:
Foh! one may smell in such a will most rank,
Foul disproportion, thoughts unnatural.—
But pardon me; I do not in position
Distinctly speak of her, though I may fear
Her will, recoiling to her better judgment,
May fall to match you with her country forms,
And happily repent.
   Oth.   Farewell, farewell.
If more thou dost perceive, let me know more;
Set on thy wife to observe.—Leave me, Iago.
   Iago. My lord, I take my leave.   [*Going*
   Oth. Why did I marry?—This honest creature, doubtless,
Sees and knows more, much more, than he unfolds.
   Iago. [*Returning*] My lord, I would I might entreat
      your honour
To scan this thing no further; leave it to time.
Although 't is fit that Cassio have his place,
For, sure, he fills it up with great ability,—
Yet, if you please to hold him off awhile,
You shall by that perceive him and his means:
Note, if your lady strain his entertainment
With any strong or vehement importunity;
Much will be seen in that.   In the meantime,
Let me be thought too busy in my fears,—
As worthy cause I have to fear I am,—
And hold her free, I do beseech your honour.
   Oth. Fear not my government.
   Iago. I once more take my leave.   [*Exit*
   Oth. This fellow 's of exceeding honesty,
And knows all qualities, with a learnéd spirit,
Of human dealings; if I do prove her haggard,
Though that her jesses were my dear heart-strings,
I'd whistle her off, and let her down the wind,
To prey at fortune.   Haply, for I am black,
And have not those soft parts of conversation
That chamberers have; or, for I am declined
Into the vale of years;—yet that's not much:
She's gone, I am abused; and my relief
Must be to loathe her.   O curse of marriage!
That we can call these delicate creatures ours,
And not their appetites.   I had rather be a toad,
And live upon the vapour of a dungeon,

Than keep a corner in the thing I love
For others' uses.   Yet, 'tis the plague of great ones;
Prerogatived are they less than the base;
'T is destiny unshunnable, like death:
Even then this forkéd plague is fated to us
When we do quicken.   Look, where she comes.
If she be false, O, then heaven mocks itself!—
I'll not believe it.

Re-enter DESDEMONA and EMILIA

    Des.   How now, my dear Othello?
Your dinner, and the generous islanders
By you invited, do attend your presence.
    Oth.   I am to blame.
    Des.   Why do you speak so faintly?
Are you not well?
    Oth.   I have a pain upon my forehead here.
    Des.   'Faith, that's with watching; 't will away again:
Let me but bind it hard, within this hour
It will be well.
    Oth.   Your napkin is too little.
        [He puts the handkerchief from him, and she drops it
Let it alone.   Come, I'll go in with you.
    Des.   I'm very sorry that you are not well.
                    [Exeunt Othello and Desdemona
    Emil.   I am glad I have found this napkin:
This was her first remembrance from the Moor:
My wayward husband hath a hundred times
Woo'd me to steal 't; but she so loves the token,—
For he conjured her she should ever keep it,—
That she reserves it evermore about her
To kiss and talk to.   I'll have the work ta'en out,
And give 't Iago:
What he will do with it Heaven knows, not I;
I nothing, but to please his fantasy.

Re-enter IAGO

    Iago.   How now! what do you here alone?
    Emil.   Do not you chide; I have a thing for you.
    Iago.   A thing for me?—it is a common thing—
    Emil.   Ha?
    Iago.   To have a foolish wife.
    Emil.   O, is that all?   What will you give me now
For that same handkerchief?
    Iago.   What handkerchief?
    Emil.   What handkerchief!
Why, that the Moor first gave to Desdemona;
That which so often you did bid me steal.
    Iago.   Hast stol'n it from her?
    Emil.   No, faith: she let it drop by negligence;

And, to the advantage, I, being here, took 't up.
Look, here it is.
    Iago.   A good wench; give it me.
    Emil.   What will you do with 't, that you have been
        so earnest
To have me filch it?
    Iago.   Why, what 's that to you?
                                            [*Snatching it*
    Emil.   If 't be not for some purpose of import,
Give 't me again: poor lady! she 'll run mad
When she shall lack it.
    Iago.   Be not acknown on 't; I have use for it.
Go, leave me.   [*Exit Emilia*
I will in Cassio's lodging lose this napkin,
And let him find it: trifles, light as air
Are to the jealous confirmations strong
As proofs of holy writ.   This may do something;
The Moor already changes with my poison:
Dangerous conceits are in their natures poisons
Which at the first are scarce found to distaste;
But, with a little act upon the blood,
Burn like the mines of sulphur.—I did say so:—
Look, where he comes!

Re-enter OTHELLO

Not poppy, nor mandragora,
Nor all the drowsy syrups of the world,
Shall ever medicine thee to that sweet sleep
Which thou owedst yesterday.
    Oth.   Ha! ha! false to me.
    Iago.   Why, how now, general? no more of that.
    Oth.   Avaunt! be gone! thou hast set me on the rack.—
I swear, 't is better to be much abused
Than but to know 't a little.
    Iago.   How now, my lord?
    Oth.   What sense had I of her stol'n hours of lust?
I saw 't not, thought it not, it harmed not me:
I slept the next night well, was free and merry;
I found not Cassio's kisses on her lips:
He that is robbed, not wanting what is stolen,
Let him not know 't and he 's not robbed at all.
    Iago.   I am sorry to hear this.
    Oth.   I had been happy, if the general camp,
Pioneers and all, had tasted her sweet body,
So I had nothing known.   O now, for ever,
Farewell the tranquil mind! farewell content!
Farewell the pluméd troop, and the big wars,
That make ambition virtue!   O, farewell!
Farewell the neighing steed, and the shrill trump,
The spirit-stirring drum, the ear-piercing fife,

The royal banner, and all quality,
Pride, pomp, and circumstance of glorious war!
And, O you mortal engines, whose rude throats
The immortal Jove's dread clamours counterfeit,
Farewell! Othello's occupation 's gone!
   Iago. Is't possible, my lord—
   Oth. Villain, be sure thou prove my love a whore,—
Be sure of it; give me the ocular proof;
Or, by the worth of mine eternal soul,
Thou hadst been better have been born a dog
Than answer my waked wrath.
   Iago.   Is't come to this?
   Oth. Make me to see't; or, at the least, so prove it
That the probation bear no hinge nor loop
To hang a doubt on; or woe upon thy life!
   Iago. My noble lord,—
   Oth. If thou dost slander her, and torture me,—
Never pray more; abandon all remorse;
On horror's head horrors accumulate;
Do deeds to make heaven weep, all earth amazed:
For nothing canst thou to damnation add
Greater than that.
   Iago.   O grace! O heaven forgive me!
Are you a man? have you a soul, or sense?—
God be wi' you; take mine office.—O wretched fool,
That liv'st to make thine honesty a vice!—
O monstrous world! Take note, take note, O world,
To be direct and honest is not safe.—
I thank you for this profit; and, from hence
I'll love no friend, sith love breeds such offence.
   Oth. Nay, stay:—thou shouldst be honest.
   Iago. I should be wise; for honesty 's a fool,
And loses that it works for.
   Oth.   By the world,
I think my wife be honest, and think she is not;
I think that thou art just, and think thou art not:
I'll have some proof. Her name, that was as fresh
As Dian's visage, is now begrimed and black
As mine own face.—If there be cords, or knives,
Poison, or fire, or suffocating streams,
I'll not endure it.—Would I were satisfied!
   Iago. I see, sir, you are eaten up with passion.
I do repent me that I put it to you.
You would be satisfied?
   Oth.   Would! nay, I will.
   Iago. And may; but how? how satisfied, my lord?
Would you, the supervisor, grossly gape on,—
Behold her tupped?
   Oth.   Death and damnation! O!
   Iago. It were a tedious difficulty, I think,

To bring them to that prospect; damn them then,
If ever mortal eyes do see them bolster,
More than their own!   What then? how then?
What shall I say?   Where's satisfaction?
It is impossible you should see this,
Were they as prime as goats, as hot as monkeys,
As salt as wolves in pride, and fools as gross
As ignorance made drunk: but yet, I say
If imputation, and strong circumstances
Which lead directly to the door of truth,
Will give you satisfaction, you might have it.
    Oth.   Give me a living reason she's disloyal.
    Iago.   I do not like the office;
But, sith I am entered in this cause so far,
Pricked to't by foolish honesty and love,
I will go on.   I lay with Cassio lately;
And, being troubled with a raging tooth,
I could not sleep.
There are a kind of men so loose of soul,
That in their sleeps will mutter their affairs:
One of this kind is Cassio.
In sleep I heard him say,—"Sweet Desdemona;
Let us be wary, let us hide our loves!"
And then, sir, would he gripe and wring my hand,
Cry,—"O sweet creature!" and then kiss me hard,
As if he plucked up kisses by the roots
That grew upon my lips: then laid his leg
Over my thigh, and sighed, and kissed; and then
Cried,—"Cursèd fate, that gave thee to the Moor!"
    Oth.   O monstrous! monstrous!
    Iago.   Nay, this was but his dream
    Oth.   But this denoted a foregone conclusion:
'T is a shrewd doubt, though it be but a dream.
    Iago.   And this may help to thicken other proofs
That do demonstrate thinly.
    Oth.   I'll tear her all to pieces
    Iago.   Nay, but be wise: yet we see nothing done;
She may be honest yet.   Tell me but this:
Have you not sometimes seen a handkerchief
Spotted with strawberries in your wife's hand?
    Oth.   I gave her such a one: 't was my first gift.
    Iago.   I know not that: but such a handkerchief—
I am sure it was your wife's—did I to-day
See Cassio wipe his beard with.
    Oth.   If it be that,—
    Iago.   If it be that, or any that was hers,
It speaks against her, with the other proofs.
    Oth.   O, that the slave had forty thousand lives!
One is too poor, too weak for my revenge.
Now do I see 't is true.—Look here, Iago:

All my fond love thus do I blow to heaven:
'T is gone.—
Arise, black vengeance, from the hollow hell!
Yield up, O love, thy crown and hearted throne
To tyrannous hate!   Swell, bosom, with thy fraught,
For 't is of aspics' tongues!

    Iago.   Yet be content.
    Oth.   O, blood, blood, blood!
    Iago.   Patience, I say; your mind perhaps may change.
    Oth.   Never, Iago.   Like to the Pontic sea
Whose icy current and compulsive course
Ne'er feels retiring ebb, but keeps due on
To the Propontic and the Hellespont;
Even so my bloody thoughts, with violent pace,
Shall ne'er look back, ne'er ebb to humble love,
Till that a capable and wide revenge
Swallow them up.—[*Kneeling*] Now, by yond marble
      heaven,
In the due reverence of a sacred vow
I here engage my words.
    Iago.   Do not rise yet.—   [*Kneeling*
Witness, you ever-burning lights above!
You elements that clip us round about!
Witness, that here Iago doth give up
The execution of his wit, hands, heart,
To wronged Othello's service!   Let him command,
And to obey shall be in me remorse,
What bloody business ever.
    Oth.   I greet thy love,
Not with vain thanks, but with acceptance bounteous,
And will upon the instant put thee to't:
Within these three days let me hear thee say
That Cassio's not alive.
    Iago.   My friend is dead; 't is done at your request:
But let her live.
    Oth.   Damn her, lewd minx!   O, damn her!
Come, go with me apart; I will withdraw,
To furnish me with some swift means of death
For the fair devil.   Now art thou my lieutenant.
    Iago.   I am your own for ever.   [*Exeunt*

SCENE IV.—Before the Castle

Enter DESDEMONA, EMILIA, *and Clown*

    Des.   Do you know, sirrah, where Lieutenant Cassio lies?
    Clo.   I dare not say he lies anywhere.
    Des.   Why, man?
    Clo.   He is a soldier; and for one to say a soldier lies,
is stabbing.
    Des.   Go to.   Where lodges he?

Clo. To tell you where he lodges, is to tell you where I lie.
Des. Can anything be made of this?
Clo. I know not where he lodges; and for me to devise
a lodging, and say, he lies here, or he lies there, were to lie
in mine own throat.
Des. Can you inquire him out, and be edified by report?
Clo. I will catechise the world for him; that is, make
questions, and by them answer.
Des. Seek him; bid him come hither; tell him I have
moved my lord in his behalf, and hope all will be well.
Clo. To do this is within the compass of man's wit; and
therefore I will attempt the doing it.   [*Exit*
Des. Where should I lose that handkerchief, Emilia?
Emil. I know not, madam.
Des. Believe me, I had rather have lost my purse
Full of crusadoes; and but my noble Moor
Is true of mind, and made of no such baseness
As jealous creatures are, it were enough
To put him to ill thinking.
Emil.   Is he not jealous?
Des. Who? he! I think the sun where he was born
Drew all such humours from him.
Emil.   Look, where he comes.
Des. I will not leave him now, till Cassio
Be called to him.—

                    Enter OTHELLO

                        How is 't with you, my lord?
Oth. Well, my good lady.—[*Aside*] O, hardness to
        dissemble!—
How do you, Desdemona?
Des.   Well, my good lord.
Oth. Give me your hand: this hand is moist, my lady.
Des. It yet has felt no age nor known no sorrow.
Oth. This argues fruitfulness and liberal heart:
Hot, hot, and moist: this hand of yours requires
A sequester from liberty, fasting and prayer,
Much castigation, exercise devout;
For here 's a young and sweating devil here
That commonly rebels. 'T is a good hand,
A frank one.
Des.   You may, indeed, say so;
For 't was that hand that gave away my heart.
Oth. A liberal hand: the hearts of old gave hands;
But our new heraldry is hands, not hearts.
Des. I cannot speak of this. Come now, your promise.
Oth. What promise, chuck?
Des. I have sent to bid Cassio come speak with you.
Oth. I have a salt and sorry rheum offends me.
Lend me thy handkerchief.

                        285

Des.   Here, my lord.
Oth.   That which I gave you.
Des.   I have it not about me.
Oth.   Not?
Des.   No, indeed, my lord.
Oth.   That is a fault.
That handkerchief
Did an Egyptian to my mother give;
She was a charmer, and could almost read
The thoughts of people: she told her, while she kept it,
'T would make her amiable and subdue my father
Entirely to her love; but if she lost it,
Or made a gift of it, my father's eye
Should hold her loathéd, and his spirits should hunt
After new fancies.   She, dying, gave it me;
And bid me, when my fate would have me wived,
To give it her.   I did so: and take heed on 't;
Make it a darling like your precious eye;
To lose 't or give 't away were such perdition
As nothing else could match.
   Des.   Is 't possible?
   Oth.   'T is true: there's magic in the web of it.
A sibyl that had numbered in the world
The sun to course two hundred compasses,
In her prophetic fury sewed the work;
The worms were hallowed that did breed the silk,
And it was dyed in mummy which the skilful
Conserved of maidens' hearts.
   Des.   Indeed! is 't true?
   Oth.   Most veritable; therefore look to 't well.
   Des.   Then would to Heaven that I had never seen 't.
   Oth.   Ha! wherefore?
   Des.   Why do you speak so startlingly and rash?
   Oth.   Is 't lost? is 't gone? speak, is it out o' the way?
   Des.   Heaven bless us!
   Oth.   Say you?
   Des.   It is not lost; but what an if it were?
   Oth.   How?
   Des.   I say, it is not lost.
   Oth.   Fetch 't; let me see 't.
   Des.   Why, so I can, sir; but I will not now.
This is a trick, to put me from my suit:
I pray, let Cassio be received again.
   Oth.   Fetch me that handkerchief: my mind misgives.
   Des.   Come, come;
You'll never meet a more sufficient man.
   Oth.   The handkerchief!
   Des.   I pray, talk me of Cassio.
   Oth.   The handkerchief!
   Des.   A man that, all his time,

Hath founded his good fortunes on your love;
Shared dangers with you;—
   Oth.   The handkerchief!
   Des.   In sooth, you are to blame.
   Oth.   Away!   *[Exit*
   Emil.   Is not this man jealous?
   Des.   I ne'er saw this before.
Sure, there's some wonder in this handkerchief:
I am most unhappy in the loss of it.
   Emil.   'T is not a year or two shows us a man:
They are all but stomachs, and we all but food;
They eat us hungerly, and when they are full
They belch us.—Look you! Cassio and my husband.

        Enter Iago *and* Cassio

   Iago.   There is no other way; 't is she must do 't:
And, lo, the happiness! go and importune her.
   Des.   How now, good Cassio? what 's the news with you?
   Cas.   Madam, my former suit.   I do beseech you,
That by your virtuous means I may again
Exist, and be a member of his love
Whom I, with all the office of my heart,
Entirely honour: I would not be delayed.
If my offence be of such mortal kind
That nor my service past, nor present sorrows,
Nor purposed merit in futurity,
Can ransom me into his love again,
But to know so must be my benefit;
So shall I clothe me in a forced content,
And shut myself up in some other course,
To fortune's alms.
   Des.   Alas! thrice-gentle Cassio,
My advocation is not now in tune;
My lord is not my lord; nor should I know him,
Were he in favour as in humour altered.
So help me every spirit sanctified,
As I have spoken for you all my best,
And stood within the blank of his displeasure
For my free speech.   You must awhile be patient:
What I can do, I will; and more I will
Then for myself I dare: let that suffice you.
   Iago.   Is my lord angry?
   Emil.   He went hence but now,
And, certainly, in strange unquietness.
   Iago.   Can he be angry?   I have seen the cannon,
When it hath blown his ranks into the air,
And, like the devil, from his very arm
Puffed his own brother;—and can he be angry?
Something of moment, then: I will go meet him.
There's matter in 't indeed, if he be angry.

Des. I pr'ythee, do so. [*Exit Iago*]—Something, sure,
  of state—
Either from Venice, or some unhatched practice,
Made demonstrable here in Cyprus to him—
Hath puddled his clear spirit; and, in such cases,
Men's natures wrangle with inferior things,
Though great ones are their object. 'T is even so;
For let our finger ache, and it indues
Our other healthful members ev'n to that sense
Of pain. Nay, we must think men are not gods;
Nor of them look for such observancy
As fits the bridal.—Beshrew me much, Emilia,
I was—unhandsome warrior as I am—
Arraigning his unkindness with my soul:
But now, I find, I had suborned the witness,
And he 's indicted falsely.
    Emil. Pray Heaven it be state-matters, as you think,
And no conception nor no jealous toy
Concerning you.
    Des. Alas the day, I never gave him cause.
    Emil. But jealous souls will not be answered so;
They are not ever jealous for the cause,
But jealous for they are jealous: 't is a monster
Begot upon itself, born on itself.
    Des. Heaven keep that monster from Othello's mind!
    Emil. Lady, Amen.
    Des. I will go seek him.—Cassio, walk hereabout:
If I do find him fit, I'll move your suit,
And seek to effect it to my uttermost.
    Cas. I humbly thank your ladyship.
                                    [*Exeunt Desdemona and Emilia*

Enter BIANCA

Bian. Save you, friend Cassio!
    Cas.   What make you from home?
How is it with you, my most fair Bianca?
I' faith, sweet love, I was coming to your house.
    Bian. And I was going to your lodging, Cassio.
What! keep a week away? seven days and nights?
Eight score eight hours? and lovers' absent hours,
More tedious than the dial eight score times?
O weary reckoning!
    Cas.   Pardon me, Bianca;
I have this while with leaden thoughts been pressed;
But I shall, in a more continuate time,
Strike off this score of absence. Sweet Bianca,
                        [*Giving her Desdemona's handkerchief*
Take me this work out.
    Bian.   O Cassio, whence came this?
This is some token from a newer friend.

To the felt absence now I feel a cause.
Is it come to this?   Well, well.
   Cas.   Go to, woman!
Throw your vile guesses in the devil's teeth,
From whence you have them.   You are jealous now
That this is from some mistress, some remembrance:
No, in good troth, Bianca.
   Bian.   Why, whose is it?
   Cas. I know not neither: I found it in my chamber.
I like the work well: ere it be demanded
(As like enough it will), I'd have it copied:
Take it, and do 't; and leave me for this time.
   Bian. Leave you! wherefore?
   Cas. I do attend here on the general,
And think it no addition, nor my wish,
To have him see me womaned.
   Bian.   Why, I pray you?
   Cas. Not that I love you not.
   Bian.   But that you do not love me.
I pray you, bring me on the way a little;
And say, if I shall see you soon at night.
   Cas. 'T is but a little way, that I can bring you,
For I attend here; but I'll see you soon.
   Bian. 'T is very good: I must be circumstanced.
                                    [Exeunt

ACT FOUR

Scene I.—Before the Castle

Enter Othello *and* Iago

   Iago. Will you think so?
   Oth.   Think so, Iago?
   Iago.   What,
To kiss in private?
   Oth.   An unauthorised kiss.
   Iago. Or to be naked with her friend a-bed,
An hour or more, not meaning any harm?
   Oth. Naked a-bed, Iago, and not mean harm?
It is hypocrisy against the devil:
They that mean virtuously and yet do so,
The devil their virtue tempts, and they tempt Heaven.
   Iago. If they do nothing, 't is a venial slip;
But if I give my wife a handkerchief,—
   Oth. What then?
   Iago. Why, then 't is hers, my lord; and, being hers,
She may, I think, bestow 't on any man.
   Oth. She is protectress of her honour too:
May she give that?
   Iago. Her honour is an essence that 's not seen;

They have it very oft that have it not:
But, for the handkerchief,—
   Oth. By Heaven, I would most gladly have forgot it.
Thou saidst,—O! it comes o'er my memory,
As doth the raven o'er the infected house,
Boding to all,—he had my handkerchief.
   Iago. Ay, what of that?
   Oth.   That 's not so good, now.
   Iago. What, if I had said, I had seen him do you
     wrong?
Or heard him say,—as knaves be such abroad,
Who, having, by their own importunate suit,
Or voluntary dotage of some mistress,
Convincéd or supplied them, cannot chose
But they must blab—
   Oth.   Hath he said anything?
   Iago. He hath, my lord; but, be you well assured,
No more than he'll unswear.
   Oth.   What hath he said?
   Iago. 'Faith, that he did—I know not what he did.
   Oth. What? what?
   Iago. Lie—
   Oth.   With her?
   Iago.   With her, on her; what you will.
   Oth. Lie with her! lie on her!—We say, lie on her,
when they belie her. Lie with her! that's fulsome.—
Handkerchief,—confessions,—handkerchief.—To confess,
and be hanged for his labour;—first, to be hanged, and
then to confess:—I tremble at it. Nature would not in-
vest herself in such shadowing passion without some in-
struction. It is not words that shakes me thus.—Pish!—
Noses, ears, and lips.—Is 't possible?—Confess—hand-
kerchief!—O devil!—   *[Falls in a trance*
   Iago. Work on,
My medicine, work! Thus credulous fools are caught;
And many worthy and chaste dames even thus,
All guiltless, meet reproach.—What, ho! my lord!
My lord, I say! Othello!—

               Enter CASSIO

                     How now, Cassio?

   Cas. What's the matter?
   Iago. My lord is fall'n into an epilepsy:
This is his second fit; he had one yesterday.
   Cas. Rub him about the temples.
   Iago.   No, forbear.
The lethargy must have his quiet course;
If not, he foams at mouth; and by-and-by
Breaks out to savage madness. Look, he stirs:
Do you withdraw yourself a little while,

He will recover straight: when he is gone,
I would on great occasion speak with you.—   [*Exit Cassio*
How is it, general? have you hurt your head?
 Oth. Dost thou mock me?
 Iago.   I mock you! no, by Heaven.
Would you would bear your fortune like a man!
 Oth. A hornéd man's a monster, and a beast.
 Iago. There's many a beast then in a populous city
And many a civil monster.
 Oth. Did he confess it?
 Iago.   Good sir, be a man;
Think, every bearded fellow that's but yoked
May draw with you: there's millions now alive,
That nightly lie in those unproper beds
Which they dare swear peculiar: your case is better.
O, 't is the spite of hell, the fiend's arch-mock,
To lip a wanton in a secure couch,
And to suppose her chaste. No, let me know;
And, knowing what I am, I know what she shall be.
 Oth. O! thou art wise; 't is certain.
 Iago. Stand you awhile apart;
Confine yourself but in a patient list.
Whilst you were here, o'erwhelméd with your grief—
A passion most unsuiting such a man—
Cassio came hither: I shifted him away,
And laid good 'scuse upon your ecstasy;
Bade him anon return, and here speak with me;
The which he promised. Do but encave yourself,
And mark the fleers, the gibes, and notable scorns,
That dwell in every region of his face;
For I will make him tell the tale anew,
Where, how, how oft, how long ago, and when
He hath, and is again to cope your wife:
I say, but mark his gesture.—Marry, patience;
Or I shall say, you are all in all in spleen,
And nothing of a man.
 Oth.   Dost thou hear, Iago?
I will be found most cunning in my patience;
But—dost thou hear?—most bloody.
 Iago.   That's not amiss;
But yet keep time in all. Will you withdraw?
           [*Othello withdraws*
Now will I question Cassio of Bianca,
A housewife, that by selling her desires
Buys herself bread and clothes: it is a creature
That dotes on Cassio, as 't is the strumpet's plague
To beguile many and be beguiled by one.
He, when he hears of her, cannot refrain
From the excess of laughter.—Here he comes.—
As he shall smile, Othello shall go mad;

And his unbookish jealousy must construe
Poor Cassio's smiles, gestures, and light behaviour
Quite in the wrong.

Re-enter CASSIO

                  How do you now, lieutenant?
    Cas.   The worser, that you give me the addition. Whose
want even kills me.
    Iago.   Ply Desdemona well, and you are sure on't.
[*Speaking lower*] Now, if this suit lay in Bianca's dower,
How quickly should you speed!
    Cas.   Alas, poor caitiff!
    Oth.   [*Aside*] Look, how he laughs already!
    Iago.   I never knew a woman love man so.
    Cas.   Alas, poor rogue! I think, i' faith, she loves me.
    Oth.   [*Aside*] Now he denies it faintly, and laughs it
    out.
    Iago.   Do you hear, Cassio?
    Oth.   [*Aside*]   Now he importunes him
To tell it o'er. Go to; well said, well said.
    Iago.   She gives it out, that you shall marry her:
Do you intend it?
    Cas.   Ha, ha, ha!
    Oth.   [*Aside*] Do you triumph, Roman! do you
triumph?
    Cas.   I marry her!—what, a customer? I pr'ythee,
bear some charity to my wit; do not think it so unwholesome:—ha, ha, ha!
    Oth.   [*Aside*] So, so, so, so. They laugh that win.
    Iago.   Faith, the cry goes, that you shall marry her.—
    Cas.   Pr'ythee, say true.
    Iago.   I am a very villain else.
    Oth.   [*Aside*] Have you scored me? Well.
    Cas.   This is the monkey's own giving out: she is
persuaded I will marry her, out of her own love and flattery,
not out of my promise.
    Oth.   [*Aside*] Iago beckons me, now he begins the story.
    Cas.   She was here even now; she haunts me in every
place. I was, the other day, talking on the sea-bank with
certain Venetians, and thither comes the bauble; and, by
this hand, she falls me thus about my neck;—
    Oth.   [*Aside*] Crying, O dear Cassio! as it were: his
gesture imports it.
    Cas.   So hangs, and lolls, and weeps upon me; so hales
and pulls me: ha, ha, ha!—
    Oth.   [*Aside*] Now he tells, how she plucked him to my
chamber. O! I see that nose of yours, but not that dog
I shall throw it to.
    Cas.   Well, I must leave her company.
    Iago.   Before me! look, where she comes.

Cas. 'T is such another fitchew! marry, a perfumed one.

Enter BIANCA

What do you mean by this haunting of me?

Bian. Let the devil and his dam haunt you! What did you mean by that same handkerchief, you gave me even now? I was a fine fool to take it. I must take out the work!—A likely piece of work, that you should find it in your chamber, and not know who left it there! This is some minx's token, and I must take out the work! There, give it your hobby-horse: wheresoever you had it, I'll take out no work on 't.

Cas. How now, my sweet Bianca! how now, how now!

Oth. [*Aside*] By Heaven, that should be my hand-kerchief!

Bian. An you'll come to supper to-night, you may; an you will not, come when you are next prepared for.

[*Exit*

Iago. After her, after her.

Cas. 'Faith, I must; she'll rail in the street else.

Iago. Will you sup there?

Cas. 'Faith, I intend so.

Iago. Well, I may chance to see you, for I would very fain speak with you.

Cas. Pr'ythee, come; will you?

Iago. Go to; say no more.   [*Exit Cassio*

Oth. [*Advancing*] How shall I murder him, Iago?

Iago. Did you perceive how he laughed at his vice?

Oth. O, Iago!

Iago. And did you see the handkerchief?

Oth. Was that mine?

Iago. Yours, by this hand: and to see how he prizes the foolish woman, your wife! she gave it him, and he hath give it his whore.

Oth. I would have him nine years a-killing.—A fine woman! a fair woman! a sweet woman!

Iago. Nay, you must forget that.

Oth. Ay, let her rot, and perish, and be damned to-night; for she shall not live. No, my heart is turned to stone; I strike it, and it hurts my hand. O, the world hath not a sweeter creature: she might lie by an emperor's side, and command him tasks.

Iago. Nay, that's not your way.

Oth. Hang her! I do but say what she is.—So delicate with her needle!—An admirable musician! O, she will sing the savageness out of a bear.—Of so high and plenteous wit and invention!

Iago. She's the worse for all this.

Oth. O! a thousand, a thousand times. And then, of so gentle a condition!

Iago. Ay, too gentle.

Oth. Nay, that's certain:—but yet the pity of it, Iago!—O, Iago, the pity of it, Iago!

Iago. If you are so fond over her iniquity, give her patent to offend: for, if it touch not you, it comes near nobody.

Oth. I will chop her into messes:—cuckold me!

Iago. O! 't is foul in her.

Oth. With mine officer!

Iago. That's fouler.

Oth. Get me some poison, Iago; this night:—I'll not expostulate with her, lest her body and beauty unprovide my mind again.—This night, Iago.

Iago. Do it not with poison, strangle her in her bed, even the bed she hath contaminated.

Oth. Good, good: the justice of it pleases; very good.

Iago. And for Cassio, let me be his undertaker: you shall hear more by midnight.

Oth. Excellent good.—[*A trumpet within*]—What trumpet is that same?

Iago. Something from Venice, sure. 'T is Lodovico, Come from the duke; and, see, your wife is with him.

Enter Lodovico, Desdemona, *and Attendants*

Lod. God save the worthy general!

Oth.   With all my heart, sir.

Lod. The duke and senators of Venice greet you.

                              [*Giving him a packet*

Oth. I kiss the instrument of their pleasures.

                              [*Opens the packet, and reads*

Des. And what's the news, good cousin Lodovico?

Iago. I am very glad to see you, signior: Welcome to Cyprus.

Lod. I thank you. How does Lieutenant Cassio?

Iago. Lives, sir.

Des. Cousin, there's fall'n between him and my lord An unkind breach, but you shall make all well.

Oth. Are you sure of that?

Des. My lord?

Oth. [*Reading*] "This fail you not to do, as you will"—

Lod. He did not call; he's busy in the paper. Is there division 'twixt my lord and Cassio?

Des. A most unhappy one: I would do much To atone them, for the love I bear to Cassio.

Oth. Fire and brimstone!

Des. My lord!

Oth. Are you wise?

Des. What! is he angry?

Lod.   May be, the letter moved him;

For, as I think, they do command him home,
Deputing Cassio in his government.
    Des.   Trust me I am glad on 't.
    Oth.   Indeed!
    Des.   My lord?
    Oth.   I am glad to see you mad.
    Des.   Why, sweet Othello?
    Oth.   Devil!   *[Striking her*
    Des.   I have not deserved this.
    Lod.   My lord, this would not be believed in Venice,
Though I should swear I saw it.   'T is very much:
Make her amends, she weeps.
    Oth.   O devil, devil!
If that the earth could teem with woman's tears,
Each drop she falls would prove a crocodile.—
Out of my sight.
    Des.   I will not stay to offend you.   *[Going*
    Lod.   Truly, an obedient lady.—
I do beseech your lordship, call her back.
    Oth.   Mistress!
    Des.   My lord!
    Oth.   What would you with her, sir?
    Lod.   Who, I, my lord?
    Oth.   Ay; you did wish, that I would make her turn:
Sir, she can turn and turn and yet go on,
And turn again; and she can weep, sir, weep,
And she's obedient, as you say, obedient,—
Very obedient.—Proceed you in your tears.—
Concerning this, sir,—O well-painted passion!—
I am commanded home.—Get you away;
I'll send for you anon.—Sir, I obey the mandate,
And will return to Venice.—Hence! avaunt!—
                           [Exit Desdemona
Cassio shall have my place.   And,—sir, to-night,
I do entreat that we may sup together:
You are welcome, sir, to Cyprus.—Goats and monkeys!
                                  [Exit
    Lod.   Is this the noble Moor whom our full senate
Call all-in-all sufficient?   Is this the nature
Whom passion could not shake? whose solid virtue
The shot of accident, nor dart of chance,
Could neither graze, nor pierce?
    Iago.   He is much changed.
    Lod.   Are his wits safe? is he not light of brain?
    Iago.   He's that he is: I may not breathe my censure.
What he might be,—if, what he might, he is not,—
I would to Heaven, he were!
    Lod.   What, strike his wife?
    Iago.   Faith, that was not so well; yet would I knew
That stroke would prove the worst.

Lod.   Is it his use?
Or did the letters work upon his blood,
And new-create this fault?
    Iago.   Alas, alas!
It is not honesty in me to speak
What I have seen and known.   You shall observe him,
And his own courses will denote him so
That I may save my speech.   Do but go after,
And mark how he continues.
    Lod.   I am sorry that I am deceived in him.   [*Exeunt*

SCENE II.—A Room in the Castle

Enter OTHELLO *and* EMILIA

Oth.   You have seen nothing then?
Emil.   Nor ever heard; nor ever did suspect.
Oth.   Yes, you have seen Cassio and she together.
Emil.   But then I saw no harm; and then I heard
Each syllable that breath made up between them.
Oth.   What, did they never whisper?
Emil.   Never, my lord.
Oth.   Nor send you out o' the way?
Emil.   Never.
Oth.   To fetch her fan, her gloves, her mask, nor nothing?
Emil.   Never, my lord.
Oth.   That's strange.
    Emil.   I durst, my lord, to wager she is honest,
Lay down my soul at stake: if you think other,
Remove your thought; it doth abuse your bosom.
If any wretch have put this in your head
Let Heaven requite it with the serpent's curse!
For, if she be not honest, chaste, and true,
There's no man happy; the purest of their wives
Is foul as slander.
    Oth.   Bid her come hither:—go.—
                                    [*Exit Emilia*
She says enough;—yet she's a simple bawd
That cannot say as much.   This is a subtle whore,
A closet-lock-and-key of villainous secrets:
And yet she'll kneel, and pray; I've seen her do't.

Re-enter EMILIA, *with* DESDEMONA

Des.   My lord, what is your will?
Oth.   Pray, chuck, come hither.
Des.   What is your pleasure?
Oth.   Let me see your eyes:
Look in my face.
    Des.   What horrible fancy's this?
    Oth. [*To Emilia*]   Some of your function, mistress;
Leave procreants alone and shut the door;

Cough or cry hem if anybody come:
Your mystery, your mystery;—nay, despatch.

[*Exit Emilia*

    Des.   Upon my knees, what doth your speech import?
I understand a fury in your words,
But not the words.
    Oth.   Why, what art thou?
    Des.   Your wife, my lord: your true and loyal wife.
    Oth.   Come, swear it, damn thyself;
Lest, being like one of heaven, the devils themselves
Should fear to seize thee: therefore be double-damned,—
Swear thou art honest.
    Des.   Heaven doth truly know it.
    Oth.   Heaven truly knows, that thou art false as hell
    Des.   To whom, my lord? with whom? how am I false?
    Oth.   Ah, Desdemona!—away, away, away!
    Des.   Alas, the heavy day!—Why do you weep?
Am I the motive of these tears, my lord?
If, haply, you my father do suspect
An instrument of this your calling back,
Lay not your blame on me; if you have lost him,
Why, I have lost him too.
    Oth.   Had it pleased Heaven
To try me with affliction; had they rained
All kinds of sores, and shames, on my bare head;
Steeped me in poverty to the very lips;
Given to captivity me and my utmost hopes;
I should have found in some place of my soul
A drop of patience: but, alas, to make me
The fixéd figure for the time of scorn
To point his slow and moving finger at,—
Yet could I bear that too; well, very well:
But there, where I have garnered up my heart,
Where either I must live or bear no life,
The fountain from the which my current runs
Or else dries up; to be discarded thence,
Or keep it as a cistern for foul toads
To knot and gender in!—turn thy complexion there,
Patience, thou young and rose-lipped cherubin;
Ay, there, look grim as hell!
    Des.   I hope, my noble lord esteems me honest.
    Oth.   O, ay; as summer flies are in the shambles,
That quicken even with blowing. O thou weed,
Who art so lovely fair, and smell'st so sweet,
That the sense aches at thee,—'would thou hadst ne'er
       been born?
    Des.   Alas, what ignorant sin have I committed?
    Oth.   Was this fair paper, this most goodly book,
Made to write "whore" upon? What committed?
Committed!—O thou public commoner!

I should make very forges of my cheeks,
That would to cinders burn up modesty,
Did I but speak thy deeds.—What committed?
Heaven stops the nose at it, and the moon winks;
The bawdy wind, that kisses all it meets,
Is hushed within the hollow mine of earth,
And will not hear it.   What committed?
Impudent strumpet!

    Des.   By Heaven, you do me wrong.

    Oth.   Are not you a strumpet?

    Des.   No, as I am a Christian.
If to preserve this vessel for my lord,
From any other foul unlawful touch,
Be not to be a strumpet, I am none.

    Oth.   What, not a whore?

    Des.   No, as I shall be saved.

    Oth.   Is 't possible?

    Des.   O, Heaven forgive us!

    Oth.   I cry you mercy then:
I took you for that cunning whore of Venice,
That married with Othello.—You, mistress,
That have the office opposite to Saint Peter,
And keep the gate of hell!

Re-enter EMILIA

                You, you, ay, you:
We have done our course: there's money for your pains.
I pray you, turn the key, and keep our counsel.   *[Exit*

    Emil.   Alas, what does this gentleman conceive?—
How do you, madam? how do you, my good lady?

    Des.   'Faith, half asleep.

    Emil.   Good madam, what's the matter with my lord?

    Des.   With who?

    Emil.   Why, with my lord, madam.

    Des.   Who is thy lord?

    Emil.   He that is yours, sweet lady.

    Des.   I have none: do not talk to me, Emilia:
I cannot weep; nor answer have I none,
But what should go by water.   Pr'ythee, to-night
Lay on my bed my wedding sheets,—remember;—
And call thy husband hither.

    Emil.   Here's a change, indeed!
                                  [Exit

    Des.   'T is meet I should be used so, very meet.
How have I been behaved, that he might stick
The small'st opinion on my least misuse?

Re-enter EMILIA *with* IAGO

    Iago.   What is your pleasure, madam?   How is 't with
        you?

    Des.   I cannot tell.   Those that do teach young babes

Do it with gentle means and easy tasks:
He might have chid me so; for, in good faith,
I am a child to chiding.
    Iago.   What's the matter, lady?
    Emil.   Alas, Iago, my lord hath so bewhored her,
Thrown such despite and heavy terms upon her,
As true hearts cannot bear.
    Des.   Am I that name, Iago?
    Iago.   What name, fair lady?
    Des.   Such as she says my lord did say I was.
    Emil.   He called her whore: a beggar in his drink
Could not have laid such terms upon his callat.
    Iago.   Why did he so?
    Des.   I do not know; I am sure, I am none such.
    Iago.   Do not weep, do not weep.   Alas the day!
    Emil.   Hath she forsook so many noble matches,
Her father, and her country, and her friends,
To be called whore? would it not make one weep?
    Des.   It is my wretched fortune.
    Iago.   Beshrew him for't!
How comes this trick upon him?
    Des.   Nay, Heaven doth know.
    Emil.   I will be hanged, if some eternal villain,
Some busy and insinuating rogue,
Some cogging cozening slave, to get some office
Have not devised this slander; I'll be hanged else.
    Iago.   Fie, there is no such man: it is impossible.
    Des.   If any such there be, Heaven pardon him!
    Emil.   A halter pardon him, and hell gnaw his bones!
Why should he call her whore? who keeps her company?
What place? what time? what form? what likelihood?
The Moor's abused by some most villainous knave,
Some base notorious knave, some scurvy fellow:—
O Heaven, that such companions thou'dst unfold,
And put in every honest hand a whip
To lash the rascals naked through the world
Even from the east to the west!
    Iago.   Speak within door.
    Emil.   O, fie upon them! Some such squire he was,
That turned your wit the seamy side without,
And made you to suspect me with the Moor.
    Iago.   You are a fool; go to.
    Des.   O good Iago,
What shall I do to win my lord again?
Good friend, go to him; for, by this light of heaven,
I know not how I lost him.   Here I kneel:—
If e'er my will did trespass 'gainst his love,
Either in discourse of thought, or actual deed;
Or that mine eyes, mine ears, or any sense,
Delighted them in any other form;

Or that I do not yet, and ever did,
And ever will—though he do shake me off
To beggarly divorcement—love him dearly,
Comfort forswear me!   Unkindness may do much;
And his unkindness may defeat my life,
But never taint my love.   I cannot say "whore:"
It does abhor me, now I speak the word;
To do the act that might the addition earn,
Not the world's mass of vanity could make me.
    Iago.   I pray you, be content; 't is but his humour:
The business of the state does him offence,
And he does chide with you.
    Des.   If 't were no other,—
    Iago.   'T is but so, I warrant.
                                          [*Trumpets*
Hark, how these instruments summon to supper!
The messengers of Venice stay the meat.
Go in, and weep not; all things shall be well.
                          [*Exeunt Desdemona and Emilia*

Enter RODERIGO

How now, Roderigo?
    Rod.   I do not find that thou deal'st justly with me.
    Iago.   What in the contrary?
    Rod.   Every day thou daff'st me with some device,
Iago; and rather, as it seems to me now, keep'st from
me all conveniency, than suppliest me with the least
advantage of hope.   I will, indeed, no longer endure it;
nor am I yet persuaded to put up in peace what already
I have foolishly suffered.
    Iago.   Will you hear me, Roderigo?
    Rod.   'Faith, I have heard too much; for your words
and performances are no kin together.
    Iago.   You charge me most unjustly.
    Rod.   With nought but truth.   I have wasted myself
out of my means.   The jewels you have had from me, to
deliver to Desdemona, would half have corrupted a votarist:
you have told me she hath received them, and returned
me expectations and comforts of sudden respect and
acquaintance; but I find none.
    Iago.   Well; go to; very well.
    Rod.   Very well! go to! I cannot go to, man: nor 't
is not very well: by this hand, I say it is very scurvy;
and begin to find myself fopped in it.
    Iago.   Very well.
    Rod.   I tell you, 't is not very well.   I will make myself
known to Desdemona: if she will return me my jewels,
I will give over my suit and repent my unlawful solicitation;
if not, assure yourself I will seek satisfaction of you.
    Iago.   You have said now.

Rod. Ay, and I have said nothing but what I protest intendment of doing.

Iago. Why, now I see there's mettle in thee; and even, from this instant, do build on thee a better opinion than ever before. Give me thy hand, Roderigo: thou hast taken against me a most just exception; but yet, I protest I have dealt most directly in thy affair.

Rod. It hath not appeared.

Iago. I grant, indeed, it hath not appeared, and your suspicion is not without wit and judgment. But, Roderigo, if thou hast that within thee indeed, which I have greater reason to believe now than ever,—I mean, purpose, courage, and valour,—this night show it: if thou the next night following enjoyest not Desdemona, take me from this world with treachery, and devise engines for my life.

Rod. Well, what is it? is it within reason and compass?

Iago. Sir, there is especial commission come from Venice, to depute Cassio in Othello's place.

Rod. Is that true? why, then Othello and Desdemona return again to Venice.

Iago. O, no! he goes into Mauritania, and takes away with him the fair Desdemona, unless his abode be lingered here by some accident; wherein none can be so determinate as the removing of Cassio.

Rod. How do you mean, removing him?

Iago. Why, by making him incapable of Othello's place; knocking out his brains.

Rod. And that you would have me do?

Iago. Ay: if you dare do yourself a profit, and a right. He sups to-night with a harlotry, and thither will I go to him: he knows not yet of his honourable fortune. If you will watch his going thence—which I will fashion to fall out between twelve and one—you may take him at your pleasure: I will be near to second your attempt, and he shall fall between us. Come, stand not amazed at it, but go along with me; I will show you such a necessity in his death that you shall think yourself bound to put it on him. It is now high supper-time, and the night grows to waste: about it.

Rod. I will hear further reason for this.

Iago. And you shall be satisfied.   [*Exeunt*

SCENE III.—Another Room in the Castle

Enter OTHELLO, LODOVICO, DESDEMONA, EMILIA, *and Attendants*

Lod. I do beseech you, sir, trouble yourself no further.

Oth. O, pardon me; 't will do me good to walk.

Lod. Madam, good night; I humbly thank your ladyship.

Des. Your honour is most welcome.

Oth.   Will you walk, sir?—
O,—Desdemona,—
   Des. My lord?
   Oth. Get you to bed on the instant; I will be returned
forthwith: dismiss your attendant there: look it be done.
   Des. I will, my lord.
            [Exeunt Othello, Lodovico, and Attendants
   Emil. How goes it now? he looks gentler than he
did.
   Des. He says, he will return incontinent;
He hath commanded me to go to bed,
And bade me to dismiss you.
   Emil.   Dismiss me!
   Des. It was his bidding; therefore, good Emilia,
Give me my nightly wearing, and adieu:
We must not now displease him.
   Emil. I would you had never seen him.
   Des. So would not I: my love doth so approve him,
That even his stubbornness, his checks, and frowns,—
Pr'ythee, unpin me,—have grace and favour in them.
   Emil. I have laid those sheets you bade me on the bed.
   Des. All's one.—Good faith, how foolish are our
     minds!—
If I do die before thee, pry'thee shroud me
In one of those same sheets.
   Emil.   Come, come, you talk.
   Des. My mother had a maid called Barbara:
She was in love; and he she loved proved mad,
And did forsake her: she had a song of "willow";
An old thing 't was, but it expressed her fortune,
And she died singing it: that song, to-night,
Will not go from my mind; I have much to do,
But to go hang my head all at one side,
And sing it like poor Barbara. Pr'ythee, despatch.
   Emil. Shall I go fetch your night-gown?
   Des.   No, unpin me here.—
This Lodovico is a proper man.
   Emil. A very handsome man.
   Des. He speaks well.
   Emil. I know a lady in Venice would have walked
barefoot to Palestine for a touch of his nether lip.
   Des. *[Singing.]*

   The poor soul sat sighing by a sycamore tree ;
      Sing all a green willow ;
   Her hand on her bosom, her head on her knee ;
      Sing, willow, willow, willow :
   The fresh streams ran by her, and murmured her moans ;
      Sing willow, willow, willow :
   Her salt tears fell from her, and softened the stones ;

Lay by these.—

Sing willow, willow, willow.

Pr'ythee, hie thee: he'll come anon.—

Sing all a green willow must be my garland,
Let nobody blame him, his scorn I approve,—

Nay, that's not next.—Hark, who is it that knocks?
  Emil. It is the wind.

  Des. I called my love, false love; but what said he then?
    Sing willow, willow, willow:
  If I court moe women, you'll couch with moe men.

So, get thee gone; good night.   Mine eyes do itch;
Doth that bode weeping?
  Emil.   'T is neither here nor there.
  Des. I have heard it said so.—O, these men, these
    men!—
Dost thou in conscience think,—tell me, Emilia,—
That there be women do abuse their husbands
In such gross kind?
  Emil.   There be some such, no question.
  Des. Wouldst thou do such a deed for all the world?
  Emil. Why, would not you?
  Des.   No, by this heavenly light!
  Emil. Nor I neither by this heavenly light:
I might do 't as well i' the dark.
  Des. Wouldst thou do such a deed for all the world?
  Emil. The world is a huge thing: 't is a great price
For a small vice.
  Des. In troth, I think thou wouldst not.
  Emil. In troth, I think I should, and undo 't when I
had done.   Marry, I would not do such a thing for a joint-
ring, nor for measures of lawn, nor for gowns, petticoats,
nor caps, nor any petty exhibition; but, for the whole
world,—why, who would not make her husband a cuckold,
to make him a monarch?   I should venture purgatory
for 't.
  Des. Beshrew me, if I would do such a wrong
For the whole world.
  Emil. Why, the wrong is but a wrong i' the world;
and, having the world for your labour, 't is a wrong in
your own world, and you might quickly make it right.
  Des. I do not think there is any such woman.
  Emil. Yes, a dozen; and as many to the vantage
As would store the world they played for.
But, I do think it is their husbands' faults
If wives do fall.   Say, that they slack their duties
And pour our treasures into foreign laps;
Or else break out in peevish jealousies,

Throwing restraint upon us; or, say, they strike us,
Or scant our former having in despite:
Why, we have galls; and, though we have some grace,
Yet have we some revenge.   Let husbands know,
Their wives have sense like them: they see and smell
And have their palates both for sweet and sour,
As husbands have.   What is it that they do
When they change us for others?   Is it sport?
I think it is.   And doth affection breed it?
I think it doth.   Is 't frailty that thus errs?
It is so too.   And have not we affections,
Desires for sport, and frailty, as men have?
Then, let them use us well; else let them know,
The ills we do, their ills instruct us so:

   Des.   Good night, good night: Heaven me such uses send,
Not to pick bad from bad, but by bad mend!   [*Exeunt*

ACT FIVE

SCENE I.—Cyprus.   A Street

Enter IAGO *and* RODERIGO

   Iago.   Here, stand behind this bulk; straight will he
     come:
Wear thy good rapier bare, and put it home.
Quick, quick; fear nothing; I'll be at thy elbow.
It makes us, or it mars us; think on that,
And fix most firm thy resolution.
   Rod.   Be near at hand; I may miscarry in 't.
   Iago.   Here, at thy hand: be bold, and take thy stand.
                             [*Retires*

   Rod.   I have no great devotion to the deed;
And yet he hath given me satisfying reasons.—
'T is but a man gone:—forth, my sword; he dies.
   Iago.   I have rubbed this young quat almost to the sense,
And he grows angry.   Now, whether he kill Cassio,
Or Cassio him, or each do kill the other,
Every way makes my gain: live Roderigo,
He calls me to a restitution large
Of gold and jewels that I bobbed from him
As gifts to Desdemona;
It must not be: if Cassio do remain,
He hath a daily beauty in his life
That makes me ugly; and, besides, the Moor
May unfold me to him: there stand I in much peril.
No, he must die:—be 't so; I hear him coming.

Enter CASSIO

   Rod.   I know his gait; 'it is he.—Villain, thou diest.
     [*Rushing out, and making a pass at Cassio*

Cas. That thrust had been mine enemy indeed,
But that my coat is better than thou know'st:
I will make proof of thine. [*Draws, and wounds Roderigo*
    Rod.   O, I am slain!
[*Iago rushes from his post, cuts Cassio behind in the leg, and
                                                        exit*
Cas. I am maimed for ever.—Help, ho! murder,
    murder!   [*Falls*

Enter OTHELLO, *at a distance*

Oth. The voice of Cassio:—Iago keeps his word.
Rod. O, villain that I am!
Oth.   It is even so.
Cas. O, help, ho! light! a surgeon!
Oth. 'T is he.—O brave Iago, honest, and just,
That hast such noble sense of thy friend's wrong!
Thou teachest me:—Minion, your dear lies dead,
And your unblest fate hies:—strumpet, I come!
Forth of my heart those charms, thine eyes, are blotted;
Thy bed, lust-stained, shall with lust's blood be spotted.
                                                    [*Exit*

Enter LODOVICO *and* GRATIANO, *at a distance*

Cas. What, ho! no watch? no passage? murder!
    murder!
Gra. 'T is some mischance; the cry is very direful.
Cas. O, help!
Lod. Hark!
Rod. O wretched villain!
Lod. Two or three groans.—It is a heavy night!
These may be counterfeits; let 's think 't unsafe
To come in to the cry without more help.
Rod. Nobody come? then shall I bleed to death.
Lod. Hark!

Re-enter IAGO, *with a light*

Gra. Here's one comes in his shirt, with light and
    weapons.
Iago. Who's there? whose noise is this that cries
    on murder?
Lod. We do not know.
Iago.   Did not you hear a cry?
Cas. Here, here! for Heaven's sake, help me!
Iago.   What's the matter?
Gra. This is Othello's ancient, as I take it.
Lod. The same, indeed; a very valiant fellow.
Iago. What are you here, that cry so grievously?
Cas. Iago? O! I am spoiled, undone by villains:
Give me some help.
Iago. O me, lieutenant! what villains have done this?

Cas.   I think that one of them is hereabout,
And cannot make away.
  Iago.   O treacherous villains!—
[*To Lodovico and Gratiano*] What are you there? come
in, and give some help.
  Rod.   O, help me here!
  Cas.   That's one of them.
  Iago.   O murderous slave! O villain!
                                        [*Stabs Roderigo*
  Rod.   O damned Iago! O inhuman dog!
  Iago.   Kill men i' the dark!—Where be these bloody
        thieves?—
How silent is this town!—Ho! murder! murder!
What may you be? are you of good, or evil?
  Lod.   As you shall prove us, praise us.
  Iago.   Signior Lodovico?
  Lod.   He, sir.
  Iago.   I cry you mercy.   Here's Cassio hurt by villains.
  Gra.   Cassio?
  Iago.   How is 't, brother?
  Cas.   My leg is cut in two.
  Iago.   Marry, Heaven forbid!—
Light, gentlemen; I'll bind it with my shirt.

Enter BIANCA

  Bian.   What is the matter, ho? who is't that cried?
  Iago.   Who is 't that cried?
  Bian.   O my dear Cassio! my sweet Cassio!
O Cassio, Cassio, Cassio!
  Iago.   O notable strumpet!—Cassio, may you suspect
Who they should be, that have thus mangled you?
  Cas.   No.
  Gra.   I am sorry to find you thus: I have been to seek
you.
  Iago.   Lend me a garter:—so.—O, for a chair,
To bear him easily hence!
  Bian.   Alas! he faints.—O Cassio, Cassio, Cassio!
  Iago.   Gentleman all, I do suspect this trash
To be a party in this injury.—
Patience awhile, good Cassio.—Come, come.
Lend me a light.—Know we this face, or no?
Alas! my friend, and my dear countryman,
Roderigo? no:—yes, sure.   O Heaven! Roderigo.
  Gra.   What, of Venice?
  Iago.   Even he, sir; did you know him?
  Gra.   Know him? ay.
  Iago.   Signior Gratiano? I cry you gentle pardon:
These bloody accidents must excuse my manners,
That so neglected you.
  Gra.   I am glad to see you.

Iago. How do you, Cassio?—O, a chair, a chair!
Gra. Roderigo!
Iago. He, he, 't is he.—[*A chair brought in*] O! that
    's well said;—the chair.—
Some good man bear him carefully from hence;
I'll fetch the general's surgeon.—[*To Bianca*] For you,
    mistress,
Save you your labour.—He that lies slain here, Cassio,
Was my dear friend. What malice was between you?
Cas. None in the world; nor do I know the man.
Iago. [*To Bianca*] What, look you pale?—O, bear him
    out o' the air.—   [*Cassio and Roderigo are borne off*
Stay you, good gentlemen.—Look you pale, mistress!
Do you perceive the ghastness of her eye?—
Nay, if you stare, we shall hear more anon.—
Behold her well: I pray you, look upon her:
Do you see, gentlemen? nay, guiltiness will speak,
Though tongues were out of use.

Enter EMILIA

Emil. 'Las! what's the matter? what's the matter,
husband?
Iago. Cassio hath here been set on in the dark
By Roderigo, and fellows that are 'scaped.
He's almost slain, and Roderigo dead.
Emil. Alas, good gentleman! alas, good Cassio!
Iago. This is the fruits of whoring.—Pr'ythee, Emilia,
Go know of Cassio where he supped to-night.—
What! do you shake at that?
Bian. He supped at my house; but I therefore shake not.
Iago. O, did he so? I charge you, go with me.
Emil. Fie, fie upon thee, strumpet!
Bian. I am no strumpet; but of life as honest
As you that thus abuse me.
Emil.   As I? foh! fie upon thee!
Iago. Kind gentlemen, let's go see poor Cassio dressed.—
Come, mistress, you must tell 's another tale.—
Emilia, run you to the citadel,
And tell my lord and lady what hath happed.—
Will you go on afore?—[*Aside*] This is the night,
That either makes me, or fordoes me quite.   [*Exeunt*

SCENE II.—A Bedchamber

DESDEMONA *in bed asleep. A light burning.*

Enter OTHELLO

Oth. It is the cause, it is the cause, my soul,—
Let me not name it to you, you chaste stars!—
It is the cause.—Yet I'll not shed her blood;

Nor scar that whiter skin of hers than snow,
And smooth as monumental alabaster.
Yet she must die, else she'll betray more men.
Put out the light, and then,—put out the light:
If I quench thee, thou flaming minister,
I can again thy former light restore
Should I repent me; but once put out thy light,
Thou cunning'st pattern of excelling nature,
I know not where is that Promethean heat
That can thy light relume.   When I have plucked thy rose,
I cannot give it vital growth again,
It needs must wither:—I'll smell it on the tree.—
                                                    [*Kissing her*
O balmy breath, that dost almost persuade
Justice to break her sword!—One more, one more.—
Be thus when thou art dead, and I will kill thee,
And love thee after.—One more, and this the last:
So sweet was ne'er so fatal.   I must weep,
But they are cruel tears: this sorrow's heavenly;
It strikes where it doth love.—She wakes.
    Des.   Who's there?   Othello?
    Oth.   Ay, Desdemona.
    Des.   Will you come to bed, my lord?
    Oth.   Have you prayed to-night, Desdemon?
    Des.   Ay, my lord.
    Oth.   If you bethink yourself of any crime,
Unreconciled as yet to Heaven and grace,
Solicit for it straight.
    Des.   Alas, my lord, what may you mean by that?
    Oth.   Well, do it, and be brief; I will walk by:
I would not kill thy unprepared spirit;
No,—Heaven forfend!—I would not kill thy soul.
    Des.   Talk you of killing?
    Oth.   Ay, I do.
    Des.   Then, Heaven
Have mercy on me!
    Oth.   Amen, with all my heart!
    Des.   If you say so, I hope you will not kill me.
    Oth.   Hum!
    Des.   And yet I fear you; for you are fatal then,
When your eyes roll so.   Why I should fear I know not,
Since guiltiness I know not; but yet, I feel I fear.
    Oth.   Think on thy sins.
    Des.   They are loves I bear to you.
    Oth.   Ay, and for that thou diest.
    Des.   That death's unnatural that kills for loving.—
Alas, why gnaw you so your nether lip?
Some bloody passion shakes your very frame:
These are portents; but yet I hope, I hope,
They do not point on me.

Oth.   Peace, and be still!
Des.   I will so.   What 's the matter?
Oth.   That handkerchief, which I so loved and gave thee,
Thou gav'st to Cassio.
Des.   No, by my life and soul!
Send for the man, and ask him.
Oth.   Sweet soul, take heed,
Take heed of perjury: thou art on thy death bed.
Des.   Ay, but not yet to die.
Oth.   Yes, presently:
Therefore confess thee freely of thy sin;
For to deny each article with oath
Cannot remove nor choke the strong conception
That I do groan withal.   Thou art to die
Des.   Then Lord have mercy on me!
Oth.   I say, Amen.
Des.   And have you mercy too!—I never did
Offend you in my life; never loved Cassio,
But with such general warranty of Heaven
As I might love: I never gave him token.
Oth.   By Heaven, I saw my handkerchief in 's hand.
O perjured woman! thou dost stone my heart,
And mak'st me call what I intend to do,
A murder, which I thought a sacrifice:
I saw the handkerchief.
Des.   He found it then;
I never gave it him.—Send for him hither;
Let him confess a truth.
Oth.   He hath confessed.
Des.   What, my lord?
Oth.   That he hath used thee.
Des.   How? unlawfully?
Oth.   Ay.
Des.   He will not say so.
Oth.   No; his mouth is stopped:
Honest Iago hath ta'en order for 't.
Des.   O, my fear interprets.—What, is he dead?
Oth.   Had all his hairs been lives, my great revenge
Had stomach for them all.
Des.   Alas! he is betrayed, and I undone.
Oth.   Out, strumpet! Weep'st thou for him to my face?
Des.   O, banish me, my lord, but kill me not.
Oth.   Down, strumpet!
Des.   Kill me to-morrow; let me live to-night.
Oth.   Nay, if you strive,—
Des.   But half an hour!
Oth.   Being done, there is no pause.
Des.   But while I say one prayer.

Oth. It is too late.   [*He smothers her*

Emil. [*Within*] My lord, my lord! what, ho! my lord, my lord!

Oth. What noise is this?—Not dead? not yet quite dead?

I, that am cruel, am yet merciful;
I would not have thee linger in thy pain.—
So, so.

Emil. [*Within*] What, ho! my lord, my lord!

Oth.   Who's there?

Emil. [*Within*] O, good my lord! I would speak a word with you.

Oth. Yes:—'t is Emilia:—by-and-by.—She's dead.—
'T is like she comes to speak of Cassio's death;
The noise was high.—Ha! no more moving?
Still as the grave.—Shall she come in? Were 't good?—
I think she stirs again:—no.—What 's best to do?
If she come in, she 'll sure speak to my wife:
My wife! my wife! what wife?—I have no wife:
O, insupportable! O heavy hour!
Methinks it should be now a huge eclipse
Of sun and moon, and that the affrighted globe
Should yawn at alteration.

Emil. [*Within*] I do beseech you
That I may speak with you, O, good my lord!

Oth. I had forgot thee. O, come in, Emilia.—
Soft,—by-and-by:—let me the curtains draw.—
Where art thou? What 's the matter with thee now?
                                    [*Unlocks the door*

Enter EMILIA

Emil. O, my good lord! yonder's foul murder done.

Oth. What! now?

Emil. But now, my lord.

Oth. It is the very error of the moon;
She comes more nearer earth than she was wont,
And makes men mad.

Emil. Cassio, my lord, has killed a young Venetian
Called Roderigo.

Oth.   Roderigo killed!
And Cassio killed!

Emil. No; Cassio is not killed.

Oth. Not Cassio killed! Then murder's out of tune,
And sweet revenge grows harsh.

Des. O, falsely, falsely murdered!

Emil.   Alas! what cry is that?

Oth. That! what?

Emil. Out, and alas! tnat was my lady's voice:—
Help! help, ho! help!—O lady, speak again!
Sweet Desdemona! O, sweet mistress, speak!

Des.   A guiltless death I die.
Emil.   O, who hath done this deed?
Des.   Nobody; I myself.   Farewell:
Commend me to my kind lord.   O, farewell!   [*Dies*
Oth.   Why, how should she be murdered?
Emil.   Alas, who knows?
Oth.   You heard her say herself, it was not I.
Emil.   She said so: I must needs report the truth.
Oth.   She's like a liar gone to burning hell:
'T was I that killed her.
Emil.   O, the more angel she,
And you the blacker devil!
Oth.   She turned to folly, and she was a whore.
Emil.   Thou dost belie her, and thou art a devil.
Oth.   She was false as water.
Emil.   Thou art rash as fire to say
That she was false: O, she was heavenly true.
Oth.   Cassio did tup her; ask thy husband else.
O, I were damned beneath all depth in hell,
But that I did proceed upon just grounds
To this extremity.   Thy husband knew it all.
Emil.   My husband?
Oth.   Thy husband.
Emil.   That she was false to wedlock?
Oth.   Ay, with Cassio.   Nay, had she been true,
If Heaven would make me such another world
Of one entire and perfect chrysolite,
I'd not have sold her for it.
Emil.   My husband?
Oth.   Ay, 't was he that told me first:
An honest man he is, and hates the slime
That sticks on filthy deeds.
Emil.   My husband?
Oth.   What needs this iterance, woman?   I say, thy
         husband.
Emil.   O mistress! villainy hath made mocks with
         love.—
My husband say that she was false!
Oth.   He, woman;
I say, thy husband: dost understand the word?
My friend, thy husband, honest, honest Iago.
Emil.   If he say so, may his pernicious soul
Rot half a grain a day! he lies to the heart:
She was too fond of her most filthy bargain.
Oth.   Ha!
Emil.   Do thy worst:
This deed of thine is no more worthy heaven
Than thou wast worthy her.
Oth.   Peace, you were best.
Emil.   Thou hast not half that power to do me harm

As I have to be hurt. O gull! O dolt!
As ignorant as dirt! thou hast done a deed—
I care not for thy sword; I 'll make thee known,
Though I lost twenty lives.—Help! help, ho! help!
The Moor has killed my mistress! Murder! murder!

Enter MONTANO, GRATIANO, *and* IAGO

  Mon.   What is the matter?—How now, general?
  Emil.   O, are you come, Iago? you have done well,
That men must lay their murders on your neck.
  Gra.   What is the matter?
  Emil.   Disprove this villain, if thou be'st a man:
He says, thou told'st him that his wife was false.
I know thou didst not, thou 'rt not such a villain.
Speak, for my heart is full.
  Iago.   I told him what I thought; and told no more
Than what he found himself was apt and true.
  Emil.   But did you ever tell him she was false?
  Iago.   I did.
  Emil.   You told a lie; an odious, damnéd lie;
Upon my soul, a lie; a wicked lie.—
She false with Cassio!—Did you say with Cassio?
  Iago.   With Cassio, mistress. Go to, charm your tongue.
  Emil.   I will not charm my tongue; I am bound to
        speak.
My mistress here lies murdered in her bed.
  All.   O heavens forfend!
  Emil.   And your reports have set the murder on.
  Oth.   Nay, stare not, masters: it is true, indeed.
  Gra.   'T is a strange truth.
  Mon.   O monstrous act!
  Emil.   Villainy! villainy! villainy!
I think upon 't,—I think,—I smell 't:—O villainy!
I thought so then:—I 'll kill myself for grief.—
O villainy, villainy!
  Iago.   What! are you mad? I charge you, get you
        home.
  Emil.   Good gentlemen, let me have leave to speak:
'T is proper I obey him, but not now—
Perchance, Iago, I will ne'er go home.
  Oth.   O! O! O!
  Emil.   Nay, lay thee down, and roar;
For thou hast killed the sweetest innocent
That e'er did lift up eye.
  Oth.   [*Rising*]   O, she was foul.—
I scarce did know you, uncle. There lies your niece,
Whose breath, indeed, these hands have newly stopped.
I know this act shows horrible and grim.
  Gra.   Poor Desdemon! I am glad thy father's dead.
Thy match was mortal to him, and pure grief

Shore his old thread in twain: did he live now,
This sight would make him do a desperate turn,
Yea, curse his better angel from his side,
And fall to reprobance.
    Oth. 'T is pitiful; but yet Iago knows,
That she with Cassio hath the act of shame
A thousand times committed: Cassio confessed it;
And she did gratify his amorous works
With that recognisance and pledge of love
Which I first gave her. I saw it in his hand;
It was a handkerchief, an antique token
My father gave my mother.
    Emil. O Heaven! O heavenly powers!
    Iago.   Come, hold your peace.
    Emil. 'T will out, 't will out:—I hold my peace, sir? no;
No, I will speak as liberal as the north:
Let Heaven, and men, and devils, let them all,
All, all, cry shame against me, yet I 'll speak.
    Iago. Be wise, and get you home.
    Emil.   I will not.
                  [Iago offers to stab his wife
    Gra.   Fie!
Your sword upon a woman?
    Emil. O thou dull Moor! that handkerchief thou
        speak'st of
I found by fortune, and did give my husband;
For often, with a solemn earnestness,—
More than, indeed, belonged to such a trifle,—
He begged of me to steal it.
    Iago.   Villainous whore!
    Emil. She give it Cassio! no, alas! I found it.
And I did give 't my husband.
    Iago.   Filth, thou liest!
    Emil. By Heaven, I do not; I do not, gentlemen.—
O murderous coxcomb! what should such a fool
Do with so good a wife? *[Iago stabs Emilia, then runs out*
    Oth.   Are there no stones in heaven
But what serve for the thunder?—Precious villain!
    Gra. The woman falls: sure, he hath killed his wife.
    Emil. Ay, ay. O, lay me by my mistress' side!
    Gra. He 's gone, but his wife 's killed.
    Mon. 'T is a notorious villain. Take you this weapon,
Which I have here recovered from the Moor.
Come, guard the door without: let him not pass,
But kill him rather. I 'll after that same villain,
For 't is a damnéd slave.   *[Exit*
    Oth.   I am not valiant neither,
But every puny whipster gets my sword.
But why should honour outlive honesty?
Let it go all.

Emil.   What did thy song bode, lady?
Hark, canst thou hear me?   I will play the swan,
And die in music.—[*Singing*] *Willow, willow, willow.*—
Moor, she was chaste; she loved thee, cruel Moor,
So come my soul to bliss, as I speak true;
So speaking as, I think, I die,—I die.   [*Dies*
    Oth.   I have another weapon in this chamber;
It is a sword of Spain, the ice-brook's temper.
O, here it is.—Uncle, I must come forth.
    Gra.   If thou attempt it, it will cost thee dear:
Thou hast no weapon, and perforce must suffer.
    Oth.   Look in upon me, then, and speak with me,
Or, naked as I am, I will assault thee.
    Gra.   What is the matter?
    Oth.   Behold, I have a weapon;
A better never did itself sustain
Upon a soldier's thigh: I 've seen the day,
That with this little arm, and this good sword,
I 've made my way through more impediments
Than twenty times your stop.—But, O vain boast!
Who can control his fate? 't is not so now.—
Be not afraid, though you do see me weaponed:
Here is my journey's end, here is my butt,
And very sea-mark of my utmost sail.
Do you go back dismayed? 't is a lost fear:
Man but a rush against Othello's breast,
And he retires.—Where should Othello go?—
Now, how dost thou look now?   O ill-starred wench!
Pale as thy smock! when we shall met at compt,
This look of thine will hurl my soul from heaven,
And fiends will snatch at it.   Cold, cold, my girl!
Even like thy chastity.
O, curséd, curséd slave!—Whip me, ye devils,
From the possession of this heavenly sight!
Blow me about in winds! roast me in sulphur!
Wash me in steep-down gulfs of liquid fire!
O Desdemona! Desdemona! dead!

Enter LODOVICO, MONTANO, CASSIO *carried in a chair, and
          officers, with* IAGO *prisoner*

    Lod.   Where is this rash and most unfortunate man?
    Oth.   That 's he that was Othello;—here I am.
    Lod.   Where is that viper? bring the villain forth.
    Oth.   I look down towards his feet,—but that 's a fable:
If that thou be'st a devil, I cannot kill thee. [*Wounds Iago*
    Lod.   Wrench his sword from him.
    Iago.   I bleed, sir; but not killed.
    Oth.   I am not sorry neither: I'd have thee live;
For, it my sense, 't is happiness to die.
    Lod.   O thou Othello, that wert once so good,

Fall'n in the practice of a damnéd slave,
What shall be said to thee?
 Oth.   Why, anything:
An honourable murderer, if you will;
For nought did I in hate but all in honour.
 Lod. This wretch hath part confessed his villainy:
Did you and he consent in Cassio's death?
 Oth. Ay.
 Cas. Dear general, I never gave you cause.
 Oth. I do believe it, and I ask you pardon.
Will you, I pray, demand that demi-devil,
Why he hath thus ensnared my soul and body?
 Iago. Demand me nothing: what you know, you know:
From this time forth I never will speak word.
 Lod. What! not to pray?
 Gra.   Torments will ope your lips.
 Oth. Well, thou dost best.
 Lod. Sir, you shall understand what hath befall'n,
Which, as I think, you know not. Here is a letter,
Found in the pocket of the slain Roderigo:
And here another: but one of them imports
The death of Cassio to be undertook
By Roderigo.
 Oth. O villain!
 Cas.   Most heathenish, and most gross!
 Lod. Now, here 's another discontented paper,
Found in his pocket too; and this, it seems,
Roderigo meant to have sent this damnéd villain;
But that, belike, Iago in the interim
Came in and satisfied him.
 Oth.   O thou pernicious caitiff!—
How came you, Cassio, by that handkerchief,
That was my wife's?
 Cas.   I found it in my chamber:
And he himself confessed but even now
That there he dropped it, for a special purpose
Which wrought to his desire.
 Oth.   O fool! fool! fool!
 Cas. There is, besides, in Roderigo's letter,
How he upbraids Iago, that he made him
Brave me upon the watch; whereon it came
That I was cast; and even but now he spake,
After long seeming dead,—Iago hurt him,
Iago set him on.
 Lod. You must forsake this room, and go with us:
Your power and your command is taken off,
And Cassio rules in Cyprus. For this slave,—
If there be any cunning cruelty
That can torment him much and hold him long,
It shall be his. You shall close prisoner rest

Till that the nature of your fault be known
To the Venetian state.—Come, bring him away.
    Oth.   Soft you; a word or two, before you go.
I have done the state some service, and they know it;
No more of that.—I pray you, in your letters,
When you shall these unlucky deeds relate,
Speak of me as I am; nothing extenuate,
Nor set down aught in malice: then must you speak
Of one that loved not wisely, but too well;
Of one not easily jealous, but, being wrought,
Perplexed in the extreme; of one, whose hand,
Like the base Indian, threw a pearl away,
Richer than all his tribe; of one, whose subdued eyes,
Albeit unuséd to the melting mood,
Drop tears as fast as the Arabian trees
Their medicinal gum.   Set you down this;
And say, besides, that in Aleppo once,
Where a malignant and a turbaned Turk
Beat a Venetian, and traduced the state,
I took by the throat the circumciséd dog,
And smote him—thus.   *[Stabs himself*
    Lod.   O bloody period!
    Gra.   All that 's spoke is marred.
    Oth.   I kissed thee, ere I killed thee:—no way but this,
                      [Falling upon Desdemona
Killing myself, to die upon a kiss.   *[Dies*
    Cas.   This did I fear, but thought he had no weapon;
For he was great of heart.
    Lod. *[To Iago]*   O Spartan dog!
More fell than anguish, hunger or the sea!
Look on the tragic loading of this bed;
This is thy work: the object poisons sight;
Let it be hid.—Gratiano, keep the house,
And seize upon the fortunes of the Moor,
For they succeed on you.—To you, lord governor,
Remains the censure of this hellish villain;
The time, the place, the torture:—O, enforce it!
Myself will straight aboard, and to the state
This heavy act with heavy heart relate.   *[Exeunt*

THE PEEBLES CLASSIC LIBRARY

BLACK BEAUTY

PRIDE AND PREJUDICE

AROUND THE WORLD IN 80 DAYS

THE VICAR OF WAKEFIELD

TREASURE ISLAND

KIDNAPPED

BARCHESTER TOWERS (2 VOLUMES)

JANE EYRE (2 VOLUMES)

GULLIVER'S TRAVELS

ROBINSON CRUSOE

A TALE OF TWO CITIES

SENSE AND SENSIBILITY

WUTHERING HEIGHTS